Broxy Kennels Fort, Souterrain and Surrounding Landscape, Perth

Broxy Kennels Fort, Souterrain and Surrounding Landscape, Perth

By Kenneth Green with John-James Atkinson,
Christina Mollie Dogherty, Charlotte Hunter,
Maureen Kilpatrick and Alun Woodward

With contributions by Torben Bjarke Ballin, Beverley Ballin Smith,
Gemma Cruickshanks, Leanne Demay, Derek Hamilton, Carol Laing,
Susan Ramsay, Catherine Smith and Clare Wilson

Illustrations by Jennifer Simonson, Gillian Sneddon with
reconstructions by Eddie Perez Fernandez

ARCHAEOPRESS ARCHAEOLOGY

ARCHAEOPRESS PUBLISHING LTD
13-14 Market Square
Bicester
Oxfordshire OX26 6AD
United Kingdom

www.archaeopress.com

ISBN 978-1-80583-293-5

Cover: Broxy Kennel Fort during sixth-fifth centuries BC. Artist's reconstruction. Back cover: Souterrain in Ditch 2N during excavation.

This book is available direct from Archaeopress or from our website www.archaeopress.com

Contents

List of Figures

List of Tables

List of Appendices

Summary

By Kenneth Green

Archaeological excavation of almost the entirety of Broxy Kennels Fort to the north of Perth, undertaken in advance of the Cross Tay link Road, revealed a multivallate fortified settlement on a hill overlooking the River Tay. The fort initially comprised two ditches that encircled the hill with a north-east entranceway that led to the interior. It was occupied from the sixth century BC.

Around the late fifth-early fourth centuries BC, part of the settlement's defences was altered to accommodate a souterrain constructed into one of the silted-up ditches. It necessitated a further short ditch either side of the entrance, followed by a final outer ditch that encircled the hill. Other changes within the enclosure may also have occurred at this time with material from clearance of structures being dumped in the ditches.

After a short hiatus, a subsequent probably unenclosed settlement across the interior of the fort persisted from the fourth century BC until around the late first century AD.

Other than traces of sporadic activity from the early medieval period to the post-medieval era, the site was to all intents and purposes lost to the plough.

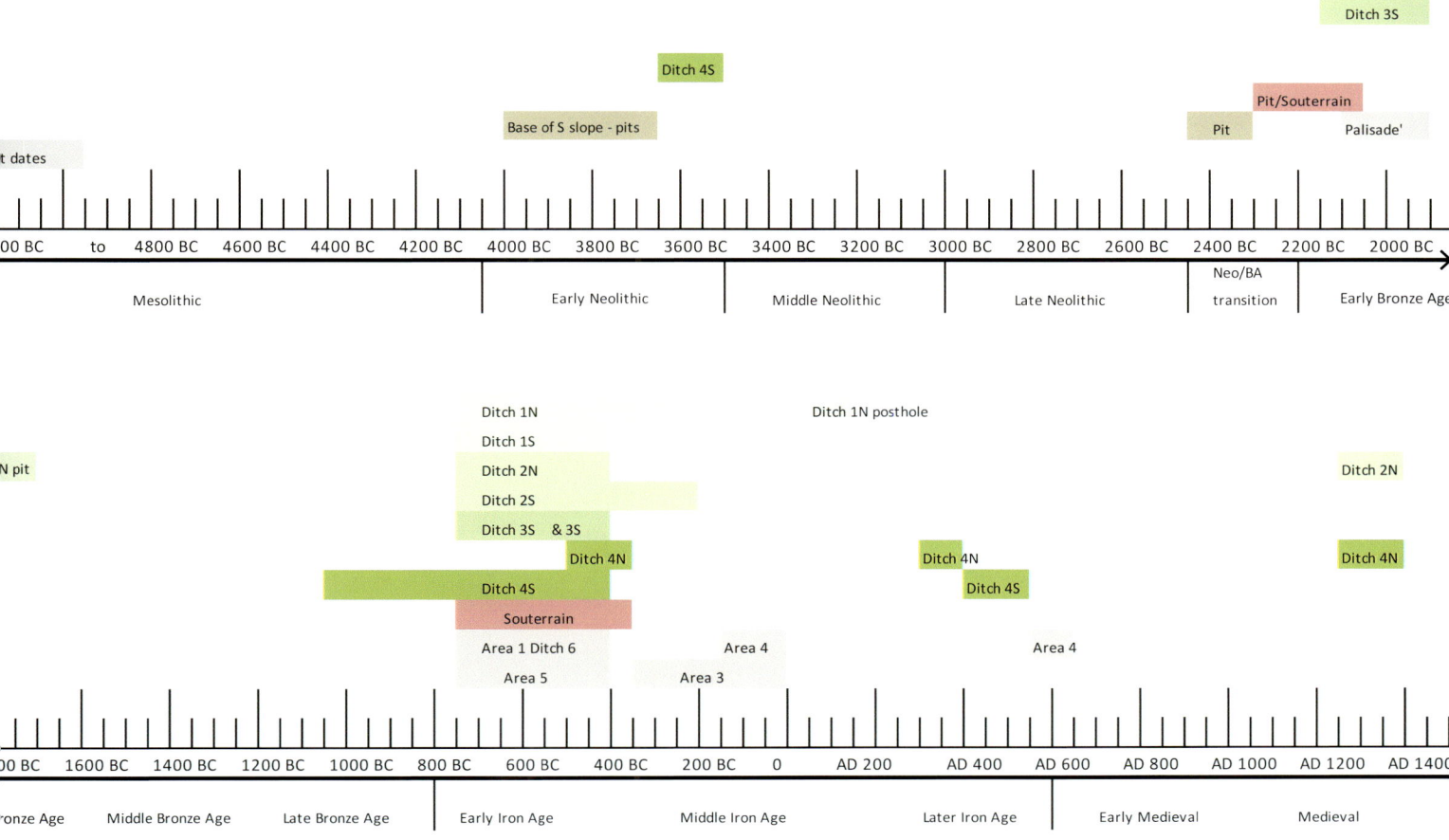

Acknowledgements

GUARD Archaeology would like to thank BAM Nuttall Ltd for commissioning us to carry out the works for this and other sites for the CTLR Project, on behalf of Perth & Kinross Council. Plant and drivers were supplied by BAM Nuttall, with managerial and site support from John Slaven, Ronald Carr, James Smith, William Diver, William O'Donoghue and Derek Walsh. GUARD Archaeology also wishes to thank Ed Danaher and Steve Lancaster of AMS Ltd and Sophie Nichol of Perth and Kinross Heritage Trust for their guidance and support throughout the work. GUARD Archaeology also thanks Susan Ramsay for her palaeobotanical expertise, advice and assessment of the sampled material, and to Tim Kinnaird of St. Andrews University for his advice and support for OSL sampling. GUARD Archaeology also thanks Bjorn Aaen and Drone Scotland for conducting the required drone surveys of the fort, supplemented by GUARD Archaeology's drone pilot, Eduardo Pérez-Fernández. Technical support for GUARD Archaeology was provided by Aileen Maule, Clark Innes and Jen Cochrane. GUARD Archaeology's Academic Advisor, Ronan Toolis provided input and advice, and the Research Framework which guided the investigations. The investigations were directed by Kenneth Green, and supervised by John-James Atkinson, Christina Mollie Dogherty and Charlotte Hunter, who were assisted by a GUARD Archaeology fieldwork team. The illustrations were produced by Jennifer Simonson and Eduardo Pérez-Fernández. The project was managed for GUARD Archaeology by Warren Bailie with assistance from Maureen Kilpatrick.

Contributors to the volume

John-James Atkinson, Beverley Ballin Smith, Christina Mollie Dogherty, Kenneth Green

Charlotte Hunter, Maureen Kilpatrick, Eddie Perez Fernandez, Jennifer Simonson, Gillian Sneddon and Alun Woodward GUARD Archaeology Ltd, 52 Elderpark Workspace, 100 Elderpark Street, Glasgow

Torben Bjarke Ballin, Lithic Research, Denny, Stirlingshire.

Gemma Cruickshanks, National Museums Scotland, Edinburgh.

Leanne Demay, National Museums Scotland, Edinburgh.

Derek Hamilton, SUERC-University of Glasgow, Scottish Enterprise Technology Park, Rankine Ave, East Kilbride, Glasgow.

Carol Laing, Lang Geoarchaeology, Hamilton, South Lanarkshire.

Susan Ramsay, Wallacestone, Falkirk, Stirlingshire.

Catherine Smith, Alder Archaeology, Perth, Perthshire.

Clare Wilson, Biological & Environmental Sciences, School of Natural Sciences, University of Stirling, Stirling.

PART 1: Introduction and Results

By Kenneth Green with John-James Atkinson, Christina Mollie Dogherty, Charlotte Hunter, Maureen Kilpatrick and Alun Woodward

Introduction

The archaeological metal detecting survey, and strip, map and sample excavation of the 1.9 ha development area Broxy Kennels fort and the evaluation and investigation of several other sites to the north of Perth (Figure 1) were delivered in advance of the construction of the Cross Tay Link Road in accordance with a condition placed upon the planning consent as set out in the 2021 Written Scheme of Archaeological Investigation prepared on behalf of Perth and Kinross Council by Archaeological Management Solutions Ltd (AMS Ltd 2021). Archaeological planning advice was provided by Perth and Kinross Heritage Trust who requested advanced archaeological investigations to determine the presence, extent and significance of any known or unknown archaeology within the footprint of the Cross Tay Link Road Project. Archaeological works were conducted by GUARD Archaeology Ltd on behalf of BAM Nuttall Ltd. The archaeological mitigation works undertaken at Broxy Kennels comprised an initial metal detecting survey in February 2022, an archaeologically monitored topsoil strip between February and March 2022 and an archaeological excavation from March to September 2022.

Broxy Kennels

Archaeological Background

The plough-truncated multivallate fort of Broxy Kennels (NRHE: NO02NE 28; HER: MPK2051) is situated on the summit of a low hill overlooking the A9 and the first major westward meander in the River Tay north of Perth (NGR: NO 09108 27875; Figure 1). The underlying geology of the site is Devonian Scone Sandstone Formation, which is overlain by Quaternary Raised Marine Deposits, Devensian Clay, Silt, Sand and Gravel (British Geological Survey: Geology of Britain Viewer). The site and its immediate environs are agricultural green fields used for arable and stock farming. It was first recorded as cropmarks on oblique aerial photography by RCAHMS (Figure 2). Four roughly concentric ditches were seen to extend around the north of the hill, broken on the north-east by an entranceway where the outer ditches turned inwards. The arrangement of the outer ditches suggested that there was phasing in the construction of the ramparts. While the same level of detail was not visible to the south of the ESE/WSW fence line due this consistently being under pasture, it was clear that fort was roughly oval in plan. The interior measures about 95 m from ENE to WSW by 50 m transversely, the ramparts enclosing an area c. 0.3 ha (Lock and Ralston 2017).

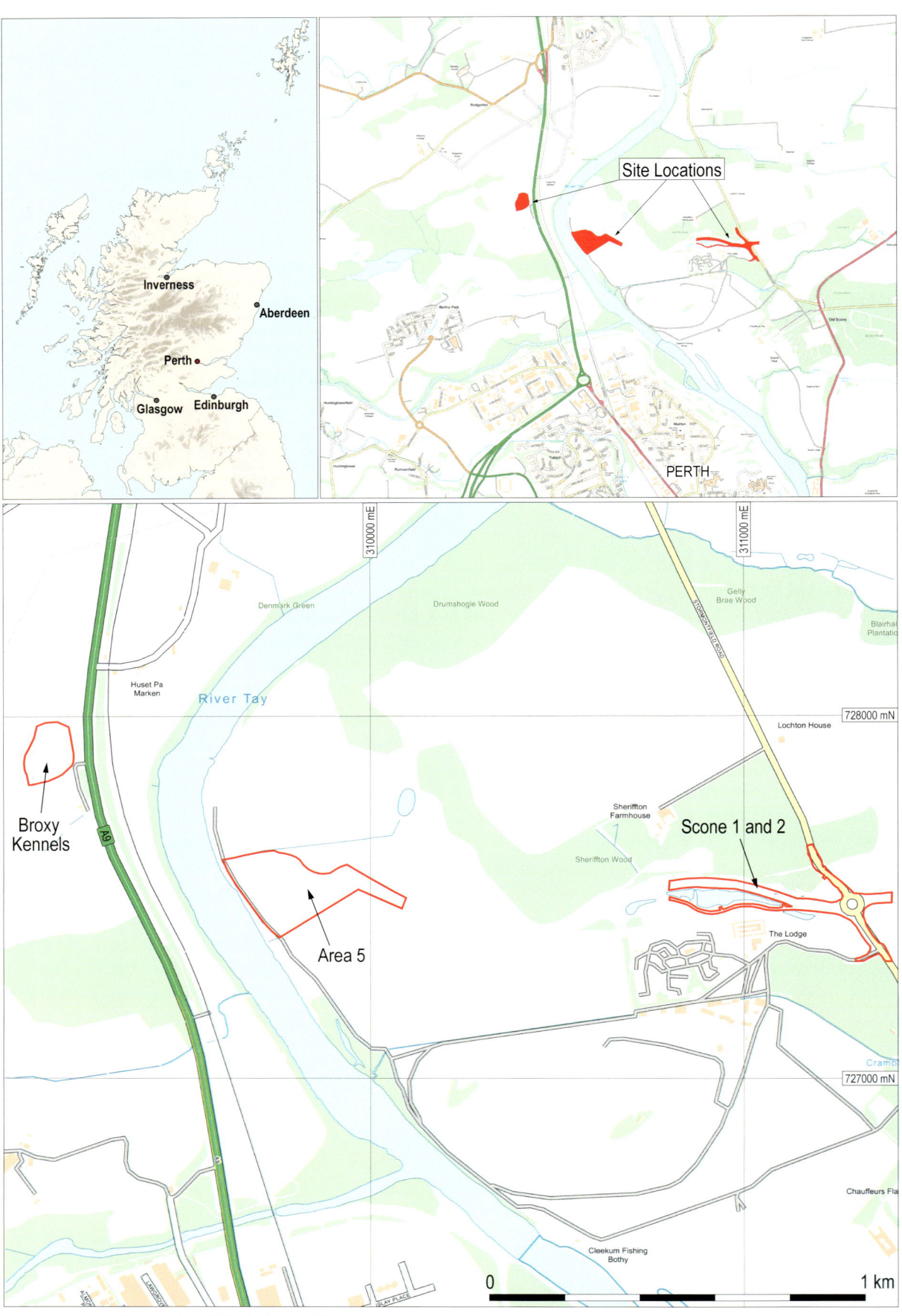

Figure 1: Site location plan.

Figure 2: Aerial view of Broxy Kennels multivallate fort, Canmore image SC01706270 © Crown Copyright: HES.

On some of the RCAHMS photographs a souterrain was observed overlying the second ditch out from the interior, immediately to the west of the entrance. It had been speculated that this represented occupation in the first and second centuries AD after the defences had gone out of use (Lock and Ralston 2017). While a geophysics survey of the northern part of the site confirmed the ditches of the multivallate fort, aside from two small amorphous areas of disturbance within the interior which were classified as 'undetermined', no other archaeological activity nor the souterrain feature were identified in the geophysical data (Burton 2018, 26).

An archaeological evaluation was undertaken in 2019 and confirmed the presence of the souterrain to the west of the fort entranceway (Pettitt and Hession 2019, 11-12). This comprised a stone-walled sunken linear feature along the alignment of the middle ditch, with a stone-flagged floor approximately 1.67m deep from the modern ground surface. The souterrain floor was overlain by four separate deposits, the second uppermost of which contained burnt wood.

The evaluation also examined several sections of the ditches previously identified in aerial photographs and the geophysics survey to reveal a fort defined by three ditches (Pettitt and Hession 2019, 12-18). The evaluation discovered the remains of only one of the ditches, perhaps the innermost ditch, around the southern side of the hill (Figure 3). The interior contained a limited number of pits, post-holes and a shallow ditch that may relate to prehistoric structures; charred hulled barley grains were recovered from these post-holes and some of the defensive ditch fills and were suggested as indicating a Bronze Age to Iron Age date (Timpany in Pettitt and Hession 2019, 31).

Figure 3: Broxy Kennels Site Plan © Rubicon Heritage Services Ltd.

The excavation of Broxy Kennels Fort was an opportunity to investigate a souterrain that had been sealed by later prehistoric deposits and which may therefore have held evidence for its original function. This evidence was considered useful to compare with that recovered from excavated souterrains in Perthshire such as Newmill, Luncarty and Loak Farm Borrow Pit as well as those further afield such as Castlelaw in Midlothian (Watkins and Barclay 1981; Sophie Nicol pers comm; Childe 1933). Any new evidence could enhance our understanding of what is a particularly important aspect of the Iron Age in Scotland.

The post-excavation analyses were also an opportunity to examine similarities with, but also what distinguishes this fort from, other forts in Tayside and beyond. There are around 4,147 forts across Britain and Ireland (Lock and Ralston 2017) of which at least 1,481 are in Scotland, though given the difficulty in drawing a line between forts and duns this figure may be even higher (Halliday 2019, 47). Proportionally the landmass of Scotland possesses more forts than anywhere else in Britain and Ireland, though given the variability in morphology, size and topographical location, it would be a mistake to view them as a unitary set (Ralston 2015, 207).

Their prominence in the archaeological record owes much to the visibility of their rampart and ditches in the modern landscape, or even through aerial photography such as the case with Broxy Kennels, but as excavations have repeatedly shown, many enclosed sites were unenclosed for large periods of their occupation (Toolis 2015, 23). Defining Iron Age sites solely by how they were enclosed at some point in time should therefore be treated with caution, especially since later prehistoric settlement architecture across Scotland spans the centuries from the late Bronze Age to the early medieval period. Nevertheless, as forts are widely distributed across the country, they represent a significant aspect of the Iron Age archaeological record of Scotland. Broxy Kennels fort is the fourth such fort in Scotland to be subject to total excavation in advance of development works; previous forts to be completely excavated, all of which also comprised cropmark sites, comprise Broxmouth in East Lothian, Braehead in Glasgow and Winchburgh in West Lothian (Armit and McKenzie 2013; Ellis 2007; Savory 2019). Occupation of these three sites extended over the latter half of the first millennium BC and into the first century AD, thus offering potentially useful contemporary comparisons with Broxy Kennels Fort.

One of amongst around 75 forts spread across Perth and Kinross (Strachan 2020, 8-9), Broxy Kennels lies within a landscape densely occupied by forts, part of a distribution spread across central and eastern Scotland. In recent decades numerous forts have been investigated in Perthshire. The Strathearn Environs and Royal Forteviot (SERF) project included excavations of 10 forts, predominantly along the Ochil hills and Strathearn and while full results are in preparation, much of the interim results, including interactive media and data structure reports, has been published online. Moreover, three forts in close proximity to Broxy Kennels have also recently been excavated as part of the Tay Landscape Partnership initiative led by Perth and Kinross Heritage Trust (Strachan 2020).

Results of the Investigations at Broxy Kennels

A detailed research framework (Toolis 2022) was prepared in consultation with the Consultant (AMS Ltd) and the Curator (PKHT), taking into consideration the relevant sections of the *Perth & Kinross Archaeological Research Framework* (PKARF). In addition, a thorough sampling strategy (Bailie and Ramsay 2022), again prepared in consultation with the Consultant and Curator, was employed throughout the excavation of Broxy Kennels Fort to ensure an appropriate level of targeted sampling with the aim of providing suitable quantities of environmental material for analysis and dating during the post-excavation stage. Sampling techniques included taking bulk soil samples, column samples, Kubiena and monolith tin samples, gridded multi-element samples from the floor deposits in the souterrain, and a number of Optically Stimulated Luminescence (OSL)[1] samples that aimed to support the radiocarbon dating in order to reconstruct the chronology and phasing of the fort, where organic material was lacking.

The monitored topsoil strip revealed the Broxy Kennels multivallate fort to comprise three main ditches (Ditches 1, 2 and 4) that appear to have completely encircled the hill and a fourth ditch (Ditch 3) that extended only partially around its northern and eastern sides. Several small groups of pits and postholes were found in the interior area of the fort at the top of the hill suggesting its possible occupation, although several modern agricultural pits were also identified there.

To the north-east, beyond the fort's ditches, were several more pits and another small ditch that were sterile. No material culture was recovered from them to suggest their possible date or function. To the south of the fort were a number of pits, postholes and deposits, some of which appeared to have been of Bronze Age date as Beaker pottery and worked flint were recovered from some of them.

Although only a few finds were recovered from the main fort ditches they, together with the stratigraphic evidence from within the ditches, generally indicate that the fort was in use during the Iron Age with other peripheral activity suggesting the site was utilised as early as the Bronze Age.

---

1   Although OSL samples were collected as a contingency, their analysis was not required for the project.

Metal Detecting and Significant Finds (Figure 4)

A Metal Detecting Survey revealed a total of 420 metal artefacts, in addition to four ceramic pieces, two lithics and one fragment of glass. The majority of these finds can be attributed to agricultural activity in the area during the nineteenth and twentieth centuries; however, some artefacts of interest were also recovered.

Of the metal artefacts recovered, 375 were made of iron and this included one Allen Key, 11 bolts, one cap or mount, one hinge, four hooks, one horseshoe, one key, 49 nails, 25 metal sheets, one sickle, four plough components and 12 sections of fencing wire. All of the iron finds were indicative of modern agricultural activity in the area. The 17 copper artefacts recovered were likewise indicative of modern agricultural activities. A further five copper alloy artefacts were recovered with only one of them being identified as archaeologically significant: a nineteenth century servant's button (SF 187). Of the total of seven lead artefacts, two were buttons (SF 014 and SF 085) and two were Dutch sack or bale seals dating to the nineteenth century (SF 182 and SF 183). Two brass artefacts were recovered and this included one button (SF 139) and one unfired .303 round of ammunition (SF 241), which was taken by the local police for safe disposal. Three steel artefacts attributed to modern machinery were also recovered.

Of particular importance were the three bronze artefacts, which included one fragment of a high-quality bronze implement (SF 019) of possible Bronze Age date or later, one bronze pommel (SF 027) possibly from a dagger dating from c. 1200 – 1600 AD, and a late-medieval penannular brooch (SF 184) (see *Metalwork* below).

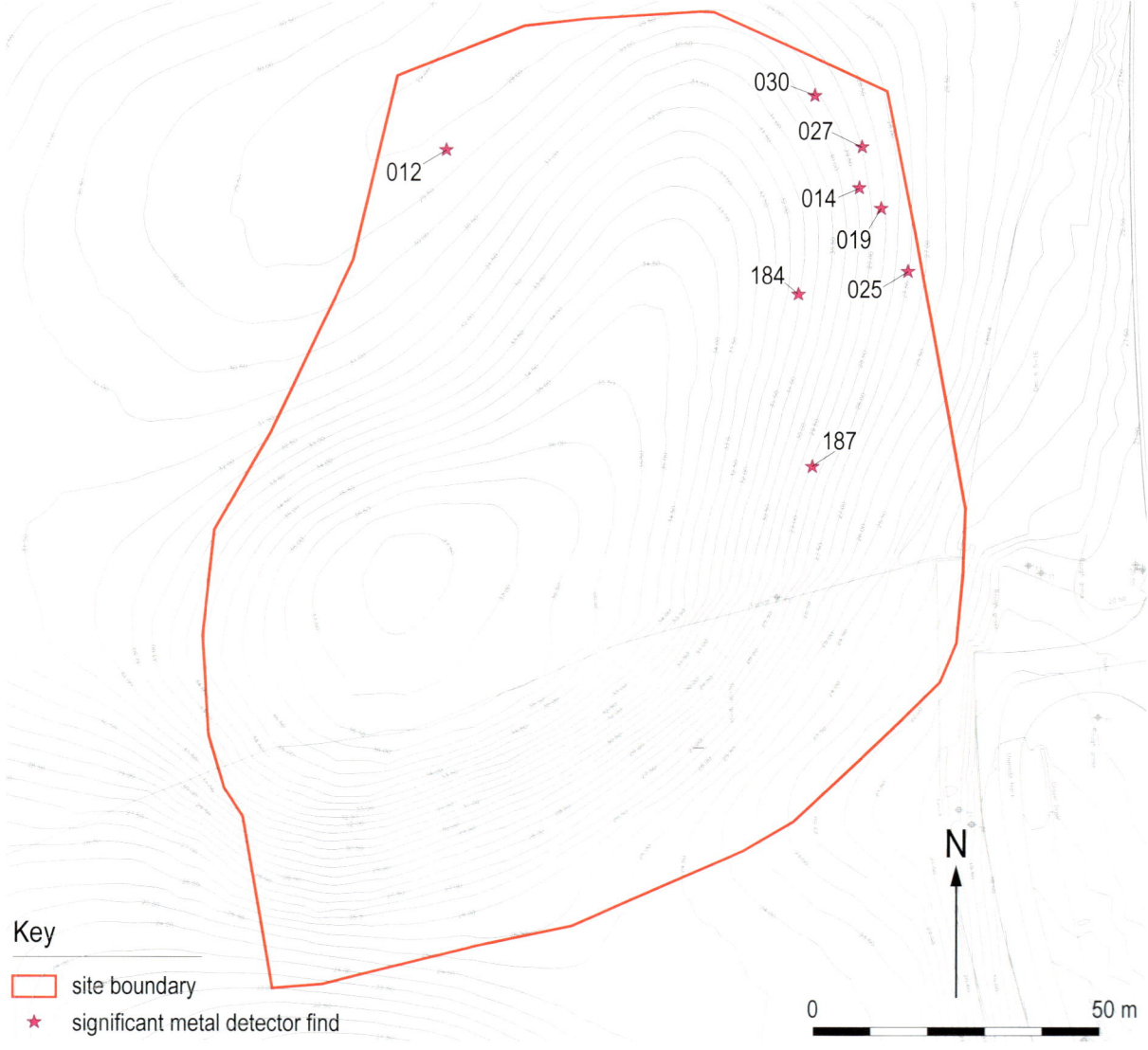

Key

☐ site boundary

★ significant metal detector find

Figure 4: Metal detecting results.

The Main Ditch Excavations

The four main ditches at Broxy Kennels Fort were divided into two parts - north and south; the terminals of all the main ditches delineated the entrance to the hillfort in the north-east and divided the fort into its northern and southern parts. The western area of the fort, beyond the area removed by the construction of the new road, remains *in situ* in agricultural land (Figures 2 and 5). The ditches were numbered 1-4 with an 'N' for north, and 'S' for south, for example, Ditch 1 South is abbreviated as Ditch 1S and so on. The hand-excavated slots trenches across each ditch were labelled A, B, C etc. with their locations of the various slots shown indicated on Figure 5.

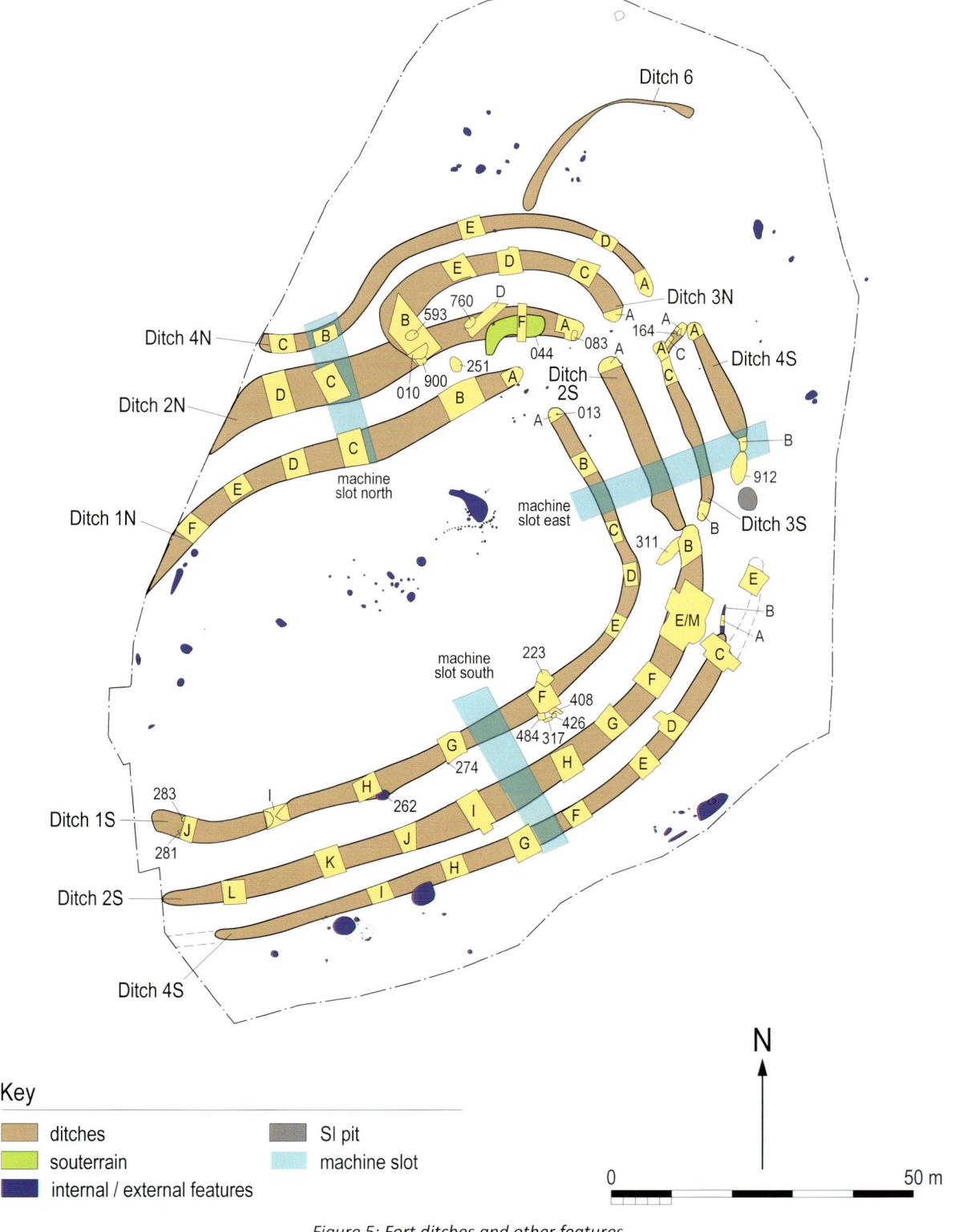

Figure 5: Fort ditches and other features.

All the ditches were filled predominantly with a variety of natural silts, sands and gravels that varied in colour, shade, hue and texture from black-brown, red-brown, yellow-brown, grey-brown, with occasional red or white lenses. Some natural clay lenses were also encountered. These deposits largely derived from the eroded sides of the ditches, from the up-cast material (or ramparts) between the ditches, and also domestic debris, which included charcoal. The ditch fills are described in detail in the DSR (Green 2023) and are illustrated in the figures below. The figures also highlight the various recuts that were identified, modern intrusions and the location of finds and samples.

The profiles of the ditches are a product of their original formation: subsequent erosion of ditch sides with deposition of eroded material in the bases of the ditches, natural infilling including blown sand, and the movement of sediments from higher to lower levels. Within this mix is the digging out of accumulated deposits in parts of the ditches when they filled in and their subsequent reshaping and recutting, in some cases at least twice. Maintenance of ditches dug into sand and silt deposits and the re-formation of ramparts, from the up-cast material, was probably a regular necessity. It is clear from the occurrence of charcoal (and the occasional finds) mixed in with the ditch fills that domestic hearth refuse was either directly or indirectly dumped into the ditches from activities within the enclosure on the top of the hill. The ditches are complex structures and understanding their formation is challenging. Their dating is discussed (see *Radiocarbon Dating and Chronological Modelling*) below.

Ditch 1S

This was the innermost ditch on the south side of the fort. It measured c. 130 m in length from its terminus in the north-east, around the eastern and southern circumferences of the hill, and up to the limit of excavation at the western extent of the site. A total of ten slot trenches A-J were hand-excavated through it indicating that the ditch varied in width from a minimum of 1.9 m to a maximum of 5.5 m and with a maximum depth of 1.6 m. Analysis of the ditch profiles from the slot trenches showed that in general the ditch

was broad at the base and slightly concave to flat. This was largely due to parts of it being re-dug at least twice, because the sandy subsoil into which it had been dug gradually filled it in. The machine trench (see below, Figure 18), reached the bottom of the ditch and reveal that it had a much narrower base originally. The emptying and recutting of the ditch widened it and produced a more rounded profile (Figures 6 and 7).

Slot A at the terminus revealed that there had been two postholes dug into the bottom of the ditch – the only evidence of wooden posts in the ditches. Small amounts of daub or pot were found in its earliest filling in Slot A, and pottery and burnt bone fragments in the base of Slot F. Slot F also produced charcoal, stone, flint, pottery sherds and further animal bone in the layers that infilled its recut suggesting that domestic debris from activities within the hillfort were discarded into the ditch at that point.

Ditch 2S

The next ditch in sequence, Ditch 2S, again began at the north-east terminus, measured c. 149 m in length, and maintain a concentric distance of between 5 m and 7 m from the south and east edges of Ditch 1S. A total of ten hand-dug slot trenches were excavated through the ditch that indicated that it varied in width from 3.35 m to just over 6 m. The maximum depth it was excavated to was 2.7 m in Slot J.

Like Ditch 1S, these ditch profiles were irregular with a tendency for a generally wider rounded or occasionally flatter basal profiles. Slot trench E/M provided a more acute and tapering base to the ditch, with a narrow flat bottom (the ankle breaker) that suggested it was the original design. There were fewer re-cuttings of this ditch than Ditch 1S, but with Slot J indicating two, and slots A, E/M and I one each. During the excavation it was noted that in the filling of the recut of Slot E/M there were accumulations of cobbles that were considered to have revetted the ditch side (Figure 8). Charcoal was located though out Slot A, the upper fills of Slots E and F, i the lower fills of Slot H, the middle fill of slot I, the middle fills of Slot J, the upper fill of Slot L and the lowest fill of Slot M. Finds were largely confined to the upper fills of the ditch: sherds of pottery and burnt bone in the re-cut fills of Slot E, and prehistoric pottery in the upper fills of slots F and Slot G, with slag fragments located in the re-cut fills of Slot I. An unidentified metal object (SF 157) was found in the lowest fill of the first re-cutting of Slot J with sherds of prehistoric pottery in the lowest fill of its second re-cut.

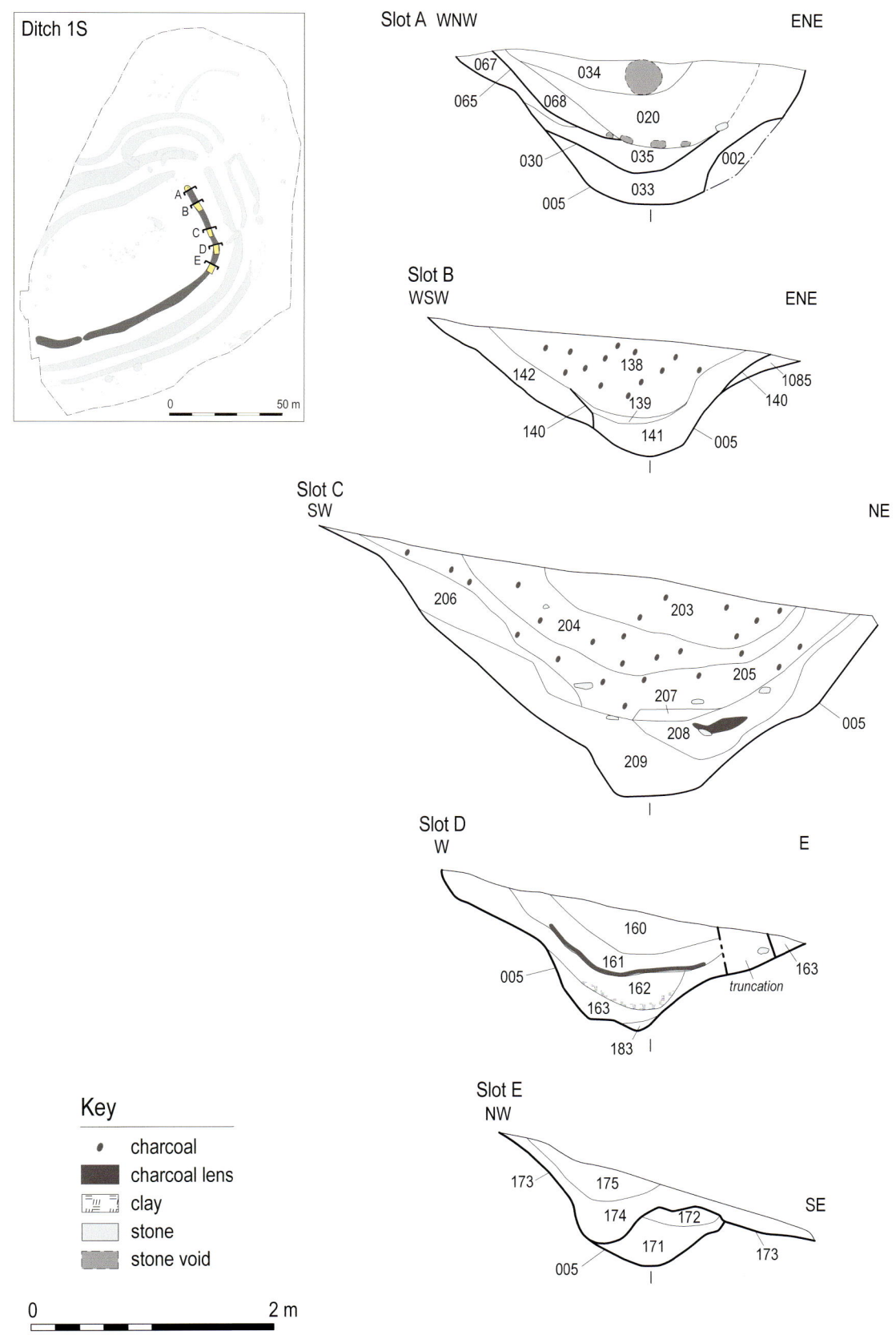

Figure 6: Ditch 1S sections of Slots A to E.

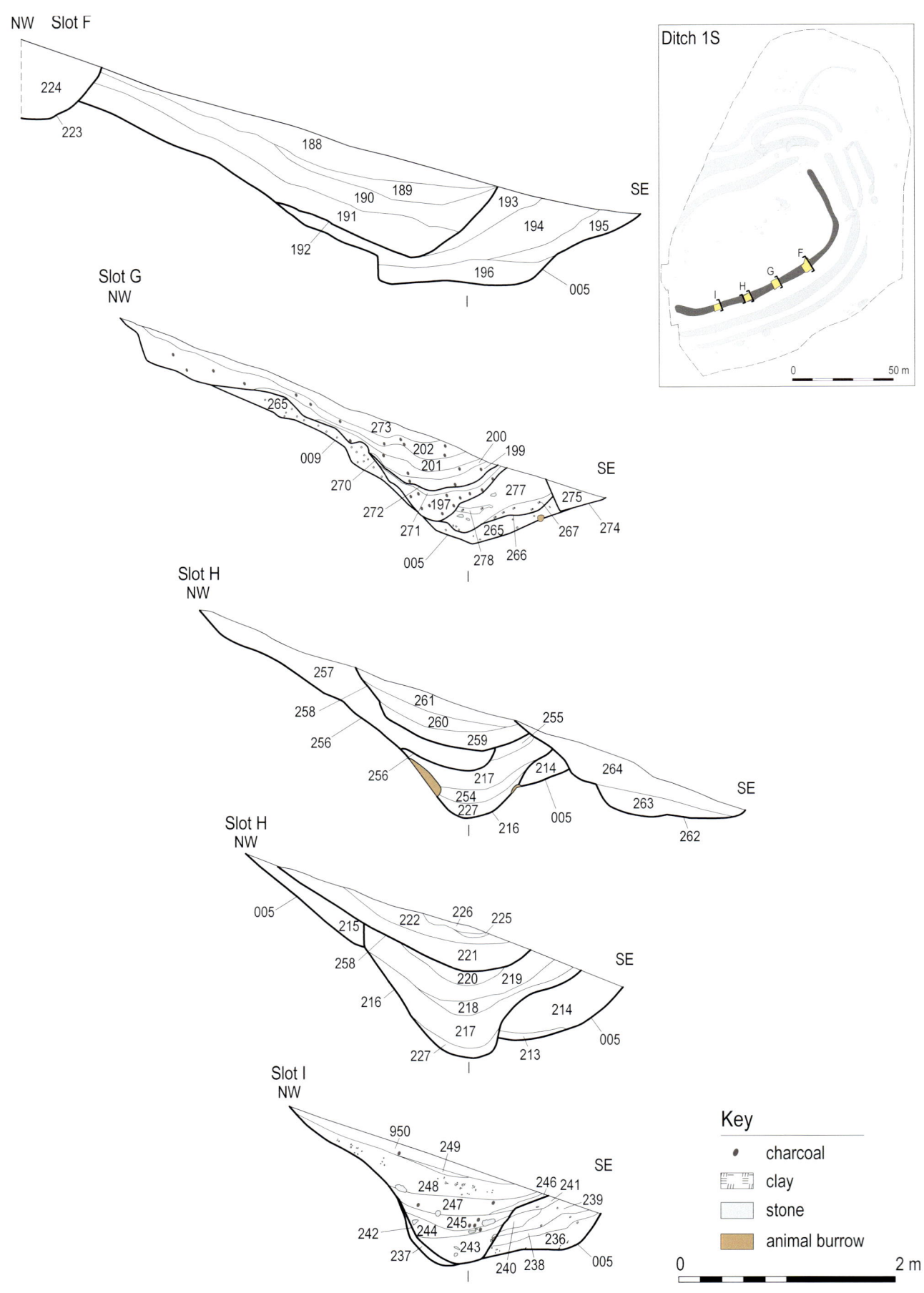

Figure 6 (continued): Ditch 1S sections of Slots F to I.

Figure 7: Ditch 1S excavation of terminal.

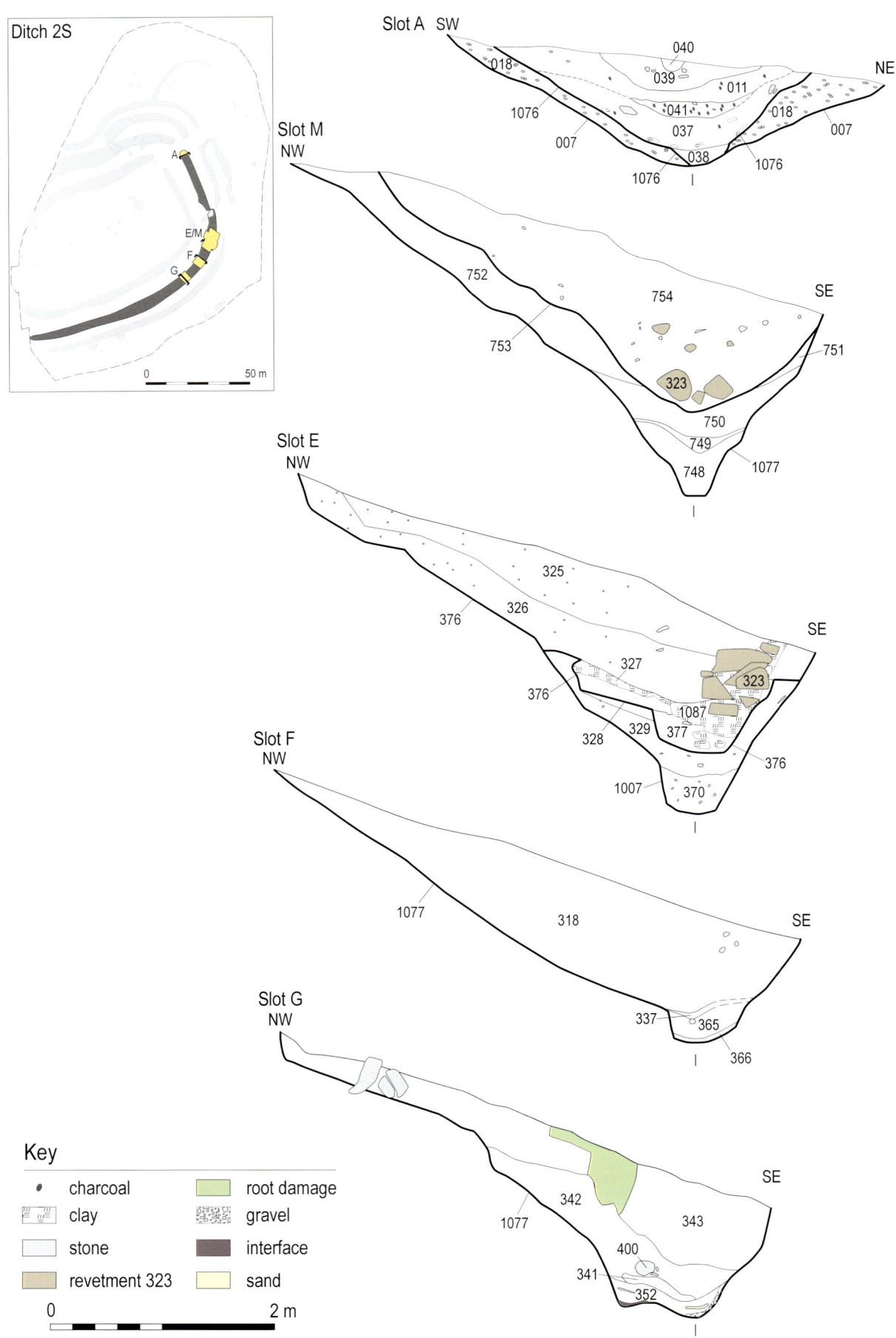

Figure 8: Ditch 2S sections of Slots A, M, E to L.

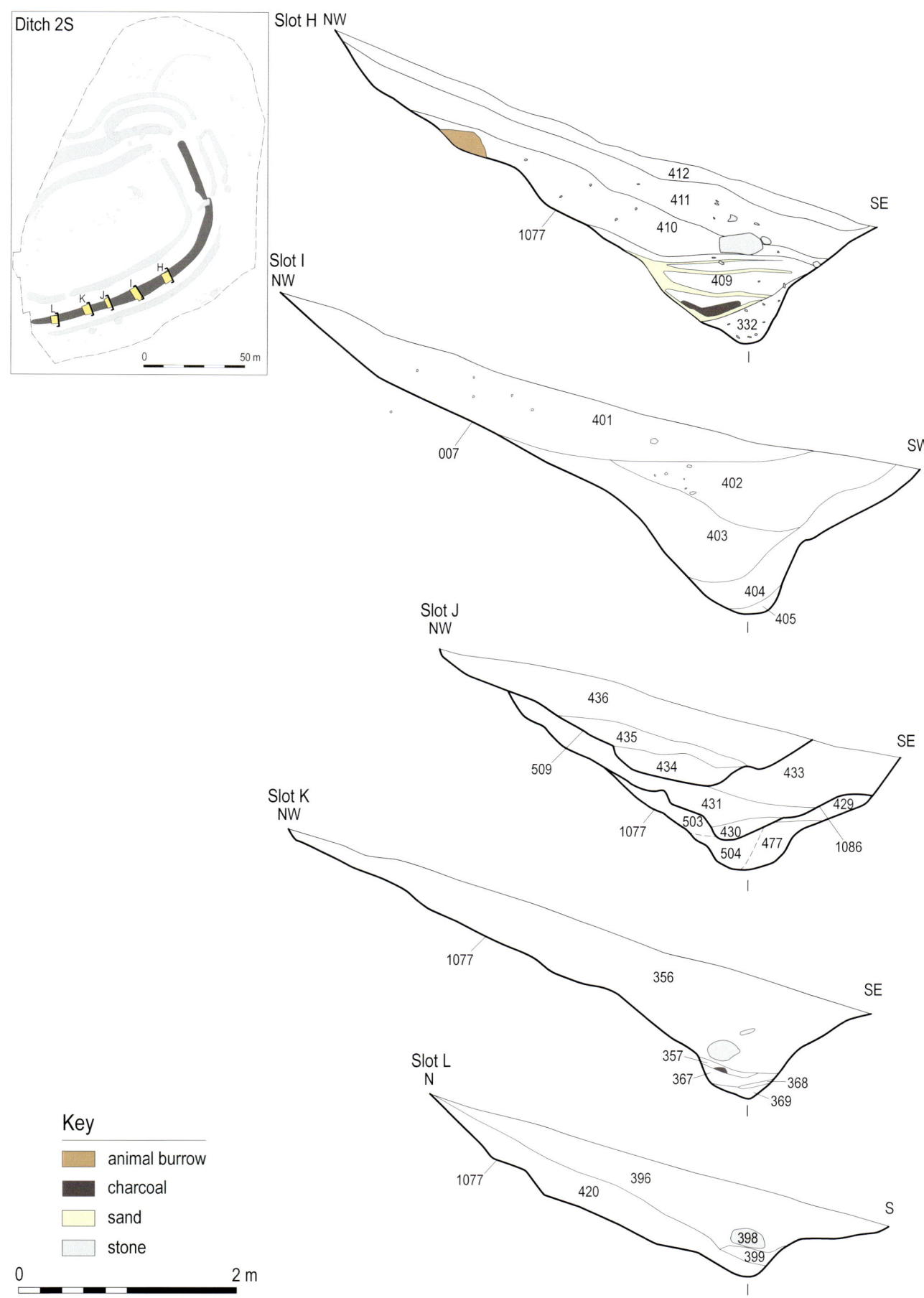

Figure 8 (continued): Ditch 2S sections of Slots A, M, E to L.

Ditch S3

The third ditch (Ditch 3S) around the eastern side of the fort measured 35.8 m in length from its terminus at the north-east entrance to where it turned inwards before terminating just short of the edge of Ditch 2S. Ditch 3S was positioned up to 5.5 m east of Ditch 2S along most of its length. It had three slot trenches dug across it (A, B and C), which revealed the ditch to be a maximum of 2 m in width with a depth of c. 1.4 m (Figures 5 and 9).

Slot A at the north end of the ditch by it terminus indicated that it was dug in a V-shape with a narrow and steep base. Further investigation in the adjoining Slot C indicated that the ditch had been re-cut and it became slightly shallower and its base was slightly wider. The southern end of this short ditch (Slot B) was only 1.4 m wide and 0.7 m deep. In this slot trench the base of the ditch was broad and almost flat. Charcoal

was found in most of the ditch fills, along with predominantly small stone and the rare flint. The occasional larger stone was located in the upper fills of Slot A by the terminus.

Ditch 4S

The fourth ditch was in two sections (Figures 10 and 11). The first section c. 31 m in length by the entrance, was positioned approximately c. 5 m to the north-east of Ditch 3S. Two slot trenches A and B were dug across it, as well as the Machine Slot East. The ditch was c. 2.2 m in width and 0.73 m in depth in Slot A at its terminus, narrowing to 1.1 m in width but increasing in depth to 2 m in Slot B. The ditch terminated in the East Machine Slot where a new short length of ditch (912) began. Although there was a gap of c. 0.20 m between the two lengths of ditch it is likely that their upper sections were stratigraphically joined and that relationship has been lost to erosion and modern agricultural truncation. A single piece of flint was found in the middle fill of Slot B.

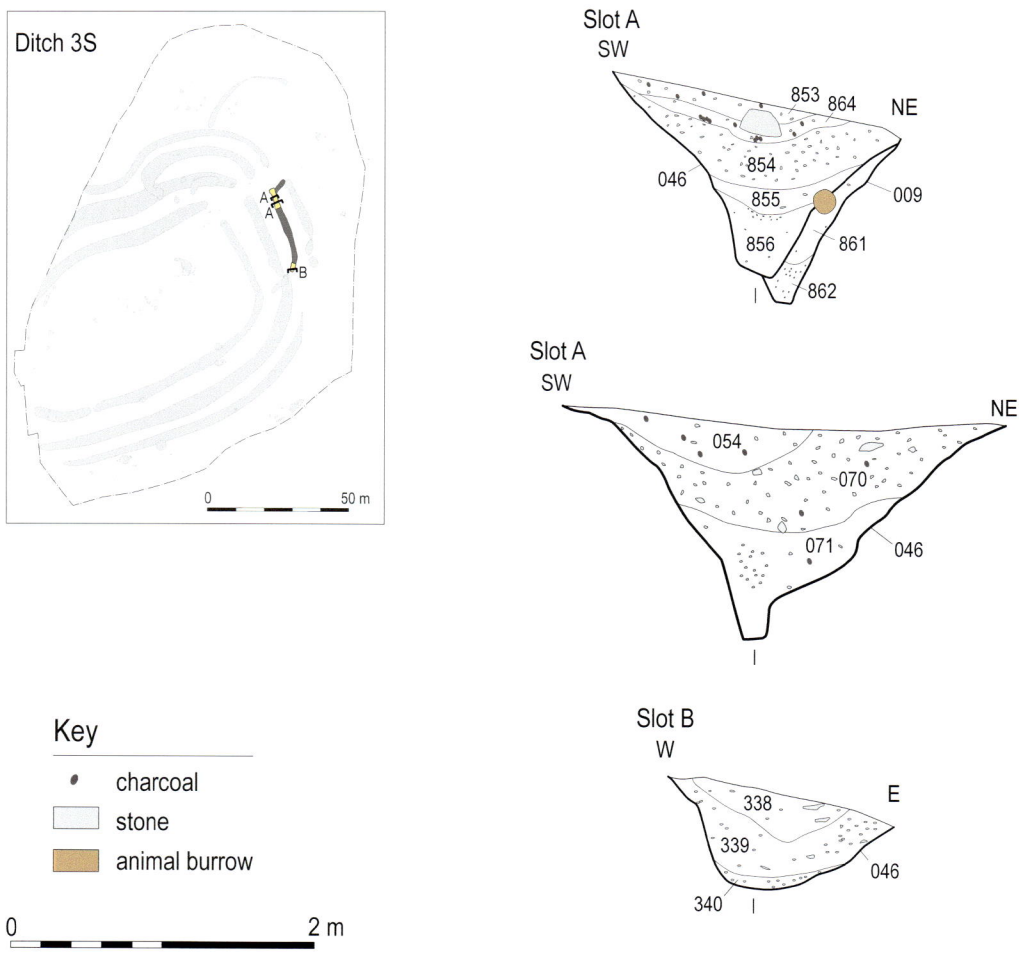

Figure 9: Ditch 3S sections of Slots A and B

A further c. 22 m to the south and seen in Slot C was the terminus of the second part of the ditch. This second ditch section was c. 114 m in length and ran concentrically with Ditch 2S but c. 5 m from it along the southern part of the hill. Seven further slot trenches were dug along this portion of the ditch (Slots C to I). In this section the ditch attained a maximum width of 4.5 m and a depth of 2 m in Slot E.

A channel or gully (535) extended from Slot C continued and tapered off to the north-east for a distance of c. 3.5 m. The gully possibly represented a continuation that may have joined with the first section, but only its 'ankle-breaker' base survived erosion and truncation. The profiles of the ditch located in the slot trenches showed

more consistency than Ditches1S to 3S, with predominantly moderately wide V-shaped bases, except for Slot E that had a narrow flat base. The ditch fills were also simple, being mainly one fill. The fills of Slot E had both charcoal and the rare stone, and only Slot H provided evidence its original acute V- shaped narrow base and of a recut. No artefacts were found in any of the ditch fills in the excavated slot trenches.

The extent of the ditches in the northern part of the fort was less than in the south due to the boundary of the excavated area in the west cutting across them. The ditches are described from the innermost to the outermost. Their termini were all situated on the northern side of the entrance to the fort.

Figure 10: Digging the ditches on the south side of the hillfort.

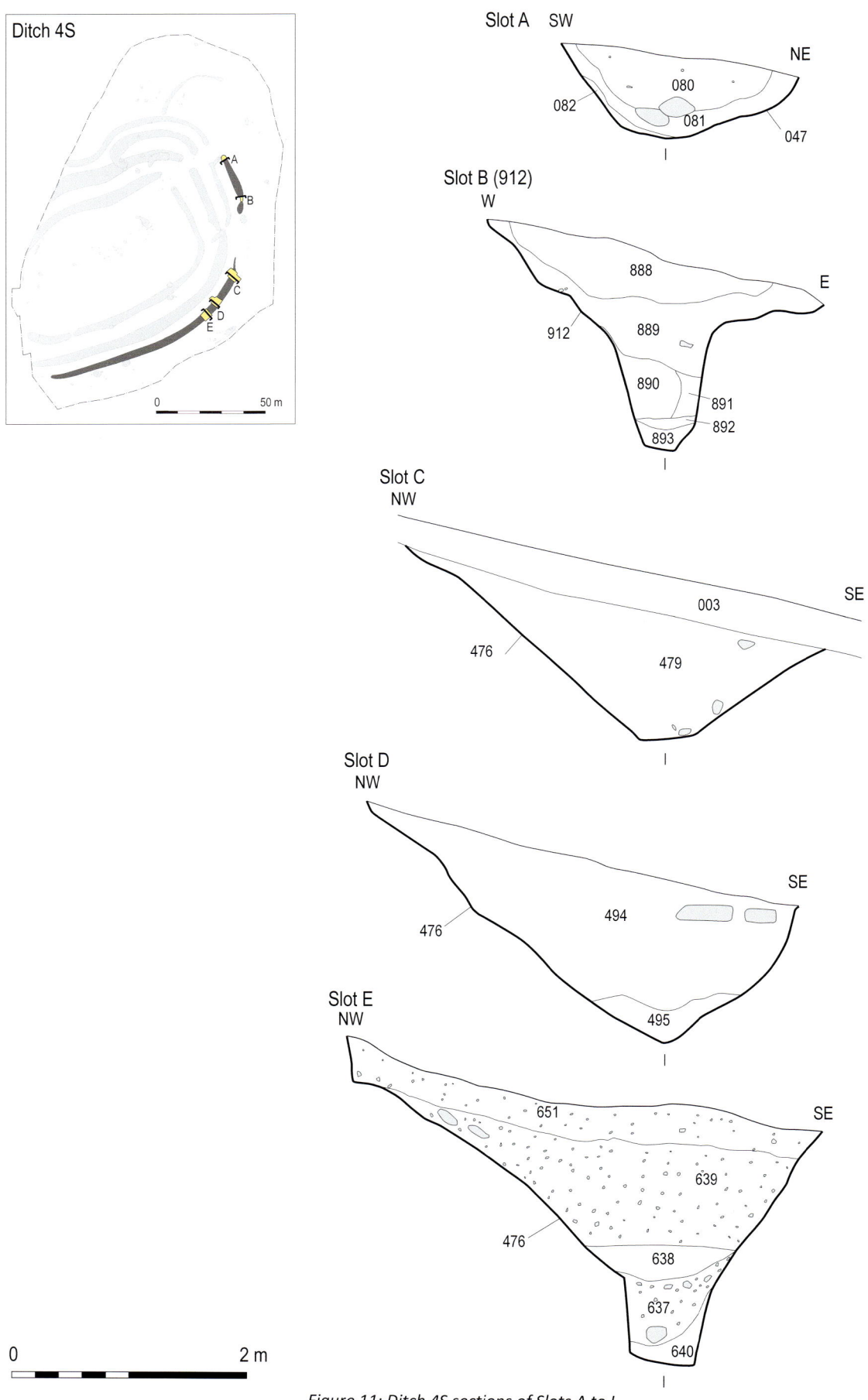

Figure 11: Ditch 4S sections of Slots A to I.

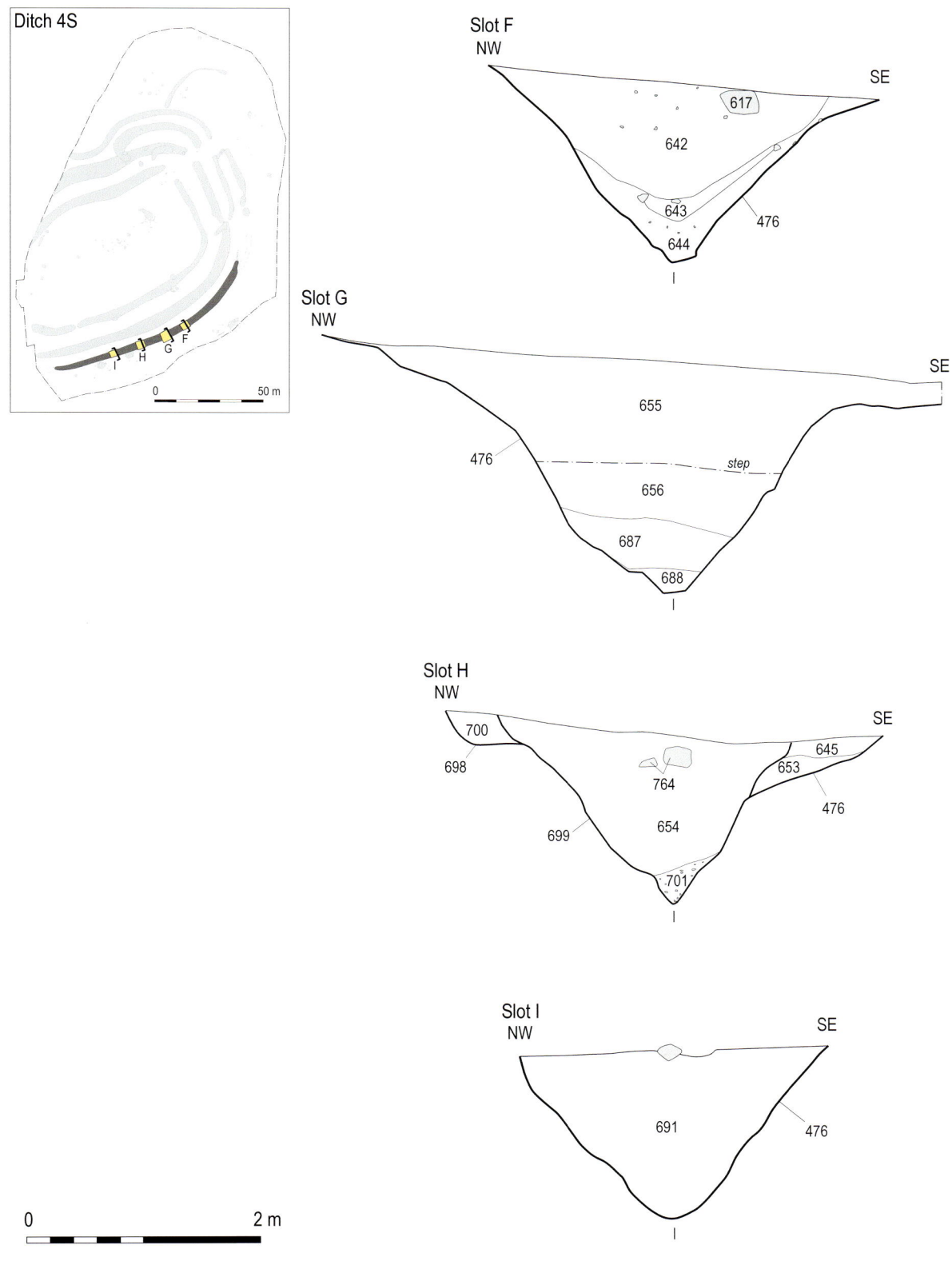

Figure 11 (continued): Ditch 4S sections of Slots A to I.

Ditch 1N

This ditch measured 71 m in length, from its terminus by the entrance up to and beyond the western limit of the site. A total of six slots trenches (A to F) were excavated across the ditch. From a minimum of 3 m in width in Slot A, the widest ditch section was in Slot C where it attained a width of 6.2 m and was also the deepest at 1.92 m. The profiles of the excavated ditch sections revealed a similar broad and open pattern as those of Ditch 1S, but with concave or uneven bases but only Slot B preserved a V-shaped profile at its base. The ditch in Slot A to D was recut once (Figure 12).

The inclusion of cobbles in the fills of the recut ditch in Slots A and B was particularly noticeable, but this may be due to their occurrence in the gravel and clay subsoil the ditch was dug through. Finds in the earliest ditch deposits were few and restricted to sherds of pottery and flint in the base of Slot B. Other finds and samples were mostly the middle or upper fills of the re-cut ditch, such as pottery, charcoal and lithics in Slot A, lithics, pottery, daub, slag and other stone in Slot B, burnt bone in Slots C and D, and daub or pottery in Slot F.

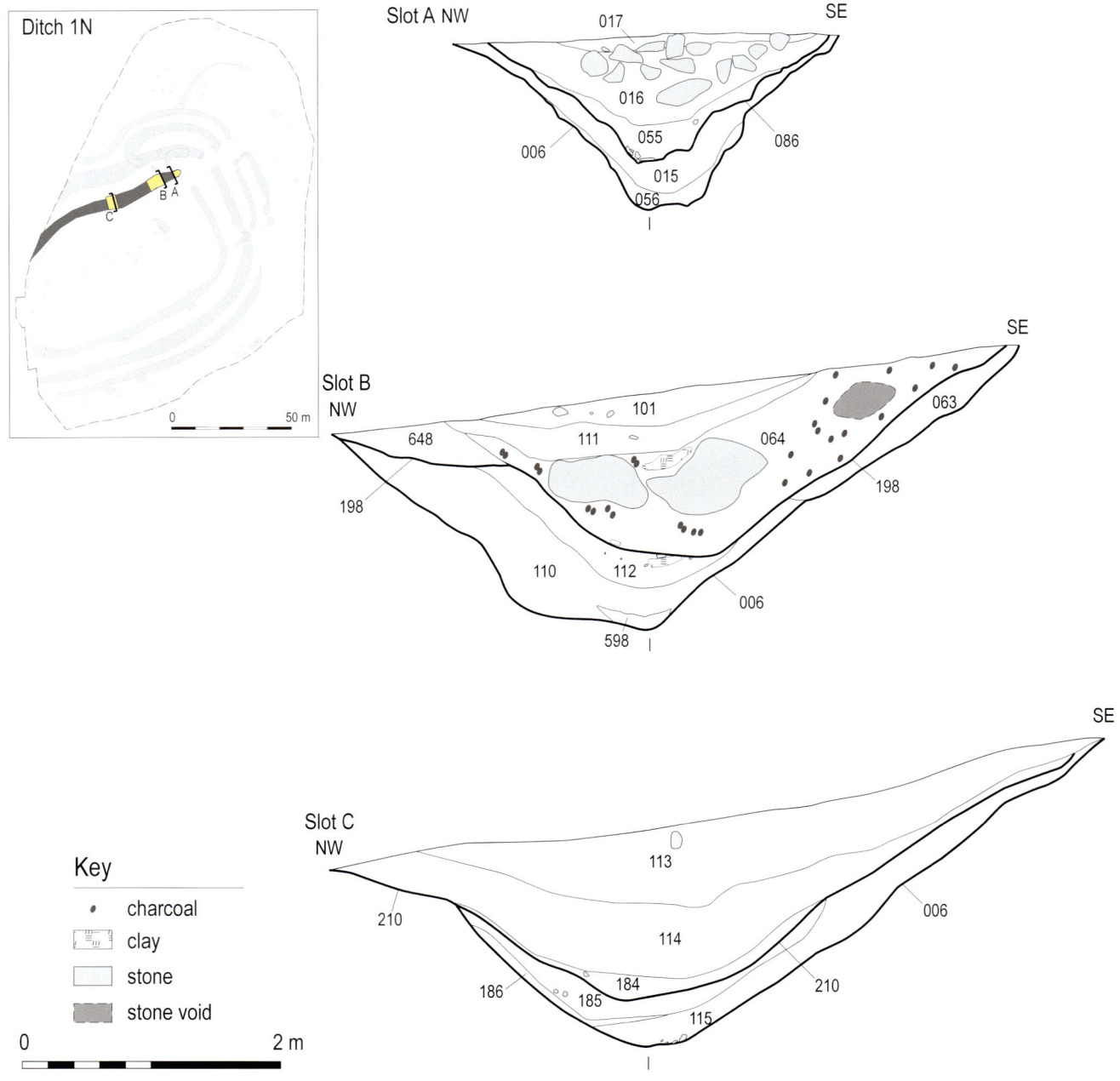

Figure 12: Ditch 4S sections of Slots A to I.

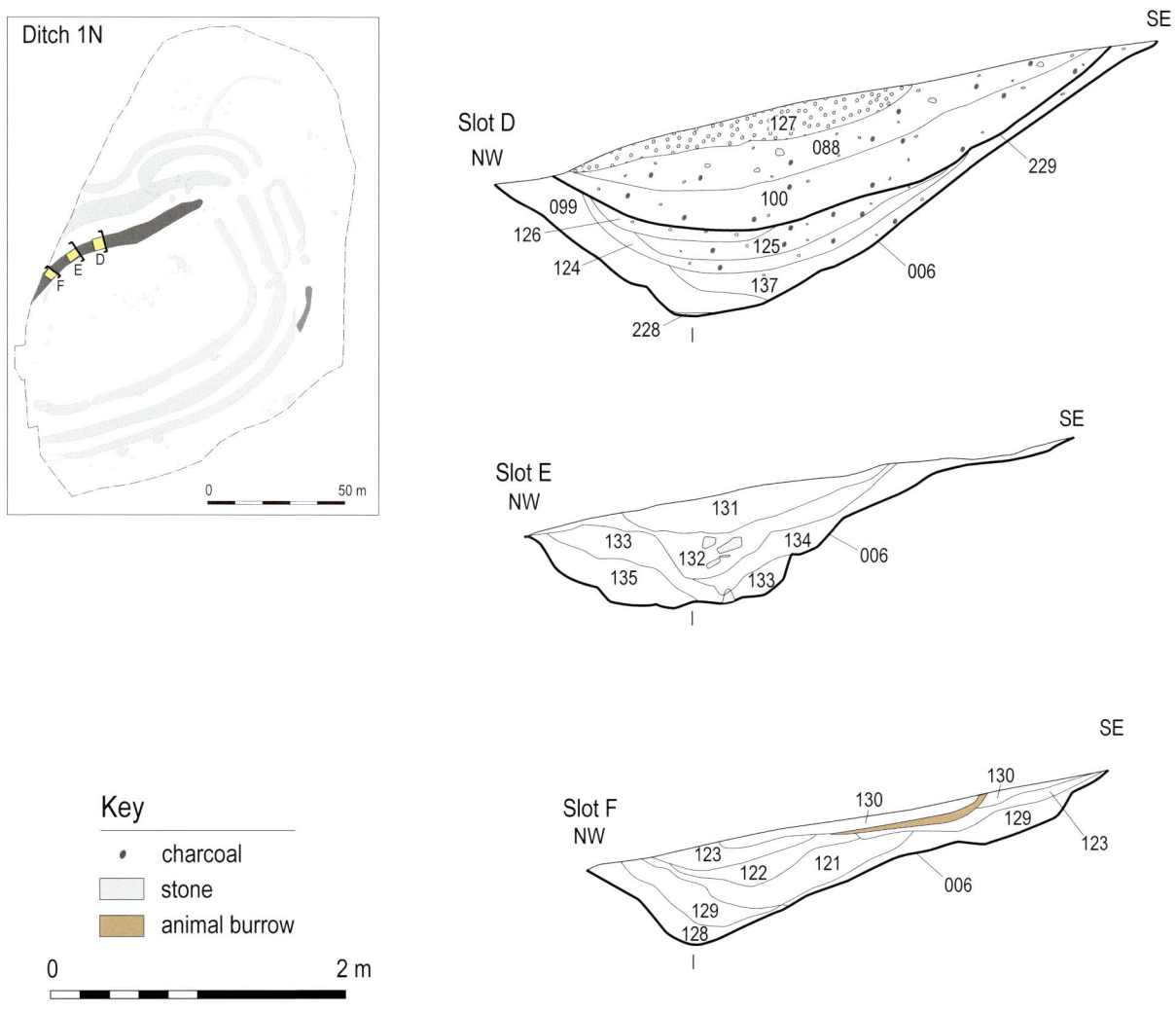

Figure 12 (continued): Ditch 4S sections of Slots A to I.

Ditch 2N

This ditch measured 65 m in length and followed a line concentric to the inner Ditch 1N, at a distance of between 5 m and 7 m from its northern and eastern edges. It extended from the north-east entrance terminal to the western extent of the site and a total of six slot trenches were hand-excavated across it. This ditch was dug into for the construction of a souterrain, which also affected Ditches 3N and 4N. An enlarged Slot B was excavated across the interface between Ditch 2N and Ditch 3N to its exterior, Slot D was excavated at an angle to the ditch north-west of the souterrain, and Slot F was dug across the ditch and the souterrain, close to the east terminal (Figures 5 and 13).

The eastern end of the ditch measured 3.7 m in width and 1.23 m in depth, but towards the western end, it had doubled in width to 7.8 m

and was deeper at 2.2 m. The terminal Slot A indicated that the ditch was recut twice, with Slots C and D re-dug once only.

Slot B was extended and widened to understand the relationship between Ditches 2N and 3N (Figure 14). During the excavation it became apparent that Ditch 2N was the earlier of the two ditches and that Ditch 3N had been excavated later, probably after Ditch 2 had gone out of use, and truncated some of its upper fills. The original deposits of Ditch 2S contained charcoal, a small number of flint artefacts and sherds of prehistoric pottery. The fills of its recut contained similar finds and included fragments of daub and a rare piece of slag. The upper fills of the recut ditch in Slots C and D contained medieval pottery and iron nails indicating that this deposit had been disturbed, possibly by ploughing in recent centuries long after the fort had fallen out of use.

Figure 13: Digging Ditch 2N by the souterrain.

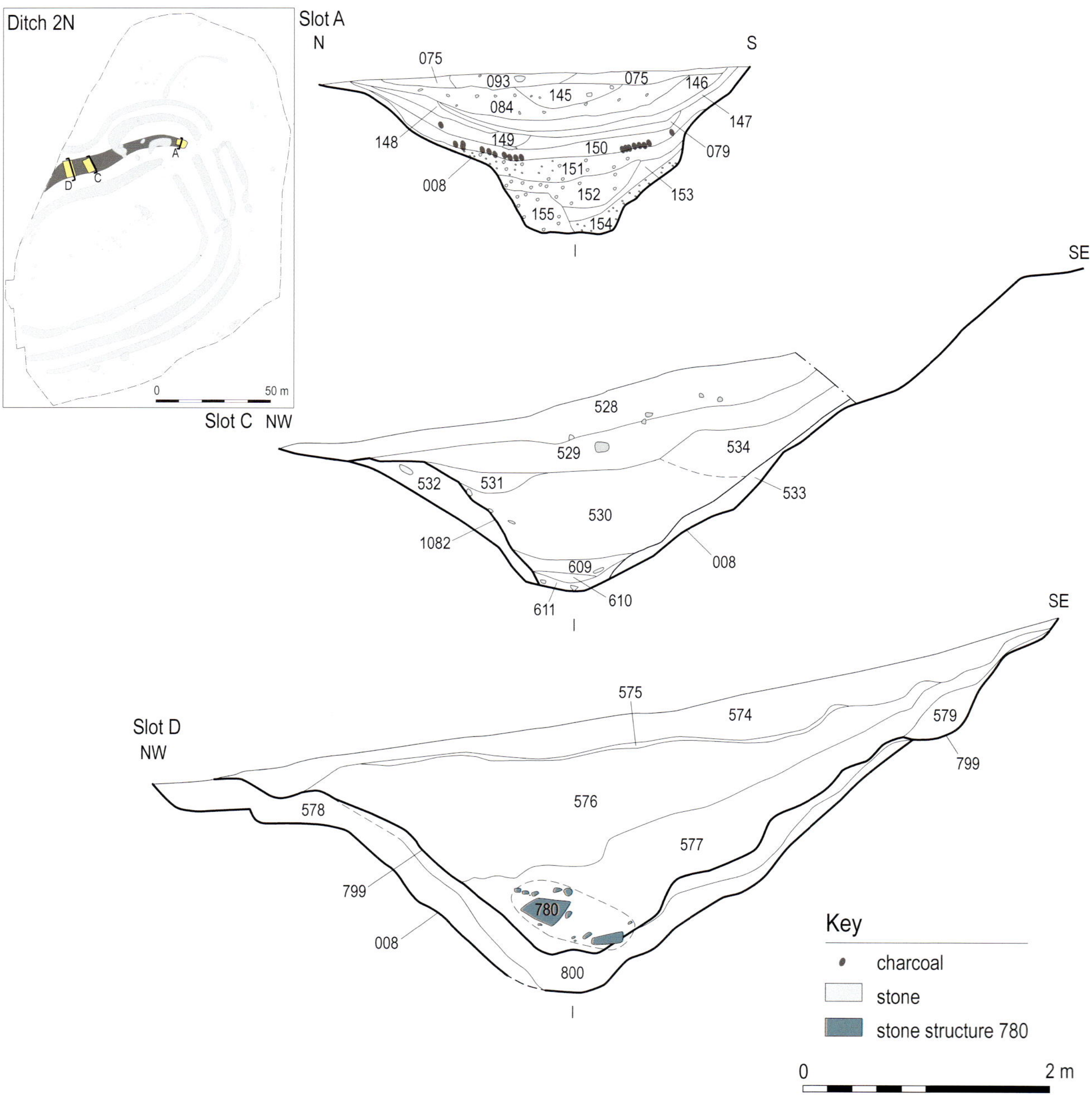

Figure 14: Ditch 2N sections of Slots A, C and D.

Ditch 3N

The third ditch on the north side, measured c. 58 m in length, but did not follow the concentric pattern of the two innermost ditches (Ditches 1N and 2N) and instead curved tightly from an east/west orientation to a north/south orientation at both ends including by the fort entrance. The construction of this ditch was probably in response to the insertion of the souterrain into Ditch 2N. It enveloped the souterrain, at a distance of c, 7 m from Ditch 2 N, before extending across the latter to the west. The ditch attained a maximum width of 4 m and maximum depth of 2 m, and its infilling deposits were largely devoid of finds.

A total of five slot trenches were hand-excavated across Ditch 3N, including Slot B (Ditch 2S). Slot A and D were recut once and Slot C recut twice (Figure 15). The profile of Slot A at the terminus was a broad flat-bottomed V, but at Slot C it was made complex by at least two recuts leaving ridges of solid natural gravel in the base of the ditch. The last recut contained noticeable natural gravelly deposits, probably slumped in from the sides of the ditch, with one containing collapsed larger stones which may have been part of a revetment on the south-east side of the ditch.

Both Slots D and E had narrow V-shaped bases with fairly steep ditch sides. Slot E indicated that the ditch at this point only had one main deposit.

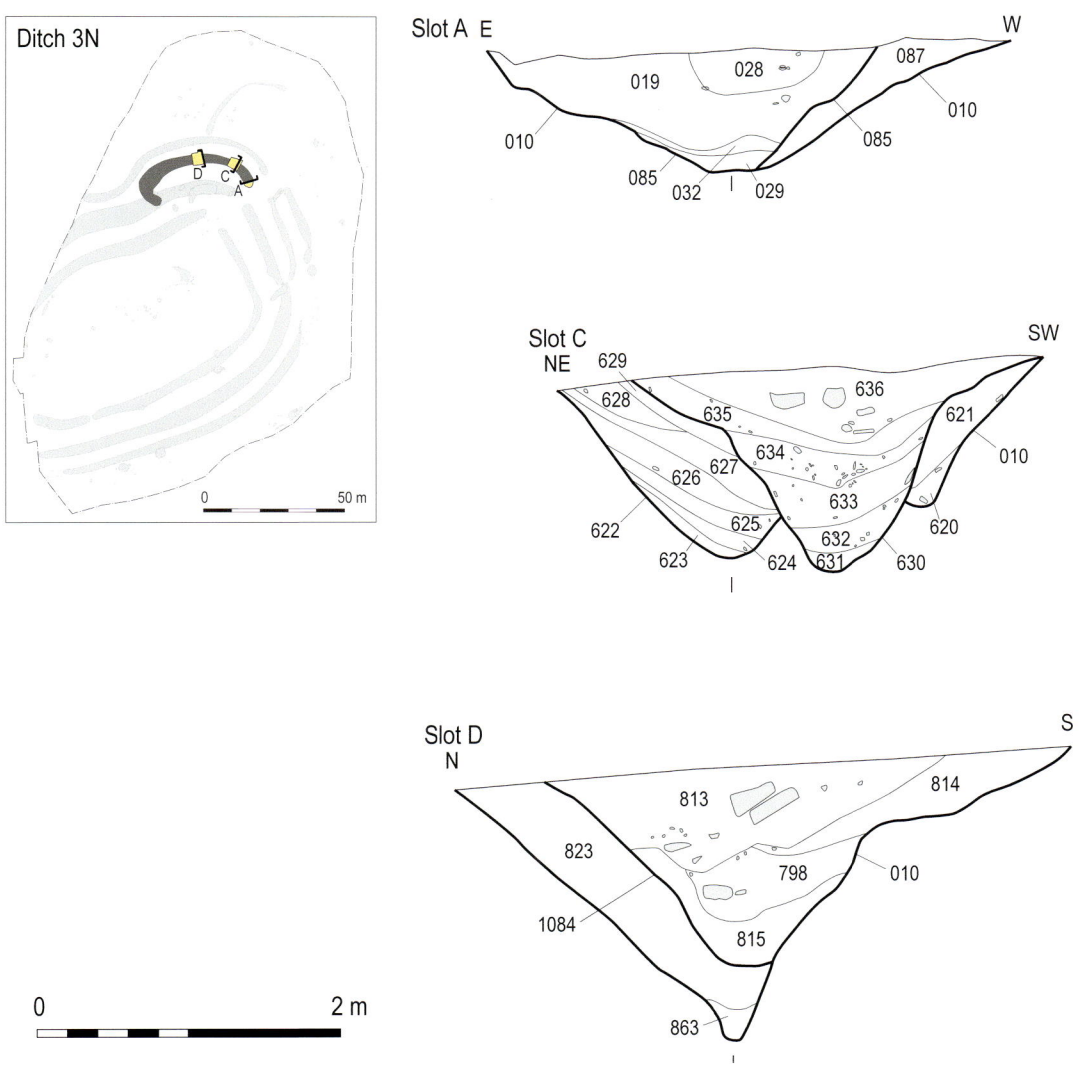

Figure 15: Ditch 3N sections of Slots A , C, D, E and B.

21

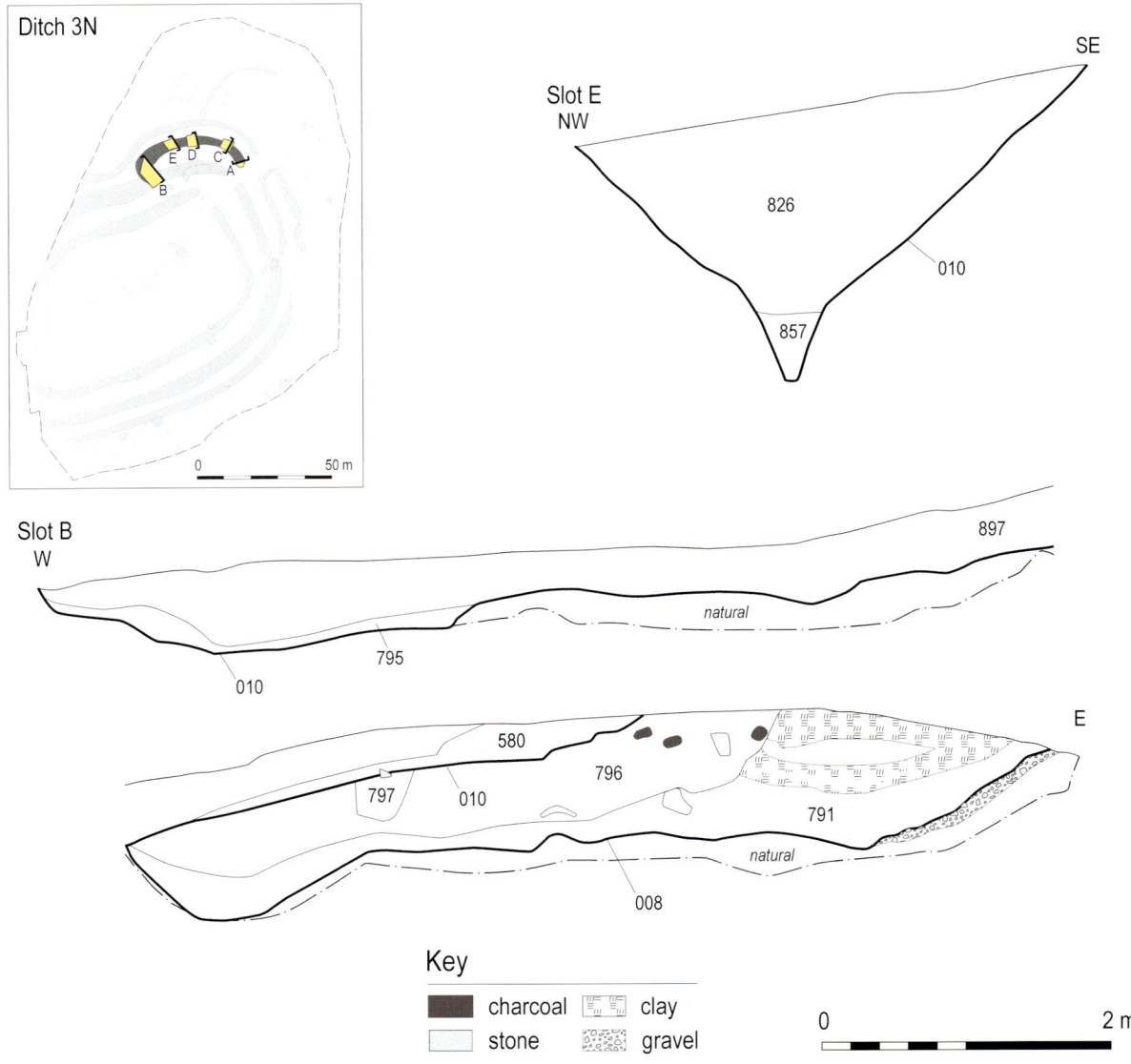

Figure 15 (continued): Ditch 3N sections of Slots A , C, D, E and B.

Ditch 4N

This ditch formed a broad S-shape as it followed a concentric line from the entrance of the fort around Ditch 3N to then curve awkwardly to follow Ditch 2N. In total it was c. 85 m in length. It was narrower than Ditches 1N-3N and its width varied from as little as 2.2 m at its terminal to c. 3.5 by the western edge of the excavation. However, it attained a depth of 2 m in the middle of its course. Five slot trenches were dug across it but only Slots A and B indicated that the ditch had been recut (Figures 16 and 17).

The ditch in Slot A at the terminus was shallow with a flattish to slightly concave base. It had been disturbed in recent times by a modern trench that cut through it and by a pit (058). Slots B and D had a V-shaped profiles that were broad at the base, while Slot C at the west end of the ditch had almost a rounded profile. Deposits of manganese were found in the lower fills of Slots B and C. Slot E, located in the middle of the course of the ditch had a distinctly V-shaped lower profile before it widened out in its upper half. No finds were found associated with the fills of this ditch.

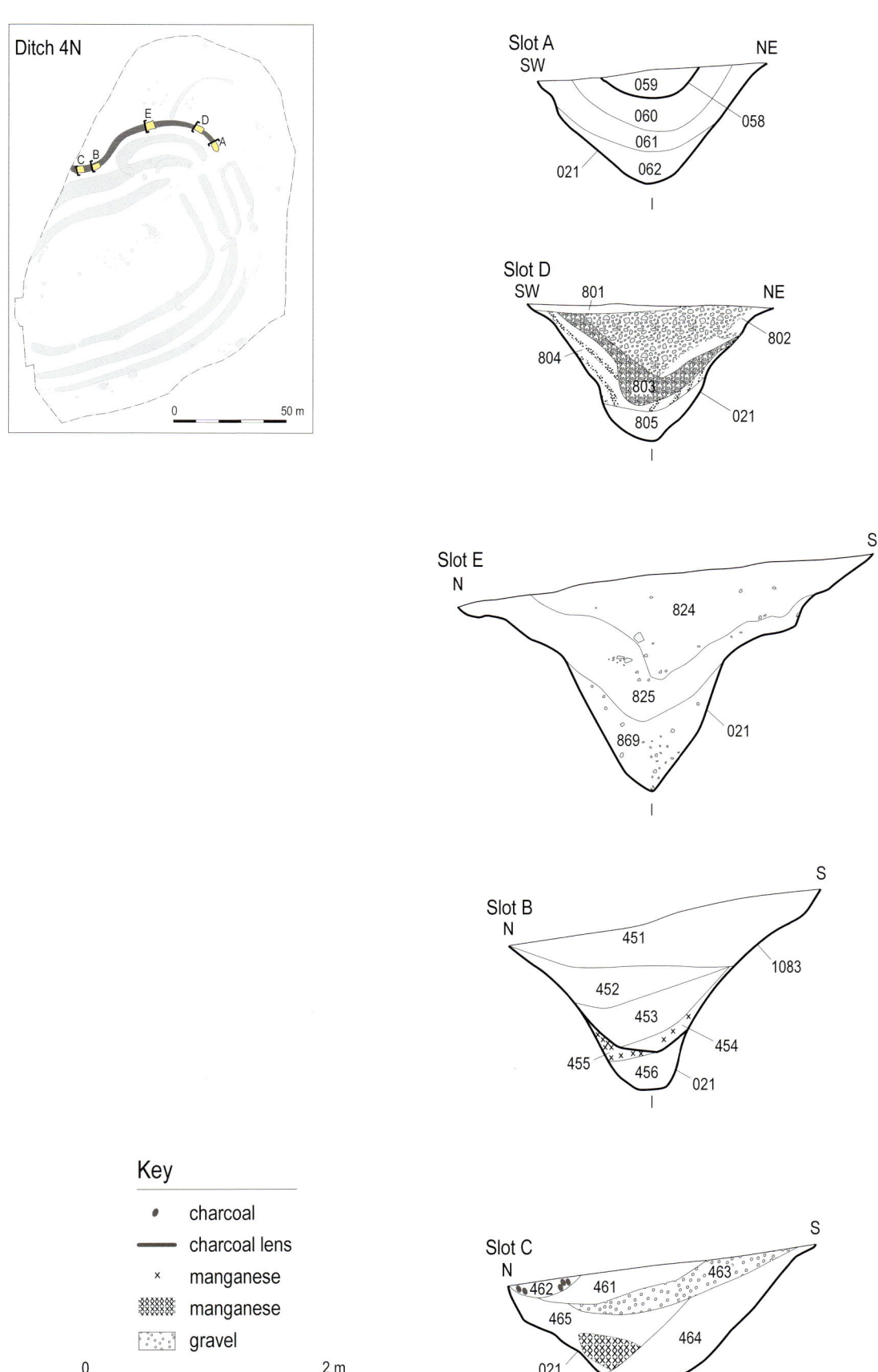

Figure 16: Ditch 4N sections of Slots A, D, E, B and C.

Figure 17: Ditch 4N during excavation.

Machine Excavated Slot Trenches

Three machine-excavated large slot trenches were also excavated across the ditches of Broxy Kennels Fort: Machine Slot 1 to the south, Machine Slot 2 to the east and Machine Slot 3 to the north. These slots allowed the ditches to be recorded in relation to each other and meant that the full extent and depth of the ditches could be recorded, something that was not always possible in the hand-excavated slot trenches due to their depth as well as the loose sandy and gravelly character of the subsoil. The machine-excavated trenches were also an attempt to distinguish soil formation processes in the ditches that were different from those found in the hand-excavated slot trenches; and to try to establish the presence of any evidence of banks or revetments between the ditches, which may have been constructed when the ditches were dug; and to provide additional opportunities for sampling, particularly for taking Optically Stimulated Luminescence (OSL) samples where organic material was lacking.

South Machine Slot Trench

The first machine excavated slot trench was dug down the south side of the fort and measured c. 31 m in length by 6.5 m in width and was generally c. 1.5 m to 2 m deep with stepped sides to prevent them from collapsing (Figure 18). It excavated new sections through Ditch 1S, Ditch 2S and Ditch 4S and revealed the natural subsoil/till it was originally dug through.

In this machine trench *Ditch 1S* was c. 4 m wide c. 1.8 m deep. The ditch from the north had a gradual slope to a gentler slope for c. 1.5 m before it became a steep slope to the base of the ditch which was a wide U-shape. The south side of the ditch had a steep incline with a gentler slope to its top.

The stratigraphy in Ditch 1S was very similar to that noted in Slots F and G (above). It was filled with sandy silt and gravels (859 and 860) before being recut by (858) and filled in by a number of thin lenses or banded layers of sands and gravels (852, 851, 859, 849 and 848). OSL samples (OSL7 to OSL9) were taken from the natural material either side of the upper edge of the ditch and from below the base of it.

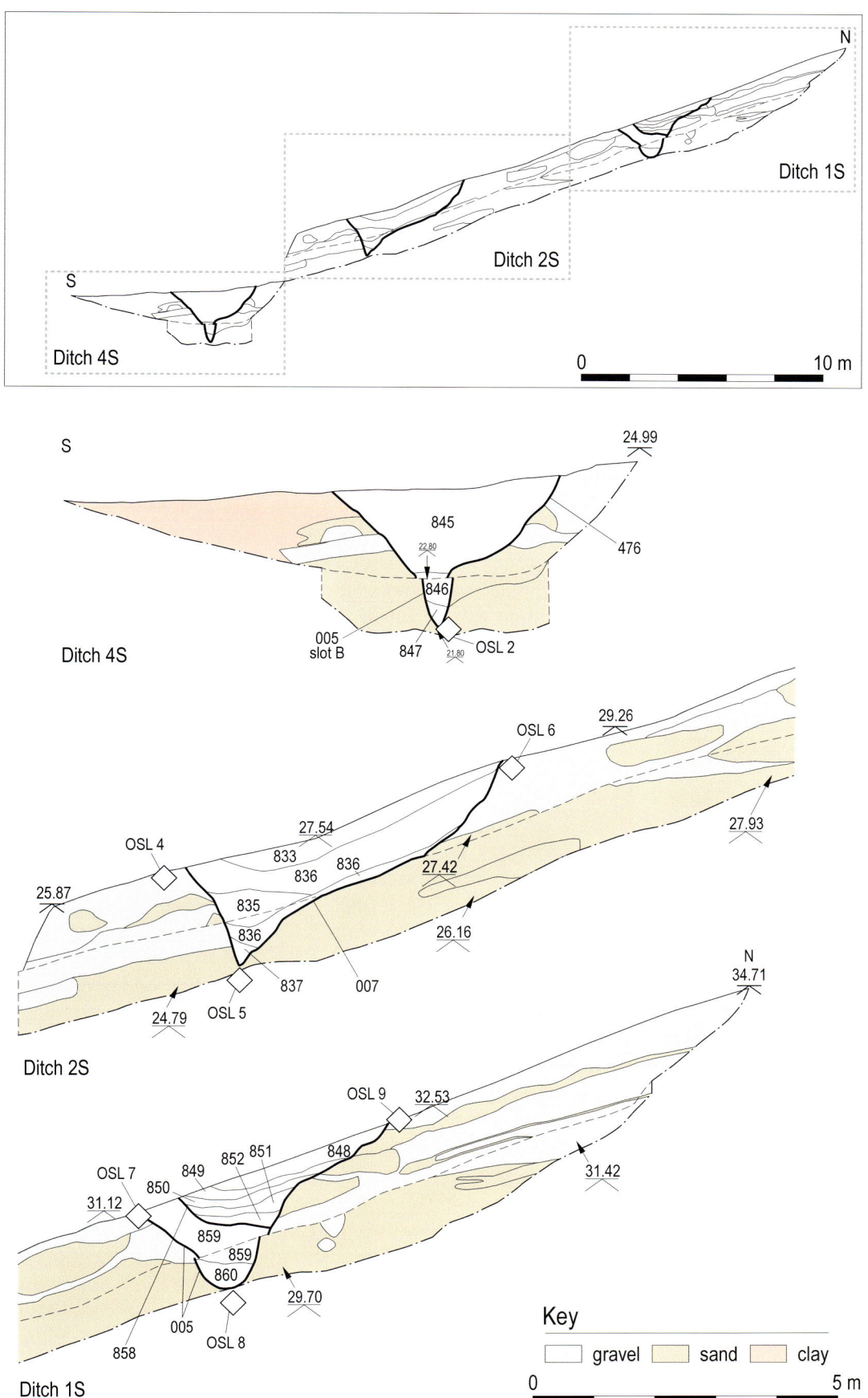

Figure 18: South Machine Slot.

Ditch 2S (1077) was c. 5 m wide with a depth of c. 2 m. It had a steeply sloping side from its top in the north with a long gentle incline with a steep slope to its pointed, V-shaped base. The south side of the ditch was sloped steeply up from the base and a slightly gentler slope at the top of the ditch.

The stratigraphy of this machine dug trench was very similar to found in Slots H and I. The ditch fills (833 834, 835, 836 and 837) mostly derived from upslope deposits to the north. OSL samples (OSL4 to OSL6) were taken from the natural material either side of the upper edge of the ditch and from below its base.

Ditch 4S was c. 3.5 m wide and c. 2.2 m deep. It had a steep incline in the north that flattened out to a near vertical side to the base of the ditch, which was a sharp V-shape. The profile on the south side was similar but it did not flatten out in the middle. Its stratigraphy of was similar to the hand-dug Slots F and G. The ditch had two basal deposits (847 and 846) and where the ditch widened out it had one (845). OSL samples (OSL1 to OSL3) were taken from the natural material either side of the upper edge of the ditch and from below its base.

East Machine Slot Trench

The second slot trench was excavated down the eastern slope of the Broxy Kennels Fort hill and was c. 33 m long and c. 5 m wide with stepped sides to prevent them from collapsing (Figure 19). This slot trench excavated new sections through Ditch 1S, Ditch 2S, Ditch 3S and Ditch 4S.

Ditch 1S was c. 3.5 m wide and c. 2.2 m deep. Its west side profile was a gently undulating but steep slope to the narrow 'ankle breaker' base. The east was equally steep at the base and curved up to the top of the ditch. It fills were similar to those recorded in Slots B and C with fine silty sand that may have naturally filled the base of the ditch while it was open. The recut (1000) was also visible. OSL samples (OSL19 to OSL21) and OSL31 were taken from the material on either side of, and from below the base of the ditch.

The measurements of *Ditch 2S* (007) were very similar to Ditch 1S and its profile was similar with the steepest slopes near the narrow almost flat-bottomed base, and gentler slopes as the ditch

sides opened up towards the west and east. The ditch had three deposits (877, 876 and 875) with the uppermost containing fragments of charcoal. OSL samples (OSL16 to OSL18) were excavated from the material on either side of the ditch and below its base.

Ditch 3S was slightly narrower than the previous two with a width of 1.9 m. It was also shallower with a depth of c. 1.4 m. Its profile was similar to Ditch 2S except at that its base was narrow and uneven. The ditch fills were similar but less complex than those in Slot A of the hand-dug Slot A. OSL samples (OSL13 to OSL15) were taken from the deposits on either side and again from below the base of the ditch.

Ditch 4S was the widest of the four, measuring 4.5 m in width and the deepest at c. 2.9 m deep. It profile very closely matched that of Ditch 2S but with a narrow V-shaped base. Its lower deposits (921, 925 and 930) were capped by a single deposit of silty sand (880). OSL samples (OSL10 to OSL12) were taken from the material to either side of the ditch and below its base.

North Machine Slot Trench

The third machine slot trench was dug down the north side of the fort and was c. 26 m long, c. 5 m wide and c. 1.5 m to 2 m deep with stepped sides (Figure 20). This slot was positioned over the locations of previously hand dug slots in Ditch 1N, Ditch 2N and Ditch 4N.

Ditch 1N, Slot C was expanded in the excavation of the North Machine Slot and revealed that the ditch was 6.5 m wide at this point and up to 3.2 m deep. From the south its profile had gentle slope downwards before becoming steeper to a near vertical drop to the V-shaped base. The return to the north was near vertical becoming more gradual as it rose towards the surface.

The stratigraphy was generally the same as that which had been recorded in Ditch 1N Slot C, although the ankle-breaker was more pronounced in the machine slot. The ditch seemed to have silted naturally particularly near the base, while the upper deposits became slightly more clayey and may have contained some domestic material from the internal area of the fort. OSL samples (OSL22 to OSL24) were taken from the material on either side of the ditch and from below its.

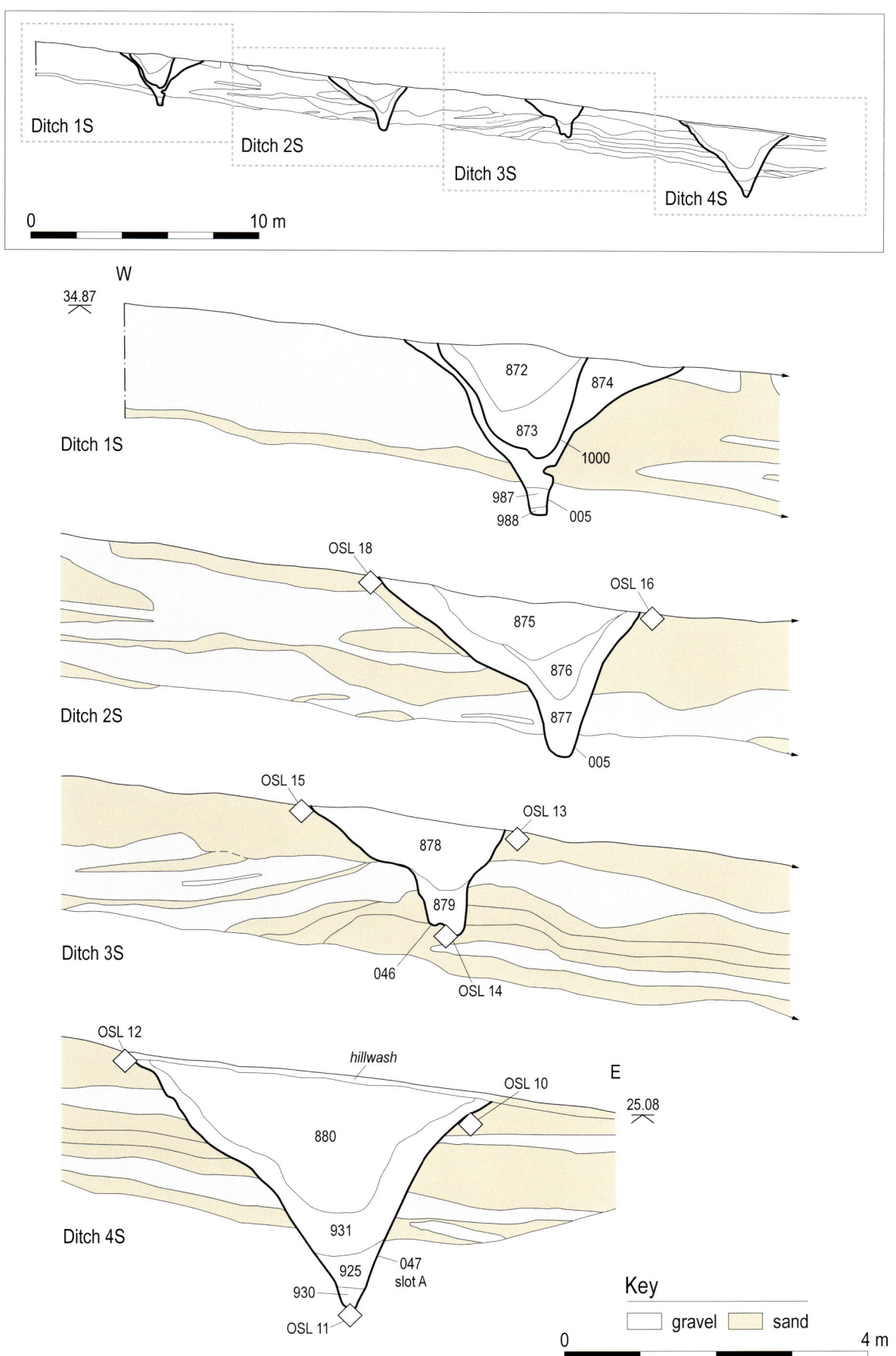

Figure 19: East Machine Slot.

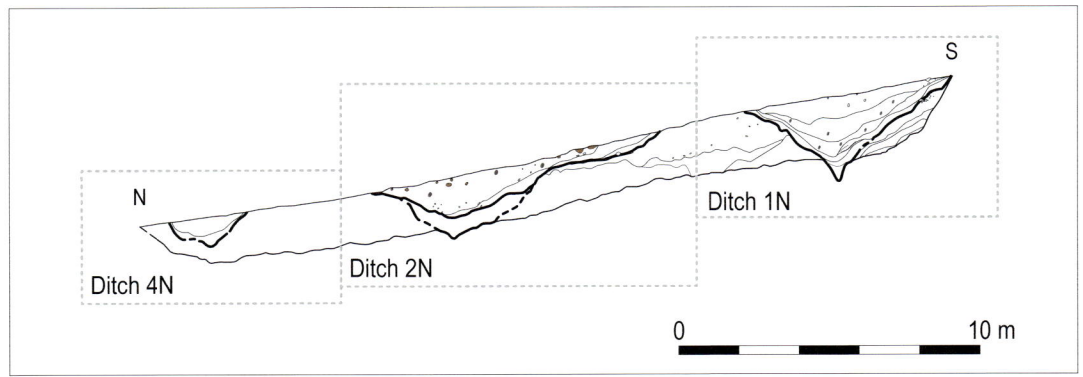

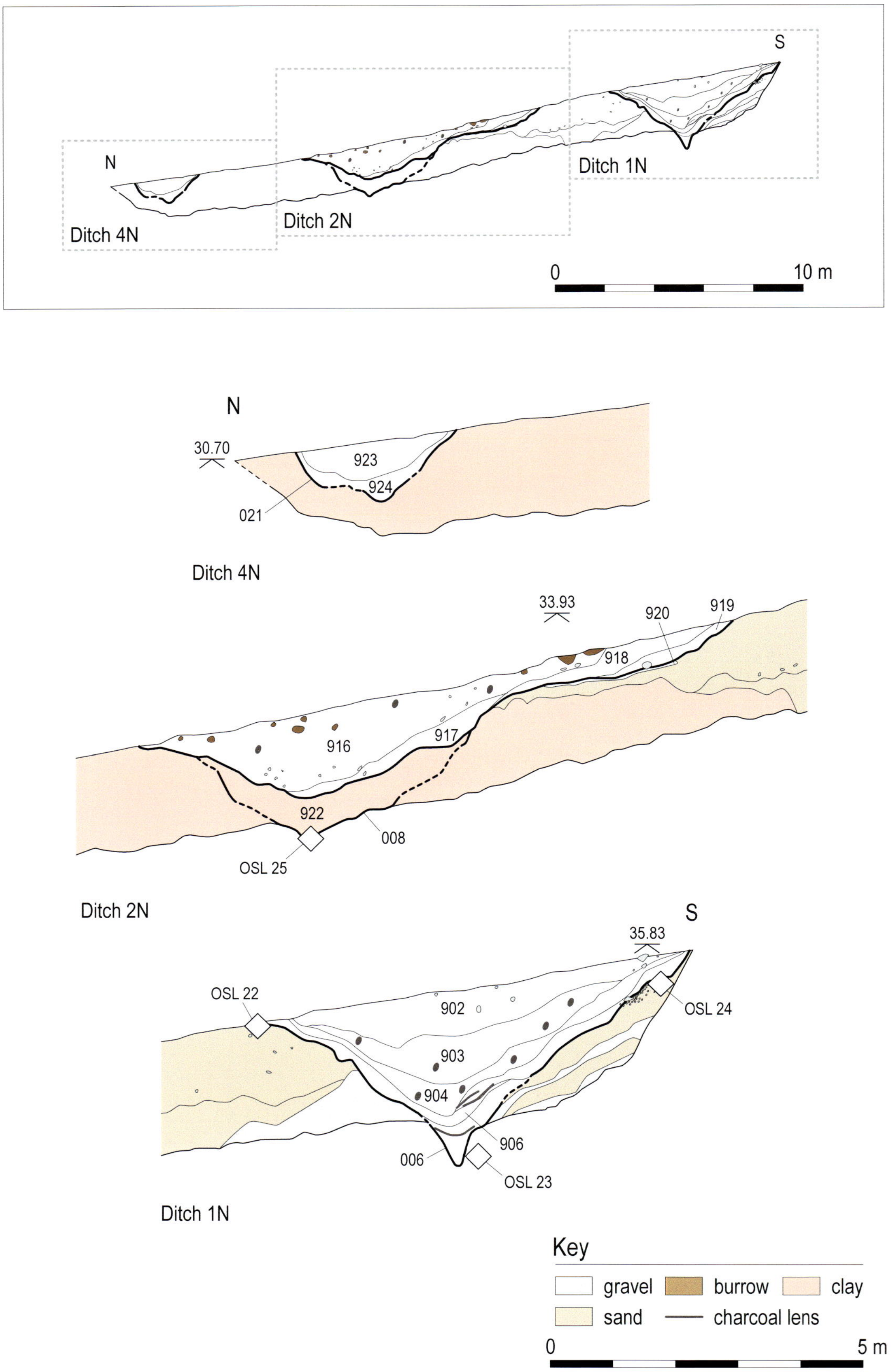

Figure 20: North Machine Slot.

The machine slot trench was also positioned over the original Slot C in *Ditch 2N*. At this point the ditch was c. 7 m wide and c. 2 m deep. From south the ditch had a gentle sloping side with a sharper gradient leading to the steep sided and narrow V-shaped base. The north side of the profile inclined more steeply to the surface. The ditch fills included sandy hill-wash material (918, 919 and 920) and was similar to the stratigraphy in Ditch 2N Slot C. OSL samples (OSL25 to OSL27) were taken from the material on either side of the ditch and below its base.

The northernmost part of the trench was positioned over the original Slot B across *Ditch 4N*. Here the ditch was 2.5 m wide and 1 m deep. Its profile was uneven and from the south it inclined steeply down to its base which was a wide V-shape. The north side of the ditch rose slightly before being flattened to then rise steeply to the surface. The stratigraphy at this point was very similar to that encountered in Ditch 4N Slot B. The two main fills (923 and 924), which were both silty clays similar to the surrounding natural deposits and filled the shallow ditch section. OSL

samples (OSL28 to OSL30) were taken from the material on either side of this ditch section.

No evidence for the remains of banks or revetments were found between any of the ditches in any of the machine excavated slot trenches. Ramparts may have existed but the soft sandy/silty deposits could have easily eroded back into the ditches, or overtime were washed downslope after the ditches had filled in. There were no buried soils between the ditches indicating the fragility of soils and the ease of removal of them from the hill.

The Souterrain

By John James Atkinson

The souterrain, a stone-built rounded end long chamber with a stone floor and with a tapering curved walled with stepped entrance was dug into the subsoil and the southern flank of Ditch 2N (Figure 21), truncating a portion of ditch and its associated fills adjacent to the entrance of the fort.

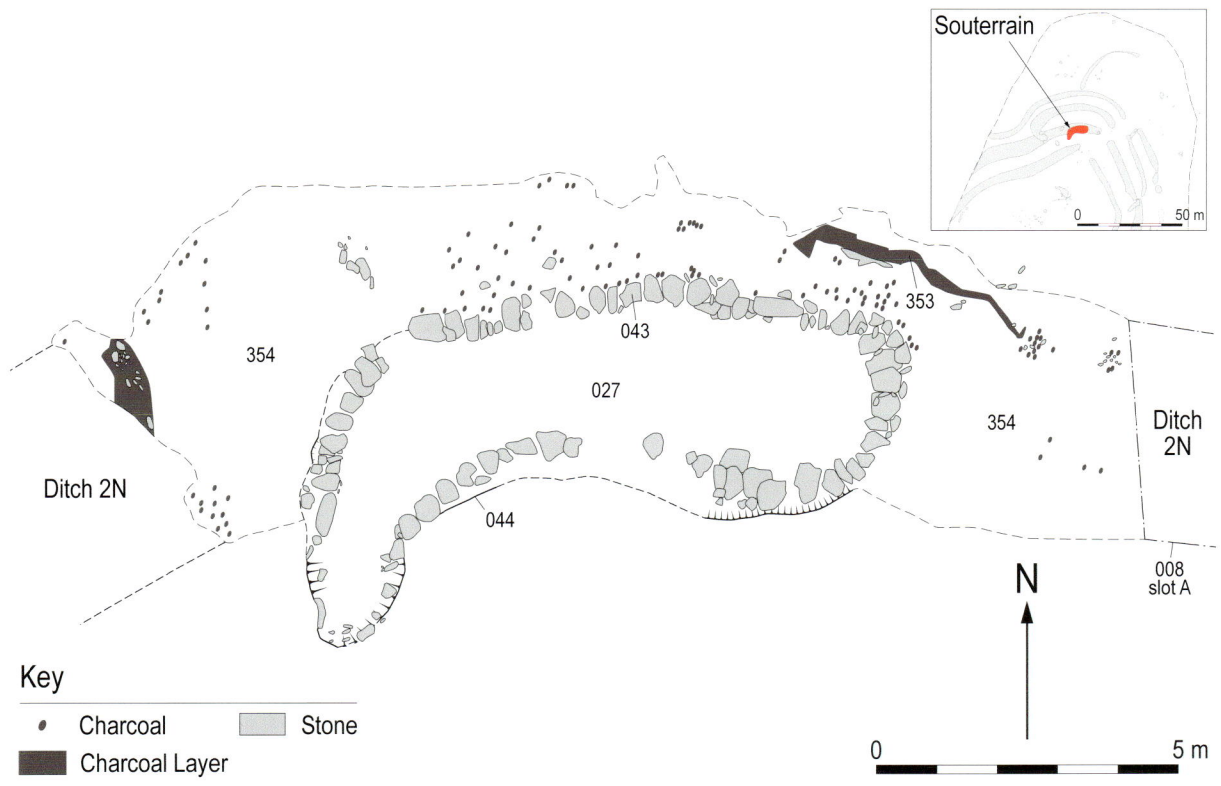

Figure 21: Location of souterrain in Ditch 2N.

Construction of the souterrain (Figure 22)

The foundation trench for the souterrain was orientated approximately east/west, and was 9.66 m in length, with a width of 5.88 m to the east and of 3.76 m to the west, where it narrowed towards the souterrain entrance, which projected to the south. The depth of the foundation trench as excavated was consistently between 1.08 m and 1.17 m. The stone wall that lined the interior of the souterrain extended above the ground surface level by c. 0.32 m, indicating the structure's overall internal height between 1.40 m and 1.49 m. At its stepped entrance, at its south-western extent, the internal space gradually sloped upwards until it reached ground level.

The sequence of construction included the initial deposition of a levelling layer of silty sand (144) within the foundation trench. The gaps between many of the larger upright boulders lining the internal space that formed the base of the souterrain walls were packed with this same material. The boulders were local, large glacial erratics of mica schist with dimensions of up to 0.78 m by 0.40 m, but other lithologies were also present. They formed a drystone wall 19.32 m in length with a width between 0.20 m and 0.67 m, and a height of 1.04 m to 1.23 m. Around most of the interior of the structure the walls were almost vertical but their upper stones were slightly corbelled to the interior.

There were two breaks in the souterrain wall. The first was the entrance passage that measured between 0.4 m and 1 m in width as it widened into the chamber. A second gap, of c. 0.70 m width, was in the north-west wall of the souterrain c. 5 m north of the entrance. During the excavation it was considered to be another possible entrance or passageway, and Ditch 2N Slot E was located behind it to determine if further structures or features associated with the souterrain existed there, but none were found. Between the foundation trench and the souterrain walls were a series of distinct infills or packing deposits (827), some of which were similar to the sandy-silty deposits (882 and 885) in Ditch 2N (008), into which the souterrain was inserted, and may represent the reuse of these materials during its construction.

The next stage in the construction of the souterrain was the laying of a bedding layer of gravelly silty sand (870/867), between 50 mm and 200 mm thick, above the levelling layer (144) onto which the stones of the floor (098) were placed. A variety of local, large and flat stones were used that created a relatively regular and level paved surface. The stones leading up to the entrance from the floor were constructed in a roughly curved and stepped ascent and long thin stones were used as pinions between the large floor stones to secure them. The stones used in the floor varied in size from c. 0.50 m by 0.50 m to 0.78 m by 0.40 m.

In the small gap in the north-west corner of the souterrain wall and below the floor level was an oval-shaped posthole (991) 0.46 m by 0.36 m 0.64 m deep. Its position suggests it was possibly associated with the function of the souterrain or a structure above it. It was filled with mixed sand and gravel (992). Near the posthole and close to the entrance were deposits of reddish silty clay (315 and 316). Both these basal deposits were sampled (see *Multi-Element Analysis*).

Use of the souterrain

Evidence for the use of the souterrain is limited as no artifacts or eco-facts survived. However, thin silty or sandy deposits generally found between the floor stones or over them (156, 157 and 182) may have been a product of its use. In the southern half of the souterrain, between the paving and deposit (156) was a small deposit (235), 30 mm thick and c. 1 m long of charcoal. It may have been the remains of a wooden plank or branch which was burnt *in-situ*. It is presumed the souterrain was capped with wooden beams resting on the corbelled wall head and this may be evidence of one of them.

Infilling of the souterrain

The primary infilling deposit (074) of mixed sand and silt that was between 0.34 m and 0.50 m thick covered the floor and the souterrain entrance (seen in Slot A). Above this, was another deposit of sandy silt (042) 0.40 m thick that entered the souterrain from its entrance and thinned out towards the eastern end of its chamber (Figure 23). Two other deposits of sandy silt (073 and 027) appeared to seal the previous deposits in the entrance area and filled the souterrain to the top of its walls.

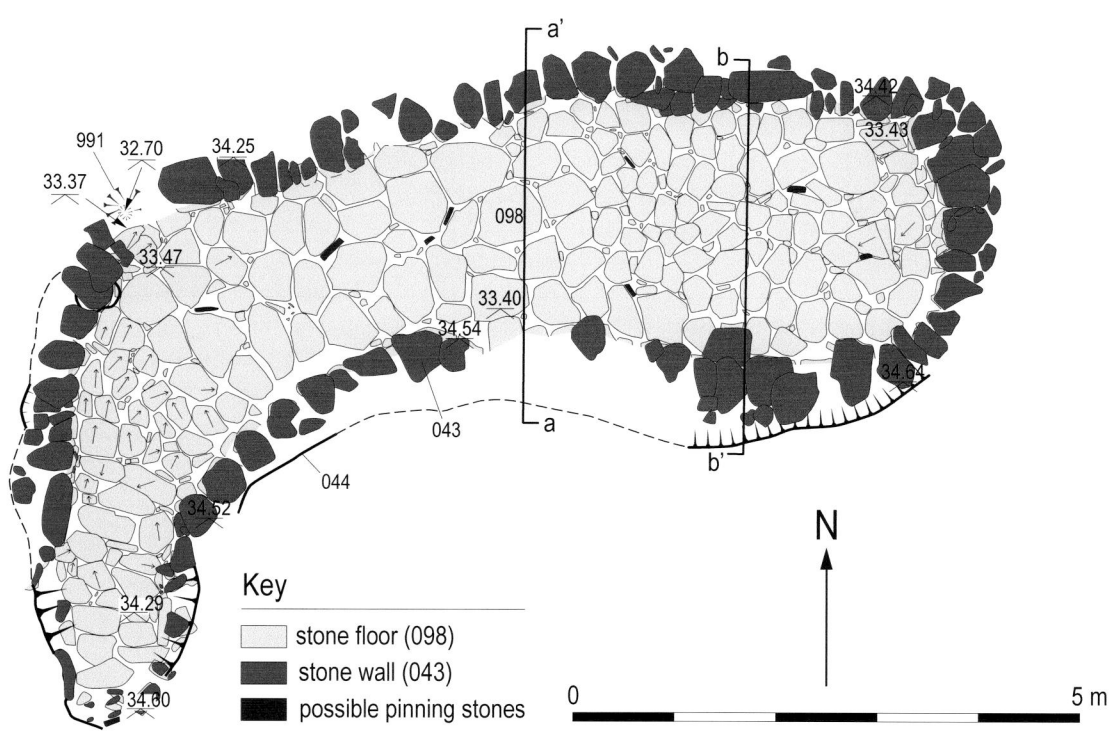

Plan of the Souterrain stone walls (043) and floor (098)

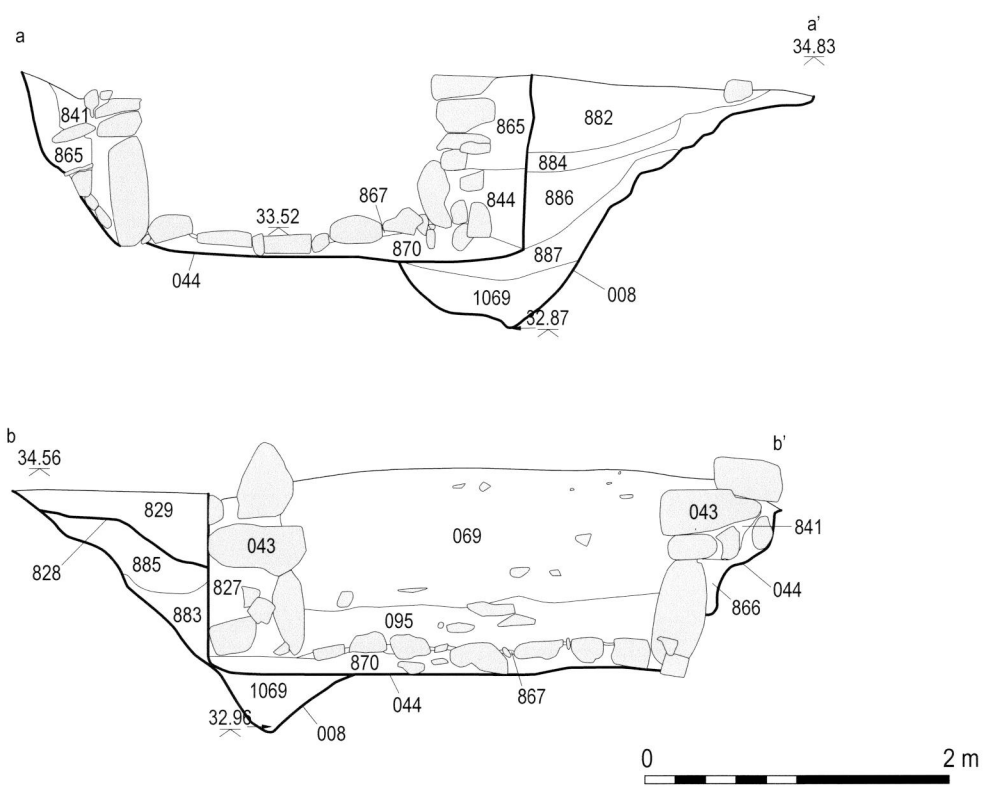

Figure 22: Souterrain plan and sections.

The initial filling (095) within the interior of the souterrain, visible in Slot F, included charcoal and fragments of burnt bone. Lying immediately above this, visible in Slot B, was a 0.86 m thick deposit of sandy clay (069) with charcoal. Sealing these deposits and much of the souterrain walls was a deposit of sandy silt (027), with stones and charcoal.

Deposits external to the souterrain

To the immediate north of the souterrain were a series of deposits relating to Ditch 2N (008). As noted above, material from them appears to have been used in the construction of the souterrain walls. These deposits were visible in the east-facing and west facing sections of Slot B. The surface deposits of the ditch (882) included stones and charcoal. These deposits showed signs of disturbance from the 2019 evaluation trench (828).

Located just north of Ditch 1N Slot B and west of the souterrain was pit (251) (Figure 5). Although there was seemingly no direct relationship between the two, it is mentioned here. The pit was large at 2.63 m by 1.92 m by 0.64 m and contained one homogenous fill (252) which a larger patch charcoal in its north-east quarter

Figure 23: Souterrain in Ditch 2N during excavation.

Other Features around the Fort

By Christina Mollie Dogherty

A number of small features found within and around the fort at Broxy Kennels. For ease of locating the features the site has been split into seven areas (Areas 1-7) as shown on Figure 24. However a number of small postholes and pits were also related to the upper levels of the ditches but more significant or relevant features are described here.

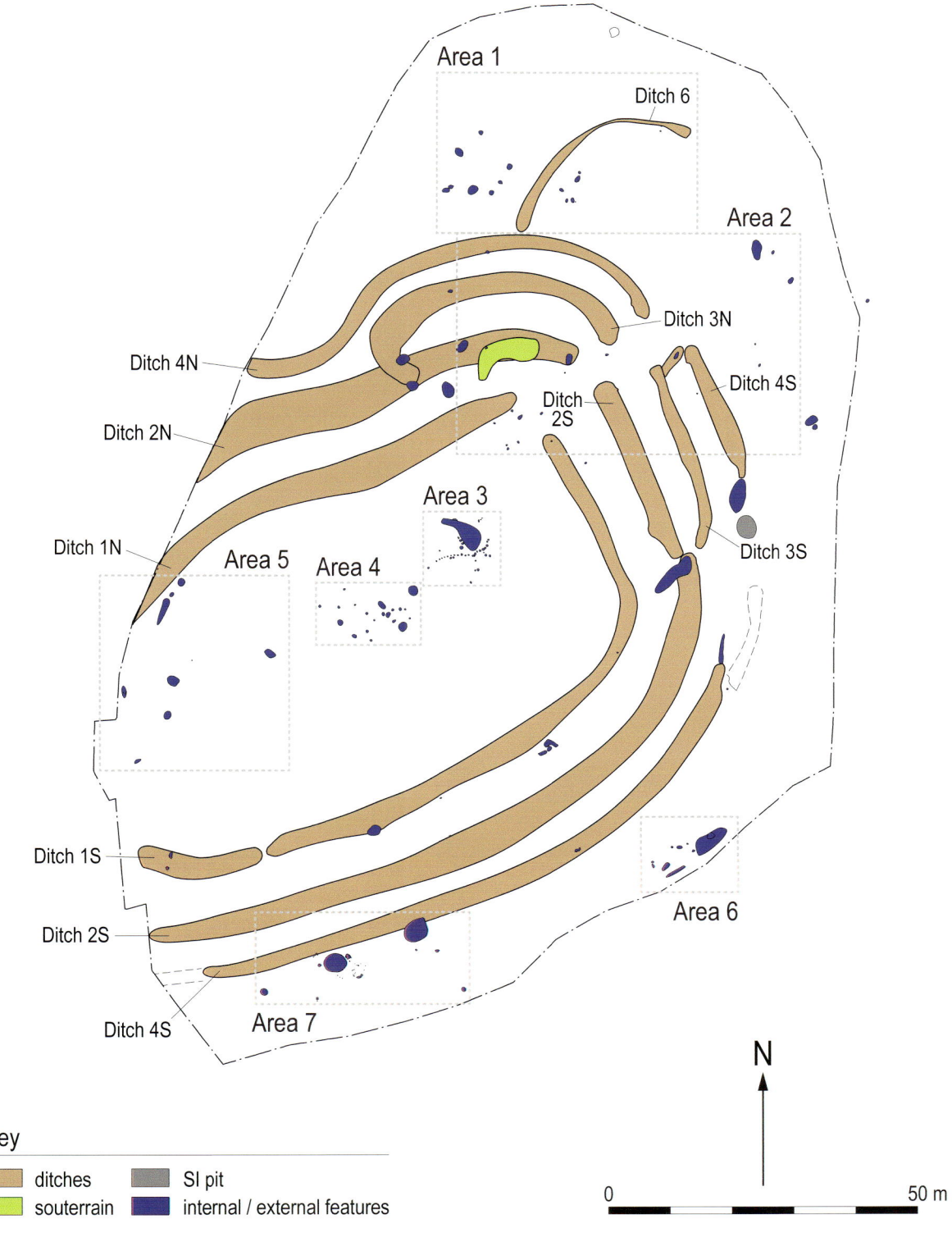

Figure 24: Location of features in Areas 1 to 7.

Features associated with the ditches

Ditch 1S

The north-east corner of the Slot F across the ditch were truncated by a large pit (223) which measured 2.83 m by 2.27 m by 1.51 m. It was filled with dark brown silty sand (224) that contained some charcoal and animal bone. Several fire-pits were identified on the south-side of Slot F (Figure 25), cutting the ditch edge and several of its fills. The earliest pit was (426), which was truncated by pit (317), which in turn was truncated on its north-west corner by pit (484). The fourth pit (408) truncated pits (426 and 317) to the east.

The earliest pit (426), 1.36 m by 0.9 m by 0.75 m was filled by mainly natural deposits some with charcoal. Pit (317) was sub-rectangular in shape and measured 1.58 m by 0.93 m by 0.53 m. A lens of charcoal lay between its primary and subsequent fill of sand. Further burnt sand or gravel layers (449 and 320) with a deposit of black sand with lumps of charcoal (321) and a burnt sand and charcoal layer (319) completed the infilling of the pit. A later oval-shaped fire-pit (484) cut pit (317) and the upper fill of Ditch 1S in Slot F. It was filled with burnt sand, charcoal and burnt bone fragments.

The final pit (408), which dug through the upper deposits of pits (317, 426 and Slot F) was a slightly curving sub-rectangular feature measuring 2 m by 0.6 m - 1.3 m by 0.4 m. It had a flue-like channel exiting from it to the south-east that was 0.7 m in length by 0.6 m in depth. This pit (408) was primarily filled with lighter and darker brown sandy layers with some charcoal but its uppermost fill was burnt sand (415) with a lens of charcoal.

Also visible in the south-west facing section of Slot H of Ditch IS was a large sub-circular pit (262) that was a modern intrusion that truncated its fills. It measured 2.6 m by 2.34 m by 0.38 m and contained several deposits including burnt sand layers with modern pottery and some charcoal.

Ditch 3S

Between c. 5 m and 6 m to the south-west of Slot B (Figure 5), across Ditch 3S, was a linear feature (311) which appeared to be a continuation of the ditch. It turned to the west and headed towards the fort interior but was shallow and heavily truncated. It was 8.3 m in length, c. 1.42 m to 2.1 m in width and between 0.24 m and 0.5 m in depth. It was oriented NE/SW and was badly affected by animal burrowing. It was filled with sandy silts and clay with some charcoal.

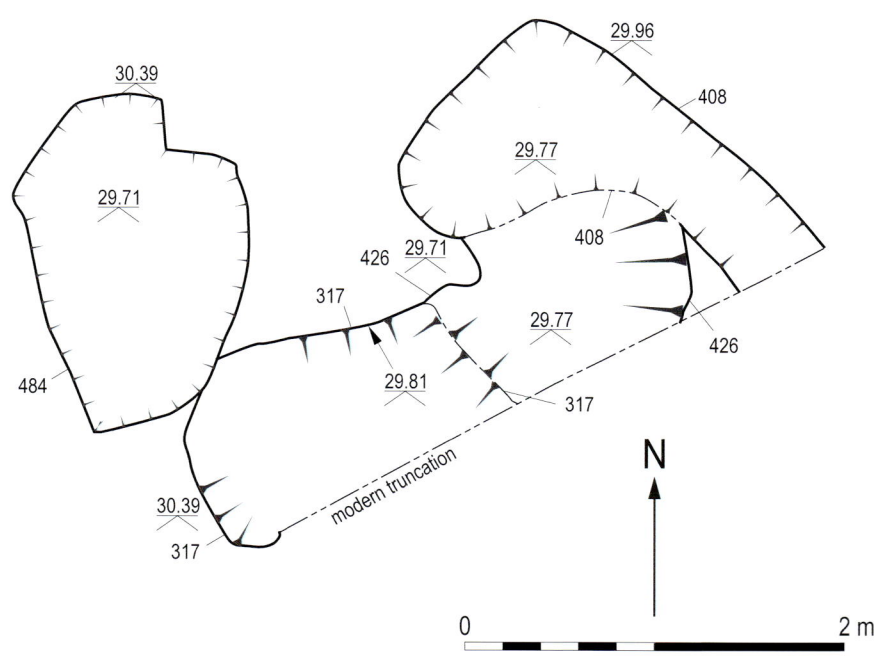

Figure 25: Features associated with the ditches: Ditch 1S fire-pits.

Ditch 2N/Ditch 3N Slot B

A pit (900) was found near the south-west corner of Slot B at the surface, possibly partially truncating the western end of Ditch 3N (Figure 5). It was 1.7 m by 0.85 m by 0.45 m and was sub-oval in shape. Its fill of dark sand and charcoal indicates it was a fire-pit.

Ditch 3N

When the section of Slot A was excavated back, two postholes on either side of the terminus were uncovered (Figure 5). The first of these (116) was located within the upper ditch fill (075) near the north side. It was sub-oval in shape and measured 0.38 m by 0.25 m by 0.25 m and was filled with sand with charcoal. The second posthole (118) was located to the north beyond the ditch terminus. It was sub-oval in shape and measured 0.60 m by 0.40 m by 0.4 m. Its two dark fills with some charcoal suggest this was a fire-pit.

Another fire-pit (811) was identified in Slot E where it was dug into the upper ditch fill. Its dimensions were 0.73 m by 0.53 m by 80 mm and it was filled with burnt silty sand, stones and charcoal.

Ditch 4N

Located c. 1.6 m to the east of Slot E and cutting the south side of the ditch, was a small sub-circular fire-pit (981) (Figure 5). It contained two burnt sandy fills.

Area 1

Ditch 6

This was located to the north of the main fort ditches in the north-east (Figures 24 and 26) of the investigated area. It was a c. 36 m long curvilinear ditch which began close to the north-east end of Ditch 4N and arced to the east which was explored by six slot trenches. The south-west end of the ditch was squared in shape, and its gravelly fill may have been caused by disturbance from an earlier evaluation trench (Pettitt and Hession 2019). Its north-east end opened into a pit and in general the ditch measured between c. 0.5 m and 2 m in width.

The first slot trench (779A) at the north-east end of the ditch was excavated across a sub-oval pit that measured 3.22 m by 1.75 m by 0.8 m. The pit contained a number of burnt deposits, but the uppermost fill (789) contained a modern nail and was likely to be a modern intrusion. The remaining slot trenches all revealed silts and gravel fills, with the final slot (779F) including some charcoal.

The following features were located in the northern half of the site (Area 1), which was divided by the curvilinear Ditch 6 (779) (Figure 26). Located to the north of this ditch was a sub-circular-shaped pit (772) with a relatively flat base that measured 1.66 m by 1.55 m by 0.56 m. It contained two fills: the upper deposit comprised brownish-yellow sand (773) with small stones/pebbles; the lower fill was orange-brown silty sand (774) with clay patches and small stones and gravel.

Other features (Figure 26)

Seven pits were arranged in a semi-circular pattern to the south-west of Ditch 6, all mostly sub-oval or sub-circular in shape and generally filled with slight variations of sandy silt with charcoal. The largest (473) measured 2.2 m by 1.58 m by 0.40 m and the smallest pit (775) was 0.85 m by 0.75 m by 0.36 m. Some of them were fire-pits and others had an unknown function.

Adjacent to the eastern terminal of Ditch 6 were two small pits (1015 and (009). The largest (1009) measured 0.45 m by 0.2 m by 0.15 m and both were filled with dark sand and pebbles.

Within the arc of Ditch 6 was a group of six small sub-circular pits, probably all fire-pits filled with dark or burnt sandy-clay layers. Only pit (985) contained visible charcoal. The largest pit (1003) measured 1.45 m by 0.74 m by 0.22 m and the smallest (998), was 0.2 m by 0.12 m by 0.09 m.

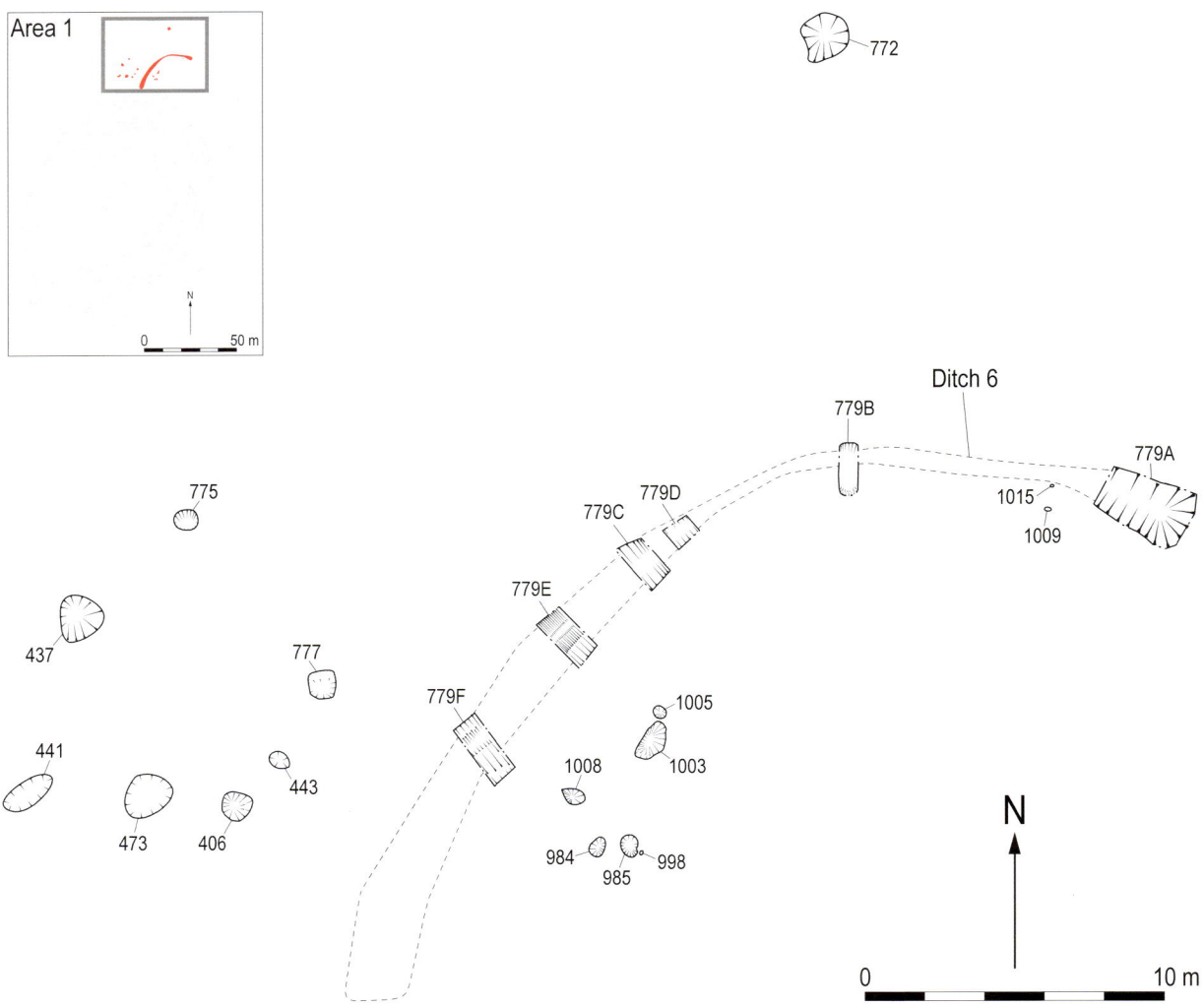

Figure 26: Plan of Area 1 with Ditch 6 and other features.

Area 2

A number of features were located in the entrance area defined by the opposing terminals of the four northern and southern ditches, and beyond the defences (Figure 27).

The following postholes (230, 346, 379, 1052 and 1070) and two possible postholes (389 and 233) were situated in the inner entrance area, close to the interior of the fort, and between the termini of Ditch 1N and Ditch 1S. None of these features were dated and it is not known if they were part of any gate system in the entrance area. Postholes (1052 and 1070) were circular features c. 0.4-0.5 m in diameter and c. 30 m deep. Both contained evidence of packing stones with some charcoal, but their central position on the inside of the inner ditch may indicate they had a deliberate

function there. Nearby posthole (346) was similar in size but of unknown function. A similar sized posthole (230) to the north-east and again in a central position between the inner terminals may have been deliberately situated there.

Posthole (379) and pit or circular posthole (233) were situated close to the edge of the terminal of Ditch 1. They measured c. 0.45 m by 0.36 m by 0.1 m but had no distinguishing characteristics. Feature (389) was probably a fire-pit. Close to the terminus of Ditch 3N was another posthole (385), which aligned with postholes (230 and 1052 and 1070). It contained charcoal but no packing stones.

East of the entrance and ditches were a small number of pits most of which contained charcoal but were undated.

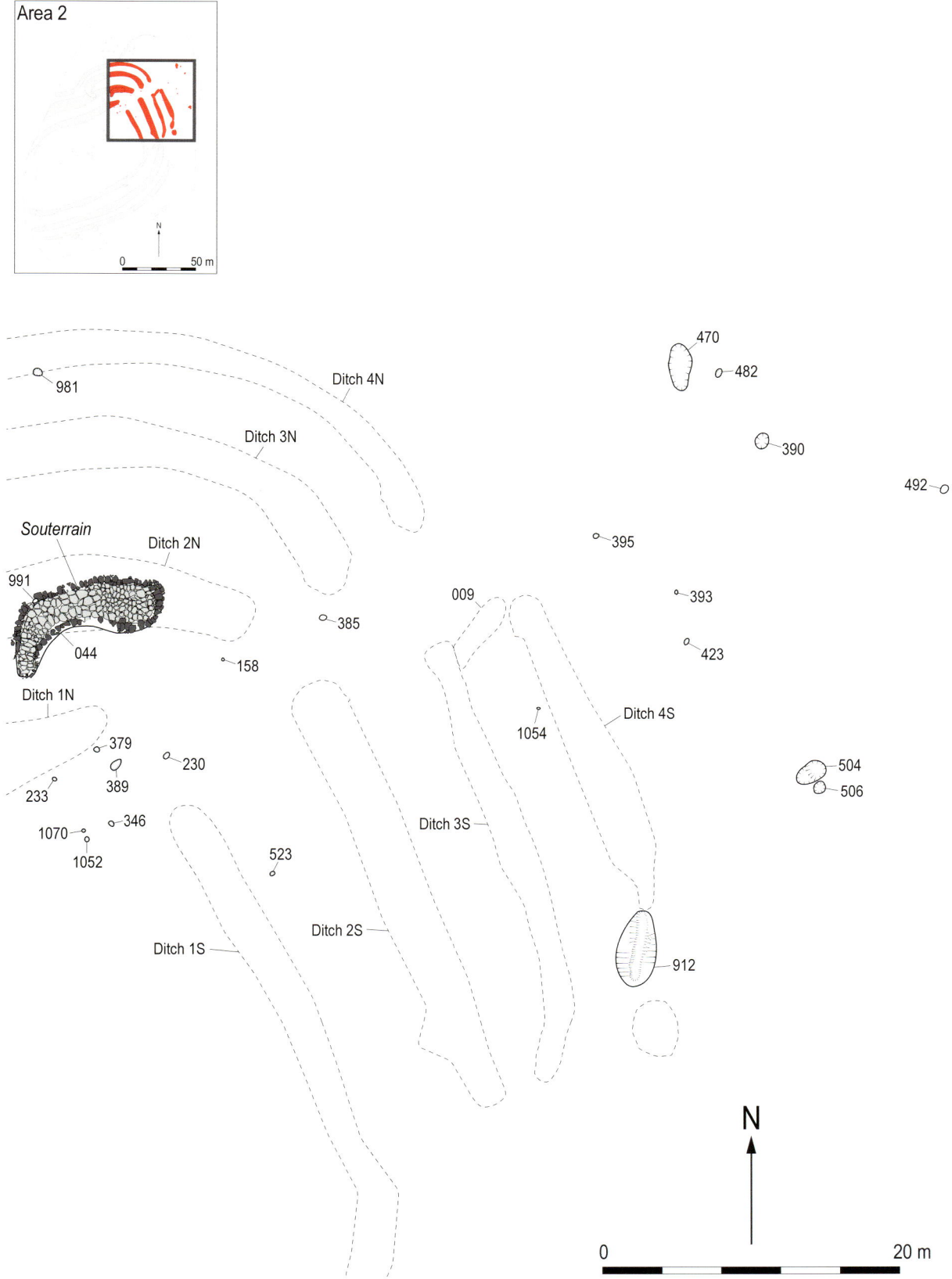

Figure 27: Plan of Area 2.

Fort Interior

Features located within the area enclosed by the fort ditches were divided into three areas, Areas 3, 4 and 5. Area 3 encompassed an area adjacent to the fort entrance, Area 4 was central within the fort interior, and Area 5 lay at the western boundary of the fort interior. It is to be noted that the top of the hill fort was badly truncated by ploughing and subsequent erosion.

Area 3

The northernmost features in this area were three truncated pits (496, 498 and 500) lying in close proximity to each other and in line (Figure 28). The first two were filled with black silt and charcoal. Pit (500) was smaller and filled with burnt silt with stones. All three pits were probably fire-pits.

To the south-east was a possible structure which consisted of two curved lines of postholes with some outlying features. The eastern line was c. 5 m long (Structure 1A) and arced from the NNE/SSW to the west, before then curving towards the south-west for a further c. 5 m. It comprised 20 postholes. Of its south-eastern postholes, none greater than 0.52 m in diameter, one contained a post-pipe (457) and only three others had charcoal in their fills. From the junction of the two structures (Structure 1A and Structure 1B), the seven remaining postholes of Structure 1A were more regularly spaced and of smaller dimensions of c. 0.22 m diameter. Four postholes had evidence of post-pipes in their fills. At a distance of 2 m south-west of the last posthole (607) was shallow pit (596) that had been subject to burrowing.

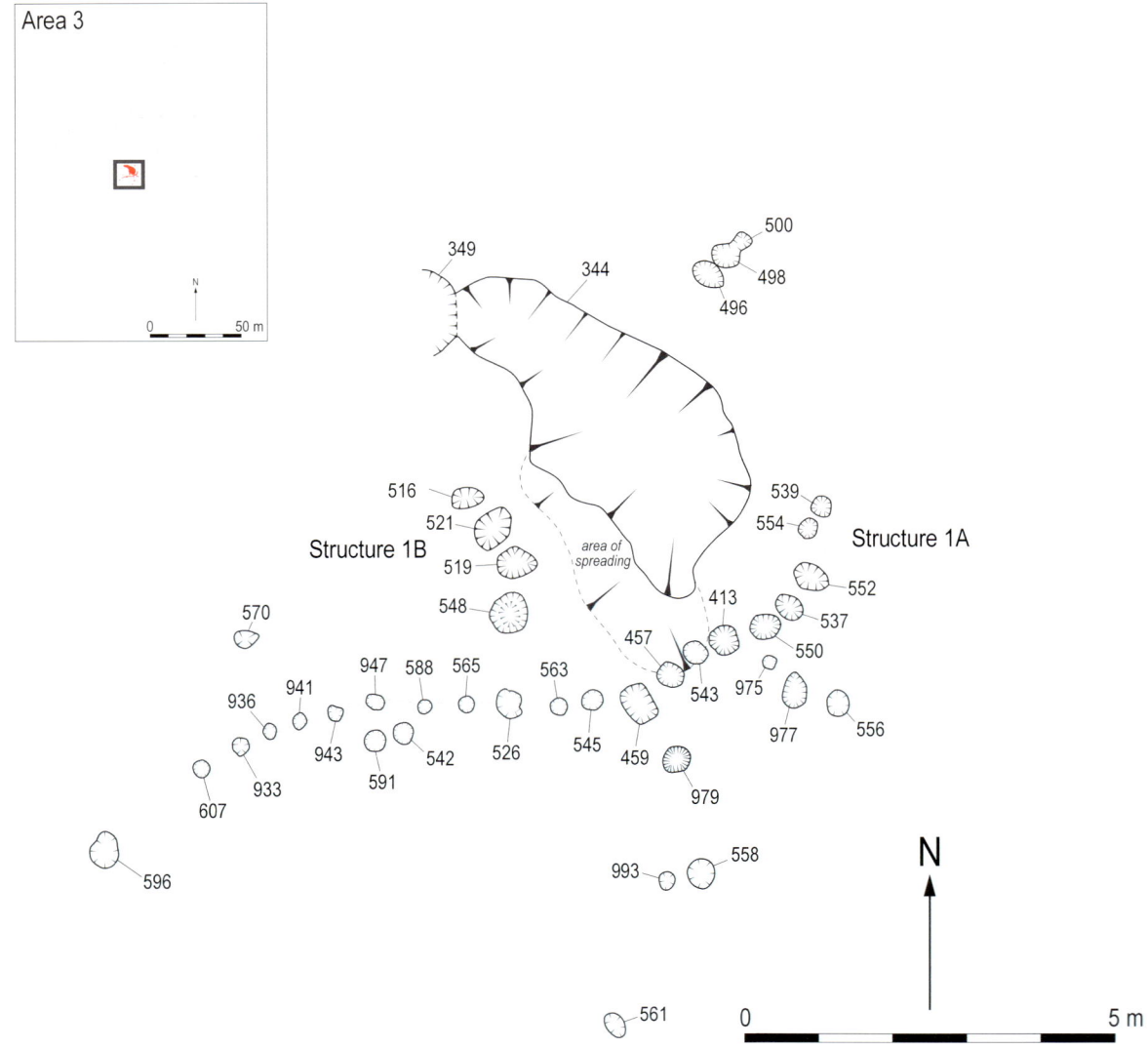

Figure 28: Plan of Area 3.

Another curved line of six posts (Structure 1B) arced from a NNW/SSE orientation to a NE/SW orientation at which point it crossed Structure 1A. The largest posthole (548) measured c. 0.60 m by 0.55 m by 0.27 m, but each contained charcoal and fragments of burnt bone. Further south-west, and to the south of Structure 1A, were two similar sized features (542 and 591), c. 0.30 m in diameter and shallow. Their fills suggested they could have been fire-pits.

The eastern and southern arcs of postholes of these structures appeared to form a boundary to a large rounded triangular feature (344) comprising grey-brown silty sand and containing some modern pottery sherds and a fragment of copper alloy (SF 149). It measured c. 6.3 m by 2.3 m by 0.32 m. At its north-western apex were the remains of a fire-pit (349) c. 0.55 m in diameter with much charcoal. The relationship of these two features to the postholes of Structure 1A is unknown

To the south of Structure 1A there were an additional number of postholes none of which aided the interpretation of the features already described. Although they varied in size, none contained finds or were dated.

Area 4

In the centre of the fort were a cluster of features of pits and postholes with no clearly discernible pattern indicative of a prehistoric structure or structures. There were several large pits and the remainder were smaller postholes, some of which may represent bonfires and later fence lines (Figure 29).

Large pits dominated this area. The north-easternmost pit (657) was large at 1.65 m by 1.54 m by 0.29 m. Its sand and gravel fill included fragments of bone. Approximately 5 m to the south-west was a deposit of dark silty sand (670) with charcoal, 90 mm thick, which covered an area of 1.72 m by 0.70 m. This could have been the site of a bonfir. A further 6.5 m to the south-west and in line with the previous two pits was another. Pit (1001) which was c. 1 m in diameter and 0.21 m in depth contained burnt sand and charcoal. Forming a triangle with pits (657 and 670) was another (581). It was the largest at 1.78 m by 1.6 by 0.28 m, and contained charcoal in both its burnt sandy fills.

Between the latter pit and (670) were two other equidistant pits of no discernible function.).

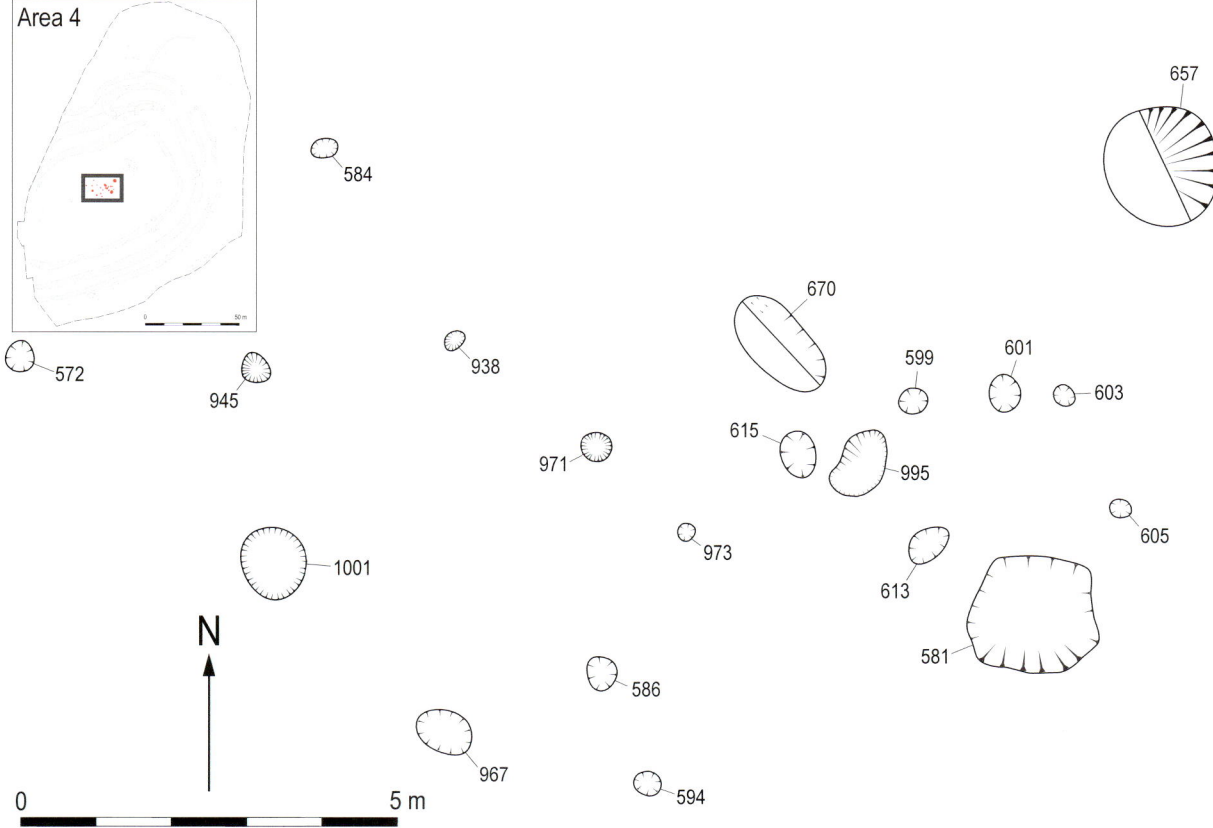

Figure 29: Plan of Area 4.

Approximately 2.5 m to the south-east of pit (1001) was another large pit (967) and interspersed between and beyond them were smaller pits and postholes, some possibly on linear arrangements but with no clear pattern. Those features west of the deposit (670) and pit (581) all contained charcoal, usually in small amounts. Some burnt bone was found in pits (945 and 971) but none of these features contained artefacts. Posthole (938) differed from the rest as it appeared to have had flat stones around its edge. These features varied in size between 0.27 m and 0.52 m in length and between 0.27 m and 0.49 m in width, with depths shallower than 0.25 m. but indicating the severe truncation of features on the hill top.

Area 5

This area on the western limits of the fort interior also contained a number of features, but how, and if, they related to those in Area 4 is not known. Again, there was no clear pattern to them (Figure 30).

Three features were present next to Ditch 1N, Slot F. Pit (958) was possibly a fire-pit with its large amount of charcoal. To the south-west was a smaller pit (1022/1057) filled with burnt sandy silt and some large stones. Further south-west was a 5 m long feature (894) that may have been an elongated fire-pit.

Across the centre of this area were four pits and a small posthole. The most easterly pit (1026) was c. 1.75 m in diameter and 0.53 m deep, contained stones and a sherd of modern pottery. The central pit (1011) was c. 2 m in diameter and shallower at 0.3 m in depth but it too contained a sherd of modern pottery. To its south was a large pit (1016) c. 2 m by 1.64 m by 0.56 m, the deepest dug of these features. It had six fills all variations of dark silty sand and gravel. The southernmost pit (1024) was situated on the west slope of the fort interior. Similar to the others, its function was unknown.

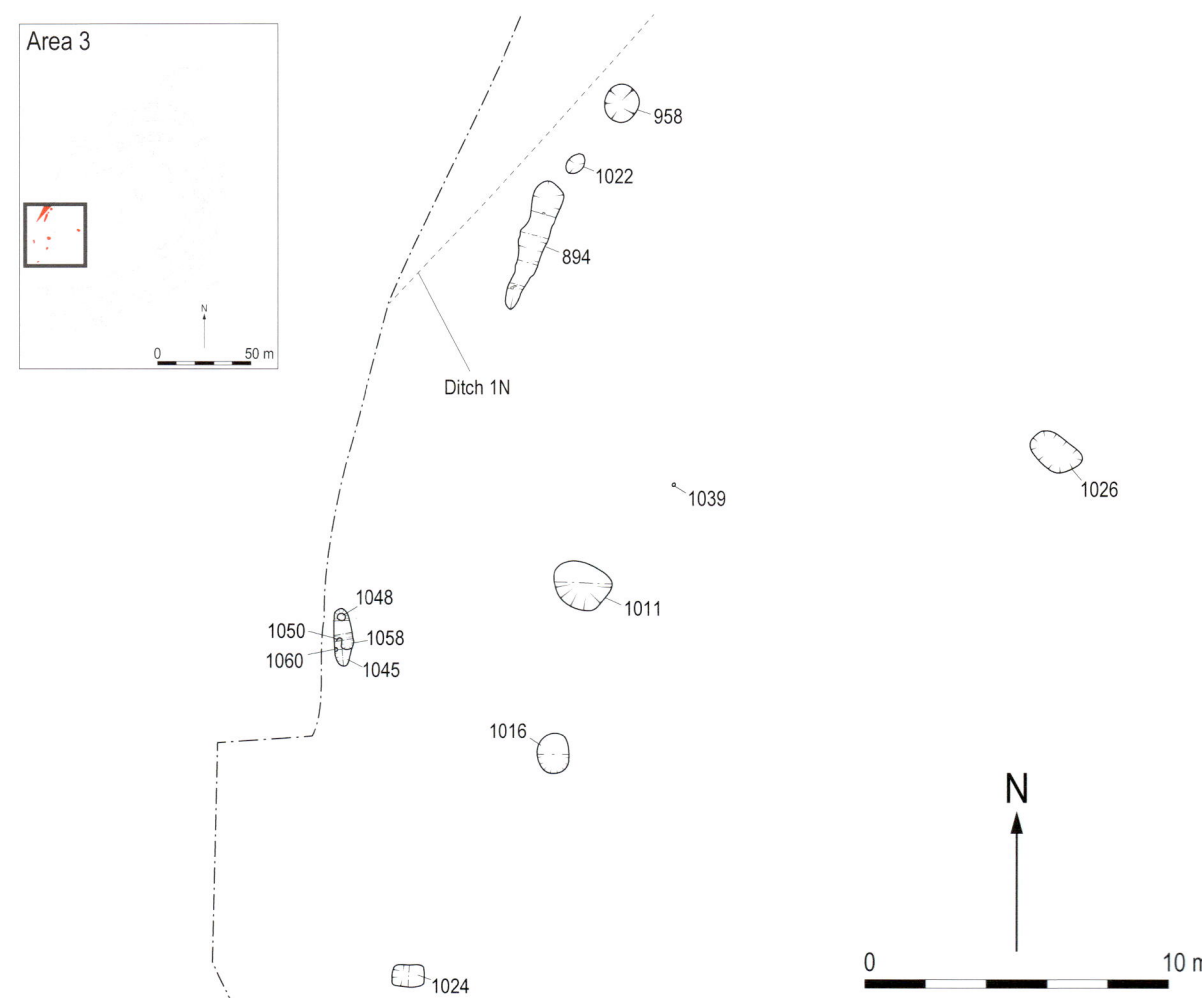

Figure 30: Plan of Area 5.

On the west side of this area close to the western boundary of the excavated area was a linear feature (1045) that measured 2.46 m by 0.74 m by 0.29 m. Its fill of burnt sand and charcoal suggested it functioned as a fire-pit. Four postholes were positioned around its perimeter, three of which contained charcoal.

South side of the Hill

Area 6

A number of prehistoric features and deposits were clustered together on the southern side of the hill (Figure 31). They were dug into the natural clayey silt subsoil below colluvium deposits (667) washed down from the hill side and appeared to be earlier than the majority of activities on the hill top.

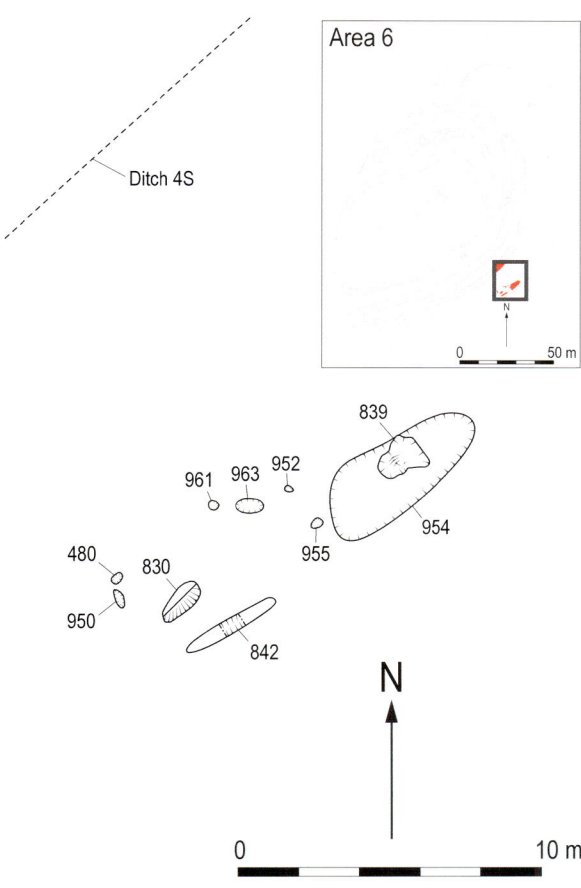

Figure 31: Plan of Area 6.

The largest feature was a 0.37 m thick deposit (954) of compacted silty sand 6 m in length and 3.3 m in width. On its northern edge was a second deposit (839) of silt with much charcoal and a small amount of burnt bone, which appeared to be a deliberate dump of hearth material.

No artefacts were recovered from either of the deposits.

To the immediate south-west of these deposits were four small pits, three of which (954, 952 and 961) averaged c. 0.4 m in length, 0.35 m in width and c. 0.16 m in depth but pit (963) was 1 m in length. Pits (952 and 963) contained some charcoal. But no finds were recovered from any of the features.

South and west of the latter group were two linear pits. Pit (830) was 1.82 m by 0.82 m by 0.22 m with three fills all with charcoal present but its middle fill (832) indicated *in situ* burning. A few metres to the east of this was another larger linear pit (842) that also contained some charcoal. These two pits were probably related by function.

West of pit (830) were two closely positioned features. Deposit (480) was a shallow and reasonably small patch of dark sandy silt with yellow-white clay patches and a large amount of charcoal. To its immediate south was pit (950), which may have been a stone hole, but its fill contained charcoal.

Two pits (504 and 506) lay outside the main group of features in Area 6 (not illustrated). They were positioned together at the base of the hill. No finds were recovered from either of the features and their function was not identified.

Area 7

At the base of the hill on its southern side were a number of features, of earlier prehistoric date than those of the fort (Figure 32). The most noticeable of these was initially identified as the remains of a possible cist (324), because of the presence of a large, flat stone (SF 205) and a sherd of early Bronze Age Beaker pottery (SF 001). During its excavation the feature was identified as a pit and not a cist and the stone was possibly a quern. The pit was 0.57 m in length by 0.38 m in width and 0.15 m in depth. It contained two similar fills of clay-silt but with pottery sherds similar to (SF 001) in it upper fill.

To the north-west of pit (324) was a large deposit, 4.50 m by 2.3 m by 0.13 m of dark silty sand (767) with stones. It represented a possible occupation layer underlying colluvium possibly derived from the digging of the southern edge of Ditch 4S near slot I (Figure 5). The deposit contained numerous sherds of prehistoric pottery (SF 219 and SF 221), with flint (SF 222) and charcoal (SF 220). A few metres to the west of (324) was a small deposit (675) which included charcoal.

The centre of this area contained a high number of features, some of which contained Bronze Age pottery, but the most dominant feature was a large and deep sub-circular pit (738), c.3.6 m by 3.3 m by 1.2 m. It had six fills (739, 741-745) of sandy silty clay with charcoal. Bronze Age pottery sherds (SF 211, SF 217 and SF 313) and lithic artefacts (SF 210, SF 214 and SF 216) were found distributed in its deposits. The pit was truncated on its south-eastern edge by a stakehole (728).

Immediately west of pit (738) was a small pit (665), 0.50 m by 0.42 m by 0.21 m, which contained charcoal and burnt bone. A fragment of a Neolithic polished stone axe head (SF 184) was found in its fill.

Two other larger features found in the vicinity of pit (738) were identified as tree boles (661 and 663). They were both irregularly shaped, less than 1 m in length and 0.70 m in width and were both quite shallow. Both contained charcoal.

Located predominantly to the south-east of pit (738) were a large number of stakeholes/small postholes, indicating the location of structures that may have been closely associated with the pit or independent of it. Some of these features were grouped together, others were more distant

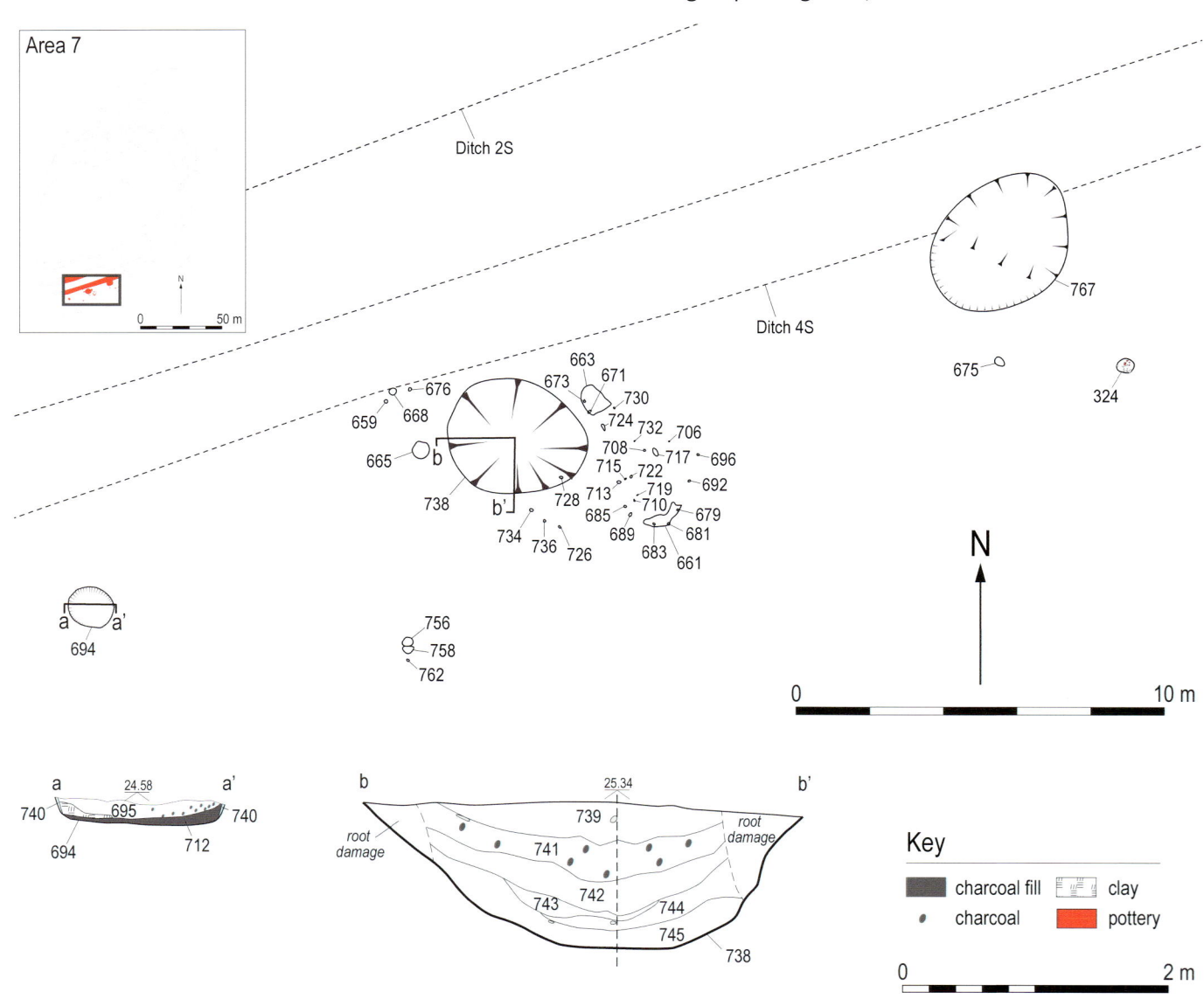

Figure 32: Plan of Area 7.

from each other, and others (734, 736 and 726, and 683, 681, 679, 692, 696 and 706) possibly formed an arc or alignment that may not have been contemporary. As there are several groups of three features (Figure 32), it is likely these may have formed wind-breaks or delineated where a temporary structure(s) were set up. Both tree boles (661 and 663) were incorporated into the arrangement of stake holes, but they gave no further evidence as to what activities the stakeholes represented.

The stakeholes were generally under 0.20 m in diameter and less than that in depth. Stakeholes (708 and 717) were not vertical but had an oblique profile. Many had evidence of charcoal in their fills.

A group of three stakeholes (676, 668 and 659) to the north-west of pit (738) lay on the edge of Ditch 4S and c. 7 m to the south was another group of three (756, 758 and 762), which were slightly larger and deeper than the rest and which contained charcoal in their fills. Their function is unknown.

Isolated at the far south-west of the area was a fire-pit (694) c. 1.2 m in diameter and 0.18 m in depth. Its basal fill of burnt clay (740) with stones and charcoal lined the pit. Above this was a layer of charcoal (712) capped with further burnt deposits (695).

The 'Palisade'

By John-James Atkinson

Initially, a possible palisade (294) extended across the base of the southern slope of the hill for c. 160 m, along the base of the north-western slope for c. 47 m, with a further 45 m being exposed across six exploratory trenches placed to the north and east of the site, a total of 234.5 m (Figure 33). Given the orientation of this feature, which linked to drainage ditch in the north west, the high numbers of modern material culture recovered from the slots trenches, the feature's position stratigraphically within the hill-wash deposits on the southern slope and the absence of post-packing material, or indeed stone agglomerations this feature is very unlikely to be a palisade and is possibly a drainage ditch of twentieth century date.

Investigations at Scone 1 and 2

By Charlotte Hunter and Maureen Kilpatrick

Introduction

An archaeological strip, map and sample excavation was carried out by GUARD Archaeology Ltd at Scone 1 and 2 (Figures 1 and 34). This phase of archaeological work was conducted as part of the wider Cross Tay Link Road (CTLR) Project and was undertaken between the 14th February and 4th March 2022. The work uncovered several prehistoric features including remnants of a burnt mound, a pit group and a possible pit alignment. Between 31st May and 2nd of June 2022, the areas around these features were extended in a further phase of topsoil stripping to investigate their extent. During this additional phase, a 10 m buffer was established mainly within the limits of the intended road line.

A total area of 600 m² was opened across the two areas of Scone 1 and 2, which were highlighted as archaeologically sensitive during the earlier archaeological evaluation phase by Rubicon Heritage Services Ltd (Pettitt and Hession 2019).

Scone 1 and 2 were located on farmland used as pasture close to the Perth Racecourse (NGR: NO11075 27516 and NO11111 27490). The topography gently undulated with a west-facing rise that sloped down towards a waterlogged area of ground. The solid geology comprises Devonian Lower Old Red Sandstone, while the drift geology is raised tidal flat deposits of silt and clay and raised marine deposits of clay, silt, sand and gravel (British Geological Survey 2025).

Results

Scone 1

A total area of 300 m² was excavated at Scone 1, with an additional 283.79 m² of topsoil removed during the additional phase of stripping to maintain an archaeology sterile 10 m buffer from those archaeological features identified, but no further feature were revealed. The machine stripping removed silty clayey topsoil (001) up to 0.5 m in depth that overlay the subsoil (002). Six archaeologically significance features, including three pits, two postholes and one small linear feature were identified cut into the subsoil. A

Key

'Palisade'

N

0   50 m

Figure 33: Possible 'Palisade'.

linear feature (011) identified as modern field drain was also uncovered. Drains such as this were common on the west side of the site and adjacent to standing water which had to be pumped away to allow investigations to proceed.

The small cluster of features uncovered at Scone 1 (Figure 35) were situated centrally and towards the east in the trench. Two sub-oval shaped possible posthole bases (009 and 010) measured between 0.65 m and 0.7 m in diameter and were between 50 mm and 0.15 m in depth. South and west of them were three similarly shaped pits (006, 008 and 083, Figure 36) over 1 m in diameter and feature (007) lay to the south-east. No artefacts were found in any of these features with their fills generally comprising silty clayey sand, often with charcoal flecks.

Figure 34: Trench plan of Scone 1 and 2.

Figure 35: Aerial photo of Scone 1.

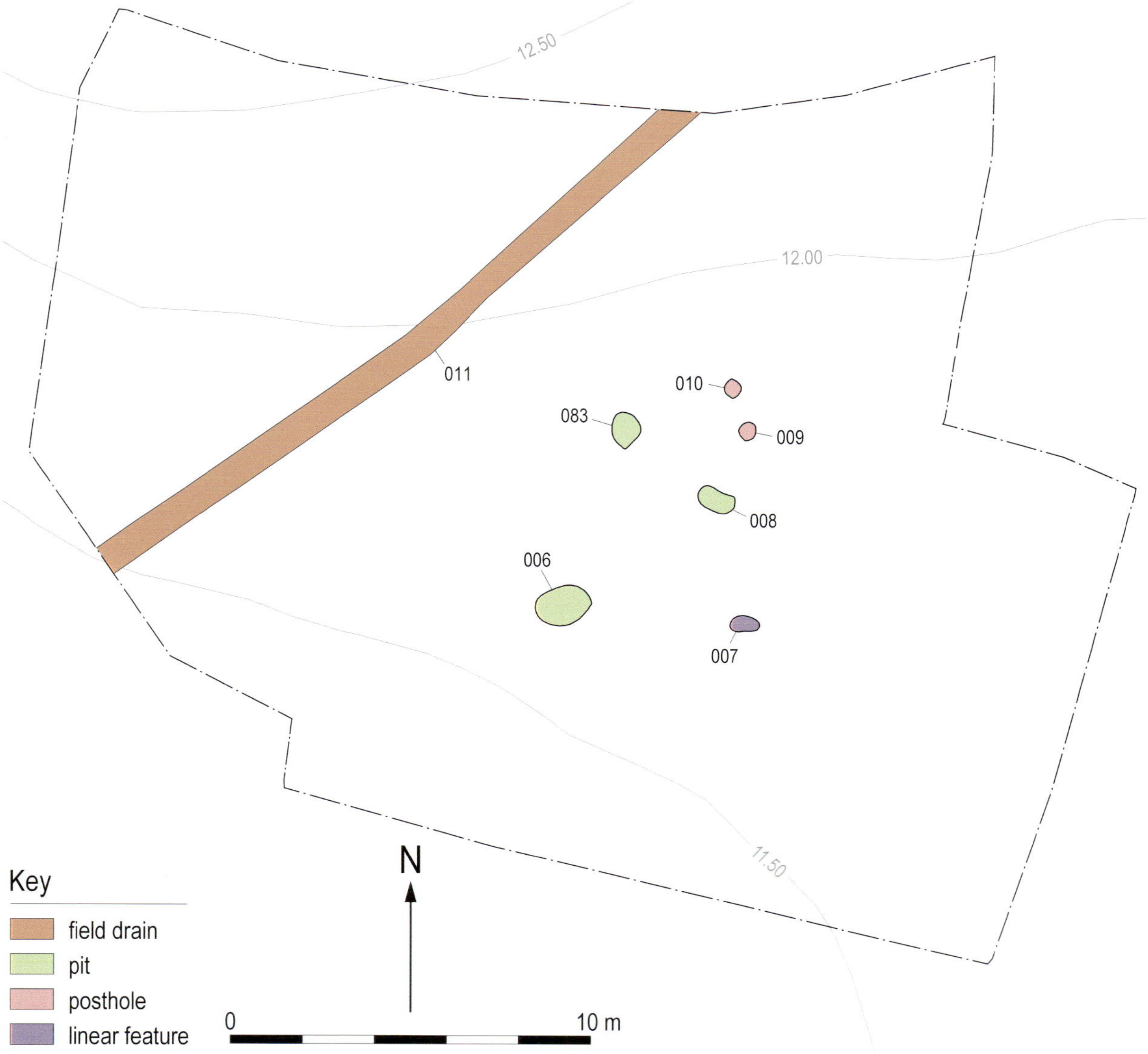

Figure 36: Plan of Scone 1.

Scone 2

An area of 300 m² was also excavated across features in Scone 2 (Figure 37) identified during the topsoil strip, with an additional 772.07 m² opened up to investigate the extent of those features, although no further features were identified, and to maintain an archaeology sterile 10 m buffer around them. During the machine stripping similar topsoil and subsoil deposits to Scone 1 were uncovered. Sixteen features of archaeological significance – 14 pits and two postholes were uncovered (Figure 38). A large deposit towards the western end of the trench was also exposed and during excavation it was discovered to be the probable remains of a burnt mound.

The main feature of interest in this area was the burnt mound. Although with a depth of only 0.15 m the feature covered an area 13 m by 6 m, and comprised two deposits, The upper deposit (044) including a large amount of burnt cobbles and pebbles in dark silty sand. The lower deposit (069) also of silty sand was only 80 mm and was also located around the perimeter of the feature. Two artefacts were recovered from the upper deposit: a polishing stone (SF 004) and a flint scraper (SF 001). A narrow trench 1 m in width was excavated across the feature and revealed the remains of a pit or possible trough (071) 1.2 m by 0.8 m by 10 mm.

Thirteen further pits and two postholes mostly found as a cluster in the south-central area, with one pit (025) further to the east, were excavated. Most features were generally oval in shape and varied in size, with the largest pit (028) measuring 1.9 m in diameter. Depths also varied although most were between 0.12 m and 0.27 m deep with others (034, 036, 038, 059, 071, 085 and 089) being between very shallow, suggesting they may had been severely truncated by later activities. Only pit (052) contained a fragment of flint debitage (SF 003). Three linear field drains, also crossing the trench.

Figure 37: Aerial photo of Scone 2.

Figure 38: Plan of Scone 2

Analysis

The investigation confirmed the presence of prehistoric remains at Scone 1 and 2. They were mostly pits, a common feature found on prehistoric sites and indicative of the presence of temporary settlement. The function of the majority of these pits was unknown, although they are often interpreted as rubbish pits or imbued with symbolic meaning or attributes (Brophy and Noble 2012). The most substantial feature uncovered was the remains of a burnt mound, a monument type which generally comprises a crescent shaped mound of fire-cracked stones, and typically found near to a fresh water source such as a burn or spring. They often contain a trough or pit which can be lined with wood, wattle, clay, stone and even moss (Brown et al. 2016). At Scone 2 a pit was identified below the main deposits of the burnt mound, although no structure or lining was identified. Burnt mounds are very common throughout the British Isles and Ireland although their functions remain indeterminate as they have been used for activities such as cooking, bathing and for industrial processing such as brewing, tanning and processing of skins or textiles. Recent environmental research by Brown et al. (2016) in Ireland has suggested their function might be associated with tanning and textile processing, but not all burnt mounds would have had the same function.

Very few artefacts were recovered to aid dating of the features at Scone 1 and 2. However, burnt mounds are generally mid to late Bronze Age in date although earlier and later similar structures have been discovered elsewhere. During the evaluation stage of the project several sherds of Bronze Age pottery was uncovered that would suggest that at least some of the activities investigated at Scone 1 and 2 were from this period (Pettitt and Hession 2019).

Within the wider locale of the present site there are numerous prehistoric monuments including the scheduled monuments of Lochton House prehistoric rectilinear enclosure (SM 6722), Blairhall House Barrow Cemetery and Cursus Monument (SM 6932) and a further barrow (SM 6946) to the north-east. To the north of the site is Sherrifton Barrow Cemetery (SM 6723), while further to the west and adjacent to the River Tay is Gold Castle rectilinear enclosure (SM 7572). These monuments attest to communities which occupied this area from the earliest prehistoric periods, possibly due to a combination of fertile land for farming and the river which would have provided both transport links and resources through fishing and hunting.

Archaeological Evaluation of Temporary Works Area 5

By Alun Woodward

Introduction

An archaeological evaluation was conducted between the 27th June and the 15th July 2022 across the proposed development area at the Temporary Works Area 5 to the north-west of Scone Village (Figure 1). This phase of work was conducted as part of the wider Cross Tay Link Road (CTLR) Project. A total of 51 trenches, 10% of the development area of 54,070 m², between 36 m and 50 m in length and 2 m in width, but with variable orientations, were excavated by machine across the area, which comprised an arable field. The aim was to establish the presence, extent and nature of any significant archaeological remains in the area. The works revealed one possible feature of archaeological significance, a small charcoal-filled pit with several burnt bone fragments which was fully excavated in Trench 3 and the remains of the nineteenth century Garragie Fishing Lodge (NO02NE 254) in Trench 24. Both features were recorded: the lodge was protected during follow-on site works and a 5m buffer zone was stripped around the pit in Trench 3 but no further archaeological features were located in this area.

Temporary Works Area 5 lay immediately to the east of the River Tay and west of the archaeological investigations at Scone 1 and 2 (NGR: NO 09813 27495; Figure 1). The area was bounded by a track to the west and by agricultural fields to the north, south and east. This field and those in the immediate vicinity were cultivated for cereal production. Geologically the area was very similar to that at Scone 1 and 2.

Results

Of the 51 trenches (Figure 39), four of them, 17, 24, 27 and 49, were extended to further evaluate possible archaeological features. The topsoil varied between sandy clay in the western part of the site to sandy silt in the east. The subsoil was sand in the west where it was closer to the River Tay and clay in the east.

The ruined nineteenth century stone and lime mortar-built Garragie fishing lodge (NO02NE 254) was located in Trench 24. At the time of the evaluation the remains comprised mainly rubble with only the one to two courses surviving *in situ*. Several fragments of slate were also noted as well as brick repairs to the building. This small structure measured c. 4.2 m by 4 m and survived to a maximum height of 1.3 m. It was completely covered in tall vegetation that obscured much of its surviving structure (Figure 40).

A small sub-circular pit (0303G) was uncovered in Trench 3 that included charcoal and burnt bone fragments in its fill but no further archaeological features were found there or in the surrounding trenches. A 5 m buffer strip around the pit (0303) was later established to determine if any related features survived in the locale but there were no new archaeological features or deposits in the machine stripped area.

The very shallow remnants of rig and furrow cultivation orientated NE/SW were observed in trenches 37, 39, 41 and 46.

Analysis

No features or artefacts of significance were encountered during the evaluation aside from the possible isolated fire-pit (0303), which remained undated. The degraded and mostly rubble footings of Garragie Fishing Lodge were also noted during the work as were the extremely truncated remnants of rig and furrow cultivation.

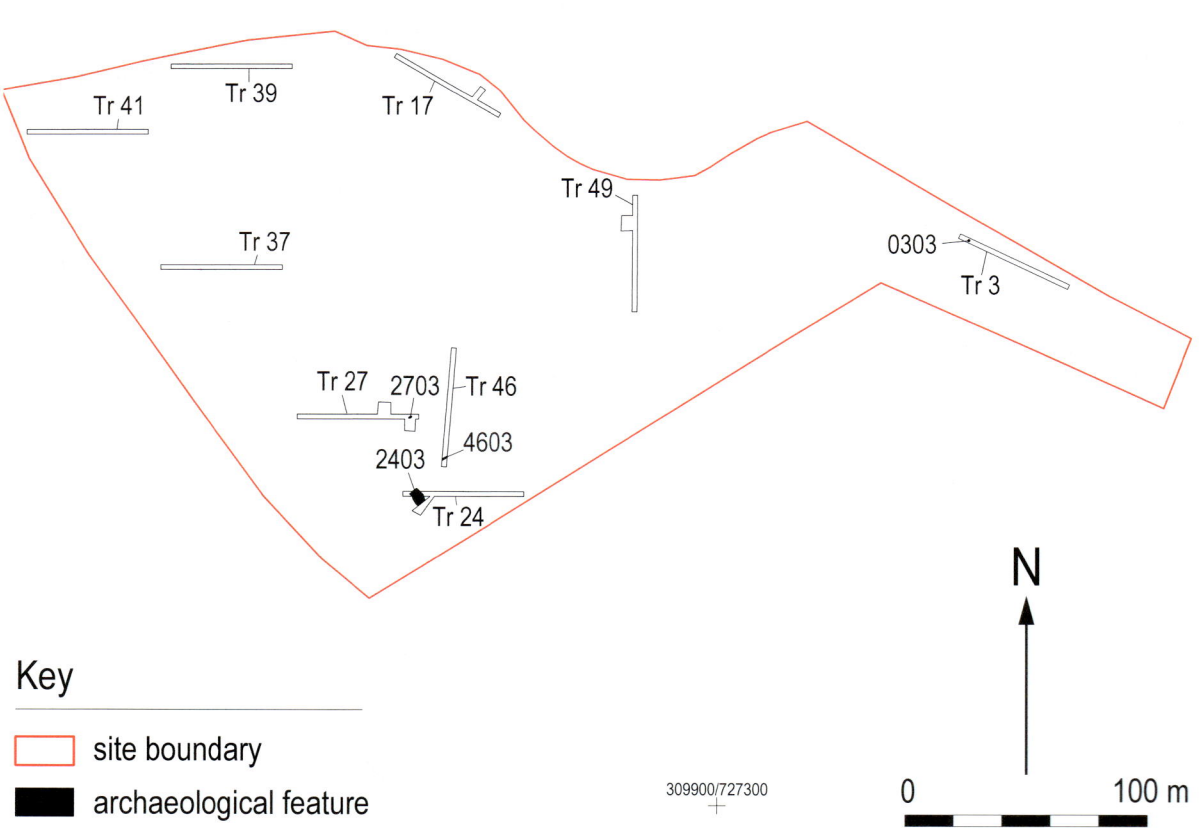

Key

- ▭ site boundary
- ▬ archaeological feature

309900/727300

N

0   100 m

Figure 39: Area 5 Trench location.

Figure 40: South facing section of southern Garragie Fishing lodge wall.

PART 2: Dating and the Environment

Radiocarbon dating and Chronological modelling

By Derek Hamilton

Introduction

A total of 56 radiocarbon dates are available from samples of charcoal from features excavated at the hilltop enclosure site of Broxy Kennels Fort (Table 1). The samples were all single entities (Ashmore 1999) and submitted to the 14Chrono Laboratory at Queen's University Belfast where they were processed following the methods described on their website (https://14chrono.org/radiocarbon-dating/pre-treatment-analysis/) by sample type and measured by accelerator mass spectrometry (AMS). The results are reported here as conventional radiocarbon ages (Stuiver and Polach 1977) and have been calibrated using the internationally agreed northern hemisphere calibration curve of Reimer et al. (2020) and the OxCal v4.4 computer program (Bronk Ramsey (2009). The simple calibrated dates are given in Figure 41 as single 95% probability ranges with the endpoints rounded outward to the nearest 10 years, while the results of any statistical modelling discussed in the text are presented in italics and with their endpoints rounded outward to the nearest five years.

Methodological approach

A Bayesian approach (Buck et al. 1996) has been applied to the interpretation of the chronology of activity at Broxy Kennels. Although simple calibrated dates are accurate estimates of the radiocarbon age of samples, this is not, usually, what archaeologists really wish to know. It is the dates of the archaeological events represented by those samples that are of interest. For example,

the start and end of the Iron Age hillfort activity is of interest. The chronology of this activity can be estimated not only by using the absolute dating derived from the radiocarbon measurements, but also by using stratigraphic relationships between samples and the relative dating information provided by the archaeological phasing.

The methodology used here allows the combination of these different types of information explicitly, to produce realistic estimates of the dates of archaeological interest. The posterior density estimates produced by this modelling are not absolute, rather they are interpretative estimates, which can and will change as further data become available and as other researchers choose to model the existing data from different perspectives. The technique used is a form of Markov Chain Monte Carlo sampling and has been applied using the program OxCal v4.4 (http://c14.arch.ox.ac.uk/). Details of the algorithms employed by this program are available in Bronk Ramsey (1995; 1998; 2001; 2009) or from the online manual. The algorithm used in the models can be derived from the OxCal keywords and bracket structure shown in Figures 41, 44-46.

Samples and model

The radiocarbon-dated samples cover practically all periods from the Mesolithic through to the medieval (Figure 41; note UBA-54851, which is Mesolithic, is not shown). While this provides good indications of when, in the past, humans were active on the hilltop, the longevity of activity increases the risks of residual material being dated in the excavated contexts. Therefore, a critical mind must be kept when considering the date of a sample and the sample's relationship to the formation of the context from which it was derived.

UB No	Sample No.	Context	Material	Radiocarbon Age BP	Calibrated 1-sigma (68.3% probability)	Calibrated 2-sigma (95.4% probability)	Period
UBA-54824	3	North - 304 part of 'palisade' ditch 294	Corylus cf avellana	3607 ± 28	2022 – 1994 cal BC 1982 – 1927 cal BC	2109 – 2107 cal BC 2034 – 1886 cal BC	EBA
UBA-54825	13	Ditch 3 North - 029 basal fill of 085	Alnus cf glutinosa	2474 ± 25	752 – 717 cal BC 710 – 682 cal BC 668 – 661 cal BC 654 – 632 cal BC 624 – 611 cal BC 592 – 542 cal BC	768 – 478 cal BC	EIA
UBA-54826	16	Ditch 4 North - 026 separating natural and upper layers	Alnus cf glutinosa	2340 ± 27	408 – 389 cal BC	512 – 505 cal BC 481 – 371 cal BC	EIA
UBA-54827	20/S2	North - 044 souterrain cut	Alnus cf glutinosa	3750 ± 28	2203 – 2134 cal BC 2081 – 2060 cal BC	2282 – 2251 cal BC 2231 – 2220 cal BC 2209 – 2117 cal BC 2098 – 2038 cal BC	EBA
UBA-54828	27	Ditch 2 South- 041 middle fill of 007	Salix sp	2421 ± 27	539 – 528 cal BC 520 – 413 cal BC	745 – 690 cal BC 665 – 645 cal BC 562 – 559 cal BC 550 – 403 cal BC	EIA
UBA-54829	28	Ditch 2 South - 037 lower fill of 007	Prunoideae	2441 ± 26	733 – 696 cal BC 663 – 650 cal BC 545 – 461 cal BC 438 – 420 cal BC	750 – 685 cal BC 666 – 636 cal BC 619 – 615 cal BC 589 – 578 cal BC 572 – 409 cal BC	EIA
UBA-54830	28/S1	Ditch 2 North - 084 fill of pit 083	Salix sp	7019 ± 36	5979 – 5945 cal BC 5922 – 5881 cal BC 5863 – 5846 cal BC	5987 – 5826 cal BC 5823 – 5803 cal BC	Mesolithic
UBA-54831	35	Ditch 1 South - 035 initial fill of recut 030 in 005	Corylus cf avellana	2411 ± 26	515 – 496 cal BC 490 – 410 cal BC	732 – 697 cal BC 663 – 650 cal BC 545 – 402 cal BC	EIA
UBA-54832	41	Ditch 3North -071 lowest fill of 046	Salix sp	2378 ± 23	472 – 434 cal BC 423 – 398 cal BC	538 – 531 cal BC 517 – 395 cal BC	EIA
UBA-54833	52	Ditch 2 North - 076 redeposited sand in pit 083	Salix sp	3471 ± 26	1875 – 1843 cal BC 1821 – 1797 cal BC 1778 – 1744 cal BC	1882 – 1738 cal BC 1714 – 1696 cal BC	EBA
UBA-54834	58	Ditch 4 South - 081 middle fill of terminus slot A	Corylus cf avellana	2443 ± 28	737 – 694 cal BC 663 – 649 cal BC 546 – 461 cal BC 438 – 420 cal BC	751 – 684 cal BC 667 – 634 cal BC 622 – 613 cal BC 591 – 409 cal BC	EIA
UBA-54835	63	Ditch 3 North - 045 top fill of 009	Alnus cf glutinosa	2442 ± 26	735 – 695 cal BC 663 – 649 cal BC 546 – 461 cal BC 438 – 420 cal BC	750 – 685 cal BC 667 – 635 cal BC 619 – 614 cal BC 590 – 577 cal BC 573 – 409 cal BC	EIA
UBA-54836	66	Ditch 4 South - 082 basal fill of terminus	Maloideae	2447 ± 25	741 – 692 cal BC 664 – 647 cal BC 547 – 471 cal BC 435 – 422 cal BC	750 – 684 cal BC 667 – 634 cal BC 621 – 613 cal BC 591 – 412 cal BC	EIA
UBA-54837	73	Ditch 1 North - 121 fill of 006, slot F	Prunoideae	2433 ± 22	719 – 708 cal BC 662 – 653 cal BC 543 – 455 cal BC 444 – 417 cal BC	748 – 687 cal BC 665 – 642 cal BC 568 – 407 cal BC	EIA

Table 1: Radiocarbon dates

UB No	Sample No.	Context	Material	Radiocarbon Age BP	Calibrated 1-sigma (68.3% probability)	Calibrated 2-sigma (95.4% probability)	Period
UBA-54838	84	Ditch 1 North - 115 basal fill of 006	Salix sp	2292 ± 26	398 – 362 cal BC 270 – 269 cal BC 240 – 236 cal BC	403 – 354 cal BC 284 – 230 cal BC	EIA
UBA-54839	105	Ditch 1 South - 141 recut of 005	Corylus cf avellana	2441 ± 25	733 – 696 cal BC 663 – 650 cal BC 545 – 462 cal BC 438 – 420 cal BC	750 – 685 cal BC 666 – 636 cal BC 618 – 615 cal BC 589 – 578 cal BC 572 – 409 cal BC	EIA
UBA-54840	162	Ditch 3 North - lower fill 166 of pit 164 in 009	Prunoideae	2402 ± 25	513 – 501 cal BC 484 – 406 cal BC	720 – 708 cal BC 662 – 652 cal BC 544 – 400 cal BC	EIA
UBA-54841	248	Ditch 3 North - lowest basal fill 181 in terminus of 009	Salix sp	2551 ± 25	746 – 690 cal BC 665 – 645 cal BC 562 – 559 cal BC 550 – 475 cal BC 434 – 423 cal BC	725 – 683 cal BC 667 – 633 cal BC 623 – 611 cal BC 592 – 411 cal BC	EIA
UBA-54842	297	Ditch 1 South - fill 191 of 192	Salix sp	2450 ± 26	746 – 690 cal BC 665 – 645 cal BC 561 – 560 cal BC 550 – 471 cal BC 435 – 422 cal BC	667 – 633 cal BC 623 – 611cal BC 592 – 413 cal BC	EIA
UBA-54843	313	Ditch 1 South - 227 bottom fill of cut 216 in 005	Corylus cf avellana	2379 ± 28	478 – 428 cal BC 426 – 398 cal BC	659 – 657 cal BC 541 – 394 cal BC	EIA
UBA-54844	326	Ditch 1 South - 197 natural silting in 005	Salix sp	2450 ± 25	745 – 690 cal BC 664 – 645 cal BC 549 – 472 cal BC 434 – 423 cal BC	751 – 683 cal BC 667 – 633 cal BC 623 – 612 cal BC 592 – 413 cal BC	EIA
UBA-54845	367	Ditch 1 South - 205 third fill of ditch	Corylus cf avellana	2460 ± 25	749 – 685 cal BC 666 – 637 cal BC 588 – 580 cal BC 570 – 514 cal BC 500 – 487 cal BC	756 – 680 cal BC 670 – 606 cal BC 597 – 456 cal BC 443 – 417 cal BC	EIA
UBA-54846	399	Ditch 1 North - 234 fill of posthole	Corylus cf avellana	1983 ± 24	32 – 30 cal BC 26 – 17 cal BC cal AD 7 – 68	41 – 9 cal BC 1 cal BC – cal AD 84 cal AD 95 – 116	MIA
UBA-54847	743	Ditch 3 South - 340 basal fill of ditch	Corylus cf avellana	3620 ± 28	2027 – 1991 cal BC 1985 – 1942 cal BC	2118 – 2097 cal BC 2037 – 1893 cal BC	EBA
UBA-54848	759	Ditch 2 South - 332 first fill of 007	Salix sp	2435 ± 25	720 – 708 cal BC 662 – 652 cal BC 544 – 456 cal BC 443 – 417 cal BC	749 – 687 cal BC 666 – 641 cal BC 587 – 583 cal BC 569 – 407 cal BC	EIA
UBA-54849	799	Ditch 2 South - 420 fill of ditch	Alnus cf glutinosa	2310 ± 25	401 – 380 cal BC	408 – 358 cal BC 277 – 258 cal BC 245 – 233 cal BC	MIA
UBA-54850	804	Ditch 2 South - 430 fill of ditch 007	Alnus cf glutinosa	2397 ± 25	513 – 503 cal BC 483 – 404 cal BC	717 – 710 cal BC 661 – 654 cal BC 542 – 399 cal BC	EIA
UBA-54851	813	North of fort - 438 fill of pit 437	Salix sp	9522 ± 43	9118 – 9078 cal BC 9058 – 9012 cal BC 8917 – 8904 cal BC 8850 – 8754 cal BC	9129 – 8970 cal BC 8938 – 8709 cal BC 8666 – 8655 cal BC	Mesolithic
UBA-54852	821	Area 3 - 458 fill of posthole 457	Corylus cf avellana	2129 ± 26	196 – 185 cal BC 178 – 102 cal BC 66 – 59 cal BC	344 – 319 cal BC 202 – 88 cal BC	MIA

Table 1 (continued): Radiocarbon dates

UB No	Sample No.	Context	Material	Radiocarbon Age BP	Calibrated 1-sigma (68.3% probability)	Calibrated 2-sigma (95.4% probability)	Period
UBA-54853	834	Ditch 4 North - 462 top fill of 021,	Alnus cf glutinosa	1030 ± 26	cal AD 994 – 1008 cal AD 1010 – 1025	cal AD 902 – 913 cal AD 976 – 1041 cal AD 1089 – 1090 cal AD 1107 – 1115	early Medieval
UBA-54854	875	Ditch 2 North - 533 erosion fill of south bank of 008	Alnus cf glutinosa	2459 ± 28	749 – 685 cal BC 666 – 637 cal BC 588 – 580 cal BC 570 – 513 cal BC 503 – 483 cal BC	756 – 680 cal BC 670 – 606 cal BC 597 – 454 cal BC 445 – 416 cal BC	EIA
UBA-54855	883	Area 3 - 549 fill of pit/ posthole	Betula sp	2126 ± 25	194 – 188 cal BC 176 – 101 cal BC 67 – 59 cal BC	342 – 322 cal BC 201 – 88 cal BC 83 – 52 cal BC	MIA
UBA-54856	900	Area 4 - 583 lower fill of pit 581	Alnus cf glutinosa	1453 ± 26	cal AD 599 – 641	cal AD 574 – 648	LIA/Pictish
UBA-54857	905	Ditch 2 North - 576 2nd fill of possible recut 799	Cytisus/ Ulex	661 ± 23	cal AD 1289 – 1306 cal AD 1364 – 1384	cal AD 1282 – 1321 cal AD 1358 – 1390	Medieval
UBA-54858	927	Ditch 4 South - 655 ditch fill	Betula sp	1582 ± 24	cal AD 434 – 466 cal AD 474 – 501 cal AD 506 – 517 cal AD 529 – 540	cal AD 424 – 547	LIA/Pictish
UBA-54859	931	Ditch 4 South - 653 lowest fill of ditch 476	Alnus cf glutinosa	2814 ± 27	1001 – 929 cal BC	1047 – 1026 cal BC 1023 – 901 cal BC	LBA
UBA-54860	932	Area 4 - 658 redeposited material in pit 657	Alnus cf glutinosa	2068 ± 27	146 – 140 cal BC 107 – 41 cal BC 10 cal BC – cal AD 1	166 – 25 cal BC 17 cal BC – cal AD 7	MIA
UBA-54861	957	Ditch 4 South - 691 primary fill 476	Alnus cf glutinosa	4824 ± 39	3645 – 3625 cal BC 3578 – 3533 cal BC	3653 – 3522 cal BC	EN
UBA-54862	971	Base of South slope - 712 primary fill of fire-pit 694	Alnus cf glutinosa	2354 ± 25	451 – 447 cal BC 415 – 391 cal BC	514 – 500 cal BC 486 – 385 cal BC	EIA/MIA
UBA-54863	983	Base of South slope - 745 fill of pit 738	Corylus cf avellana	3891 ± 26	2457 – 2394 cal BC 2389 – 2343 cal BC	2464 – 2293 cal BC	EBA
UBA-54864	1003	Ditch 2 South - 748 basal fill of 007	Alnus cf glutinosa	2451 ± 23	746 – 609 cal BC 665 – 645 cal BC 550 – 476 cal BC 432 – 425 cal BC	751 – 683 cal BC 667 – 643 cal BC 622 – 612 cal BC 591 – 414 cal BC	EIA
UBA-54865	1013	Ditch 3 North - 631 basal fill of 2nd recut of 630	Salix sp	2461 ± 23	749 – 685 cal BC 666 – 637 cal BC 588 – 580 cal BC 570 – 515 cal BC	755 – 680 cal BC 670 – 606 cal BC 596 – 458 cal BC 440 – 418 cal BC	EIA
UBA-54866	1021	Area 1 Ditch 6 - 787 basal fill of ditch 779	Betula sp	2432 ± 23	717 – 709 cal BC 661 – 654 cal BC 542 – 457 cal BC 442 – 418 cal BC	746 – 690 cal BC 665 – 645 cal BC 564 – 557 cal BC 551 – 407 cal BC	EIA
UBA-54867	1066	Ditch 2 South - 837 basal fill of 007	Alnus cf glutinosa	2434 ± 23	719 – 708 cal BC 662 – 653 cal BC 543 – 457 cal BC 442 – 418 cal BC	747 – 689 cal BC 665 – 644 cal BC 565 – 408 cal BC	EIA

Table 1 (continued): Radiocarbon dates

UB No	Sample No.	Context	Material	Radiocarbon Age BP	Calibrated 1-sigma (68.3% probability)	Calibrated 2-sigma (95.4% probability)	Period
UBA-54868	1069	North - 841 fill behind souterrain wall	Corylus cf avellana	2314 ± 23	401 – 385 cal BC	408 – 361 cal BC 274 –264 cal BC 241 – 235 cal BC	MIA
UBA-54869	1072	Base of South slope - 838 basal fill of pit 830	Corylus cf avellana	4977 ± 35	3788– 3705 cal BC 3673 – 3658 cal BC	3932 – 3923 cal BC 3915 – 3877 cal BC 3804 – 3650 cal BC	EN
UBA-54870	1074	North - 844 basal fill behind souterrain walls	Alnus cf glutinosa	2444 ± 29	739 – 693 cal BC 664 – 648 cal BC 547 – 460 cal BC 449 – 419 cal BC	751 – 683 cal BC 667 – 633 cal BC 622 – 612 cal BC 591 – 410 cal BC	EIA
UBA-54871	1091	Ditch 3 South - 856 basal fill of 046	Corylus cf avellana	2440 ± 29	734 – 696 cal BC 663 – 650 cal BC 545 – 459 cal BC 440 – 418 cal BC	750 – 684 cal BC 667 – 635 cal BC 621 – 613 cal BC 590 – 408 cal BC	EIA
UBA-54872	1102	North - 867 bedding layer for floor stones of souterrain	Prunoideae	2372 ± 29	476 – 432 cal BC 424 – 395 cal BC	540 – 391 cal BC	EIA/MIA
UBA-54873	1104	North - 870 bedding layer for floor stones of souterrain	Alnus cf glutinosa	2458 ± 28	749 – 685 cal BC 666 – 637 cal BC 588 – 580 cal BC 570 – 511 cal BC 505 – 481 cal BC	755 – 680 cal BC 670 – 607 cal BC 596 – 452 cal BC 446 – 416 cal BC	EIA
UBA-54874	1121	Ditch 4 South - 889 intermediate fill of 912 terminus	Alnus cf glutinosa	2432 ± 28	719 – 708 cal BC 662 – 653 cal BC 543 – 451 cal BC 446 – 416 cal BC	749 – 686 cal BC 666 – 638 cal BC 588 – 580 cal BC 570 – 405 cal BC	EIA
UBA-54875	1175b	Base of South slope - 964 fill of pit 963	Corylus cf avellana	4943 ± 37	3763 – 3737 cal BC 3714 – 3651 cal BC	3791 – 3644 cal BC	EN
UBA-54876	1187	Ditch 4 North - 982 fill of pit 981	Alnus cf glutinosa	1247 ± 21	cal AD 691 – 695 cal AD 703 – 740 cal AD 773 – 775 cal AD 790 – 806 cal AD 809 – 821	cal AD 678 – 747 cal AD 759 – 767 cal AD 771 – 775 cal AD 787 – 833 cal AD 851 – 876	Pictish/ early Medieval
UBA-54877	1123	Inner - 1053 fill of posthole 1052	Corylus cf avellana	2093 ± 25	150 – 132 cal BC 118 – 88 cal BC 83 – 52 cal BC	175 – 42 cal BC 8 – 2 cal BC	MIA
UBA-54878	1225a	Area 5 - 1057 fill of pit 1022	Alnus cf glutinosa	2390 ± 22	478 – 428 cal BC 426 – 402 cal BC	540 – 526 cal BC 522 – 399 cal BC	EIA
UBA-54879	1227	Area 5 - 1049 fill of linear feature 1045?	Salix sp	2410 ± 27	515 – 496 cal BC 490 – 409 cal BC	733 – 696 cal BC 663 – 650 cal BC 546 – 401 cal BC	EIA
UBA-54880	SF 167	Ditch 1 North - 064 fill of recut 198	Corylus cf avellana	2443 ± 24	735 – 695 cal BC 663 – 649 cal BC 546 – 465 cal BC 436 – 421 cal BC	750 – 685 cal BC 666 – 636 cal BC 618 – 615 cal BC 589 – 578 cal BC 572 – 410 cal BC	EIA
UBA-54881	SF248	North - 095 lowest fill of souterrain slot B	Corylus cf avellana	2350 ± 25	413 – 390 cal BC	513 – 502 cal BC 482 – 383 cal BC	EIA/MIA

Table 1 (continued): Radiocarbon dates

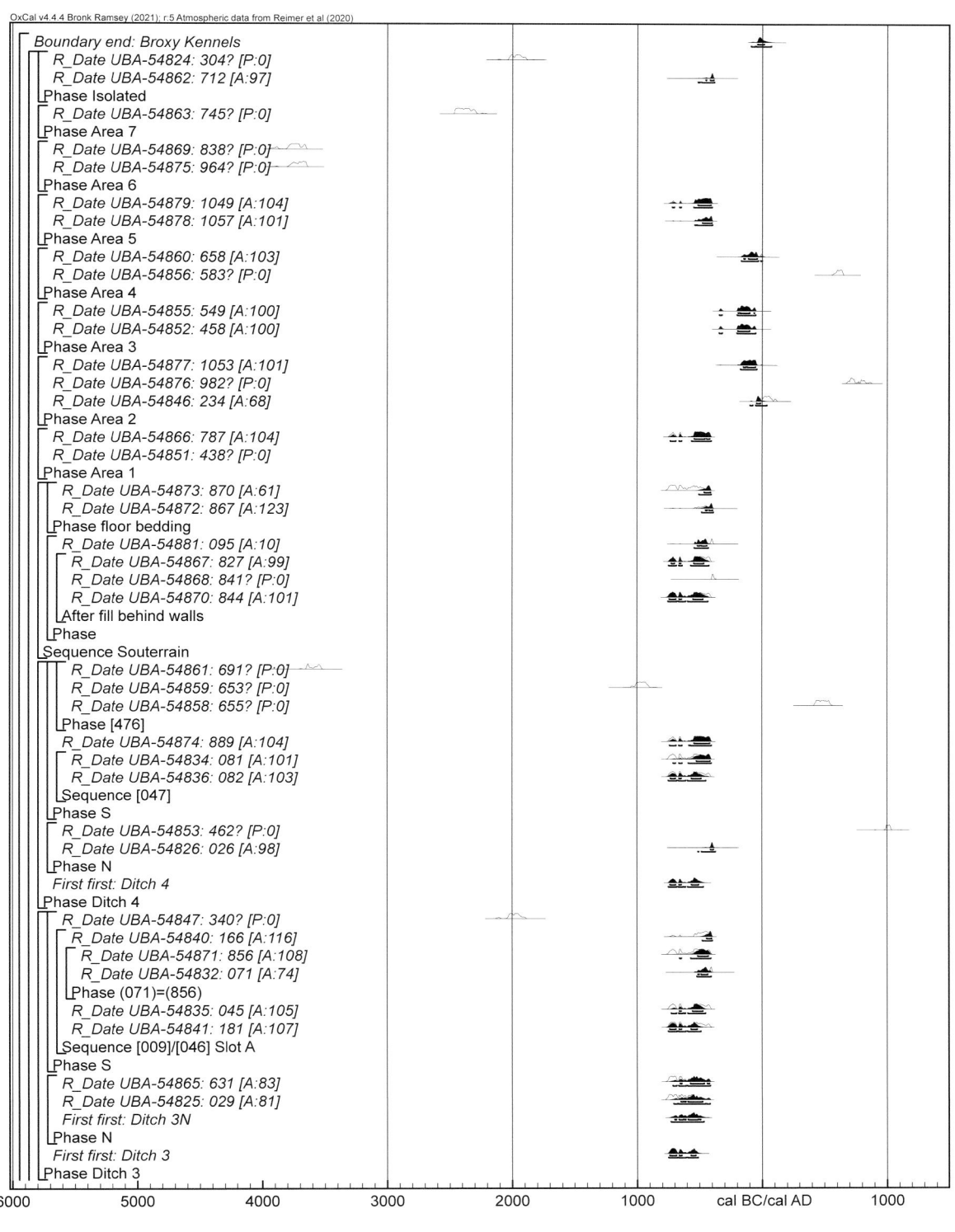

OxCal v4.4.4 Bronk Ramsey (2021); r:5 Atmospheric data from Reimer et al (2020)

Modelled date (cal BC/cal AD)

Figure 41: Broxy Kennels MODEL. Overall chronological model from Broxy Kennels Fort. Each distribution represents the relative probability that an event occurred at some particular time. For each of the radiocarbon measurements two distributions have been plotted, one in outline, which is the result of simple radiocarbon calibration, and a solid one, which is based on the chronological model use. The other distributions correspond to aspects if the model. For example, 'start: Broxy Kennels' is the estimated date that Iron Age activity began at the site, based on the radiocarbon dating results. The large square 'brackets' along with the OxCal keywords define the overall model exactly.

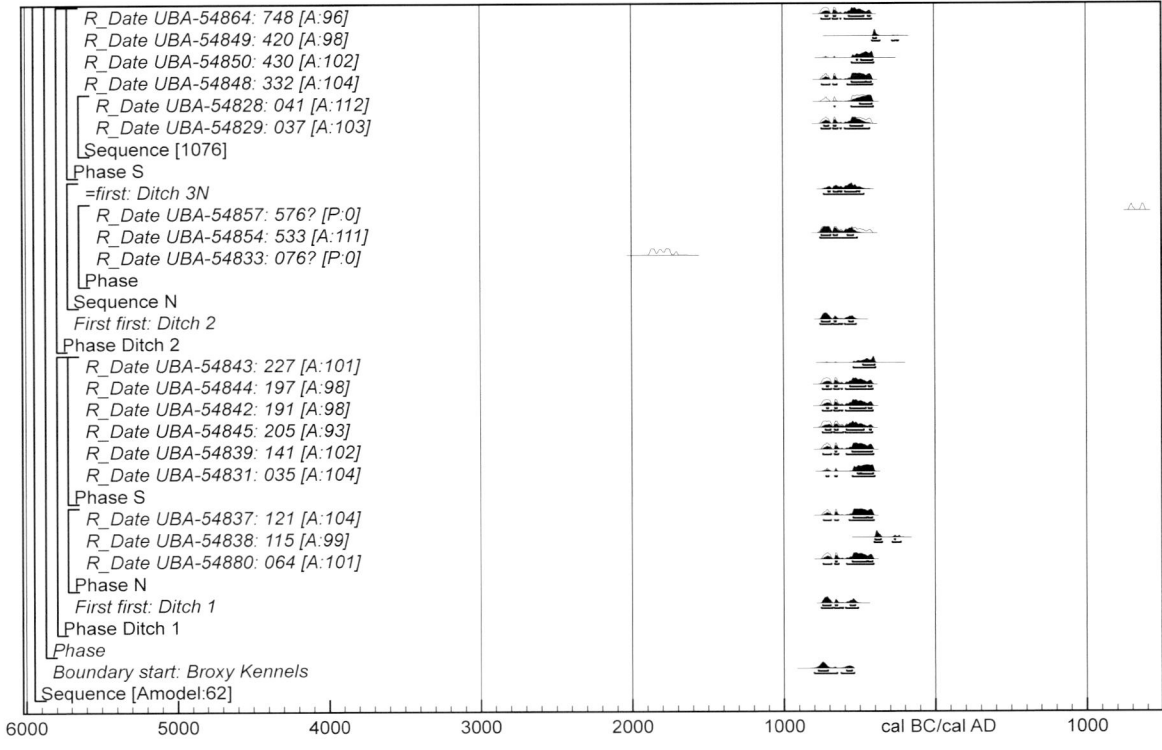

Modelled date (cal BC/cal AD)

Figure 41 (continued): Broxy Kennels MODEL. Overall chronological model from Broxy Kennels Fort. Each distribution represents the relative probability that an event occurred at some particular time. For each of the radiocarbon measurements two distributions have been plotted, one in outline, which is the result of simple radiocarbon calibration, and a solid one, which is based on the chronological model use. The other distributions correspond to aspects if the model. For example, 'start: Broxy Kennels' is the estimated date that Iron Age activity began at the site, based on the radiocarbon dating results. The large square 'brackets' along with the OxCal keywords define the overall model exactly.

Below, the dated samples are discussed by feature/feature group. Typically, only the direct stratigraphic relationships are modelled, but here a hybrid approach has been used. For the enclosure ditches, the model groups the radiocarbon dates by ditch and separates the north and south halves but calculates the earliest probability for each ditch circuit using the First parameter in OxCal. Furthermore, each ditch has at least one episode of recutting visible in the sections and these have radiocarbon dates. While it is possible a recut seen in multiple sections could represent multiple recutting events, the model is conservative and places dates from the lowest cut of a ditch into an unordered group and then all dates from any recuts into an unordered group that is later. The Date parameter is then used to estimate the date of the recut and to provide an estimate for how long a ditch might be in use prior to a major recutting episode. Additionally, if there is a later feature (e.g. pit or posthole) cutting a ditch anywhere along its circuit, this has been placed further up the sequence from the dates in the recut fills.

Ditch 1

The north circuit of Ditch 1 has three contexts with radiocarbon dates. Slot C has a date (UBA-54838) on willow charcoal from the basal fill (115) of the initial ditch cut (006), which contained considerable amounts of charcoal and ash along with some burnt bone. A fragment of Prunoideae charcoal was dated (UBA-54837) from a dumped middle fill (121) in the primary ditch (006), as observed in Slot F. In Slot B there is a date (UBA-54880) on hazel charcoal from the charcoal-rich primary fill (064) of the recut (198) of ditch (006).

There are six radiocarbon dates from fills within the south circuit of Ditch 1. The main ditch (005) had a fragment of hazel charcoal dated (UBA-54845) from its third fill (205) in Slot C. Hazel charcoal was dated (UBA-54831) from the basal fill (035) of the ditch recut (030) in Slot A. Hazel charcoal was also dated (UBA-54839) in the primary fill (141) of the recut (140) of the main ditch (005), as observed in Slot B. Willow charcoal was dated (UBA-54842) from the basal fill (191) of the recut (191) in Slot F, and another sample of willow was dated (UBA-54844) from the basal fill (197) of recut (270) in Slot G. Finally, a fragment of hazel charcoal was dated (UBA-54843) from the bottom fill (227) of recut (216) in Slot H.

Ditch 2

The north circuit of Ditch 2 has two radiocarbon dates from its fills. A fragment of alder charcoal was dated (UBA-54854) from the erosion fill (533) of the main ditch (008) in Slot C, while broom/gorse charcoal was dated (UBA-54857) from the second fill (576) of a possible recut (799) in Slot D. UBA-54857 is late medieval in date and has been excluded from the modelling. There is a pit (083) that cuts the ditch recut (089) in Slot A and willow charcoal was dated (UBA-54833) from what was described as a slumped of redeposited sand (076). The result is Bronze Age and out of sequence, thus suggesting the fill was redeposited and resulting in it being excluded from the modelling of the Iron Age activity at Broxy Kennels.

There are six radiocarbon dates from fills in the south circuit of Ditch 2. The main enclosure ditch (007) was dated in three slots. Willow charcoal was dated (UBA-54848) from the basal fill (332) in Slot H. Alder charcoal was dated (UBA-54849 and -54864) from basal fills (420 and 748, respectively) of (1077) the main ditch in Slots L and M. In Slot A there is a sequence of dated fills. The lower fill (037) of recut (1076) of main ditch (007) has a date (UBA-54829) on a fragment of Prunoideae charcoal, while willow charcoal was dated (UBA-54828) from the middle fill (041). In Slot J, there is a result (UBA-54850) on alder charcoal from the basal fill (430) of recut (1086). This fill had extensive evidence of burning, though it is unclear if that occurred *in situ* or the material was deposited shortly after the event.

Ditch 3

There are two radiocarbon results from recuts of the northern circuit of Ditch 3. Alder was dated (UBA-54825) from the basal fill (029) of recut (085) of the main ditch in Slot A, while willow charcoal provides a date (UBA-54865) for the basal fill (631) of the second recut (630) identified in Slot C. Ditch 3N cuts Ditch 2N in the area of Ditch 3N Slot B.

Five radiocarbon dates are available from fills in the south circuit of Ditch 3. Slots A and C intersect and form two tails (009) and (046) of the ditch terminus. In Slot A, ditch (046) is recorded cutting (009). The basal fill (181) of (009) was dated (UBA-54841) by a fragment of willow charcoal. The final fill (045) of (046) was dated (UBA-54835) with a fragment of alder charcoal. A fragment of willow charcoal was dated (UBA-54832) in the basal fill (071) of the recut (046), recorded in Slot A, and a fragment of hazel charcoal was dated (UBA-54871) from the basal fill (856) of the same ditch (046) in Slot C. It is possible, based on the recorded archaeology, that (071) and (856) are equivalent contexts. Hazel charcoal was dated (UBA-54847) in the basal fill (340) of the ditch (046) in Slot B.

Finally, there is a radiocarbon result (UBA-54840) from the charcoal-rich lower fill (166) of pit (164) that is cut into the top fill (179) of ditch (009) in Slot A.

Ditch 4

The two radiocarbon dates from Ditch 4N are from alder charcoal (UBA-54826) from the basal fill (026) of main ditch (021) in Slot A and alder (UBA-54853) from the charcoal-rich top fill (462) of (021) in Slot C. Fill (462) was noted as possibly redeposited. The result (UBA-54853) is medieval and so has been excluded from the modelling.

The southern circuit of Ditch 4 is made of three primary ditch cuts – (047), (912), and (476) – which have radiocarbon dates from six of their fills. In Slot A there is a sequence of dated fills for the main enclosure ditch (047). A fragment of Maloideae charcoal was dated (UBA-54836) from the basal fill (082), while hazel charcoal was dated (UBA-54834) from the charcoal-rich middle fill (081). The main cut (912) of Ditch 4 in Slot B has a date (UBA-54874) on a fragment of alder charcoal from an intermediate fill (889). Ditch (476) has dates from Slots G–I. In Slot G, a fragment of birch charcoal was dated (UB-54858) from the top fill (655), which contained remnants of structure (641). The result is medieval and has been excluded from the modelling. The second to last fill (653) was dated (UBA-54859) by a fragment of alder charcoal. Finally, a fragment of alder was dated (UBA-54861) from the single fill (691) in Slot I. This slot was in the vicinity of the earlier prehistoric activity just outside the enclosure on the south, and the Neolithic result from the fill has been excluded.

Souterrain

There are six radiocarbon dates from fills associated with the souterrain that is dug into the top of Ditch 2N. Four of the results are from either fills behind the souterrain walls or that from the matrix surrounding the stone walls. A fragment of alder charcoal was dated (UBA-54870) from the basal fill (844) behind the walls, while a hazel charcoal fragment was dated (UBA-54868) from an upper fill (841) from behind the walls. There are two dates (UBA-54867 and -54881) from alder and hazel charcoal, respectively, in fills that formed part of the matrix within wall (043). Finally, there are two results (UBA-54872 and 54873) from Prunoideae and alder charcoal, respectively in the bedding layers (867=870) on the stone floor of the souterrain.

Area 1

Area 1 lies to the far north of the site, just outside the outer ditches, consisted of Ditch 6 and two groups of pits and postholes. A fragment of willow charcoal was dated (UBA-54851) from the fill (438) of a pit (437), which was to the west of Ditch 6 and contained a small amount of charred plant remains. The result is Mesolithic and has been excluded from the chronological model. Ditch 6, (779) Slot A, off of Ditch 4N in this area had a fragment of birch charcoal dated (UBA-54866) from its basal fill (787).

Area 2

Area 2 comprises features in and around the entranceway of the enclosure, in the north-east of the site. There is a date (UBA-54876) on alder charcoal from the charcoal-rich fill (982) of pit (981), a potential fire-pit, which is cut into the top of Ditch 4N. The date is early medieval and has been excluded from the chronological model. In the entrance area around Ditch 1 there is a result (UBA-54846) on a fragment of hazel charcoal from fill (234) of posthole (233) and another piece of hazel charcoal dated (UBA-54877) from the fill (1053) of posthole (1052).

Area 3

Area 3 is slightly further within the enclosed area and is focussed on arcs of postholes that have been grouped to form overlapping Structures 1A and 1B. Hazel charcoal was dated (UBA-54852) from the fill (458) of posthole (457) in Structure 1A, and birch charcoal was dated (UBA-54855) from the fill (549) of posthole (548) in Structure 1B.

Area 4

Moving further south-west into the enclosed space is Area 4, which is characterised by a cluster of pits and postholes. There are radiocarbon dates on single fragments of alder charcoal from two of the pits. The radiocarbon result (UBA-54856) from the lower fill (583) of pit (581), a fill that was charcoal-rich but not the result of *in situ* burning, is early medieval and has been excluded from the modelling. The radiocarbon date (UBA-54860) from the fill (658) of pit (657) is late pre-Roman Iron Age in date, however, the context also contained Victorian pottery.

Area 5

In the furthest south-west portion of the enclosed space lies Area 5. Alder charcoal was dated (UBA-54878) from fill (1057) of pit (1022), while willow charcoal was dated (UBA-54879) from primary fill (1049) of posthole (1048).

Areas 6 and 7

To the south of the enclosure ditches lies Areas 6 and 7. There is a date (UBA-54875) on a fragment of hazel charcoal from the single fill (964) of pit (963) in Area 6, and another piece of hazel was dated (UBA-54869) from the basal fill (844) of pit (830). Another fragment of hazel charcoal was dated (UBA-54863) from the initial fill (745) of pit (738) in Area 7. The dates from these three features are Neolithic and so the dates are excluded from the modelling.

Other dated features

There is a radiocarbon result (UBA-54862) on a fragment of alder charcoal from the charcoal-rich primary fill (712) of fire-pit (694). At the bottom of the hill was excavated a palisade ditch (294) and a radiocarbon result (UBA-54824) on a fragment of hazel charcoal from fill (304) has suggested it dates from the Bronze Age, though it has been noted the context could comprise hillwash. As the result is Bronze Age it has been excluded from the modelling.

A chronological model was created that grouped the results by the time periods used above. Where there were four or more dates from a period, the OxCal program was used to apply the modelling algorithm to each phase or activity, independent of one another. The method follows the simple bounded phase model described in Hamilton and Kenney (2015). Radiocarbon dates on samples that appear to be residual in a feature group or from features not positively identified as part of a group have been excluded from the modelling and are shown with a '?' next to their label in Figures 41 and 44-45.

Results

The initial run of the chronological model, following the stratigraphic relationships noted above and including only Iron Age dates has poor agreement (Amodel=2.6). The model shows a number of reversals in the stratigraphy, if the sample dated from each context closely dates when each context formed. In these situations, it is common for there to be reworked deposits where the dated sample is either residual or intrusive.

Going through the model, there are three radiocarbon results that have very low individual agreement indices. In Ditch 1N, UBA-54838 appears to be too recent given it is from the basal fill (115) of the primary ditch (006) in Slot C. The context is described, though, as being full of ash and some burnt bone, which suggests it is a dump of material and should provide a more secure date for the formation of the deposit than some of the other ditch fills. Similarly, the second result with low agreement (UBA-54849) is from the basal fill (420) of the primary ditch (1077) in Ditch 2S Slot L, and it is also too recent given its location in the stratigraphy. Finally, the third result with poor agreement (UBA-54868) is from the upper fill (841) behind the souterrain walls. It too is too recent given the dating from the souterrain, though being an upper deposit could potentially be intrusive in this context.

The primary issue to resolve is the occurrence of material from a robust and secure dating context (UBA-54848: 115) that is too recent given the stratigraphy. Since the context appears to be a dump of burnt material, there is little reason to regard the result as inaccurately dating the context. Therefore, the conclusions that can be drawn are either the result is incorrect or what has been viewed as the primary cut in Slot C is actually a recut that removed the original ditch

in this location. If the latter can be true in Ditch 1N Slot C, it can be the case in all other slots through the enclosure ditches. An alternative model was constructed that only incorporated the directly observed stratigraphic relationships within individual slots and allowed for the dated contexts between the slots to remain unordered as it is possible the observed 'primary' cut is actually a recut.

This revised model has good agreement (Amodel=62; Figure 41) and estimates the Iron Age activity at Broxy Kennels spanned *495–840 years* (*95% probability*; Figure 42; *span: Broxy Kennels*) or either *525–585 years* (*15% probability*) or *680–795 years* (*53% probability*). The model is imprecise in its estimate for the start date of the Iron Age activity on the site in *805–535 cal BC* (*95% probability*; Figure 42; *start: Broxy Kennels*) or either *780–710 cal BC* (*52% probability*) or *595–550 cal BC* (*16% probability*). It estimates the activity ended in *90 cal BC–cal AD 75* (*95% probability*; Figure 42; *end: Broxy Kennels*) or *40 cal BC–cal AD 15* (*68% probability*).

Rarely should the radiocarbon dates be used to inform on phasing at a site, since there is always the risk of sampling bias as a result of past activity or choices made during the excavation. An examination of the radiocarbon results and the summed probability distribution (Figure 43) suggests the distribution is far from uniform. In fact, the radiocarbon samples that date from the first millennium cal BC show a clear pattern with approximately two-thirds of the samples from the site dating to the earlier Iron Age and five dating to the later pre-Roman Iron Age. This later activity appeared to be centred on the interior of the enclosure in Areas 2, 3, and 4.

With this in mind, a third model was constructed that separated these three areas into a separate 'Later Iron Age' phase of activity. This model has good agreement (Amodel=66; Figure 44). This model estimates the early Iron Age activity at the site began in *575–465 cal BC* (*95% probability*; Figure 45; *start: EIA Broxy Kennels*) or *560–500 cal BC* (*68% probability*). This earlier period ended in *405–370 cal BC* (*95% probability*; Figure 45; *end: EIA Broxy Kennels*) or *400–380 cal BC* (*68% probability*). The total span of this earlier activity was *70–200 years* (*95% probability*; Figure 47; *span: EIA Broxy Kennels*) or *115–175 years* (*68% probability*).

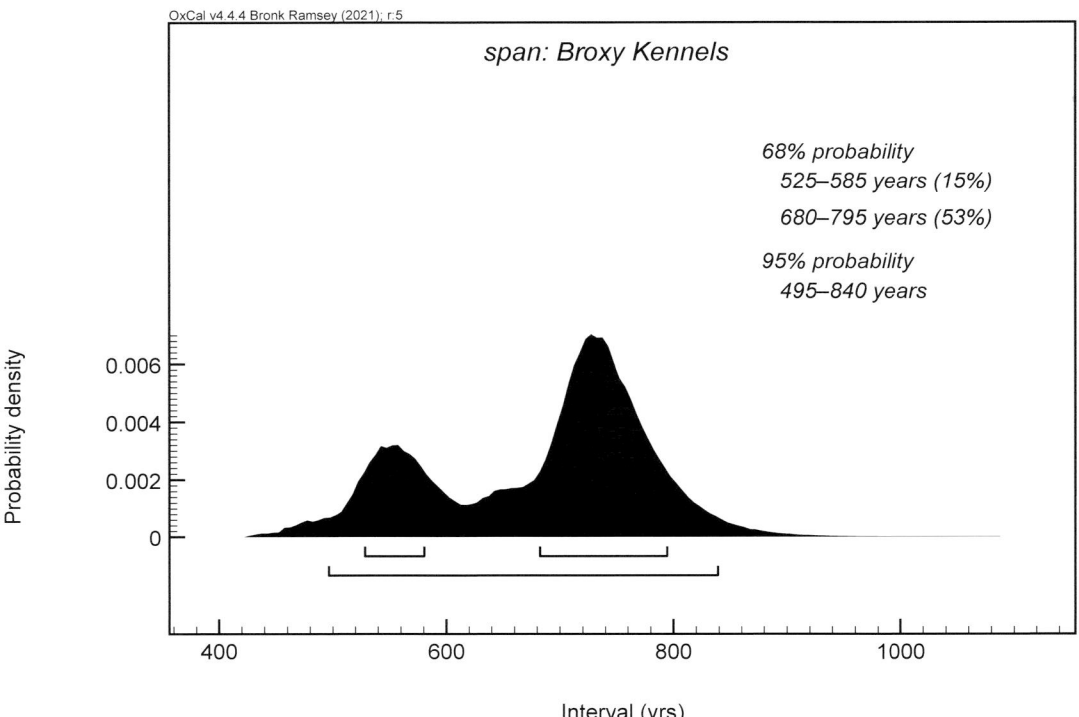

Figure 42: Broxy Kennels MODEL. Estimated spans of the Iron Age activity modelled at Broxy Kennels as shown in Figure 41.

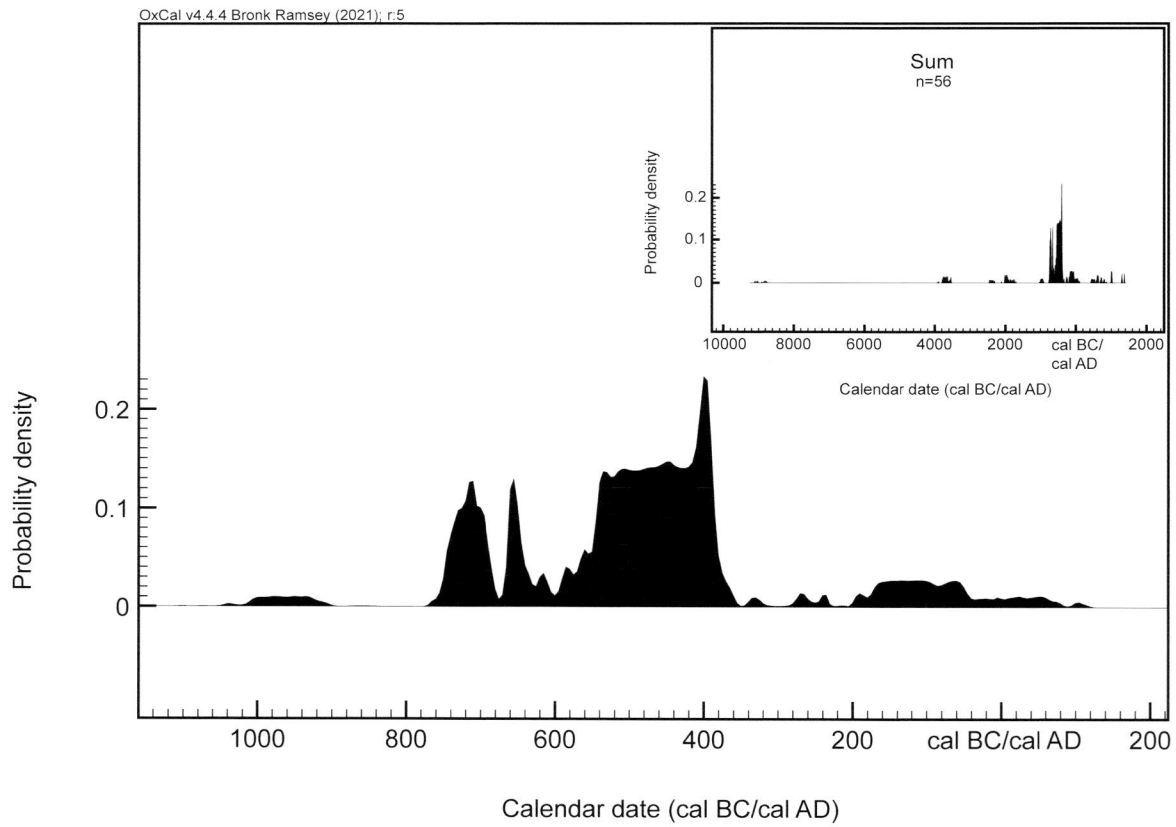

Figure 43: Combined Broxy Kennels SUM. Sum of all the calibrated dates for the Iron Age from Broxy Kennels Fort, Perth, Perthshire. The inset shows the sum of all the dates from Broxy Kennels. The figure provides a rough approximation of the distribution of the dated samples and, by extension, a proxy for the intensity of activity (caveats discussed in the text).

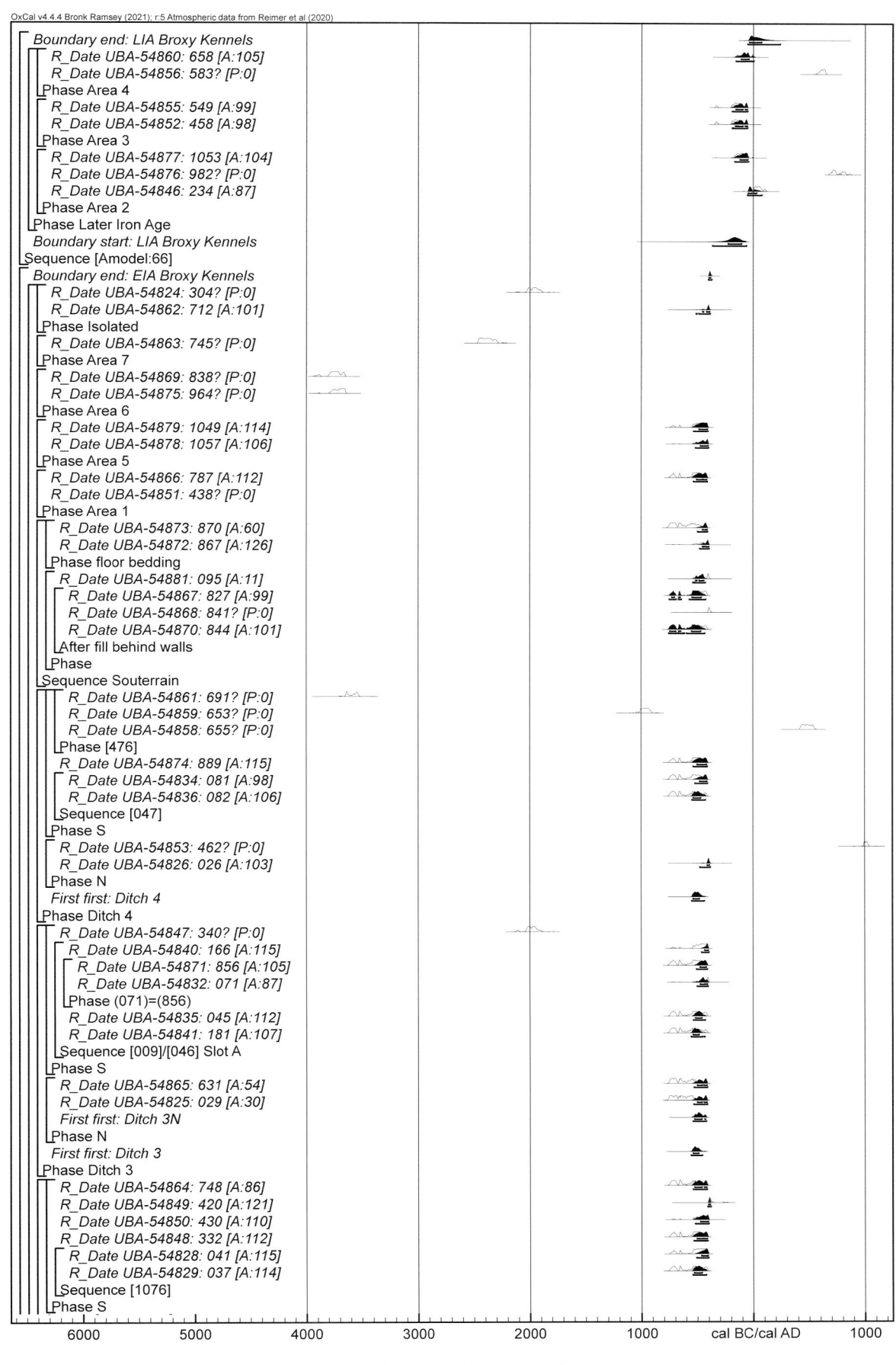

Figure 44: Broxy Kennels MODEL. Revised chronological model that separates the earlier and later Iron Age activity into two distinct phases. The model is as described in Figure 41.

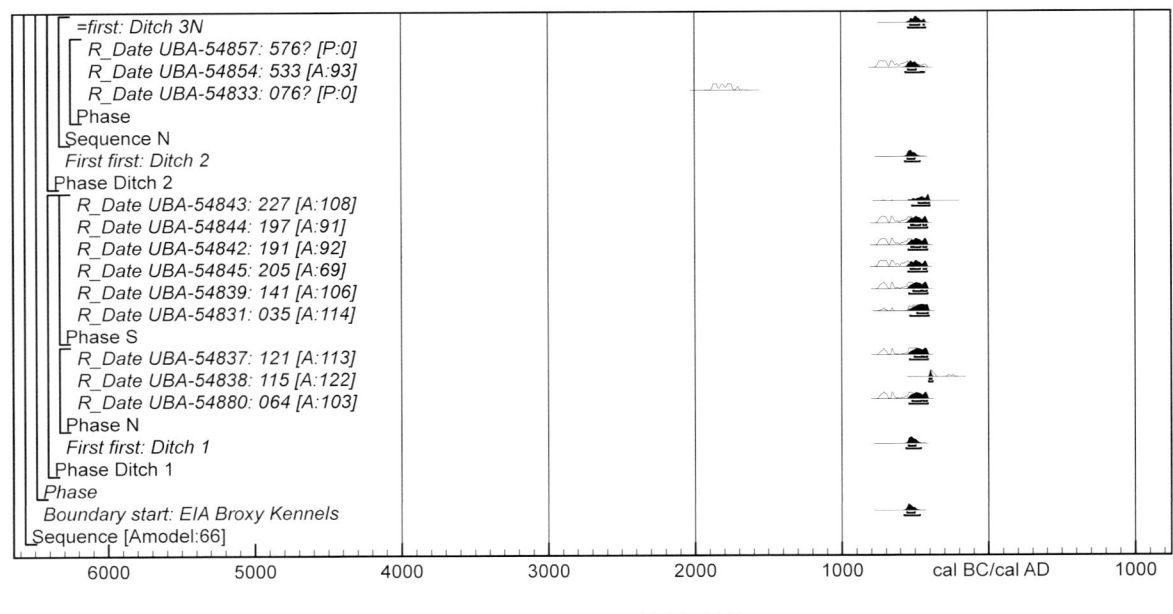

Figure 44 (continued): Broxy Kennels MODEL. Revised chronological model that separates the earlier and later Iron Age activity into two distinct phases. The model is as described in Figure 41.

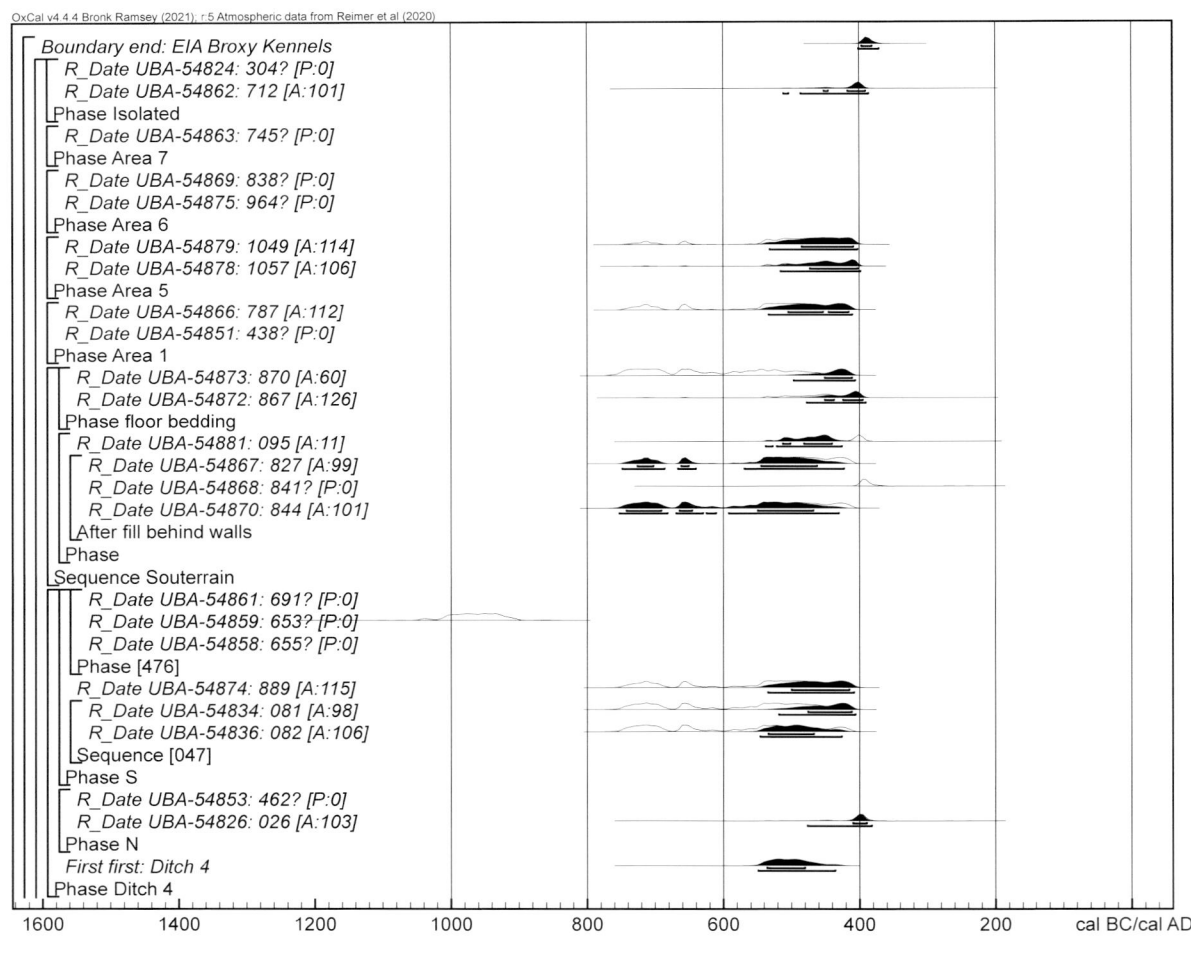

Figure 45: Broxy Kennels MODEL. Chronological model for the earlier Iron Age activity at Broxy Kennels. The model is excerpted from the overall model shown in Figure 44.

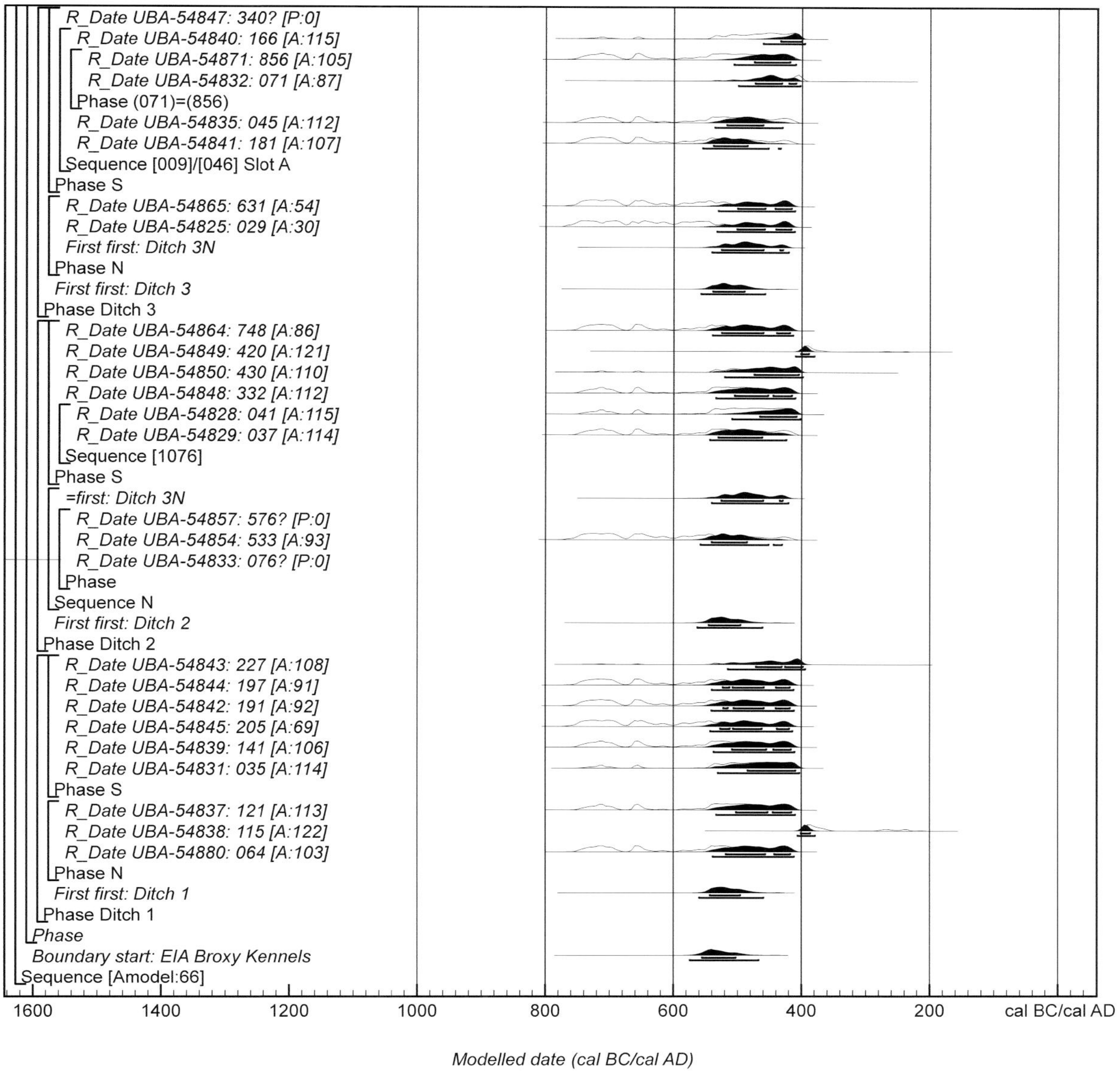

R_Date UBA-54847: 340? [P:0]
R_Date UBA-54840: 166 [A:115]
R_Date UBA-54871: 856 [A:105]
R_Date UBA-54832: 071 [A:87]
Phase (071)=(856)
R_Date UBA-54835: 045 [A:112]
R_Date UBA-54841: 181 [A:107]
Sequence [009]/[046] Slot A
Phase S
R_Date UBA-54865: 631 [A:54]
R_Date UBA-54825: 029 [A:30]
First first: Ditch 3N
Phase N
First first: Ditch 3
Phase Ditch 3
R_Date UBA-54864: 748 [A:86]
R_Date UBA-54849: 420 [A:121]
R_Date UBA-54850: 430 [A:110]
R_Date UBA-54848: 332 [A:112]
R_Date UBA-54828: 041 [A:115]
R_Date UBA-54829: 037 [A:114]
Sequence [1076]
Phase S
=first: Ditch 3N
R_Date UBA-54857: 576? [P:0]
R_Date UBA-54854: 533 [A:93]
R_Date UBA-54833: 076? [P:0]
Phase
Sequence N
First first: Ditch 2
Phase Ditch 2
R_Date UBA-54843: 227 [A:108]
R_Date UBA-54844: 197 [A:91]
R_Date UBA-54842: 191 [A:92]
R_Date UBA-54845: 205 [A:69]
R_Date UBA-54839: 141 [A:106]
R_Date UBA-54831: 035 [A:114]
Phase S
R_Date UBA-54837: 121 [A:113]
R_Date UBA-54838: 115 [A:122]
R_Date UBA-54880: 064 [A:103]
Phase N
First first: Ditch 1
Phase Ditch 1
Phase
Boundary start: EIA Broxy Kennels
Sequence [Amodel:66]
1600
1400
1200
1000
800
600
400
200
cal BC/cal AD
Modelled date (cal BC/cal AD)

Figure 45 (continued): Broxy Kennels MODEL. Chronological model for the earlier Iron Age activity at Broxy Kennels. The model is excerpted from the overall model shown in Figure 44.

OxCal v4.4.4 Bronk Ramsey (2021); r:5 Atmospheric data from Reimer et al (2020)
Boundary end: LIA Broxy Kennels
R_Date UBA-54860: 658 [A:105]
R_Date UBA-54856: 583? [P:0]
Phase Area 4
R_Date UBA-54855: 549 [A:99]
R_Date UBA-54852: 458 [A:98]
Phase Area 3
R_Date UBA-54877: 1053 [A:104]
R_Date UBA-54876: 982? [P:0]
R_Date UBA-54846: 234 [A:87]
Phase Area 2
Phase Later Iron Age
Boundary start: LIA Broxy Kennels
Sequence [Amodel:66]
600
400
200
cal BC/cal AD
200
Modelled date (cal BC/cal AD)

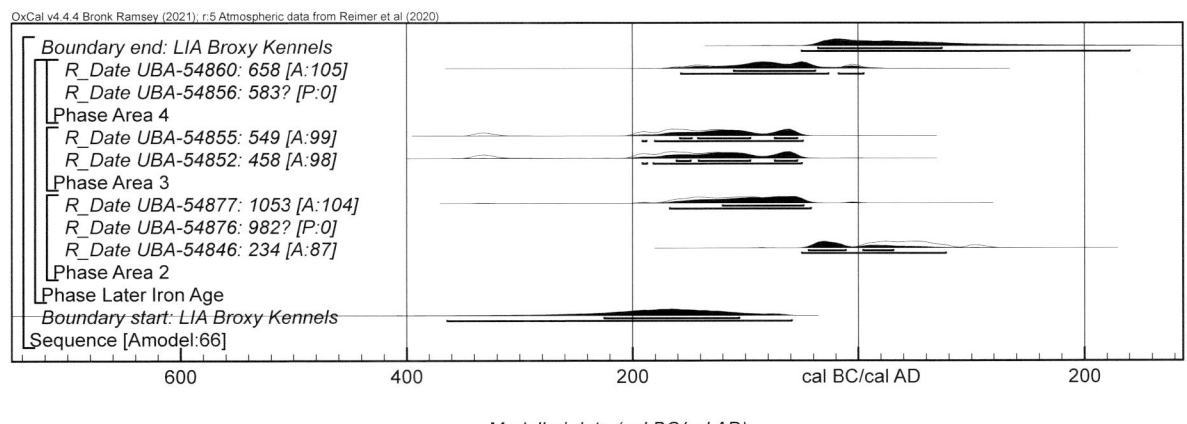

Figure 46: Broxy Kennels MODEL. Chronological model for the later Iron Age activity at Broxy Kennels. The model is excerpted from the overall model shown in Figure 44.

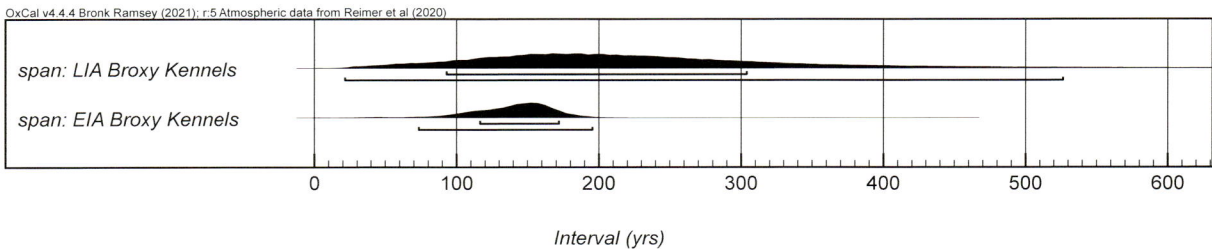

Figure 47: Broxy Kennels MODEL. Estimated spans of the activity for the earlier and later Iron Age periods modelled at Broxy Kennels as shown in Figure 44.

According to the modelling, the later Iron Age activity began in *365–60 cal BC* (*95% probability*; Figure 46; *start: LIA Broxy Kennels*) or *225–105 cal BC* (*68% probability*). It ended in *55 cal BC–cal AD 245* (*95% probability*; Figure 46; *end: LIA Broxy Kennels*) or *40 cal BC–cal AD 75* (*68% probability*). The later Iron Age activity spanned *20–530 years* (*95% probability*; Figure 47; *span: LIA Broxy Kennels*) or *90–305* years (*68% probability*).

In this revised, and preferred model, the combination of a large number of radiocarbon dates and the shape of the calibration curve falling off the 'Hallstatt' plateau has resulted in a precise date for the start of earlier Iron Age activity and an even more precise end date for the activity. This stands in contrast to the much less precise ranges for the start and end date probabilities for the later Iron Age activity, which suffer because of the low number of results (Steier and Rom 2000).

The chronological model for Broxy Kennels included the First parameter within the groups of dates from each ditch circuit. This parameter calculates the earliest probability within the group, which could potentially inform on the order of construction, if we assume any offset between digging and infilling of the ditches is relatively equal across the circuits given the spatial spread of dated material from many discrete excavation slots. In comparing these probabilities using the Order function, there is little to suggest Ditches 1–3 were not broadly contemporary – other than the fact Ditch 3N overlaps part of Ditch 2N. However, there is a 64% probability *first: Ditch 3* occurred prior to *first: Ditch 4*, and a 71% and 74% probability, respectively, that *first: Ditch 1* and *first: Ditch 2* occurred prior to *first: Ditch 4*. While the assumption may be incorrect, if not, it suggests the hillfort evolved over the period of its use rather than being initially constructed with the four complete circuits.

Discussion

The radiocarbon dating demonstrates there was punctuated activity on the hill at Broxy Kennels that spanned millennia. Despite the existence of considerable earlier prehistoric activity along the southern edge of the hilltop, the dating demonstrates the main enclosure activity occurred in the earlier Iron Age. The sealed deposits in the enclosure ditches are filled with material dating almost exclusively dating to the period 800 – 400 cal BC. While not every dated context can be considered ideal for selection of a radiocarbon dating sample, there are a large number that represent dumps of charred debris that are interpreted as being the result of clearing out such things as hearths or fire-pits. Therefore, these samples are not likely to be of an original date that is much removed from the date of their redeposition and provide a reliable framework for interpreting the chronology of the hillfort ditch circuits.

In considering these earlier Iron Age dates and the activities on the site, it is necessary to turn attention to the souterrain. In both models, the souterrain 'dates' to the earlier Iron Age activity. Souterrains, as a structure type, are understood to typically date to the closing centuries BC or earliest centuries AD in Scotland. Most of the dates from souterrain-related deposits are from backfills and the matrix of the walls. These contexts are most likely repositories of residual material from earlier activity on the site and so only provide a *terminus post quem* for the construction of the souterrain. Therefore, the dating attribution is solely dependent upon the interpretation of the floor layers (867 and 870), as bedding layers on the floor contain material that is contemporary with the use of the souterrain. The two results are not statistically consistent (T'4.5; df=1; T'(5%)=3.8; Ward and Wilson 1978) and suggests the floor contains material of mixed ages. This is not what is expected when submitting multiple taphonomically secure samples from a context or feature that represents either a single event or activity over a short period of time. It is reasonable to conclude the dates associated with the souterrain are all from charcoal associated with earlier Iron Age activity that has been redeposited in the later Iron Age during a period of potential reuse of the hilltop. In this period of reuse, the souterrain was constructed, being dug into the top fills of Ditch 2N and the chronology of the associated activity 'recorded' in the features in Areas 2 to 4 just to the south of this structure.

With regards to the taphonomic processes on site and the complications with both understanding and relating ditch cutting sequences across the individual slots, Broxy Kennels is a site where the implementation of the secondary scientific tool, specifically portable optically-stimulated luminescence profiling, might have been useful. As a tool, it could have enabled a better understanding of the sediment packages from which material was being dated and even the phasing of infilling periods as a result of the mapping of the pOSL sensitivities of the sediments. That said, by having a mix of dated samples coming from clearly defined contexts of charcoal-rich material and noted natural erosion infills, the dating programme has been able to help elucidate the taphonomic complexity of the site.

The dating of Broxy Kennels Fort provides another example of a mid-first millennium hilltop enclosure in the vicinity of Perth, with dating very similar to Moncreiffe (Strachan et al. 2023). Furthermore, it aligns this earlier Iron Age activity with enclosure activity seen across much of Britain at this time (Hamilton and Haselgrove 2019). It is within this broader chronological and spatial context that the archaeology of the hillfort can best be understood.

Archaeobotany

By Susan Ramsay

Introduction

The following archaeobotanical report details the processing, analysis and interpretation of botanical remains recovered from samples taken during excavations at Broxy Kennels Fort and Scone, Perth.

Methodology

Bulk Sample Processing

A programme of bulk sampling was undertaken in order to examine the carbonised archaeobotanical remains from Broxy Kennels and Scone. In total, 400 bulk samples and 18 Spot Find (SF) samples were analysed for the presence of botanical remains. The bulk samples were processed by flotation for the recovery of carbonised remains, using standard methods and sieves of mesh diameter 1 mm and 500 µm for flots and 2 mm and 4 mm for retents from flotation.

Macrofossil Analysis

Dried flots and sorted retents were examined using a binocular microscope at variable magnifications of x4 - x45. For each sample, an estimation of the total volume of carbonised material >4 mm was made. For each sample, all the charcoal >4 mm was identified unless this proved to be too large an amount, in which case a known percentage of the total charcoal >4 mm was identified. All carbonised cereal grains and seeds were also identified and any other plant macrofossil remains were noted.

The testa characteristics of small seeds and the internal anatomical features of all charcoal fragments were further identified at x200 magnification using the reflected light of a metallurgical microscope. Reference was made to Schweingruber (1990), Gale and Cutler (2000) and Cappers et al. (2006) to aid identifications and vascular plant nomenclature follows Stace (1997).

Pollen analysis

Pollen analysis was undertaken on three monolith tins, from a section through Ditch 1, taken during the excavation by the archaeologists on site. The three monolith tins <290>, <291>, <292> came from the North facing section of Slot B, within Ditch 1 and overlapped to give a single sequence through the ditch sediments. A total of 15 samples for pollen analysis were taken at between 4-5 cm intervals throughout the sequence. Pollen samples were prepared by the University of Reading, using standard methodologies with sodium polytungstate heavy liquid separation to remove the mineral component and final mounting of the samples in glycerine jelly stained with safranin.

Pollen identification and nomenclature follows Moore et al. (1991), whilst vascular plant nomenclature follows Stace (1997). A minimum of 500 total land pollen grains (TLP) were counted for every sample. The pollen diagram was constructed using Tilia.Graph v.3.0.3 (Grimm, 2022), with percentages calculated using a sum based on TLP for all terrestrial higher plants. Aquatics were presented using percentages based on a sum of TLP + Aquatics and Pteridophytes/Moss using percentages based on a sum of TLP + Pteridophytes + Moss.

Results

Results will be discussed by area, following the order and groupings contained within the Results (see Summary of Broxy Kennels ditch excavations). The full results are given in Tables 2-27 in Appendix 1 and Tables 28 and 29 in Appendix 2.

The fort was defined by four ditches, which are each split into two parts, North and South. The terminals of the ditches were all located in the north-east of the fort, thus dividing the fort into its northern and southern parts. However, the western part of the fort lay outside the area investigated and so remains unexcavated. The ditches were numbered 1-4, north or south and then by slot number. The innermost ditch was allocated D1 and the outermost ditch, D4. The souterrain was located within Ditch 2N.

Ditch 1S

Ditch 1S Slot A (Table 2)

Slot A of Ditch 1S covered the ditch terminus in the north-east corner of the fort. The basal fill (033) did not contain any carbonised remains. This fill was cut by two postholes (048 and 052). The fill (049) of posthole (048) produced only trace amounts of birch charcoal and a single indeterminate cereal grain, while fill (053) of posthole (052) produced only traces of birch, hazel and oak charcoal. These fills suggest scattered hearth waste rather than the remains of posts burnt *in situ*. Above (033) was a natural silting deposit (012), which also produced traces of birch, hazel and oak charcoal with a single indeterminate cereal grain, suggesting small amounts of this carbonised material may have been scattered across this part of the site.

These basal fills were truncated by a recut (030), that was initially filled by (035), which produced a mixed charcoal assemblage of alder, hazel, oak and willow, suggesting the remains of scattered hearth waste rather than deliberate dumping of material into the ditch recut. A further recut (065) was filled by (068) on its west side and (020) on the east side. These fills produced very different carbonised assemblages. Fill (020) produced only traces of alder and oak charcoal but fill (068) produced much more significant amounts of charcoal, with alder, birch, hazel, cherry type, oak and willow all present. This assemblage would be consistent with domestic hearth waste and may represent dumping of this material into the ditch recut.

A pit (013) had been cut into the upper fills of Slot A, truncating (012, 020 and 035). The fill (014) produced only traces of hazel and broom/gorse charcoal. A further small pit (050) showed evidence of burning and the fill (051) produced significant quantities of charcoal, carbonised grain and weed seeds. The charcoal assemblage was comprised mainly of birch and hazel, with small amounts of oak and willow also present. Over 600 carbonised cereal grains were recorded but the vast majority were too poorly preserved to be further identifiable. Of those that were in better condition, it was possible to identify barley and small amounts of oats. Large numbers of fathen and redshank seeds, along with traces of brome grass, black bindweed and dead nettle type were also recorded. This assemblage would be consistent with waste from cereal processing, with the cereal grains perhaps having fallen into the base of a hearth and consequently were subjected to multiple burning episodes causing the poor preservation.

Ditch 1S Slot B (Table 2)

The primary fill (142) of Ditch 1S-B did not produce any carbonised remains. This fill was truncated by recut (140), but the lower fills (141 and 139) of this recut produced only traces of hazel and cherry type charcoal. However, the uppermost fill (138) contained significant quantities of willow charcoal, with hazel and oak also present. This assemblage may represent the remains of a burnt wattle structure rather than hearth waste.

Approximately 2.7 m NE of D1S-B was a posthole (523), fill (524), but the charcoal assemblage was sparse with only traces of hazel and willow charcoal, a few grains of possible barley and a fragment of hazel nutshell. This assemblage is consistent with scattered hearth waste rather than being the remains of a post burnt *in situ.*

Ditch 1S Slot C (Table 2)

The fills of this slot comprised (209, 208, 206 and 205), from the lowermost fill to the uppermost. All fills contained small amounts of charcoal, with hazel, oak, and willow all represented, with traces of hazel nutshell. The charcoal could be representative of burnt wattle, but the quantities involved are too small to be able to state this confidently.

Ditch 1S Slot D (Table 3)

The carbonised assemblages from lower fills (161, 163 and 183) of Ditch 1S Slot D were very similar, with hazel, oak and willow charcoal present in all, with the addition of small amounts of alder charcoal in (161) and hazel nutshell in (183). As with the other Ditch 1S slots, these assemblages may suggest burnt wattle forms at least part of the assemblage.

The uppermost fill (160) produced a more diverse charcoal assemblage, with alder, birch, hazel,

cherry type, oak, willow and hazel nutshell all represented. This assemblage would suggest the remains of domestic hearth waste rather than structural remains.

Ditch 1S Slot E (Table 3)

The primary fill (171) of Slot E produced only traces of oak and willow charcoal, with traces of hazel nutshell. The ditch was recut (173), with primary fill (174) and secondary fill (175) producing mixed charcoal assemblages with alder, hazel, cherry type, oak and willow all represented, along with fragments of hazel nutshell in (175). These assemblages are consistent with scattered domestic hearth waste having become incorporated into the fill. Towards the north-east corner of Slot E was a posthole (167), which truncated fill (175). The posthole fill (168) produced a very similar charcoal assemblage to that from fill (175) and it would appear that the posthole was probably filled with material from (175).

Ditch 1S Slot F (Table 3)

The basal fill (196) of Ditch 1S Slot F produced only traces of oak charcoal, with fills (195 and 193) overlying this basal fill. The ditch was recut (192), truncating (193). The basal fill (191) of recut (192) produced only traces of oak and willow charcoal, with hazel nutshell. Overlying this was fill (190), which produced some animal bone and a very diverse charcoal assemblage of alder, birch, hazel, cherry type, oak and willow, with traces of hazel nutshell. Fill (189) overlay (190) and produced a very similar charcoal assemblage suggesting dumped hearth waste or midden material. However, in addition a spot find of charcoal SF 106 consisted entirely of hazel and oak small roundwood, suggesting that some structural material may also have been dumped into this fill. The uppermost fill (188) contained significantly less charcoal than the lower fills but still a diverse assemblage of birch, hazel, heather type, oak and will, with hazel nutshell, again suggesting hearth waste.

Several fire-pits or possible kilns were recorded from the south side of Ditch 1S Slot F. Fire-pit (317), fill (321) produced large quantities of oak charcoal and a few traces of hazel nutshell. The selection of oak as fuel for this feature suggests a possible industrial use for the fire-pit or kiln.

Ditch 1S Slot G (Table 4)

The primary fill (265) of Slot G produced only traces of heather type charcoal, which could be the remains of the surface vegetation into which this ditch was dug. This basal fill was recut by (266), with a fill containing a small lens deposit (267) that produced traces of hazel, cherry type, oak and willow charcoal, suggesting domestic hearth waste.

A further recut (270) had a basal fill (197) that contained significant amounts of hazel charcoal, with smaller amounts of birch and willow charcoal, with a trace of hazel nutshell. Fill (197) was sealed by (271), which in turn was sealed by (199). Fill (199) produced a diverse charcoal assemblage of alder, birch, hazel, cherry type, oak and willow with a trace of hazel nutshell, suggesting dumped domestic hearth waste.

Ditch 1S Slot H (Table 4)

The basal fill (213) of Ditch 1S Slot H produced significant amounts of alder, hazel and willow charcoal, with traces of hazel nutshell. A second basal fill (215) was located on the upslope on the northern side of the ditch. This fill produced a more diverse charcoal assemblage of alder, hazel, cherry type, oak and willow. The main fill (214) of this ditch slot produced only traces of hazel, cherry type, oak and willow charcoal, suggesting this may be reworked from the earlier basal fills. A significant recut (216) almost entirely truncated the earlier ditch cut. The basal fill (227) of the recut produced significant amounts of hazel charcoal, with alder, cherry type, oak and willow also present. A further recut (258) had a basal fill (221) that contained a similar carbonised assemblage to that from the basal fill (227) of recut (216).

The above recuts and fills were present on the north-east facing section. On the south-west facing section recut (256) was filled by (257), which contained alder, birch, hazel and willow charcoal. A further recut (258) was filled by (259), which was unusual in containing large amounts of alder charcoal with only traces of hazel also present. Alder charcoal is sometimes indicative of industrial processes.

Ditch 1S Slot I (Table 4)

The initial fills of D1S Slot I were truncated by recut (242). The basal fill (243) contained a mixed charcoal assemblage of alder, birch, hazel, oak and willow. Above this was a silty clay (247) that was then overlain by (248), which contained a very similar carbonised assemblage as that from (243) but with the addition of traces of hazel nutshell. A further recut (279) visible on the north-east section had a basal fill (291), also with a similar carbonised assemblage to those from (243 and 248).

Ditch 1S Slot J (Table 4)

The basal fill (285) of Ditch 1S Slot J was overlain by fill (286), which produced a similar carbonised assemblage of alder, birch, hazel, oak and willow as seen in the fills in Slot I.

Ditch 2S

Ditch 2S Slot A (Table 5)

Ditch 2S Slot A was located at the north-east terminus of Ditch 2S. The original cut (007A} was filled by (018) but this produced only a trace of oak charcoal. The ditch was recut by (1076), but the basal fill (038) also contained only a trace of oak charcoal. This basal fill was overlain by a light coloured clayey sand (037) and then by a slightly darker clayey sand (041). These fills produced similar diverse carbonised assemblages with alder, birch, hazel, cherry type, oak and willow present in both. Fill (041) also produced traces of rowan type charcoal and fill (037) contained small amounts of hazel nutshell. These fills are consistent with domestic hearth waste.

Ditch 2S Slot D (Table 5)

Ditch 2S Slot D covered a north-west facing terminus of Ditch 2S. The primary fill (358) produced only small amounts of alder, hazel and oak charcoal.

Ditch 2S Slot E/M (Table 5)

The initial excavation of Slot E was extended to the north-east to investigate a line of stones that formed a possible revetment within the ditch (Slot M).

The original ditch cut was initially filled by (370), which produced small amounts of burnt bone and a diverse charcoal assemblage of alder, birch, hazel, cherry type, oak and willow. This is similar to the assemblages from the fills from Ditch 2S Slot A. The ditch was recut by (376), with a basal fill (377) and a stone deposit (323). At the base of (323) and reaching up the north side of the section was fill (327), with small amounts of alder, hazel, oak and willow charcoal. Overlying (323) and (327) was a sandy silt and clay (326) that produced several fragments of prehistoric pot and bone but only traces of birch and hazel charcoal.

The ditch cut revealed in extension Slot M had a basal fill (748) that produced a couple of large fragments of alder charcoal. Overlying the basal fill were fills (749 and 750) that were not assessed and finally fill (751) that produced only a trace of alder charcoal.

Ditch 2S Slot F (Table 5)

Basal fill (366) produced only a trace of indeterminate charcoal, while the overlying fill (365) produced only traces of oak and willow charcoal. The main fill (318) of this ditch slot again produced a diverse charcoal assemblage of alder, birch, hazel, oak and willow, similar to the charcoal assemblages from the fills from other parts of this ditch.

Ditch 2S Slot G (Table 6)

The basal fill (352) produced only a trace of oak charcoal, while the overlying fill (341) had only a trace of alder charcoal. Fill (342) overlay (341) but was not analysed and was, in turn, overlain by fill (343), which produced fragments of prehistoric pottery and a possible sling0shot stone but only traces of hazel and willow charcoal.

Ditch 2S Slot H (Table 6)

The primary fill (332) of Ditch 2S Slot H was thought to represent silting from erosion into the ditch. The charcoal assemblage was similar to that seen elsewhere with alder, birch, hazel, oak and willow all present in small amounts.

Ditch 2S Slot I (Table 6)

The basal fill (405) in Ditch 2S Slot I produced only traces of hazel and oak charcoal. The original fills

were recut by (1080) and the basal fill (403) of this recut produced only traces of alder charcoal. Overlying (403) and extending to the top of the ditch was fill (402), which contained a fragment of slag and a mixed charcoal assemblage of alder, hazel, cherry type, oak and willow, together with a fragment of hazel nutshell.

Ditch 2S Slot J (Table 6)

The primary fill (477) of the ditch cut in Ditch 2S Slot J produced only traces of hazel and oak charcoal with a single carbonised barley grain and may represent slumping or erosion into the ditch rather than deliberate dumping of material. The original fills were recut by (1086), with basal fill (430) that produced large fragments of alder charcoal, with smaller amounts of hazel, oak and willow also present. In addition, this fill contained some carbonised weed seeds, including brome grass, sedge and heath grass suggesting that these species may have grown on the original ground surface during construction and/or occupation. Overlying this was (431), again with significant amounts of alder charcoal, but with traces of cherry type and oak also present. A further recut (509) had a basal fill (434) with only small amounts of alder and cherry type charcoal, with a fragment of hazel nutshell.

Ditch 2S Slot L (Table 6)

Ditch 2S Slot L had a basal fill (420) with small amounts of alder, hazel and willow charcoal but this may the remains of background scatter of domestic hearth waste that eroded into the ditch. The main fill in this ditch slot was (396) but this produced only a trace of alder charcoal.

Ditch 3S

Ditch 3S Slot A (Table 7)

Slot A in Ditch 3S was located at the terminus, which was split into two (009 and 046). The original cut (009) of the terminus had a basal fill (181) with only traces of oak and willow charcoal. Above this was fill (180) followed by upper fill (179) that contained a fragment of prehistoric pottery and charcoal of birch, hazel, cherry type and oak, with a fragment of hazel nutshell. This may be the remains of midden waste that was dumped into the ditch. The upper fill (179) was cut by a shallow pit (164), with a basal fill (166) that was rich in charcoal, with large amounts of hazel and alder and smaller amounts of cherry type, oak and willow also present. Burnt bone was also present in this fill suggesting it may represent the remains of midden waste that had been dumped into the pit.

At the interface between (009 and 046) cut (009) was filled by (096) and (097), but these produced only traces of mixed charcoal. Overlying these fills were (057) and above this (045) which produced small amounts of mixed charcoal that may be scatter from domestic hearth waste along with several fragments of prehistoric pottery. These fills were recut by (046), with basal fill (071), which also produced small amounts of mixed charcoal consistent with domestic hearth waste.

An extension to the excavation in this area of Ditch 3S, located a further expanse of cut (009) with basal fill (862) but this produced no carbonised remains. The basal fill (856) of recut (046) contained basal fill (856) which produced a small amount of mixed charcoal with fragments of hazel nutshell, again suggesting domestic hearth waste.

Ditch 3S Slot B (Table 7)

The basal fill (340) in cut (046) of Ditch 3S Slot B produced a mixed charcoal assemblage of hazel, cherry type, oak, willow, and hazel nutshell, similar to the fills of (046) recorded elsewhere

Linear Feature 311 (Table 7)

A linear feature (311) was located around 5-6 m to the southwest of the southern terminus of Ditch 3S Slot B. It was not clear whether this feature was a truncated continuation of Ditch 3 or whether it was an unrelated linear feature. The fills (313 and 314) produced similar carbonised assemblages of birch, hazel, oak and willow, with a fragment of hazel nutshell in (314). These assemblages are similar to those seen elsewhere from ditch fills, which might suggest that this linear feature is broadly contemporaneous with Ditch 3.

Ditch 4S

Ditch 4S Slot A (Table 8)

Slot A was located at the terminus of Ditch 4S in the north east corner. The basal fill (082) and the overlying fills (081 and 080) produced

very similar mixed charcoal assemblages with traces of hazel nutshell in (080 and 081). These assemblages are consistent with domestic hearth waste. Approximately 2 m south-south-east of Ditch 4S Slot A was a small pit (1054) but the fill (1055) did not produce any carbonised remains.

Ditch 4S Slot B (Table 8)

This slot through ditch 4S revealed the southern terminus of ditch cut (047) and the northern terminus of ditch cut (912).The basal fill (893) of ditch (912) produced only traces of hazel charcoal. Several fills were then present within the ditch that were not investigated but an upper fill (889) produced a more mixed charcoal assemblage with traces of alder, hazel, cherry type, oak, and hazel nutshell.

Approximately 4 m to the east of Ditch 4S was a further ditch cut (299) but it was not clear how this related to the other ditches on this site. The fill (306) contained a mixed charcoal assemblage of hazel, alder, oak and willow, together with some carbonised barley and hazel nutshell fragments. This assemblage is consistent with domestic hearth waste and is one of the few on site with more than traces of cereal grain present.

Ditch 4S Slot C (Table 8)

There was a gap of 22 m between (912) and another terminus of Ditch 4S, with a new cut (476). However, the primary fills (479) produced only traces of hazel and oak charcoal. A gully (535) may represent a continuation of ditch 4S but the fill (536) did not produce any carbonised remains. Approximately 2 m south of Ditch 4S Slot C was a small pit or posthole (468), with fill (469), but this produced only a trace of oak charcoal that was not enough to suggest any evidence for a post burnt *in situ*.

Ditch 4S Slot D (Table 9)

Ditch 4S Slot D showed a continuation of ditch cut (476). The primary fill (495) did not produce any carbonised remains.

Ditch 4S Slot E (Table 9)

The fills (637), (638) and (640) of Ditch 4S in this slot were generally lacking carbonised remains, with only a trace of oak charcoal in (637).

Ditch 4S Slot F (Table 9)

Ditch 4S Slot F showed a continuation of ditch cut (476). The primary fill (644) produced only traces of

Ditch 4S Slot G (Table 9)

Ditch 4S Slot G also showed a continuation of ditch cut (476). The primary fill (688) produced small amounts of oak charcoal. The uppermost fill (655) contained some large cobbles that may have formed part of a wall or revetment. The charcoal assemblage contained significant amounts of cherry type charcoal, with birch, hazel and traces of hazel nutshell. Cherry type charcoal is relatively common on this site but is not usually the dominant type in any of the assemblages.

Ditch 4S Slot H (Table 9)

Ditch 4S Slot H also showed a continuation of ditch cut (476). The primary fill (653) produced only a single fragment of alder charcoal.

Ditch 4S Slot I (Table 9)

Ditch 4S Slot G contained a further continuation of ditch cut (476). The only fill (691) produced small amounts of alder, cherry type and oak charcoal. Within this deposit was a charcoal rich deposit (746) that contained only hazel charcoal. This could be the remains of a burnt wattle object rather than just dumped hearth waste.

Ditch 1N

Ditch 1N Slot A (Table 10)

This first slot was located at the terminus of the ditch (006) in the north-east corner. The basal fill (056) contained small amounts of mixed charcoal, as did the fill (055) of recut (086). Overlying this was (016), which also contained mixed charcoal with a single indeterminate cereal grain. This material is consistent with domestic hearth waste. The uppermost fill (017) in this slot did not produce any carbonised remains.

Ditch 1N Slot B (Table 10)

The ditch cut (006) on the south-west facing section was initially filled by (598), a silty sand, with small amounts of hazel, oak and willow

charcoal. This basal fill was overlain by (110). The bulk sample <088> from this fill did not produce any carbonised remains other than a single fragment of hazel nutshell but two spot finds produced large fragments of willow roundwood (SF 175) and significant amounts of oak (SF 225). These charcoal finds may be from burnt structural elements that were dumped into the ditch. Above (110) was reddish-brown silty sand (112) with pottery, flint and charcoal. The bulk sample <089> produced only small amounts of oak and willow charcoal but (SF 169) contained large fragments of hazel and willow roundwood charcoal and a single fragment of roundwood cherry type. Again, this tends to suggest the remains of burnt wattle that had been dumped into the ditch in a discrete deposit.

These lower fills were truncated by recut (198). The basal deposit (648) was not analysed but this was sealed by (064) with organic clayey lenses, flint, pottery, possible daub and charcoal spot finds. Very large quantities of charcoal were recovered from (064), with large fragments of hazel and willow roundwood, smaller amounts of oak roundwood and occasional fragments of alder and cherry type roundwood. The large amounts of hazel and willow roundwood would suggest the remains of burnt wattle-work that had been dumped into the ditch. This may have been as part of midden waste, considering the other occupation material identified from this context.

The north-east facing ditch section had a fill (109) overlying (112) but this did not produce any carbonised remains. The recut (198) had a basal fill (107) that contained large amounts of hazel charcoal, with willow and oak also present, again suggesting structural remains. This was overlain by a number of fills (187, 108, 106 and 105), which produced more willow and hazel charcoal but with alder actually being the commonest type. Alder is not usually considered a wood chosen for construction (other than in waterlogged situations) and so this deposit may contain some structural material along with charcoal from another origin. Fill (105) was overlain by (103), again producing large amounts of willow and hazel charcoal, with traces of oak and birch also recorded.

Pollen analysis results from ditch fills (110, 112, 107, 187 and 108) (Figure 48)

The full pollen counts and percentages for this section are given in Table 29 and Table 30 in Appendix 2. Pollen percentages <1% are shown using a black dot for presence in the tables. This stratigraphic section covered a depth of 68 cm and included ditch fills (110, 112, 107, 187 and 108). The initial cut (006) of Ditch 1 contained fills (110 and 112) and then the ditch was recut (198) with fills (107, 187 and 108) from the base upwards. The recutting of the ditch may have resulted in some redeposition or mixing of the sediments within this section. It is unlikely that the sequence is a result of entirely natural siltation processes and the pollen diagram shows potential discontinuities at the boundaries between contexts. The pollen diagram will be discussed in terms of the context numbers assigned to each of the ditch fills.

The basal ditch fill (110) was covered by samples 57 cm, 62 cm and 67 cm. The basal samples 67 cm and 62 cm showed very high percentages of devil's-bit scabious (*Succisa pratensis*) pollen, suggesting that this species was probably growing in the ditch itself and so is significantly over-represented in the pollen diagram. Devil's-bit scabious grows in grasslands, meadows and heathlands, especially in wetter areas. It is an insect-pollinated species and so does not produce lots of pollen as it does not need to be dispersed into the air. The quantities of pollen recorded probably came from plants growing either on or very close to the sample site. It is likely that the large quantities of polypody fern spores that were also recorded in this context were also from plants growing within or around the ditch. Traces of aquatics species including bog bean (*Menyanthes trifoliata*) and whorled milfoil (*Myriophyllum verticillatum*) were also present in this zone suggesting period standing water in the ditch.

The main tree/shrub pollen in context (110) was hazel, with only small amounts of alder (*Alnus)*, oak *(Quercus)*, ash (*Fraxinus*) and willow (*Salix*) also present. Hazel pollen increased from the base to the top of the pollen zone covering this context. The charcoal from this context was mainly oak and willow, suggesting that these types were not growing in the near vicinity of the site.

Grass (Poaceae) pollen also increased towards the top of this zone, with sedge (Cyperaceae) and herbs such as pink family (Caryophyllaceae), meadow buttercup type (*Ranunculus acris* type), dandelion type (Lactuceae), ribwort plantain (*Plantago lanceolata*) and mustard type (*Sinapis* type). These are all types associated with open grassland, with the ribwort plantain suggesting the land around the site may have been grazed at this time. Heather pollen is relatively high at the base of this zone suggesting heathland was present, perhaps when the initial ditch was dug. By the end of this zone, heather has declined significantly, perhaps as heathland was replaced by open grazed grassland.

Above basal fill (110) was (112) that produced hazel, willow, oak and cherry type charcoal. Pollen samples from 53 cm and 48 cm covered this context but very little tree or shrub pollen was recorded in this zone, with only small amounts of alder and hazel recorded, with a trace of ash. This might suggest the felling of nearby woodland but could also be a mathematical artefact of the extremely high percentages of devil's-bit scabious recorded in this zone. Heather pollen declines significantly in this context, while grass pollen increases along with other herbaceous types from the bottom of this zone to the top. Herbaceous types such as pink family, dandelion type, ribwort plantain, meadow buttercup type and mustard type all increased but devil's-bit scabious was by far the commonest type present, reaching 88% TLP. No aquatics were present in this zone suggesting the ditch may have become drier as it silted up but that it was still damp enough for devil's-bit scabious to grow in abundance.

The ditch was then recut (198), with the initial fill (107) of the recut being represented by samples 20 cm, 25 cm, 29 cm, 34 cm, 39 cm and 43 cm in the pollen sequence. The lowest part of this fill, at 43 cm, had very high percentages of grass pollen, with associated grassland weeds. Tree and shrub pollen was very low, as was heather pollen. This indicates a very open grassland landscape during the period immediately after the recut of the ditch. This may have been a period during which occupation activity on the site and in the immediate area increased. This is the only level in the pollen diagram in which cereal type pollen is present at >1%, suggesting arable fields were

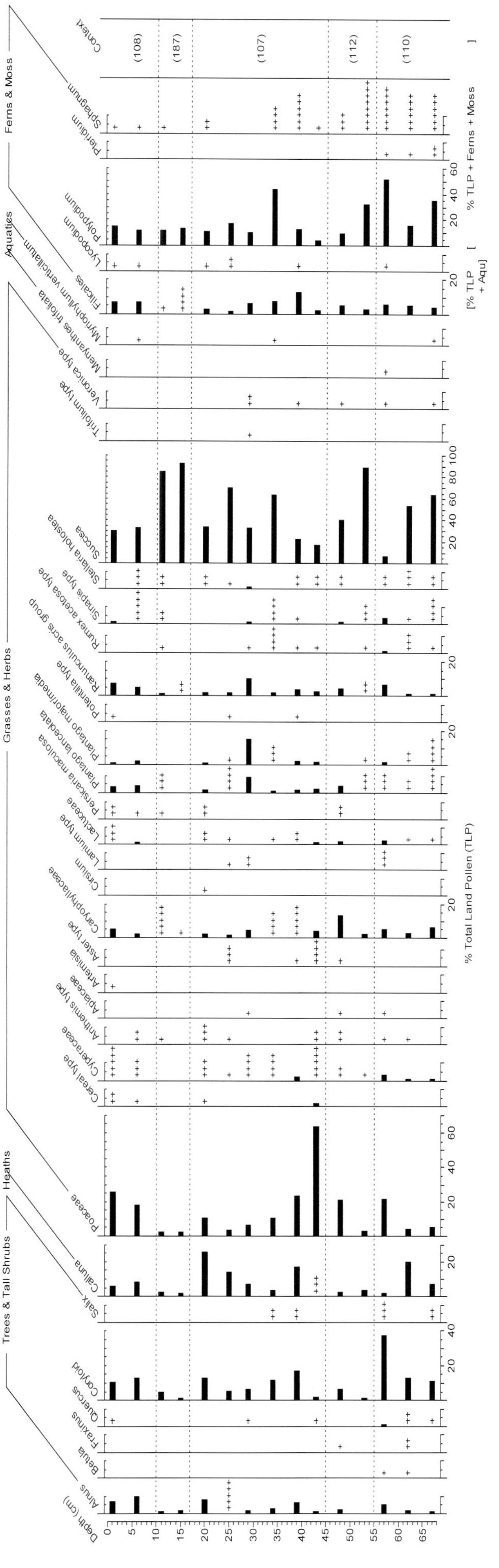

Figure 48: Pollen analysis results from Ditch 1N Slot B.

located nearby. Charcoal of hazel, willow and oak was common in this fill, suggesting that this wood must have been collected some distance from the site. Moving upwards through the pollen sequence within (107), grass pollen declines but tree and tall shrub pollen increases, with alder and hazel increasing most significantly, but willow and oak were present in trace amounts. Heather pollen also increased significantly. This suggests that some areas of grassland were recolonised by heather heathland and by hazel and alder scrub, perhaps because of a decrease in human activity in the area. The pollen spectrum from 29 cm was notable in having more significant amounts of herbaceous pollen, including pink family, ribwort plantain, broad-leaved/hoary plantain (*Plantago major/media*), meadow buttercup type, mustard type and stitchwort (*Stellaria holostea*), although grass pollen was relatively low. This suggests these taxa were growing very close to the ditch and the abundance of plantains might indicate the site itself was being grazed at this time.

Above fill (107) was a relatively thin fill (187) that ran down the side of the ditch into fill (107). Fill (187) was represented by pollen samples at 11 cm and 15 cm depth in the sequence. The pollen spectra in this context show extremely high percentages of devil's-bit scabious (85% and 93%) indicating on-site growth, presumably on the sides of the ditch. These large quantities of devil's-bit scabious pollen mask much of the other pollen taxa within the spectra. Tree and shrub pollen is very low with only alder and hazel represented at less than 5%, grass and heather only reach around 2%, while herbaceous types (other than devils-bit scabious) only occur at trace levels.

Above (107) was a further thin fill running down the side of the ditch and across the base. Fill (108) was represented by pollen samples 6 cm and 1 cm. More significant amounts of alder and hazel pollen were present, corresponding with the charcoal types that were recorded from this ditch. Oak charcoal was also commonly found but only traces of oak pollen are present in this zone. Higher levels of grass pollen were noted, along with weeds of open grassland including pink family, dandelion, ribwort plantain, broad-leaved/hoary plantain, meadow buttercup and mustard type. Devil's-bit scabious pollen was still around 30% of the total pollen but significantly lower than in much of the sequence. This still

suggests that devil's-bit scabious is growing within the ditch but perhaps not directly on the site of the pollen sequence. Traces of cereal pollen were recorded from both pollen samples, suggesting that arable agriculture was taking place nearby.

Ditch 1N Slot C (Table 11)

The basal fill (115) of ditch cut (006) produced a mixed charcoal assemblage that was dominated by alder, with a trace of hazel nutshell. This was overlain by a whitish grey clay (186) and then by (185) with similar mixed charcoal assemblages as found in (115). The ditch was recut by (210), with a primary fill (184) that was very similar in composition to that from the fills of the original ditch cut and may be the result of erosion from these deposits into the newer recut.

Ditch 1N Slot D (Table 11)

The ditch cut (006) in Slot D contained basal fill (228) with small amounts of hazel and oak charcoal, with a single carbonised barley grain. Overlying this were fills (137) and (124), followed by (125), with a mixed charcoal assemblage of alder, birch, hazel and willow charcoal. This was overlain by (126), which contained a very similar assemblage but with the addition of cherry type and oak charcoal. The ditch was recut by (229), with an initial fill (100) that was very similar in charcoal composition to (125) with the addition of a single indeterminate cereal grain. This material may be reworked from the original ditch fills into the recut fill.

Ditch 1N Slot E (Table 11)

The basal fill (135) of (006) in Slot E produced small amounts of alder, hazel and oak charcoal with traces of hazel nutshell. Overlying this was (133) but this fill produced only trace amounts of hazel nutshell. Overlying (133) was fill (134) with traces of alder, oak and willow charcoal. The charcoal quantities present in these fills does not suggest deliberate dumping of material into the ditch fills and is more likely to be erosion from scattered hearth waste on the surface of the site.

Ditch 1N Slot F (Table 11)

The basal fill (128) of (006) in Slot F produced only traces of oak and willow charcoal, with a couple of indeterminate cereal grains. Overlying this was fill (129) with only traces of alder and oak charcoal. Above this was (121) with more abundant charcoal, dominated by oak but with willow, hazel and cherry type also present. This fill also produced degraded ceramic or daub and, combined with the charcoal assemblage, suggests a component of burnt wattle and daub structural material may be present. Overlying this was (123) but this fill contained much smaller quantities of charcoal, with birch, hazel, oak and willow present.

Ditch 2N

Ditch 2N Slot A (Table 12)

The terminal of Ditch 2N was located in the north-east. The cut (008) contained primary fill (090), with a small quantity of mixed charcoal types, with animal bone or possible horn. This suggests redeposited midden material. This was recut by (089) with primary fill (079), which produced a similar carbonised assemblage to that from (090). Above this lay fill (078) and fill (084), which contained degraded pottery and possibly daub. There was only a small amount of charcoal present with hazel and cherry type represented. The quantity of charcoal involved was not enough to suggest the presence of wattle and daub remains. The above fills were truncated by a possible pit (083) in the ditch. The fills (076 and 077) of the pit both contained mixed charcoal assemblages consistent with domestic hearth waste.

The excavation was continued to the west where cut (008) had lower fills (155, 154, 153 and 152), which produced only traces of charcoal. The upper fill (150) produced larger quantities of mixed charcoal with willow being the commonest type present. Recut (089) probably truncated the top of these deposits. The lower fills (149, 148 and 147) were not examined but the next two fills (146 and 145) produced only traces of hazel charcoal.

Two postholes were located on either side of the terminus. Postholes (116), fill (117) produced small amounts of cherry type and oak charcoal, probably from hearth waste rather than providing any evidence for a post burnt *in situ*. The second posthole (118) had a basal fill (136) again with just traces of mixed charcoal, with no evidence for the post having been burnt *in situ*.

Ditch 2N Slot E and F (Table 12)

Slots E and F related to the souterrain that truncated the ditch just west of Slot A. Slot F was excavated across the souterrain and will be discussed in the souterrain part of the report. Slot E was located on the north-west side of the souterrain. The ditch cut (008) in Slot E was initially filled by (807) but produced only a trace of oak charcoal.

Ditch 2N / Ditch 3N Slot B (Table 13)

This slot covered both Ditch 2N and 3N. This slot showed that Ditch 2 was earlier than Ditch 3 and had probably gone out of use when Ditch 3 was excavated and that Ditch 3 truncated the upper fills of Ditch 2. Ditch 2N, cut (008), was initially filled by (791) but only produced traces of oak and willow charcoal with traces of hazel nutshell. This fill was overlain by fills (790 and 796), which were not investigated. A pit (957) was cut into (796), but the fill (797) produced only traces of mixed charcoal.

In the north facing section of the slot the fills were truncated by the cut for Ditch 3 (010). The basal fill (580) of this cut produced significant amounts of alder and hazel charcoal, with birch, cherry type and willow also present suggesting dumped hearth or midden waste. The south facing section had a different basal fill (795), which also produced a mixed charcoal assemblage but, unlike (580), no hazel charcoal was present.

A pit (593) was located between the two ditches. The fill produced prehistoric pottery, worked stone and animal bone, but only small amounts of hazel, cherry type and oak charcoal, suggesting this may be midden waste. Another pit (900) was located in this area, possibly truncating the western end of Ditch 3N. The fill (898) produced only traces of alder and willow charcoal.

Ditch 2N Slot C (Table 13)

The primary fill of this ditch (008) was split into (533) on the south-east side and (532) on the north-west side. The fills produced only traces of mixed charcoal. The basal fill (611) of the recut did not produce any carbonised remains. The upper fills (529 and 528) also produced only traces of charcoal, although (529) did produce a carbonised barley grain and an indeterminate cereal grain.

Ditch 2N Slot D (Table 13)

Slot D was the final slot in Ditch 2N, with ditch cut (008) being initially filled by (578), then (800, 579 and 577) although these fills produced only traces of charcoal and a single barley grain in (579). The next deposit was (576), which produced some sherds of pottery along with abundant carbonised heather stems and fragments of broom/gorse charcoal. This material could be the remains of burnt surface vegetation or may represent fuel for a specific activity such as bread ovens? The uppermost deposit (574) in the slot did not produce any carbonised remains.

Ditch 3N

Ditch 3N Slot A (Table 14)

Slot A was located at the east terminus of Ditch 3N (010), with the initial deposit (087) producing a diverse range of charcoal types, including alder, hazel, cherry type, oak and elm. This find of elm charcoal was one of only two on the whole site, with the other being from Area 7. The basal fill was recut by (085) and initially filled by (029). The bulk sample <013> from fill (029) produced only traces of alder charcoal. However SF67 produced very large quantities of oak charcoal with significant amounts of willow roundwood and a single fragment of hazel. This assemblage is consistent with burnt structural material such as wattle panels. Overlying this were fills (032 and 019) but these produced only traces of mixed charcoal.

Ditch 3N Slot C (Table 14)

The initial cut (010) of Slot C had a basal fill (620) but this produced only a single fragment of hazel nutshell. The first recut (622) was filled by a number of layers of silty gravel that may be redeposited form the side of the ditch. The layers included (623 and 624) but neither fill produced any carbonised remains. A second recut (630) contained trace amounts of mixed charcoal in the basal fill (631) and only a single fragment of alder charcoal in the overlying fill (632).

Ditch 3N Slot D (Table 14)

The cut (010) was initially filled by (863) but produced no carbonised remains. The ditch was recut (1084) with a primary fill (815) that was overlain by (798). Fill (798) contained large amounts of alder charcoal, with small amounts of hazel, cherry type and a trace of hazel nutshell. The predominance of alder within this fill might indicate an industrial origin for this carbonised material.

Ditch 3N Slot E (Table 14)

The ditch cut {010) was initially filled with (857) but this fill contained only traces of hazel and willow charcoal.

Ditch 4N

Ditch 4N Slot A (Table 15)

Slot A was located at the terminus of Ditch 4N. The ditch cut (021) was initially filled with (026) containing small amounts of alder, oak and willow charcoal. This fill was then recut by (031), with the initial fill (026) having a charcoal assemblage dominated by significant amounts of alder, with hazel, cherry type, oak and willow also present.

The section was extended and a further extent of ditch cut (021) was located. The basal fill (062) produced no carbonised remains. A further recut (058) was filled by (059) and produced a mixed charcoal assemblage of alder, birch, hazel, cherry type and willow, suggesting scattered or dumped domestic hearth waste.

Ditch 4N Slot B (Table 15)

The ditch cut (021) was initially filled with (456) but this produced no carbonised remains. Overlying this was (455) with only a trace of alder charcoal. These deposits were recut by (1083), which was initially filled by (454) but again, no carbonised remains were present.

Ditch 4N Slot C (Table 15)

The cut (021) in the east facing section of this slot was initially filled by (464) but this produced only a trace of oak charcoal. Overlying this was (465, 463 and 461) with the uppermost deposit (462). Fill (462) produced significant amounts of mixed charcoal, with alder, birch, hazel, broom/gorse, oak and willow all present. This suggests domestic hearth waste or midden material having been dumped into the ditch.

In the west facing ditch section, the initial cut was filled with (466) but only produced a fragment of indeterminate charcoal.

Ditch 4N Slot D (Table 15)

The cut (021) in Slot D was filled with (805), with no carbonised remains. This was overlain by (804) with only traces of hazel and willow charcoal. In the north-west section similar deposits were identified to those from the south-east section but with an additional deposit (809), but that fill did not produce any carbonised remains.

Ditch 4N Slot E (Table 15)

The cut (021) in this slot was initially filled by (869) but this fill produced only a trace of oak charcoal. Overlying this was (825), which produced a sherd of prehistoric pottery and a small amount of mixed charcoal of hazel, oak and willow.

To the east of Ditch 4N Slot E was a small pit (981). The lower fill (990) produced only traces of oak charcoal but the upper fill (982) contained large amounts of charcoal, with alder, oak, hazel, broom/gorse and cherry type. It is suggested that this may be the remains of a fire-pit.

Ditch 6 (Table 16)

Ditch 6 (779) was located to the north of the main fort ditches in the north-east part of the site. The ditch was curvilinear, approximately 36 m long and opened into a pit at the north-east end.

The first slot (779A) covered the pit at the north-east end and had a primary fill (787), which produced small amounts of mixed charcoal, as did the overlying fill (786) but with the addition of small amounts of hazel nutshell.

At slot (779C) the ditch was filled with five deposits but only the basal fill (785) was investigated. The fill produced only a trace of oak charcoal.

Slot (779D) was initially filled by (911) but this did not produce any carbonised remains.

Slot (779E) had a basal fill (915) that produced only traces of hazel charcoal.

Slot (779F) was located near the south-west end of Ditch 6. It contained three fills, the first of which (928) produced traces of hazel and oak charcoal. The middle fill (929) also produced only traces of hazel and willow charcoal, with a fragment of hazel nutshell. The upper fill (927) produced a more diverse charcoal assemblage of alder, birch, hazel, oak and willow but at traces levels.

The fills from Ditch 6 are generally indicative of domestic hearth waste. The quantities involved do not suggest large amounts of dumped material and may represent accidental incorporation of scattered hearth waste from an occupation layer.

Souterrain (Table 17)

The souterrain was cut into the natural subsoil (002) and the southern side of Ditch 2N, truncating part of (008) and the associated fills, adjacent to the entrance of the fort. Fill (353) is the top fill surrounding a possible fence line north of the souterrain. It produced moderate amounts of willow and hazel charcoal, suggesting that the fence may have been formed from willow and hazel wattle.

The main cut (044) of the souterrain was orientated East/West, 9.66 m in length and a maximum of 5.88 m wide. The souterrain was lined with stone walls (043) that extended to a height of 1.49 m. The first phase of construction after the cut (044) was the use of yellow brown silty sand (144) as bedding material between many of the stones. Fill (144) produced significant amounts of charcoal, with alder, birch, hazel, oak and willow suggesting that hearth waste or midden material had been used for this bedding material and for packing around the boulders in the stone wall. Between the cut (044) of the souterrain and the stone walls (043) were a series of fills (844, 865 and 866). These fills produced only traces of charcoal and so appear to have a different origin to the bedding material (144).

Above these basal fills between the souterrain cut (044) and the stone walls (043) were a further two fills (827 and 841). The first of these (827) was located above (844) but produced significant amounts of charcoal, with alder, birch, hazel, cherry type, oak and willow, with traces of hazel nutshell. This seems to be further evidence for hearth waste or midden material having formed part of the infill for the stone walls. Fill (827) appeared similar to fills (882 and 885) that were part of Ditch 2N (008), into which the souterrain was cut and might have suggested reuse of these ditch fills in the souterrain construction. Fills (882 and 885) also produced mixed charcoal assemblages but the quantities of alder charcoal in (827) were significantly larger and so may suggest additional hearth waste was added. The second fill (841) was located above (866) but produced slightly more charcoal than (866) but less than that seen in (827).

On the exterior of the souterrain cut (044) at the northern extent were a series of fills that related to Ditch 2N (008) and which may have been used in the construction of the souterrain. These fills (1069, 886, 884 and 882) produced small amounts of mixed charcoal with traces of hazel nutshell in (882). Immediately above (1069) was fill (883), which produced only traces of alder charcoal. This was overlain by (885), which produced a mixed charcoal assemblage similar to that seen in other fills that were reused from the ditch to form this packing material.

The next phase of construction was the souterrain floor (098) that began with a gravel rich bedding layer (870), with a similar mixed charcoal assemblage seen elsewhere. The stones of the souterrain floor were placed onto this bedding layer. Between the stones was fill (867) but this produced only traces of birch and cherry type charcoal.

Below the level of the floor stones, within a small gap in the souterrain wall in the north-west corner was a possible posthole (991). The fill (992) produced small amounts of mixed charcoal and so does not provide evidence for a post burnt *in situ*.

The next phases encompass the use of the souterrain and then infilling following abandonment. This was excavated in two slots. The first excavation Slot A was located at the souterrain entrance and identified four fills (027, 042, 073 and 074) and the second excavation Slot B covered the structure of the souterrain and its relationship with the fills of Ditch 2 and identified fills (069, 094 and 095). The earliest fills on the souterrain floor were (074) near the entrance and (095) across the main chamber. Deposit (074) produced significant amounts of hazel and willow charcoal, with small amounts of alder and oak also present. This might suggest burning of a wattle structure or panel in this area. Immediately above (074) at the souterrain entrance was (042) that sloped from the entrance

into the main chamber of the souterrain. The fill produced very large quantities of oak and willow charcoal with smaller amounts of hazel also present. This strongly suggests the presence of burnt structural material, probably willow wattle-work with oak supports. Overlying this was (073), which also produced significant amounts of oak and willow charcoal, but with the addition of alder, birch and cherry type suggesting there may be a mix of structural material and hearth waste in this deposit. Overlying this, and filling much of the rest of the souterrain depth, was fill (027), which also produced significant amounts of oak, hazel and willow charcoal, but with large amounts of alder also present, together with small amounts of cherry type and birch. Again, this suggests a possible mix of structural material with hearth waste.

The initial fill over the main floor area was (095), which produced significant amounts of alder and hazel charcoal, with small amounts of birch, rowan type, cherry type, oak and willow also present. This suggests the remains of domestic hearth waste. Lying above this was fill (069), which also produced a mixed charcoal assemblage but with the addition of a couple of carbonised barley grains and two indeterminate cereal grains. These quantities of grain are not sufficient to indicate either cereal processing or storage. This fill was sealed by (027) described above.

Separate context numbers were given to deposits in the primary fills (074 and 095) in the main chamber that appeared to be significantly different to the main fill. The contexts included (157, 182 and 156). These fills all produced mixed charcoal assemblages, with hazel usually being the commonest type present. A small deposit (235) approximately 30 mm thick and 1 m long was located in the southern half of the souterrain. It was thought this might be the remains of a plant or branch burnt *in situ*. However, this deposit contained a mixed charcoal assemblage of birch, hazel and cherry type but with carbonised heather stems being the commonest type present. It is not clear what this deposit represents but it is not a single plank or branch.

In the north-west corner of the souterrain was deposit (315) but this produced only a trace of oak charcoal and an indeterminate cereal grain. In the south-west corner, close to the entrance, was deposit (316), which produced a mixed charcoal assemblage with traces of indeterminate cereal grain, similar to that seen elsewhere and which is consistent with domestic hearth waste.

Internal and External Features

This section details features found within and around the fort and have been divided into seven areas (Areas 1-7) (Figure 24).

Area 1 (Table 18)

Area 1 was located in the northern half of the site and this area was divided into two by curvilinear Ditch 6. North of the ditch was pit (772) but the fill produced only a trace of hazel nutshell. To the south of (772) were a further series of pits (777, 775, 406, 437, 441 and 443) but most of these pits produced only traces of charcoal or no charcoal. Only fill (407) of pit (406) and fill (438) of pit (437) produced slightly more charcoal, although the assemblages were all mixed charcoal and probably the remains of scattered hearth waste.

South of Ditch 6, near to the eastern terminal were small pits (1015 and 1009). However, the fills (1014 and 1010) did not produce any carbonised remains.

To the south of Slots E and F in Ditch 6 were a cluster of pit features (1005, 1003, 1008 and 984). Only the fill (1007) of pit (1008) produced any carbonised remains with traces of birch and oak charcoal and a single carbonised barley grain.

Area 2 (Table 19)

Area 2 covered the entrance area of the fort, encompassing the terminals of all four ditches. Four pits (492, 482, 470 and 390) were located in the north-east of this area but the fills from these did not produce any significant carbonised remains.

Further up the slope, close to the terminus of Ditch 4, was a group of three pits (393, 395 and 423). Fill (397) of pit (395) did not produce any carbonised remains. Fill (394) of pit (393) produced significant amounts of oak charcoal but no other carbonised remains. This might suggest it contains the remains of a burnt oak post or other structural remains. The fill (424) of

pit (423) produced a mixed charcoal assemblage, dominated by alder. This would be consistent with the remains of hearth waste.

Two postholes (158 and 385) were located near the terminal ends of Ditch 2N and Ditch 3N. The fill (159) of (158) produced only traces of alder and hazel charcoal. The fill (386) of posthole (385) produced slightly more charcoal, with hazel, cherry type and oak present. Neither posthole appears to contain evidence for a post burnt *in situ.*

Just north of Ditch 1N Slot B and west of the souterrain was pit (251). It contained a single fill (252), which produced large quantities of oak charcoal and traces of hazel nutshell. The oak charcoal may represent the remains of an oak post or other structural remains.

A number of features were located in the entrance to the interior of the fort between terminus for Ditch 1N and the terminus for Ditch 1S. Postholes (230) fill (231), (233) fill (234), (346) fill (347) and (1071) fill (1072) all produced traces of mixed charcoal but no evidence for the posts having been burnt *in situ.* The fill (1053) of pit (1052) contained possible packing stones, a possible whetstone and some daub, along with traces of hazel and oak charcoal and hazel nutshell.

Area 3 (Table 20)

Area 3 was located within the interior of the fort. The northernmost features were two truncated pits (496 and 498). The fills (497 and 499) produced only traces of hazel and oak charcoal.

Pits

To the south of these pits was a possible structure (Structure 1) that consisted of two curving lines of posts and some outlying features.

Structure 1A

The first line of posts (Structure 1A) included postholes (539, 554, 552, 537, 413, 543, 457, 563, 526, 588, 947, 943, 941, 936, 933, and 607). The majority of the fills of these postholes produced either very small amounts of mixed charcoal or no carbonised remains at all. Fill (553) of (552) produced small amounts of cereal grain recovered with oats and barley both represented. The quantities of cereal grain involved are not sufficient to suggest cereal processing on site and seem to be scatter from domestic hearth or midden waste.

Structure 1B

Another line of posts, Structure 1B, crossed Structure 1A and included postholes (516, 521, 519, 548, 542 and 591). The posthole fills generally contained small amounts of mixed charcoal although fill (520) of posthole (519) contained more significant amounts of charcoal, though nothing to suggest a post burnt *in situ*. The fills (549 and 551) of posthole (548) contained a mixed charcoal assemblage but with more significant numbers of carbonised cereal grain, with oats, barley and possible wheat all represented.

One outlying feature was posthole (570) to the north of Structure 1A and west of Structure 1B. However, the fill (571) did not produce any carbonised remains.

Outlying features to the south

There were a series of eight outlying features outside Structure 1, to the south. To the south-east of posthole (550) was a series of three postholes (556, 975 and 977). The fill (557) of (556) produced hazel, oak and willow charcoal together with small amounts of cereal grain, with oats, barley and possible wheat identified. The fill (975) of posthole (976) did not produce any carbonised remains while the fill (978) of posthole (977) produced small amounts of mixed charcoal and a single carbonised grain of oats. South of (459) was posthole (979), with fill (980) that produced only a fragment of heather charcoal and a barley grain.

Approximately 2 m south of pit (959) were two postholes (993 and 558). The fill (560) of posthole (558) did not produce any carbonised remains. The fill (994) of posthole (995) produced only a single fragment of alder charcoal and a carbonised barley grain. A further 2 m to the south was a third posthole (561) with fill (562) that produced only traces of birch, hazel and willow charcoal.

To the north of the postholes that formed Structure 1 was a large feature (344) that was filled with silty sand, gravel, boulders along with some modern pottery and a fragment of copper

alloy. The fill (345) produced a mixed charcoal assemblage of alder, birch, hazel, cherry type, oak and willow, together with traces of oats, barley and hazel nutshell. This fill is consistent with midden waste and is unlikely to be modern, so the modern pottery may be a later intrusion.

Under (345) at the north-west end was a large fire-pit (349) that was filled by (350 and 351). Upper fill (350) produced small amounts of mixed charcoal but the basal fill (351) produced very large quantities of oak charcoal, suggesting that this fire-pit may have had an industrial use.

Area 4 (Table 21)

Area 4 was located in the centre of the fort interior.

Central cluster of features

A central cluster of pits and postholes included pits (581, 613, 615 and 657) with postholes (599 and 605). Their fills generally contained mixed charcoal assemblages, with a few grains of barley also located within fill (600) of posthole (599). A large deposit of dark silty sand (570) produced very large amounts of oak and willow charcoal, with smaller amounts of alder and hazel. It is possible that this feature contained a proportion of burnt structural material.

Western cluster of features

To the west of the above features was a further group of pits (967 and 1001) and postholes (572, 584, 586, 594, 938, 945, 971 and 973). As with the features in the central cluster, the fills generally contained small amounts of mixed charcoal and hazel nutshell, suggesting this internal part of the fort had scattered hearth waste on the occupation surface and that this material became incorporated into cut features.

Area 5 (Table 22)

Area 5 was located in the western part of the interior of the fort. Three features were present next to Ditch 1N Slot F: pit (958), pit (1022) and linear (894). The northernmost feature was pit (958), which was noted in the DSR as having large amounts of charcoal present, suggesting *in situ* burning or dumping of burnt waste. However, the fill (960) only produced small amounts of charcoal and so this may suggest that there had been some burning of the soil to give the appearance of a large amount of carbonisation. South-east of this was pit (1022), with fill (1057) that contained large stones but only a trace of alder charcoal. To the south was a small linear (894), approximately 5 m in length that contained two fills (895 and 896). The lower fill contained significant amounts of willow and hazel charcoal, with small amounts of oak also present and a couple of grains of carbonised barley. The upper fill (895) produced large amounts of oak and hazel roundwood, with smaller amounts of willow roundwood also present. This suggests the presence of a burnt wattle structure, possibly with oak supports. The linear feature may have once been a wattle fence line or partition.

Further west were pit (1011) and posthole (1039) on the western side of the interior of the fort. Posthole (1039), fill (1040) produced only a trace of alder charcoal and so there is no evidence for the post having been burnt *in situ*. Pit (1011) lay 4 m to the south-west and measured around 2 m in diameter. The lower fill (1013) produced significant amounts of conifer wood, rather than charcoal. This might suggest a more modern origin for this feature. The upper fill (1012) produced some modern pottery and only a trace of indeterminate cinder, again suggesting a modern date for this feature.

Linear feature (1045) was orientated north-south and contained fills (1046 and 1047). The lower fill (1047) produced only small amounts of hazel charcoal. The upper fill (1046) produced large amounts of hazel charcoal, with alder, oak, willow and broom/gorse also present. Although hazel was the dominant charcoal type it is more likely that this material is the remains of hearth waste rather than wattle. This linear was truncated by posthole (1048), fill (1049), which contained only traces of hazel and willow charcoal, so no evidence for the post having been burnt *in situ*. To the south of this was posthole (1050), fill (1051), again with only traces of mixed charcoal present.

Area 6 (Table 23)

Area 6 was located on the southern side of the site, outside the ditches defining the fort. A number of features were clustered together in this area and were thought to be prehistoric in date.

Deposit (839) contained significant amounts of oak charcoal, with hazel and willow also present, together with traces of hazel nutshell. The soil was not heat affected and so it appeared that this material had been dumped, possibly from burnt structural material elsewhere.

Immediately to the south-west was pit (955), fill (956) that produced small amounts of mixed hazel, oak and willow charcoal that is thought to have been deposited through natural silting, possibly from deposit (839). To the north was pit (952), fill (953), but this did not produce any charcoal. To the west of this was pit (963), fill (964), with small amounts of mixed hazel, oak and willow charcoal. Next to this was pit (961), fill (962), but this produced no carbonised remains.

To the south of pit (961) was pit (830), which contained three fills. The lower fill (838) and upper fill (831) produced very similar carbonised assemblages with alder, hazel, oak and willow charcoal and traces of hazel nutshell. This material is probably the remains of domestic hearth waste. A few metres to the east of this as a linear pit (842) approximately 3.7 m in length. The fill contained hazel charcoal and traces of hazel nutshell. This could be the remains of a burnt hazel hurdle, although more charcoal may have been expected if this was the case.

To the south-west were two more pits (480 and 950). Fill (481) of pit (480) produced significant amounts of oak charcoal, with small amounts of hazel and willow also present. This assemblage may contain burnt structural material. Immediately to the south was pit (950), but the fill (951) did not produce any carbonised remains.

Two features, pits (504 and 506), lay outside the main cluster of features in Area 6. Pit (504) contained a single fill (505), which produced only a single fragment of hazel charcoal. Pit (506) contained two fills (507 and 508). The upper fill (507) produced only traces of alder and hazel charcoal, whilst the lower fill (508) produced traces of oak and willow, with a fragment of hazel nutshell.

Area 7 (Tables 24-27)

Area 7 was located to the south-west of the site, at the base of the hill.

Features associated with deposit (767)

In the north-east of Area 7 was a large deposit (767), that was thought to represent a possible occupation layer that lay under the hillwash that covered part of the southern edge of Ditch 4S. Finds included prehistoric pottery and flint, with significant amounts of oak and hazel charcoal, with some alder, birch and willow also present together with two grains of barley. This might suggest that structural material formed part of the assemblage but that hearth waste was also present.

Pit (324) was originally thought to be the remains of a cist as it was associated with a large flat stone and possible Bronze Age pottery. However, the stone was later thought to be a saddle quern and the feature was a pit rather than a cist. The first fill (721) of the pit produced only traces of hazel and oak charcoal. Overlying this was (348), which was excavated in four spits but produced a mixed charcoal assemblage of alder, hazel, oak and willow charcoal.

A few metres to the north-west of (324) was deposit (675), which was thought, during excavation, to be the remains of a post or stake that had been driven into the ground and then burnt, rather than a post located within a posthole. The fill (675) produced significant amounts of alder charcoal but no other types, suggesting that this may well be the remains of an alder stake burnt *in situ*.

Bronze Age structure

A 5 m diameter structure, formed by an irregular ring of stakeholes, was thought to date to the Bronze Age. The stakeholes included (679, 681, 683, 689, 692, 696, 706, 708, 710, 713, 715, 717, 719, 722 and 732). The majority of the stakeholes contained only traces of charcoal, with alder, hazel, oak and willow represented together with traces of carbonised barley and hazel nutshell. However, the fill (718) of stakehole (717) produced significant amounts of carbonised barley grain and indeterminate cereals together with hazel charcoal. This material may be evidence of cereal processing waste that had been used as packing for the stakehole. A possible tree bole (661), fill (662) also contained very large quantities of cereal grain, with around 600 grains recorded. The majority of the grains

were identifiable as barley or possible barley. In addition, large amounts of hazel charcoal were recorded, with traces of oak. This would appear to be the remains of either cereal processing waste or stored cereal grain that had accidentally been burned. The hazel charcoal might suggest these cereals had been contained in a woven hazel container.

Southern stakeholes

To the south of the structure was a semi-circular line of stakeholes (726, 734 and 736). However the fills (727/726) and (735/734) produced no carbonised remains and fill (737/736) produced only a trace of alder charcoal.

Stakeholes around tree bole (663)

To the west of the structure was a tree bole (663), which was surrounded by a number of stakeholes (671, 673, 724 and 730). The fills produced only traces of charcoal and carbonised barley grains, probably from scattered occupation debris nearby.

Bronze Age Pit (738)

To the west of tree bole (663) was a large Bronze Age pit (738) that contained six fills (739, 741, 742, 743, 744 and 745). The fills generally produced moderate quantities of mixed charcoal and hazel nutshell, with hazel charcoal being particularly abundant in fills (739 and 741) and willow charcoal in fill (742). Of particular note were moderate amounts of carbonised cereal grain in the upper fill (739), with barley and possible barley making up just over half the grain recorded, with the rest being too poorly preserved to be further identifiable. A stakehole (728), fill (729), did not produce any carbonised remains.

On the western edge of pit (738) there appeared to be a fire affected deposit (755) but this only produced small amounts of hazel and willow charcoal with traces of hazel nutshell. If a large fire had been set here then the majority of the charred remains must have been removed from the site.

Other pits and postholes

To the west of pit (738) was pit (665), fill (666), which contained stones, burnt bone and a stone tool. The charcoal was a mixed assemblage of alder, hazel, oak willow and a single fragment of elm. This is only one of two fragments of elm on the site and may suggest this pit dates to the earlier prehistoric period.

To the north of pit (665) were three possible stakeholes (676, 668 and 659). The fill (660) of (659) contained significant amounts of alder charcoal, with hazel and hazel nutshell. Although the main stake may have been made of alder, the mixed nature of the assemblage may also just be the remains of scattered hearth waste. Fill (669) of stakehole (668) produced only small amounts of hazel and willow charcoal, while fill (fill (677) of stakehole (676) produced only traces of hazel and oak charcoal.

A short distance to the south-west of the above features were a further three stakeholes (756, 758 and 762). The fills (757, 759 and 763) were dominated by oak charcoal, although hazel charcoal was also present in (757 and 759). This might suggest that these stakeholes once held oak stakes, possibly with woven hazel branches between them.

To the far south-west of the site was a possible fire-pit (694) that contained three fills (695, 712 and 740). Fills (695 and 712) produced very large quantities of alder charcoal, with traces of hazel in (712). Fill (740) produced only small amounts of alder charcoal. There was evidence for *in situ* burning confirming that this was a fire-pit. The predominance of alder as the main fuel might also indicate this fire-pit had an industrial use.

'Palisade' (Table 28)

During excavation, a possible palisade/small ditch was revealed extending around the lower slopes of the hill on the southern side of the fort. The ditch (294) extended for approximately 140 m across the southern slope, for 47 m across the base of the north-western slope and a further 45 m to the north and east of the site. Only two fills (295) from Slot F and (304) from Slot G were examined. Fill (295) did not produce any carbonised remains but (304) produced significant amounts of alder and hazel charcoal, with traces of oak. Finds from the dith trenches suggest that this might be a relatively modern feature.

Scone

Scone 1 (Table 28)

Excavations at Scone 1 revealed three pits and two postholes. However, only the fill (084) of pit (083) was examined and it produced only small amounts of willow charcoal.

Scone 2 (Table 28)

Excavations at Scone 2 revealed a number of pits and postholes along with the possible remains of a burnt mound.

The burnt mound measured 13 m by 6 m. The upper, deepest deposit (044) contained heat affected stones and a mixed charcoal assemblage of alder, birch, hazel, oak and willow suggesting collection of fuel from the local area.

Pit (052), fill (053), produced a small amount of mixed alder, hazel and oak charcoal. The fill (061) of a possible posthole (058) produced mixed hazel, oak and willow charcoal with traces of hazel nutshell. There is no evidence for a post having been burnt *in situ*.

Discussion

Woodland and Heathland Resources

The samples examined from Broxy Kennels produced an extremely diverse range of charcoal types, all of which were native trees or shrubs that could have been sourced locally. However, the pollen sequence suggests that only hazel and alder were growing nearby during the period in which the fills of Ditch 1 were formed. Although, oak, birch, ash and willow pollen were recorded, they were only ever present at trace levels suggesting these taxa were not growing in significant numbers in the area around the fort.

Hazel, oak, willow and alder charcoal were the commonest charcoal types recorded from the site but charcoal assemblages that were identified as domestic hearth waste often contained smaller amounts of other charcoal types including birch, rowan type, cherry type, and heather type. This suggests that wood collected for domestic fuel was not deliberately selected but just used what was available at the time.

There were a few contexts where there was some evidence for deliberate selection of wood types for fuel. A fire-pit (317) located on the south side of Ditch 1S Slot F produced very large quantities of oak charcoal and a similar assemblage was recorded from the base of fire-pit (349) located under a possible midden deposit (344) to the north of Structure 1. The abundance of oak, with only traces of other types suggests that these features may have had industrial purposes that required the higher temperatures that can be generated by burning oak as the main fuel source (Gale and Cutler 2000). Further evidence for deposits of industrial fuel waste may be present in a few contexts where large quantities of alder charcoal were recorded. These included deposits in the fills of Ditch 1S Slot H, Ditch 1N Slot B, Ditch 3N Slot D and fire-pit (694) in Area 7. Although alder is not often considered a good wood for burning, it does burn very well and with a high heat if it has been properly seasoned first. It is also one of the favoured wood types for making charcoal, which can then be burned to provide the higher heat often required by industrial processes (Gale and Cutler 2000).

Possible evidence for the remains of structural materials was recorded in several contexts. Evidence for large quantities of hazel and willow charcoal in linear features including Ditch 4S Slot I and fills to the north of the souterrain suggest the remains of wattle fence lines as does a mix of oak and hazel charcoal in linear feature (894) in Area 5.

Several deposits of charcoal that had been dumped in ditch fills were also thought to be the remains of structural material because they contained abundant quantities of a mixture of all or some of oak, hazel and willow. Several fills in Ditch 1N Slot B and Slot F produced these types of assemblages, sometimes with evidence for burnt daub as well. Of the four main ditches, only Ditch 1 produced this evidence for burnt structural remains, perhaps suggesting these deposits are the remains of the first buildings constructed within the initial hillfort ditch. Similar assemblages were also recorded within the initial souterrain floor deposits perhaps as a result of this material being present over the site when the souterrain was first constructed. It could also represent the remains of a wicker structure or

object that was burned within the souterrain but this might be a less probable explanation.

Evidence for structural remains that had been burnt *in situ* were less common but pits (393 and 251), associated with the entrance to the fort, both produced large quantities of oak charcoal, suggesting they contained the remains of burnt oak posts. The only other possible evidence for *in situ* burnt structural remains were associated with stakeholes (756, 758 and 762) in Area 7, which produced large amounts of oak and hazel charcoal that may be the remains of a structure with oak uprights and woven hazel wattle panels between the uprights.

It is clear that areas of heathland were present in the vicinity of the site from pollen present at various points throughout the pollen sequence from Ditch 1N Slot B but heather charcoal was generally not common in the samples from this site. However, two contexts did contain large quantities of carbonised heather stems. An unusually shaped deposit (235) that was only 3 cm thick but around 100 cm in length was initially thought to be the remains of a plank but analysis has shown that it contained mixed charcoal with significant quantities of heather. There is no obvious explanation for the shape and content of this feature, other than it is not a burnt plank of wood. The second context with large amounts of heather type charcoal was fill (576) in Ditch 2N Slot D, which also produced small amounts of gorse/broom type charcoal. It is possible that this dump of material could represent clearing of vegetation growing on site but, as this seems to be a single deposit that is not replicated elsewhere it may be more likely that this material is rake-out from a bread-oven. Gorse/broom wood and, to a lesser extent, heather stems were often used to fuel bread ovens as they are easy to light, burn quickly and produce the hot temperature required for baking bread (Gale and Cutler, 2000).

Cereals and Weeds

Cereal grain was relatively uncommon on the site, particularly in association with the hillfort. Small numbers of cereal grains were identified in fill (306) in Ditch 4S Slot B, from posthole (548) in Structure 1B and posthole (556) to the south of Structure 1. Ditch fill (306) produced barley grains, while the posthole fills produced small amounts of mixed cereals, with barley, oats and possible wheat all represented. The quantities involved are not sufficient to suggest any cereal processing was being undertaken on the site. Mixed cereal assemblages such as these are often more associated with medieval or later sites, since oats are really only common in mainland Scotland from the medieval period onwards. Throughout most of prehistory, barley has been the commonest cereal type grown in much of Scotland. Although wheat is present in prehistoric contexts in Scotland, it is much less common and often restricted to higher status sites. There was no evidence for any carbonised cereal chaff or arable weeds in the hillfort samples. For the size and apparent status of the hillfort, the quantities of cereal grain recorded are extremely small and so this may suggest that cereal processing was taking place elsewhere.

Cereal pollen, probably from barley, was identified in the pollen diagram but only at trace levels in occasional samples. Only the pollen sample at 39 cm showed cereal pollen above 1% TLP, which is enough to suggest cereal growing nearby. Although cereals are wind pollinated, cereal pollen does not travel far from the parent plant and so anything more than a trace of cereal pollen is enough to suggest arable agriculture nearby.

In contrast, three contexts with larger quantities of cereals were identified from Bronze Age features in Area 7. A stakehole (717) forming part of a possible Bronze Age structure produced over 100 grains of barley or possible barley, with hazel charcoal. This might suggest re-use of cereal processing waste as packing for the stakehole. Barley would have been the main cereal type grown in Scotland during the Bronze Age and so is consistent with the suggested date for this feature.

A feature identified as a possible tree bole (661) also contained very large quantities of cereal grain, with around 600 grains recorded. The majority of the grains were identifiable as barley or possible barley. In addition, large amounts of hazel charcoal were recorded, with traces of oak. This would appear to be the remains of either cereal processing waste or stored cereal grain that had accidentally been burned. Later in the excavation it was noted that there may have been a line of stakeholes under this 'tree bole' and so it may be that this deposit is associated with another structure rather than being a natural feature. The oak and hazel charcoal could be further evidence for a structure having been destroyed by fire or could be from some kind of wattle container in which the cereal grain had been stored.

Only two contexts from the entire site produced evidence for 'weed' seeds. Fill (431) in Ditch 2D Slot J produced various sedge and grass seeds, suggesting these were species growing on the ground where the fire was set. The second context was the fill (051) of fire-pit (050) which produced large numbers of fathen and redshank seeds, with single seeds of brome grass, black bindweed and dead nettle type. Both fathen and redshank plants can produce many hundreds of seeds per plant and so the large numbers of seeds may just be from a few plants growing on the site on which the fire was set. They are particularly common on nutrient-rich soils associated with human habitation.

Other Food Plants

Other than cereal grains, the only other food plant remains recorded from the site were fragments of hazel nutshell. Traces of hazel nutshell were found in many samples across the site, suggesting that it was a relatively commonly eaten foodstuff but there is no evidence for any large quantities of nutshell that might suggest processing or storage of hazel nuts on the site.

Micromorphology

By Carol Laing

Introduction

This report summarises the findings arising out of the micromorphological analysis of undisturbed sediment samples collected from the archaeological investigation by GUARD Archaeology of Broxy Kennels Fort. Micromorphological investigation of the soil thin sections will provide high resolution analysis of the pedological features and determine depositional processes and composition of the sediment in the sample locations. Additionally, micromorphological investigation will determine if there is any visible evidence to indicate anthropogenic alterations to the fill.

Geoarchaeological and archaeological significance

The application of micromorphological techniques to the Broxy Kennels Fort samples - the microscopic analysis of soil/sediment thin sections - can play a significant role in archaeological and palaeoenvironmental investigation particularly when carried out with a methodical approach to observations and their interpretation.

Soil/sediment properties reflect the environment in which they have been formed, and so the recovery of known anthropic sediments from archaeological contexts has the potential to assist archaeologists to understand complex site formation processes related to past land use and the palaeo-environment. By applying micromorphological investigation to undisturbed soils it enables soil development properties to be examined: thickness, bedding, particle size, sorting, coarse to fine ratios, composition of the fine material, groundmass, colour, related distribution, microstructure, and distribution of inclusions, the shape of inclusions, and finally the inclusions to be identified and quantified. Additionally, these analyses can provide details of micro-artefacts, not seen by the naked eye during macromorphological analysis.

Methodology

The four undisturbed sediment samples were collected during archaeological excavation of Broxy Kennels Fort. They were from Ditch 1S Slot B, Ditch 3S (interface between the original ditch and its recut) and the lowest fills in the Souterrain. The samples were dried and then impregnated using an epoxy-based resin under vacuum. The impregnated soils were cured, and then sliced, bonded to glass slides and precision lapped to 30μm thickness to produce soil thin sections.

By following procedures laid out in the International Handbook for Thin Section Description (Bullock et al. 1985) and Guidelines to Analysis and Description of Soil Regolith Thin Sections (Stoops 2003) soil properties were recorded semi-quantitatively and adapted specifically for the Broxy Kennels Fort samples. The thin sections were analysed using an Olympus polarizing microscope at a range of magnifications (x10–x400) and under Plane Polarized Light (PPL), Crossed Polarized Light (XPL) and where applicable Oblique Incident Light (OIL). Each light source allowed identification of specific microscopic features, such as, mineral and organic components, pedology and feature classification. All features observed were recorded on an Excel spread sheet with the limit of the coarse to fine material being 20 μm (c/f20 μm).

Results and Interpretation

The following sections show characterisation and interpretations of seven micromorphological thin sections from Broxy Kennels Fort, with a summary of the frequency and type of pedofeatures in each thin section recorded in a supplementary table (Table 31).

Macro Analysis

Macro analysis of the soil thin section from CTLR indicated that there were similar pedogenic processes occurring in sample TS137 (Ditch 1S, Slot B) and TS534 (lowest fill in the Souterrain), both displaying a moderately developed blocky microstructure. In contrast, sample TS118 (Ditch 3S) exhibited a homogenous, massive,

Course Material

Thin Section No	Region	Related Distribution	c/f [20µm] distribution (ratio)	Rock/Mineral Quartz	Basalt	Feldspar	Glauconite	Organic Charcoal	Woody Material	Groundmass PPL	XPL	Peds	Voids	Development	Pedofeatures Redoximorphic nodules	Clay infillings
118		Enaulic	4:1	****	***	**	**	*		Dotted	Speckled	Apedal /Massive	Chambers, Vughs	Weak	**	
137		Enaulic	3:2	****	***	**		***		Dotted	Speckled	SA-B	Channels, Chambers Vughs	Strong	**	
533	1	Enaulic	3:2	****	***	**		**		Dotted	Speckled	SA-B	Channels, Chambers Vughs	Moderate	**	
533	2	Enaulic	3:2					****	*****	Dotted	Speckled	SA-B	Channels, Chambers Vughs	Moderate	**	
533	3	Enaulic	3:2					**		Dotted	Speckled	SA-B	Channels, Chambers Vughs	Moderate	**	
534	4	Enaulic	3:2	****	***	**		***		Dotted	Speckled	SA-B	Channels, Chambers Vughs	Moderate	**	***

All measurements indicated are semi quantitative

*Key: Peds: SA-B-Sub-angular blocky; Frequency: * Infrequent (<2%); *Low (2-5%); ***Moderate (5-10%); **** High (10-20%); *****Very High (>20); N/A: Not applicable*

Table 31: Supplementary table with a summary of the main micromorphological observations and the frequency of the feaures from the thin section collected at Broxy Kennels Fort.

apedal microstructure. TS533 (lowest fill in the Souterrain) displayed diffused boundaries between depositional layers; Region 2 and the lower Region 1 and upper Region 3. The lower Region 1 and Region 2 both exhibiting weakly developed blocky microstructures, while Region 3 has an apedal microstructure.

The coarse mineral and rock materials observed in the thin sections from this location are comprised mainly of rounded and sub rounded quartz (~40%) and quartzite (~10%), sub rounded and angular basalt (~10%) and feldspar (~2%). There are infrequent inclusions of rounded glauconite (2%) evident in sample TS118 (Ditch 3S). The

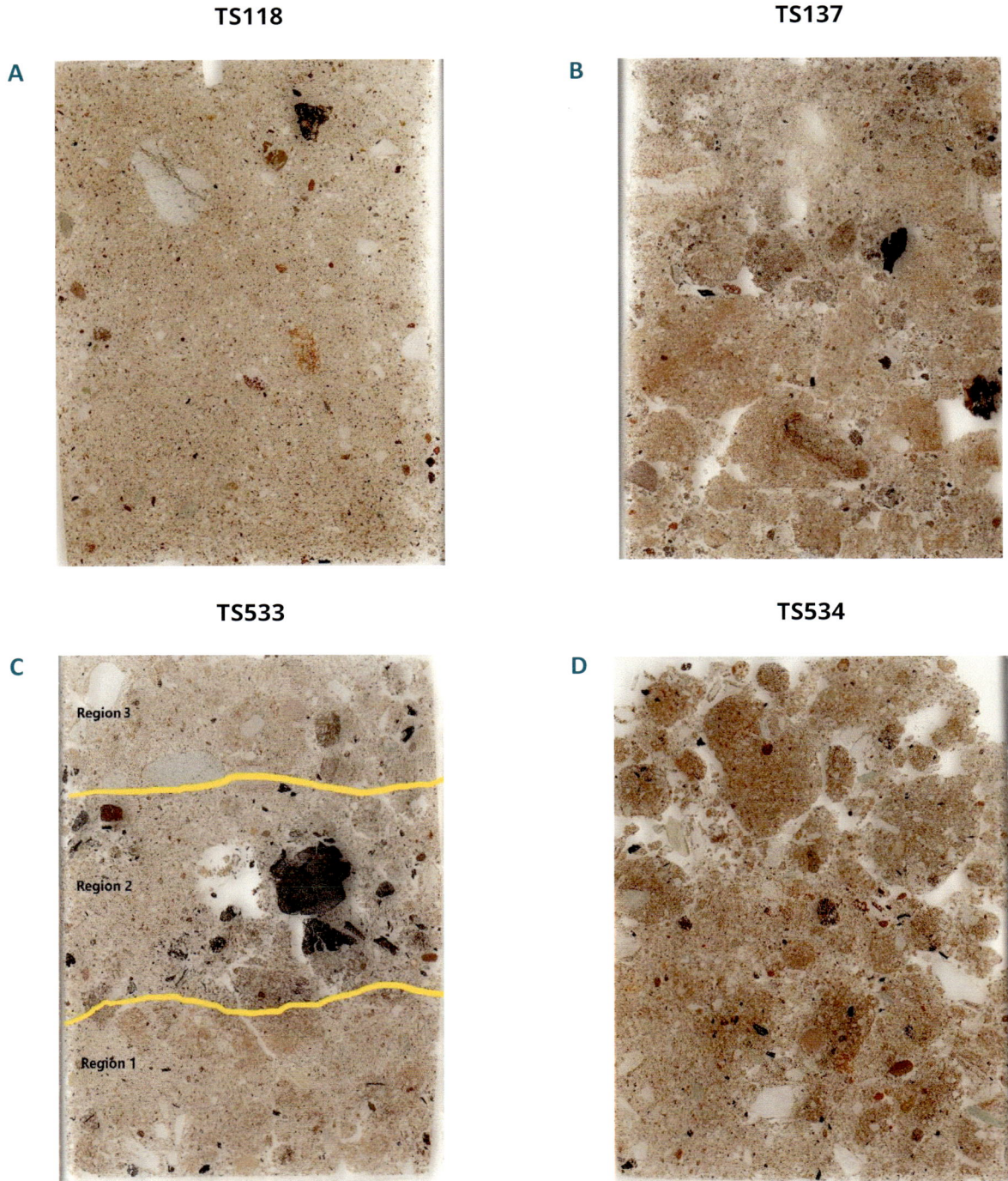

TS118

A

TS137

B

TS533

C

Region 3

Region 2

Region 1

TS534

D

Figure 49: Thin sections TS118 (Ditch 3S), TS137 (Ditch 1 S, Slot B), TS533 and TS534 (both lowest fills of the Souterrain) from the sample collected at Broxy Kennels Fort. Sample TS533 is annotated to indicate the difference in the composition of Region 2 compared to Region 1 below and Region 3 above. The boundaries between the regions being defused.

composition of the ground mass in the thin section deriving from the localised geology. The coarse to fine ratio (c/f) was similar in samples TS137, TS533 and TS534 (3:2), with sample TS118 displaying a 4:1 c/f ratio. The samples displayed an enaulic related distribution; derived from the configuration of the coarse and fine material in the sediment (Stoops 2003). The limpidity of the groundmass in PPL illumination was similar in all the samples; displaying a dotted appearance due to the presence of dark micro-fragments (>20 μm) (Macphail and Goldberg 2010). The b-fabric identified under XPL was speckled in all samples due to the presence of clay colloids in the fine matrix. Charcoal was exhibited in all sample (OIL), sample TS118 (Ditch 3S) displaying the lowest frequency (~<2%) with most fragment being microcharcoal <20 μm, Region 2 of sample TS533 displayed the highest frequency of charcoal (~20%). Wood-like material, in varying stages of degradation, was observed in samples TS137 and TS533 (Figure 49B and 49C), sample TS533 (from the lowest Souterrain fills) displaying the highest frequency (>20%) (Table 31) and largest inclusions (>2500 μm) (Figure 49C).

The moderately developed microstructure identified in samples TS137, TS533 and TS534 was sub-angular block and the peds were separated by inter-pedal channel voids, while intra-pedal chambers and vughs were identified in the peds. Sample TS534 (from the Souterrain floor) displayed large channel voids, indicating greater distance between peds, see in Figure 1. Sample TS118 (Ditch 3S) displayed apedality with the massive microstructure exhibiting intra-pedal chambers and vughs. Redoximorphic nodules were evident in samples TS118, TS134 and TS534, reduction and oxidation processes continuing to occur in sample TS533 and TS534 (both from the lowest Souterrain fills) with iron (Fe) rich accumulations observed. Clay translocation was observed in TS534, with the formation of limpid clay infilling in intra-pedal voids of the fine matrix (Figure 49D).

Discussion

Micromorphological investigation determined that the composition of the coarse rock and mineral inclusions in the samples (TS118, TS134, TS533 and TS534) were derived from the localised geology. The rock and mineral inclusions

identified in all of the samples were weathered or partially weathered, with only sample TS118 (Ditch 3S) displaying angular basalt and weather glauconite. These inclusions within the samples would indicate that there has been incorporation of material from another area, due to their infrequency. Glauconite forms in geological time in shallow seas not indicative of the locale, while the angularity of the basalt would suggest there was little weathering after the fragment had broken off a larger piece.

The microstructure in samples TS137, TS533 and TS534 were moderately developed, displaying sub-angular blocky peds. The moderate frequency of organic matter in the form of charcoal and the presence of intra-pedal vughs indicates aggregation of the soil colloids allowing the formation of the peds in the groundmass (Oades 1984). The formation of Fe nodules and Fe inclusions also requires the presence of organic matter, this acting as a catalyst in the reduction, precipitation and dissolution of Fe (Lindbo et al. 2010). A high frequency of charcoal inclusions was observed on Region 2 of sample TS533 (the lowest fill of the souterrain), additionally a high level of wood-like material was also observed, in varying degrees of degradation. The presence of charcoal inclusions, microcharcoal and wood like material suggest that there has been anthropogenic activity in the local environment (Adderley et al. 2010). The difference in the degradation of the wood-like material would suggest an amalgamation of the sediments took place prior to deposition in Region 2, with wood-like material incorporated into the soil at different times. The diffused boundaries between Region 2 and the lower Region 1 and upper Region 3 of sample TS533 (the lowest fill of the Souterrain) point to mixing of the deposits after they had been laid down during different depositional events. The mixing of the soil to form the diffused boundary indicates that there had been no compaction prior to Region 2 being deposited on Region 1, and again when Region 3 was deposited onto Region 2. There are no indications of compaction pedofeatures, the frequency of wood-like material and charcoal being the only significant indicator of different depositional processes forming the 3 regions. Once the regions had been deposited in phase one of soil formation, phase 2 of the soil pedogenesis occurred with the formation of voids between the regions thus the overall microstructure developed.

The formation of compound limpid clay infillings observed in sample TS534 (lowest fill of the Souterrain) indicates that there has been clay eluviation at this location, the movement of soil down the soil profile by water action. The formation of the compound infillings occurred through a series of depositional events forming the compound infilling morphology. Clay colloids percolate through the soil profile dissolved in soil water, this occurs due to changes in the pH of the soil above (Kühn et al. 2018). This suggests that there were processes in the soil above the sample location that would alter the soil pH; such as the incorporation of organic matter.

It is evident (Figures 49 and 50) that sample TS118 (Ditch 3S) is apedal and displays no microstructure, with only intra-pedal chambers and vughs present within the massive soil matrix. Apedality in sample TS118 suggests several possible hypotheses: 1) settling of the soil in this sample region had occurred or; 2) high aggregation levels had resulted in the development of large peds not identified through micromorphology. It is evident that there were reduction and oxidation processes taking place in this sample location, thus the translocation of Fe through the soil profile. As stated earlier in this report, organic matter is required in this process, and due to the presence of organic matter soil aggregation would be taking place. If the soil were to have settled then there would be no intra-pedal chamber voids and vughs visible in the thin section, however this is not the case. It is therefore concluded, that the peds are too large to be observed through micromorphology (Lang 2014).

Conclusions

The undisturbed soil samples collected from the archaeological investigation of the site at Broxy Kennels Fort indicated that the sediment in the samples was derived from localised parent material. It is evident that there is differentiation in the pedogenic processes between the samples at the site. However, there is little notable difference between the composition of the groundmass in samples. Sample TS118 (from Ditch 3S) being the exception.

Glauconite and angular basalt in sample TS118 indicates that there have been inclusions into the soil not derived from the localised area. Glauconite does not match the local geological signature. However, this is a singular event. While the inclusion of angular basalt indicates fragmentation of basalt, however there is no evidence to indicate the method of fragmentation.

Although charcoal is apparent in all the samples there is a distinct difference in the size of the charcoal fragments, with TS118 containing infrequent charcoal and micro-charcoal. It was evident the Region 2 of sample TS533 (from the lowest fill of the Souterrain) that there was a mix of charcoal and wood-like material, the latter displaying varying stages of degradation, thus indicating they were incorporated into the soil over different events or from different locales, as the groundmass composition was the sample. The formation of sample TS533 occurring over three different deposition events, the surface of the event not being compacted due to diffusion of the boundaries between the deposits

The presence of compound limpid clay infillings in sample TS534 (lowest fill of the Souterrain) is evidence that there was a change in the pH of the soil in the upper horizons. The compound morphology indicating that the eluviation of the clays had been deposited during several events.

It is evident that micromorphological analysis has provided high resolution data on the pedogenic formation of the soil thin sections. The analysis has identified soil formation in the samples was similar in three of the four samples; TS118 displaying difference in microstructure. It is however evidence that there is anthropogenic signature in all the samples, in the form of charcoal and wood-like material, this indicating human activity in the localised environment.

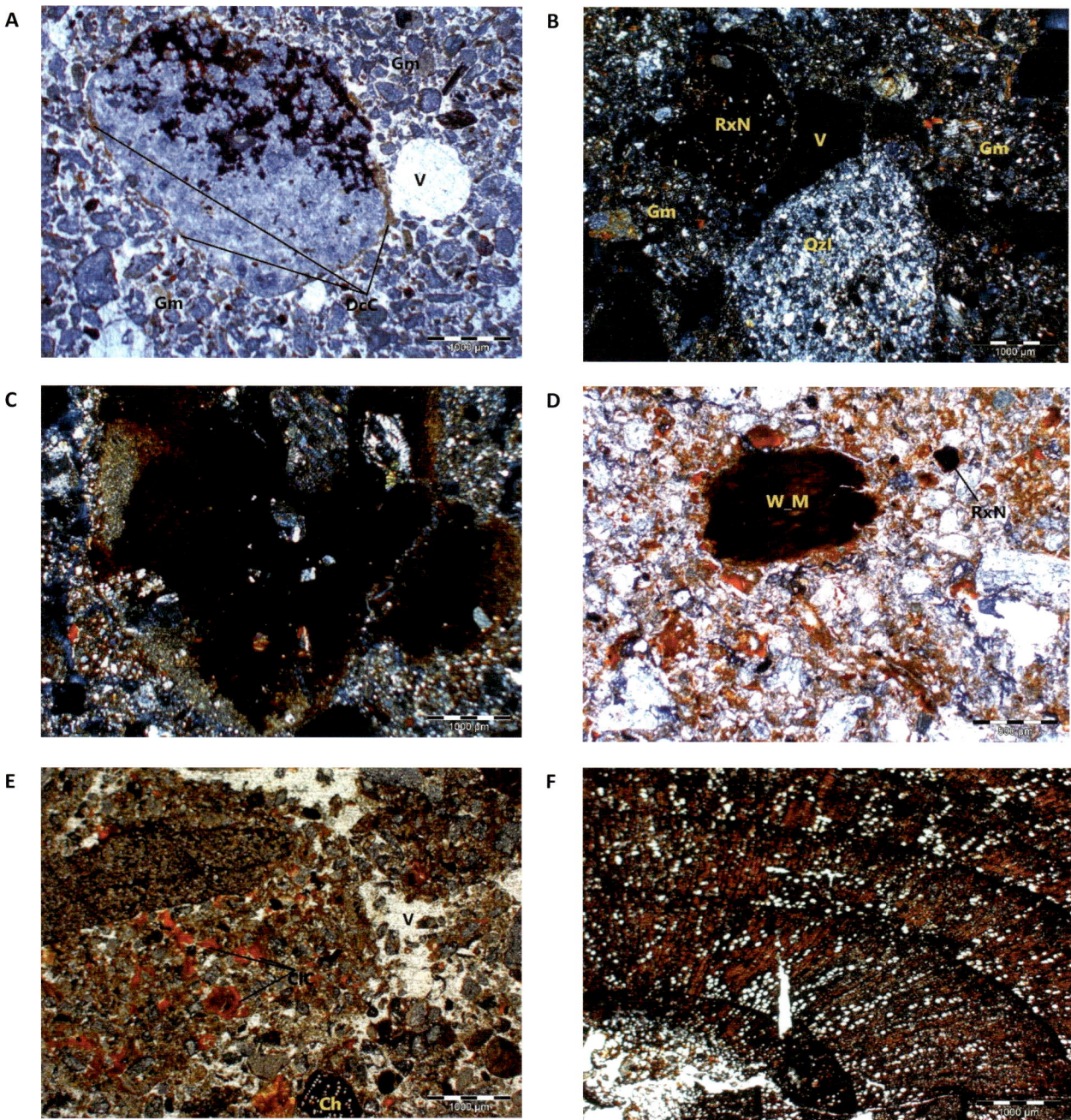

Figure 50: A. Dusty coatings (DcC) formed on a large rock/mineral inclusion and next to a chamber void (V) in TS118 (Ditch 3S) (PPL); B. Redoximorphic aggregate nodule (RxN) formed in the groundmass (Gm) of sample TS137 (Ditch 1S, Slot B) adjacent to a quartzite inclusion (QzI) (XPL); C. D. Wood-like material (W_M) in the matrix of sample TS137 and the formation of a small, typic redoximorphic nodule (RxN), E. Fragmented clay infillings (ClC) in the groundmass of sample TS534 (lowest fill of the souterrain) (PPL); F. Large woody material exhibited in sample TS533 (lowest fill of the Souterrain) (PPL).

Multi-element analysis of souterrain deposits

Dr Clare Wilson

Background and Aims

Broxy Kennels multivallate Fort was first identified based on crop marks in RCAHMS oblique aerial photographs. The possible presence of a souterrain overlying the 2nd ditch was also identified in the aerial photographs and it has been speculated that the souterrain indicates occupation in the 1st and 2nd centuries AD after the fort defences had gone out of use (Lock and Ralston 2017). No trace of the souterrain was identified by geophysical survey (Burton 2018), however, the presence of a stone-built souterrain was confirmed to the west of the fort's entranceway during the archaeological evaluation in 2019 (Pettitt and Hession 2019). This structure comprised a stone-walled sunken linear feature with a stone-flagged floor, approximately 1.67 m deep from the modern ground surface. The souterrain floor was overlain by four separate deposits, the second uppermost of which contained burnt wood. The fort and souterrain were excavated by GUARD Archaeology Ltd in 2022 as part of the Cross Tay Links Road archaeological works.

This report presents the results of the geochemical analyses of samples from the basal deposits of the souterrain with the aim of identifying differential patterns in the elemental composition that may help to identify patterns of space use and activity.

Environmental background

The local bedrock geology of the site is mapped by the BGS as sedimentary, Devonian Sandstone of the Scone Sandstone Formation, this is overlain by superficial Quaternary raised marine deposits of clay, silt, sand and gravel, and Quaternary fluvio-glacial deposits of silt, sand and gravel (British Geological Survey, 2024). The local soils are mapped by the Soil Survey of Scotland as Corby series humus-iron podzols of the Corby association, with areas nearby of Carey series imperfectly drained brown earths of the

Carpow association and Harviestoun series non-calcareous gleys of the Carbrook association (Soil Survey of Scotland 2024). The current land use is agricultural with improved pasture and arable.

Methods

The basal deposit of the souterrain structure was sampled using a 0.2 m grid system covering the base of almost the entire surviving structure. A sub-sample of these (50 small bulk samples) were provided for multi-element analysis. Eight of these samples were control samples taken from the local subsoil (context 002). Three of the control samples were taken from the south slope (359, 360 and 361) of the site, the other control samples were taken from the north slope (362, 363, 364 and 365). The remaining 42 samples represent a transect along the length (long axis) and width (short axis) of the souterrain as shown in Figure 51. The souterrain samples represented three different contexts:

- Context 95: firm light greyish-brown sandy clay with frequent small stone and charcoal fleck inclusions,

- Context 156: dark greyish-black sandy clay area, which was very charcoal rich,

- Context 157: firm greyish-brown silty clay, with frequent small sub-rounded pebble and charcoal fleck inclusions.

Samples were oven dried at 105°C and sieved through a 1 mm stainless steel sieve to remove any gravels and coarse sands. Compressed sample pellets 2 cm in diameter were created using a Perkin-Elmer hand operated press with 12 tonnes of applied pressure.

For the multi-element analysis a bench-mounted portable X-ray fluorescence analyser (NITON XL3t-Goldd+, Thermo Scientific was operated in Cu/Zn mining mode with a run time of 60 seconds per analysis. Four analyses were made of each sample (2 on each side of the pellet) with the sample moved between each analytical run so that a representative area of the pressed pellet surface was analysed. Elemental concentrations were calculated using a theoretical calibration model (Hf/Ta) from the resultant spectra.

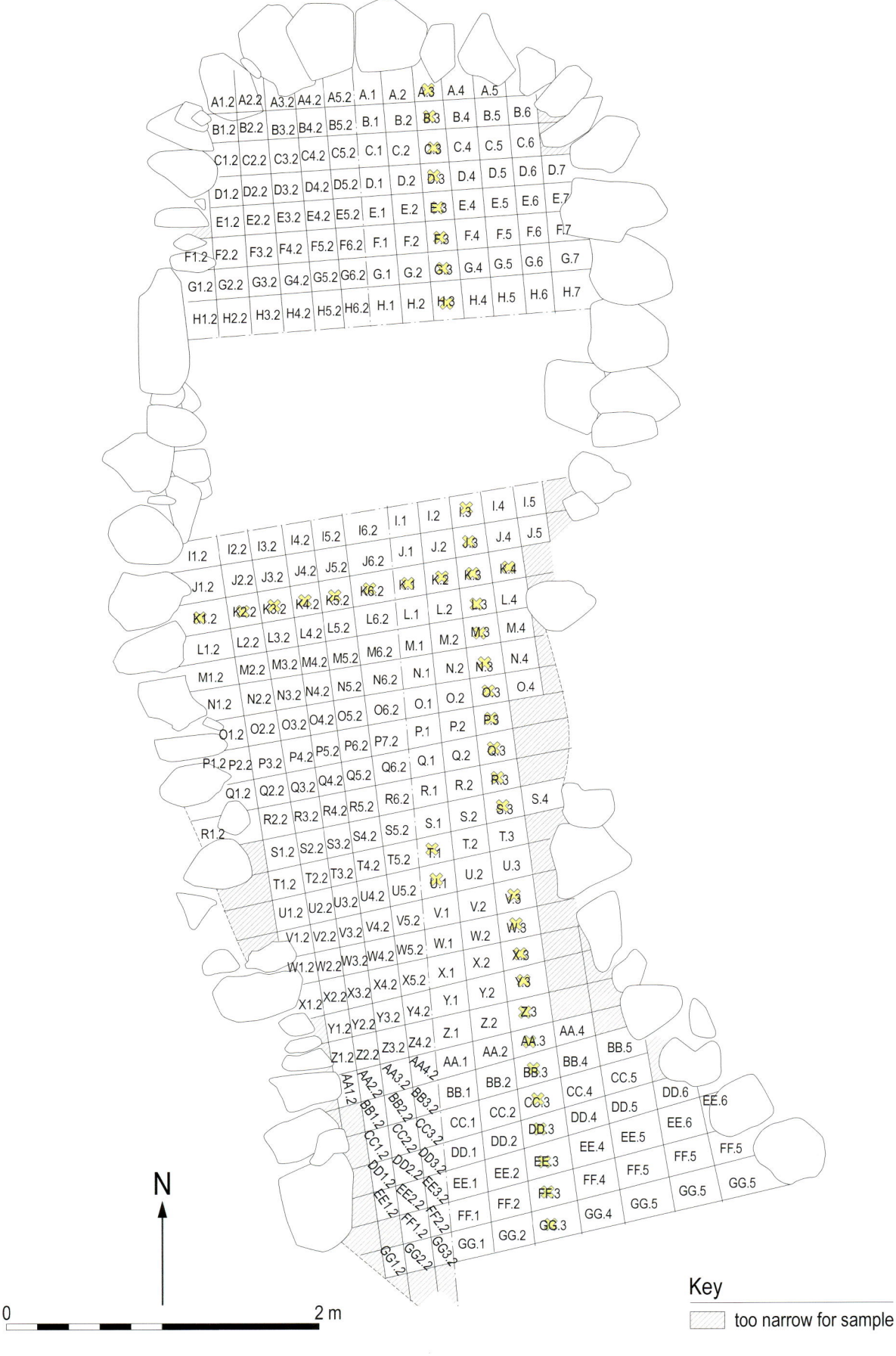

Figure 51: Excavation plan of Trench 4 showing the grid used for soil sampling, the sub-set of samples subject to multi-element analysis is marked with yellow crosses.

Mean concentrations were calculated from the four replicate analyses, for all elements within the instrumental limits of detection. Data analysis used SPSS 29.0 and R Studio 3.1.4.0. Missing values that were below detection limit were replaced with proxy values 10% below the detection limit, rounded to 1 significant figure for the purposes of analysis. Mann-Whitney U tests were applied to test for differences in concentrations between the controls and the souterrain floor samples, Kruskal-Wallis analysis was applied to test for differences between contexts, and a Principal Components Analysis with varimax rotation was used to identify groupings of elemental responses and groupings of samples along the first three component axes.

Results

The complete table of average soil sample concentrations is presented in Appendix 3. Elemental concentrations in the souterrain samples were first compared with those of the control samples using an independent samples Mann Whitney U test to identify significant differences. The results are presented in Table 32. This identified that chemically the controls and souterrain samples are generally similar, however statistically significant differences were identified for iron (Fe), aluminium (Al), phosphorus (P), titanium (Ti) and silicon (Si).

Element	Significance (p value)	Element	Significance (p value)
Barium (Ba)	0.576	Manganese (Mn)	0.507
Zirconium (Zr)	0.524	Chromium (Cr)	0.397
Strontium (Sr)	0.13	Vanadium (V)	0.805
Rubidium (Rb)	0.168	Titanium (Ti)	<.001
Zinc (Zn)	0.185	Calcium (Ca)	0.524
Iron (Fe)	<.001	Potassium (K)	0.354
Aluminium (Al)	<.001	Silicon (Si)	<.001
Phosphorus (P)	<.001	Sulphur (S)	0.969
Magnesium (Mg)	0.746		

Table 32: Results of the independent samples Mann-Whitney U Test of concentrations between the souterrain and control samples.

Of those elements demonstrating a significant difference in concentration between the souterrain and the control samples, for Si, Al, Ti and P the concentrations were markedly higher in the souterrain samples than in the controls, whilst for Fe the concentrations were higher in the control samples (Figure 52). In general, the variance in concentrations was either similar between the controls and souterrain samples or was higher in the controls.

Kruskal-Wallis analysis identified significant differences between contexts for Fe, Al, P, Ti and Si, but additionally also for Cr and S. Pairwise analysis between contexts for Fe, Al, P, Ti and Si revealed no significant differences other than between each of the souterrain base contexts and the control samples (context 002). For Cr and S (Figure 53) significant differences between souterrain contexts do emerge. For S, there is no significant difference between the controls (002) and any of the souterrain contexts. However, concentrations of S in context 95 are significantly lower than in either contexts 156 or 157. For Cr, there is no significant difference between the controls (002) and any of the souterrain contexts. However, concentrations of Cr in context 156 are significantly higher than in either contexts 95 or 157. Whilst concentrations between the souterrain contexts differ, not context differs significantly from the controls which exhibit a high variance in concentrations.

To better understand the element patterns and behaviours at the site a Principal Components Analysis was conducted using all the samples and all the detected elements. The first three components account for 48% of the variance in the dataset and the plotted elements against these first three components (Figure 54) demonstrates the relationship between component 1 and these five significantly different elements with Fe having the lowest score on component 1 and Si, Al, Ti and P the highest. Plotting sample regression scores against components 1 and 2, highlights the importance of control (context 002) versus souterrain sample (contexts 95, 156, 157) origin with respect to component 1. Against components 2 and 3, there is also separation of souterrain contexts 95 and 156 as suggested by the S and Cr results.

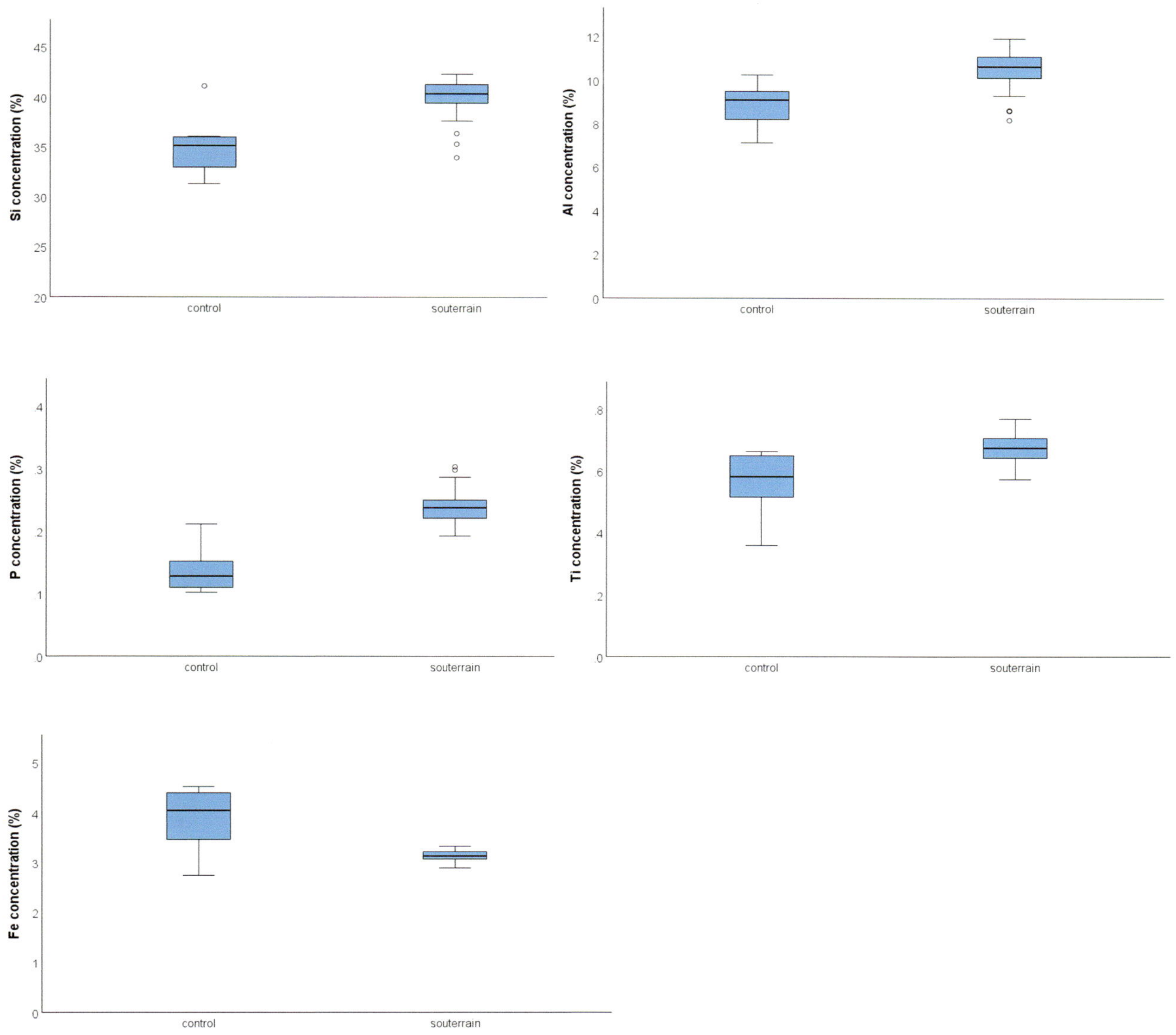

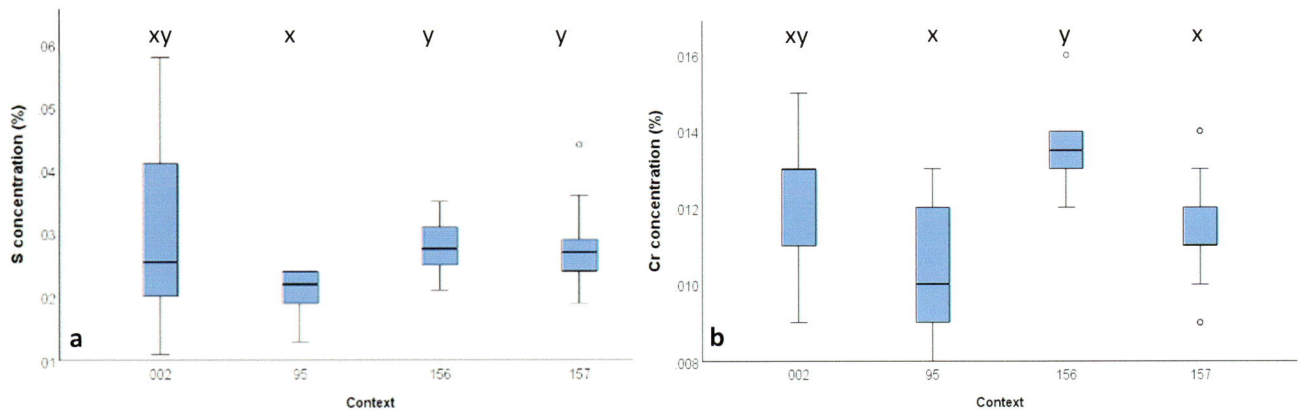

Figure 52: Box plots showing concentrations of Fe, Al, P, Ti and Si in the souterrain and control samples.

Figure 53: Boxplot of a) S and b) Cr concentrations by context. Shared letters indicate no significant difference between contexts.

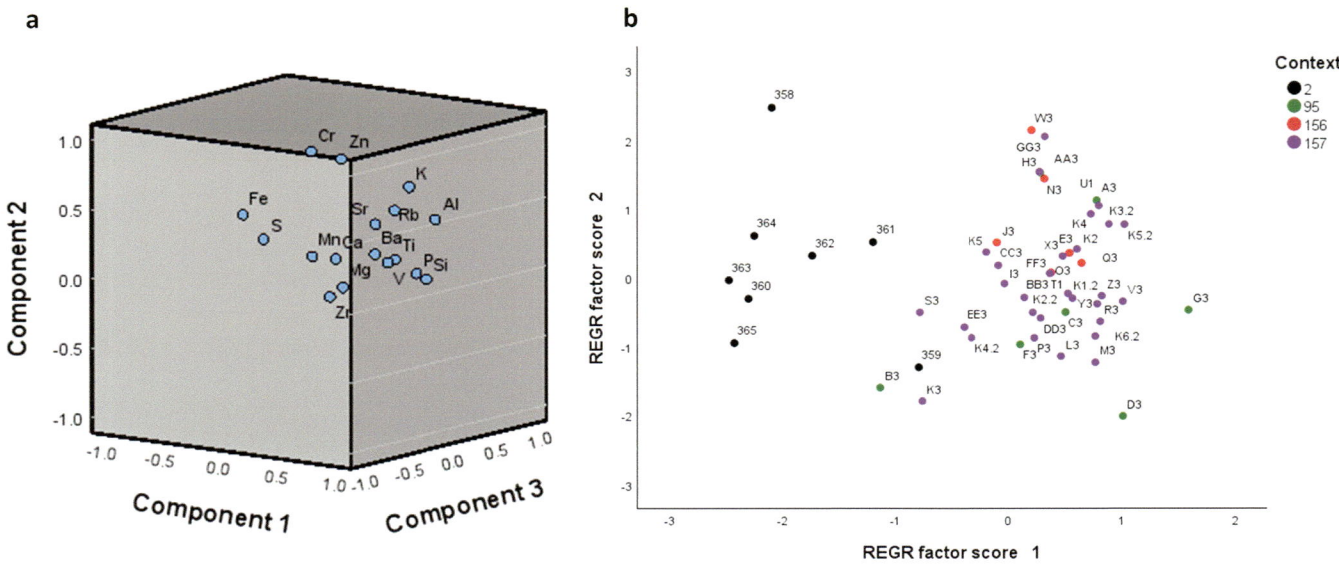

Figure 54: a) Elements plotted against the first three components, b) Sample regression factor scores plotted against component 1 and 2.

Plotting elemental concentrations along the length and width of the souterrain revealed few clear trends. Concentrations of S tend to increase from east to west (Figure 55) along the length of the souterrain. Fe, Si, Ti, Cr and P concentrations showed no such trend, nor were any distinct areas of concentration or depletion identified; variance in concentrations appeared random along the length of the souterrain. Across its width, from north to south, there was a noticeable drop in Fe concentrations. No other trends or patterns were identified.

Discussion

The local Corby series soils are inherently free draining and acidic with low concentrations of exchangeable cations and low concentrations of P and trace elements in the mineral soil (Laing 1976). The naturally low trace element soil concentrations in the local soils are supported by the below detection limit concentrations of elements such as copper (Cu) and cobalt (Co) in these samples. The low cation exchange capacity of these soils (Laing 1976) is one reason for this, and this may also affect the soil's ability to retain the elemental signatures of added materials.

The elements that have most commonly been associated with anthropogenic activity in archaeological contexts are variously P, N, Ca, Pb, Zn, Cu, K and Mg (Wilson et al. 2008; Oonk et al. 2009; Arroyo-Kalin 2014; Salisbury 2020).

The Broxy Kennels site is interesting as the only one of these elements that demonstrates an elevated concentration within the souterrain structure compared to the controls is P, the other significant patterns are for Si, Fe, Ti and Al. These are elements that traditionally are more strongly associated with geological and pedogenic processes rather than being anthropogenic markers (Wilson et al. 2007; Oonk et al. 2009). Of these geogenic elements Fe concentrations are lower in the souterrain samples than in the controls, whilst Si, Ti and Al have significantly higher concentrations in the souterrain samples. The main sources of Si in Scottish soils are from silicate minerals, predominantly quartz, whilst Si and Al are associated with alumina-silicate clay minerals and Ti is a common soil element associated with mafic minerals such as ilmenite.

Phosphate concentrations in the control sub-soil samples from Broxy Kennels range from a minimum concentration of .102% and a maximum of .211% with an average concentration of .137%. In the Souterrain samples the minimum concentration of P was .193% and the maximum .304% with a mean concentration of .237% (Figure 52). There was no significant difference in the concentrations of P within the different contexts that were analysed from in the souterrain. Total concentrations of P in similar podzolic Corby association sub-soils are recorded elsewhere in the region of 0.07-0.21% (Laing 1976), which

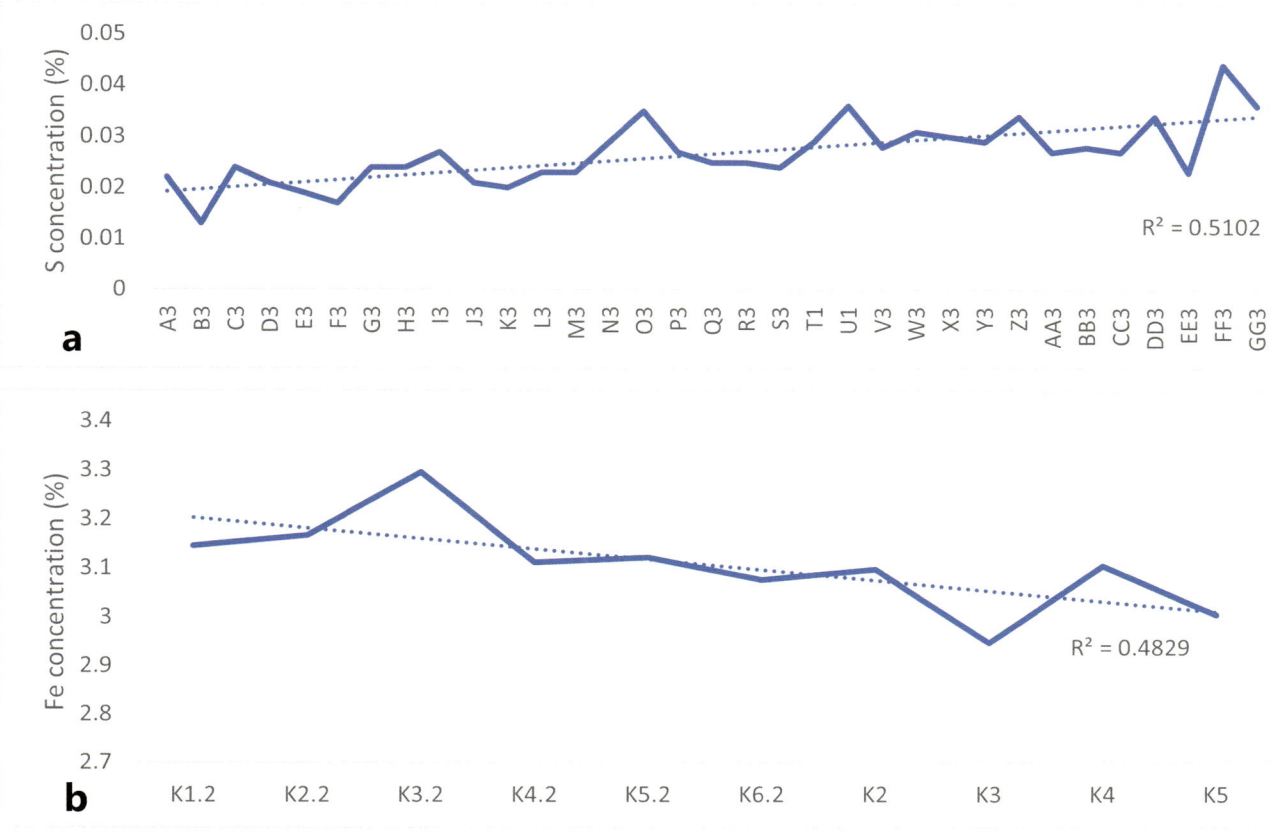

Figure 55: Element concentrations plotted by sample locations within the souterrain. a) S concentrations along the length (east A3 to west GG3); b) Fe concentrations across its breadth (north K1.2 to south K5).

is in line with the concentrations recorded in the control samples. However, the elevated concentrations seen within the archaeological soils would place these soils within the upper 95% quartile for P concentrations in mineral soils in Scotland (Paterson 2011) and clearly indicates anthropogenic enhancement.

Phosphate is typically enhanced in any area with sustained human activity. It is indicative of organic material and whilst particularly enhanced in grave and midden soils (for example Davidson et al. 2007; Pickering et al. 2018), more moderate levels of enhancement as seen at Broxy Kennels can result from any activity that adds small amounts of organic material to the soils. In archaeological contexts P is often associated with enhanced levels of other elements such as Ca, Cu, Zn, Pb, K and Mg. The fact that these, often co-occurring elements were absent at Broxy Kennels and that P was most closely correlated with Si (Figure 52a) perhaps suggests that 'fresh' organic materials were being added (deliberately or accidently) in relatively limited amounts, directly

to 'clean' locally derived sub-soil type materials. However, the presence of charcoal suggests that these soils have been subject to the addition of burnt material residues which would normally add a wider suite of elements such as K, Mg, S and various metals such as Pb and Cr (Pierce et al. 1998; Wilson et al. 2008). Another explanation is that in these acidic free draining soils, which have a low capacity to bind and retain cation elements, other elements have been leached away and only P remains. Phosphorus is always found naturally in its oxidised phosphate form. As an anion phosphate behaves differently to other soils elements and can be strongly bound by clay minerals and Fe oxides (Ahmed et al. 2023).

Concentrations of Cr and S also differed between the archaeological contexts (Figure 53), with the highest concentrations in context 156 which was also noted to contain the highest quantities of charcoal so there may be a correlation between these elements and inputs of burnt residues to the soils. It was also noted (Figure 55a) that sulphur concentrations are highest towards the western entrance of the souterrain and decrease along its length, perhaps suggesting more intense activity towards the entrance area. However, it must be noted that the local variance of these elements in the sub-soil is high and no significant difference was identified between the concentrations in context 156 and the control samples.

Patterns of Fe concentration (Figures 52 and 55b) likely reflects podzolisation and drainage patterns in these soils and sediments rather than anthropogenic inputs. In these free drained podzolic soils Fe is mobilised from the upper horizons and deposited in the sub-soil horizons (Ashman and Puri 2013) explaining the higher concentrations in the sub-soil derived controls. It's also possible that the stone base of the souterrain impeded drainage and created localised waterlogging (gleying) which may also lower Fe concentrations in the souterrain deposits although the lack of correlation between Fe and Mn (Figure 54) suggests this is not an important process here.

Conclusion

Overall, the geochemistry of the Broxy Kennels souterrain samples indicates past anthropogenic activity but is inconclusive as to the nature of that activity or its intensity. Given the free draining and podzolised nature of these soils, the wider suite of elements that we might expect associated for example with the charcoal in the sediments appear to have been lost due to leaching leaving only the natural minerals and an enhanced concentration of more tightly bound phosphate.

Animal Bone

By Catherine Smith

Introduction and condition of the bone

Animal bone fragments were recovered from the excavations at Broxy Kennels Fort. Recovery methods were hand excavation and sieving of soil samples during the post-excavation process. With the exception of the fore parts of a horse, thought to be of relatively modern origin, bone fragments from the site were of very small size, were much affected by erosion and frequently showed signs of having been subjected to high temperatures. The majority of the bone fragments recovered from soil samples were burnt or calcined.

Condition of the bone is described in the accompanying catalogue in terms of observed surface abrasion, density and friability, using a numerical scoring system. On this basis the most poorly preserved bone would score only 4 points while the best could potentially score 17 points. Across the site, preservation scores were low; the highest scoring bone was part of a rabbit pelvis which can be assumed was fairly recent (score: 12) while the lowest score (5) was applicable to some very small tooth enamel fragments.

Species present

The Catalogue (Appendix 4) and Tables 33 and 34 present details of the elements found and the areas from which the fragments originated. The following species or taxon groups were identified at the site:

- cattle/cf cattle (5), large ungulate (2),
- sheep/goat (1; BS sample only), ?small ungulate (1)
- ungulate (100; tooth enamel fragments in BS sample only)
- pig (1; BS sample only)
- horse/cf horse (10, possibly modern)
- rabbit (1, probably modern)
- indeterminate mammal (270 in hand-excavated component; fragments in sieved soil samples (BS) not counted/included).

Cattle, sheep/goat and pig remains came from archaeological deposits likely dating to the Iron Age while those of horse and rabbit were thought to be of more recent origin. The horse bones, with the exception of an upper cheek tooth, consisted of parts of the left and right scapulae, several thoracic vertebrae and a few rib fragments, likely also horse. The size of the scapulae indicated an animal of moderate size, perhaps of the stature of a pony. Slight new bone formation around the vertebral articulations indicated some degree of arthritis. The rabbit bone is probably from an animal which had burrowed into the site deposits but in any case is thought to be of medieval date at the earliest.

Locations of bone across the site (Tables 33 and 34)

Hand-excavated bone fragments were recovered from deposits within the series of ditches surrounding the fort, from souterrain fills and from miscellaneous posthole or pit fills (Table 33). With the exception of some small mandible fragments, probably from cattle and from which the teeth were absent (Ditch D1N-Slot D, 124, SF 110), none of the hand-excavated fragments found in the ditches could be identified as anything other than indeterminate mammal. Souterrain fills were similarly lacking in faunal material - one bone shaft fragment could have come from an immature small ungulate (069, SF 180) but most of the fragments associated with the souterrain were from indeterminate mammal.

Although numerous soil samples were collected from the ditches surrounding the fort, their faunal inclusions, as with the hand-excavated assemblage, consisted mainly of tiny fragments of calcined bone which could only be described as indeterminate mammal (Table 34). However, cattle and ungulate (sheep/goat/cattle) fragments were also noted in sieved samples. Part of a calcined cattle third phalange came from Ditch D1N, Slot B (105, BS 112), some large ungulate cf cattle tooth enamel from Ditch D1S Slot A (035, BS 035) and fragments of ungulate tooth enamel from a later pit in Ditch D4N Slot E (982, BS 1187).

Soil sampling provided the only evidence of sheep/goat and pig on the site. A calcined fragment of sheep/goat distal metapodial was extracted from a sample taken from Area 4 (946, BS 1171) and a pig tooth enamel fragment from a small pit in Area 3 (499, BS 1100). For full list of samples, see Appendix 4.

Discussion

As is so often the case with rural archaeological sites in Tayside and Fife, soil conditions are not conducive to good bone preservation. Acidic soils are the main culprit in poor bone survival, particularly if they are free-draining. Waterlogged deposits, which exclude the aerobic micro-organisms which contribute to bone decomposition, were unfortunately not found at Broxy Kennels Fort. The preservative action of deposition in a waterlogged environment of a similar date is amply illustrated by the excellent condition of bone recovered from a cistern at the hillfort of Castle Law, Abernethy. When excavated in the Victorian period, the cistern had contained 'about two feet of water' and the bones were dyed 'jet black', a characteristic of well-preserved bone (Christison and Anderson 1899, 24; Robertson 2023, 224). Calcined bone however does survive slightly better than unburnt bone in poor soil conditions, due to recrystallisation of the bones' inorganic structure, and it was notable that many of the fragments recovered in the soil samples from Broxy Kennels Fort had indeed been exposed to high temperatures.

The souterrain was equally disappointing in the amount of faunal evidence which it contained - although sieved soil samples contained burnt bone, much of this consisted of small fragments of indeterminate mammal, with the exception of one bone from a small ungulate, possibly sheep. However, souterrains in this part of Scotland have rarely produced much in the way of bone; for example Watkins and Barclay (1981, 189, 197) report that at the souterrain of Newmill, near Bankfoot, there was a 'scant harvest of animal remains' and of these all were identified as belonging to cattle. At Shanzie Souterrain near Alyth, although no horse bones or indeed those of other animal species were found, a copper alloy ring from a horse bridle bit was recovered from a side chamber (Coleman and Hunter 2002, 90). Horse gear in the form of a bronze terret, used to guide harness traces, was also found at Carlungie Souterrain in Angus (ibid 98) so it seems that horses were indeed present in this part of Scotland at the time when souterrains were in use.

The direct bone evidence from Broxy Kennels Fort does however indicate that cattle, sheep/goats and pigs were being kept during the Iron Age, as they were elsewhere in Scotland at this period. (The Broxy horse bones probably represent a more recent burial). Unsurprisingly, given the poor preservation of the material, there was no evidence for hunting of wild animals or birds, and fish bones were similarly absent.

At other hillforts in the area for example at Clatchard Craig, Newburgh, a small animal bone assemblage reviewed and re-catalogued by Lin Barnetson (1986) also consisted mainly of cattle, sheep/goats, pig and horse with at least one incidence of red deer, while the assemblages from the hillforts of Castle Law, Abernethy, and Moredun on Moncreiffe Hill overlooking the Tay, confirm the importance of cattle, sheep and pigs and notably the relative scarcity of deer (Robertson 2023, 183-4; 225). Broxy Kennels Fort therefore fits within a local pattern of exploitation first and foremost of domestic animals with only slight reliance on wild game.

PART 3: Material Culture

The Lithic Assemblages

By Torben Bjarke Ballin

Introduction

In 2022, GUARD Archaeology Ltd carried out surveys of a number of areas as part of the wider Cross Tay Link Road (CTLR) Project. Two main areas were defined: Scone 1 with Scone 2 (NGR: NO11075 27516 and NO11111 27490) and Broxy Kennels (NGR: NO 09108 27875 centred).

An archaeological strip, map and sample excavation was carried out at Scone 1 and 2. The work uncovered several prehistoric features, including remnants of a burnt mound, a pit group and a possible pit alignment which were subsequently excavated. Three lithics were recovered from Scone 2.

The topsoil-stripping of Broxy Kennels revealed up to four ditches encircling the hill, a souterrain and a series of pits and postholes across the interior and exterior of the fort. All archaeological features were fully hand-excavated, with the exception of the ditches, which were 30-60% hand-excavated. Over the course of the topsoil-stripping and excavation, several previously unknown sections of ditch and other features were revealed, along with a complex stratigraphic sequence of hill-wash, pre- and post-dating the fort. A total of 251 lithic pieces were recovered from Broxy Kennels.

This report characterizes the lithic artefacts in detail, with special reference to raw-materials, typological composition and technology. From this characterization, it is sought to date and interpret the finds to the degree this is possible.

The evaluation of the lithic material is based upon a detailed catalogue of all the lithic finds from Scone 2 and Broxy Kennels, and in the present report the artefacts are referred to by their catalogue (CAT) number.

The Assemblage

During the excavations of the Scone and Broxy Kennels sites near Perth, 254 lithic artefacts were recovered (Table 35). In total, 93% of the artefact assemblage is debitage, 2% is cores, and 5% is tools. Table 35 also indicates the relative composition of the collection's raw materials. Only flint has a high proportion of tools (7%), whereas all other raw materials are characterised by 0-1% tools. The lithic typology applied in the present report follows (Ballin 2021). The abbreviation 'GD' is used for 'greatest dimension'.

Scone 2

Only three pieces were recovered from Scone 2: one blade (CAT 6), one microblade (CAT 66) and one bipolar core (CAT 5) (Figure 56). CAT 6 and CAT 66 were recovered from the fill of pit (052), whereas CAT 5 was recovered from burnt mound context (044).

CAT 6 is the medial section of a broad blade in flint, and it has a width of 9 mm. CAT 66 is a soft-hammer microblade in black, aphyric Arran pitchstone (Ballin 2009; Ballin and Faithfull 2009), and it measures 15 by 3 by 1 mm. CAT 5 is a small bipolar core in carnelian, and it measures 20 by 18 by 8 mm; it is a bifacial specimen with one reduction axis (one set of opposed terminals).

The bipolar core from the burnt mound is probably a residual piece, indicating domestic activities in the area at an unspecified point of time during prehistory. Given what we know today about intentional depositions of Arran pitchstone across the British Isles during in particular the early Neolithic (Ballin 2015; 2017; Ballin et al. 2018), the two blades are most likely to represent ritual activity in the area during this period.

Broxy Kennels

Raw material – types, sources and condition

This assemblage includes four groups of raw materials (Tables 35-36): flint, materials of the chalcedony family, quartz and pitchstone.

In total, 152 pieces of flint were recovered. These pieces include fine-grained brown and grey/mottled-grey flint which may all have been procured from the local shores of the North Sea c. 50 km towards the west. CAT 55 (Figure 56) is the only piece of dark-brown (so-called 'black') flint, and this raw material may have been imported from the general Yorkshire area during the late Neolithic period (e.g. Ballin 2011; 2025; forthcoming a).

As shown in Table 35, the chalcedony group includes predominantly carnelian (64%), supplemented by agate (33%), with one piece of chalcedony also being present. This composition corresponds to that of the Mesolithic site of Freeland Farm just south of Perth (Nicol and Ballin 2019), which is also dominated by carnelian. Assemblages (especially Mesolithic ones) from the Tay estuary tend to be dominated by materials from the chalcedony group (e.g. Morton Site A; Coles 1971), whereas earlier and later sites include a larger proportion of flint. Sites north of the estuary are usually dominated by flint and sites south of the estuary by chert.

Type	Scone 2 Various raw mats	Broxy Kennels Flint	Chalc family	Quartz	Pitch-stone	Total
Debitage						
Chips		93	23	34		150
Flakes		20	4	28		52
Blades	1	6		1	1	9
Microblades	1	11		2	1	15
Indeterminate pieces		3	3	1		7
Crested pieces		2		1		3
Total debitage	2	135	30	67	2	236
Cores						
Split pebbles		1				1
Cores w 2 platfs at angle		1				1
Bipolar cores	1	1				2
Core fragments		2				2
Total cores	1	5				6
Tools						
Edge-blunted microliths		1				1
Leaf-shaped arrowheads		1				1
Double-scrapers				1		1
Truncations		1				1
Combined scraper/knives		1				1
Pieces w edge-retouch		3				3
Pieces w invasive retouch		1				1
Fire-flints		3				3
Total tools		11		1		12
Total	3	151	30	68	2	254

Table 35: General artefact list.

Materials of the chalcedony family have been discussed on a number of occasions (e.g. Ballin 2018; Nicol and Ballin 2019). The group may be subdivided into a number of different sub-categories on the basis of colours and patterns, such as chalcedony proper (grey or bluish-grey), jasper (usually red), carnelian (brown), agate (characterized by concentric banding), and bloodstone/plasma (green jasper). Bloodstone is almost exclusively found around the extinct volcanoes on the Isle of Rhum in the Scottish Inner Hebrides.

All the quartz is white milky quartz, which may have been procured from local streams, such as the Tay, or in the form of erratic nodules (Ballin 2008). Three pieces of pitchstone (CAT 26, 66 and 139; popularly referred to as Scottish obsidian) are all black and aphyric, and this raw material was almost certainly procured from sources in eastern Arran (Ballin 2009; Ballin and Faithfull 2009) and brought to the site through an extensive exchange network which covered all of the British Isles, apart from Shetland (a pitchstone microblade was recently recovered from Herefordshire, not far from the English Channel; Stafford 2024).

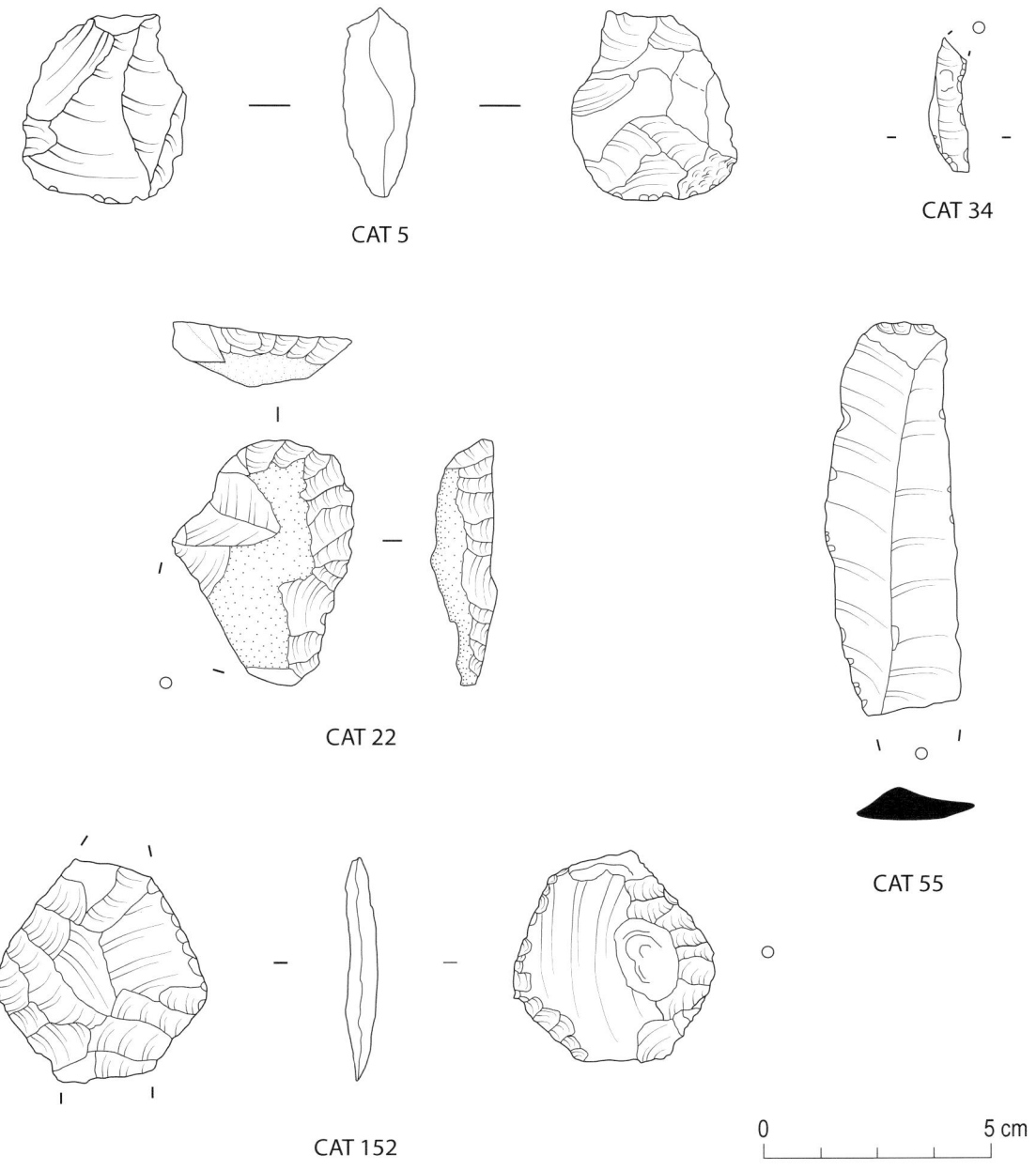

Figure 56: Flint artefacts - CAT 5, 22, 34, 55, 152.

105

Type	number	%
Agate	10	33
Carnelian	19	64
Chalcedony	1	3
Total	30	100

Table 36: Composition of the chalcedony group.

Debitage

The 234 pieces of debitage include 150 chips, 52 flakes, eight blades, 14 microblades, seven indeterminate pieces and three crested pieces (Table 35). A total of 135 pieces are flint, 30 pieces are of the chalcedony family, 67 pieces are quartz and two pieces are Arran pitchstone.

As shown in Table 37, the flint, chalcedony and quartz include large numbers of chips, suggesting that during the Mesolithic, Neolithic and Bronze Age periods these raw materials were reduced at Broxy Kennels. However, none of these knapping floors survived the Iron Age construction work at the site. Blades and microblades were produced in flint, quartz and pitchstone, indicating a Mesolithic/Neolithic presence at the location. The 11 microblades in flint probably relate to a late Mesolithic visit to the site.

A total of three crested pieces were retrieved: one flake (CAT 4), one broad blade (CAT 7) and one microblade (CAT 10). The width of the blades varies between 8 mm and 13 mm.

Cores

In total, six cores were recovered from the site: one split pebble, one core with two platforms at an angle, one bipolar core and two core fragments. Apart from bipolar core CAT 5, which is carnelian, all cores are in flint.

Split pebble CAT 53 is roughly one half of an elongated pebble, and it has a GD of 33 mm. Only one intact platform core CAT 29 was recovered. This piece is a core with two platforms at an angle, and it is basically an exhausted conical blade core, which at the end of its 'life' had a secondary platform added at a perpendicular angle to the original platform. It measures 32 by 29 by 15 mm. Two bipolar cores represent the completely exhausted remains of cores which became too small to be reduced further by the application of free-hand platform technique. CAT 5 (carnelian) measures 20 by 18 by 8 mm, whereas CAT 88 (flint) measures 11 by 5 by 5 mm. Two fragments (CAT 69 and 14) of platform cores have GDs of 27 mm and 38 mm, respectively.

Tools

The 12 tools include one microlith, one leaf-shaped arrowhead, one scraper, one truncation, one combined scraper/knife, three pieces with edge-retouch, one piece with invasive retouch, and three fire-flints (Table 35). Apart from quartz scraper CAT 250, all tools are in flint.

CAT 34 (Figure 56) is the medial-distal fragment of an edge-blunted microlith with full blunting along its left lateral side and fine ancillary retouch along the opposed lateral side. This piece is based on a microblade and measures 14 by 4 by 1 mm.

CAT 152 (Figure 56) is a leaf-shaped point which missing its outermost proximal and distal ends. With its angled lateral sides, this piece falls into the category of kite-shaped arrowheads. One face is covered entirely by invasive retouch, whereas the ventral face has invasive retouch along both lateral sides. It measures 23 by 21 by 3 mm. One ventral potlid flake has been detached, either due exposure to frost or fire.

	Numbers					Per cent				
	Flint	Chalc family	Quartz	Pitch-stone	Total	Flint	Chalc family	Quartz	Pitch-stone	Total
Chips	93	23	34		150	69	77	50		64
Flakes	20	4	28		52	15	13	41		22
Blades	6		1	1	8	4		2	50	4
Microblades	11		2	1	14	8		3	50	6
Indeterminate pieces	3	3	1		7	2	10	2		3
Crested pieces	2		1		3	2		2		1
Total debitage	135	30	67	2	234	100	100	100	100	100

Table 37: Relative composition of the debitage by raw material.

CAT 250 is a robust double-scraper of quartz. It has a regular steep, convex scraper-edge at either end. Both working-edges are abraded, suggesting that the piece was used extensively for the processing of hard materials, such as wood, bone or antler. It measures 47 by 40 by 26 mm.

CAT 55 is a medial-distal segment of a blade with straight to slightly convex distal truncation, based on 'black', possibly exotic flint. The blank is a broad blade, and the piece measures 43 by 14 by 4 mm. The fact that the distal modification is on relatively soft cortex suggests that this is not a scraper, and that the function of the retouch was not to serve as a working-edge but as blunting. Fine, shallow use-wear along both lateral edges suggests that CAT 55 was used as a knife.

CAT 22 (Figure 56) is the medial-distal fragment of a combined scraper/knife. It is based on a small flake (26 by 18 by 5 mm), and it has a convex, steep scraper-edge at the distal end and a scale-flaked cutting-edge along the right lateral side.

A total of three pieces with edge-retouch were also recovered from the location (CAT 13, 16 and 51). Two pieces are based on flakes, and one is on a blade. These pieces are probably tools and tool fragments with different functions. CAT 8 is a very thin lateral fragment with bifacial invasive retouch (GD = 8 mm; th = 1.6 mm). It is most likely a fragment of a leaf-shaped point.

In addition to these prehistoric lithic artefacts, three probably post-medieval fire-flints were also recovered (CAT 1-3). In prehistory and post-Bronze Age times (Iron Age to the post medieval period), several different techniques were applied to produce fire, with the main prehistoric manner of fire-making involving a flint and a piece of pyrite (or other forms of sulfuric iron), whereas the main later manner of fire-making involved a flint and a mostly bullhorn-shaped steel implement (Ballin 2005). It is suggested that the use of the term 'strike-a-light' is limited to the implements doing the actual striking (subject), and not the material which is being struck (object). This means that, in prehistoric fire-making, the flint is the strike-a-light (as it strikes the pyrite), whereas, in later fire-making, it is not (as it is being struck by the steel strike-a-light). It is suggested that the struck post-Bronze Age lithics are referred to as 'fire-flints'. CAT 1-3 are all in mottled-grey flint, with a GD of 26-54 mm, and one is based on a pebble another on a shaped piece ('core'), and one on an indeterminate piece. They all have battered, in some cases concave, edges, where the pieces were struck by a steel strike-a-light.

Distribution

As shown in Table 38, approximately three-quarters of the finds are likely residual pieces which entered ditches, pits, the souterrain, etc. with the back-fill, whereas one-fifth were retrieved from possible occupation layers (306 and 767), both on the southern slope of the site.

Location	n	%
Ditches	117	46
Pits	47	19
Post-/stakeholes	8	3
Occ. layer 306	34	13
Occ. layer 767	18	7
Souterrain	13	5
Various structures	3	1
Various disturbed	7	3
US	7	3
Total	254	100

Table 38: Distribution of lithic finds across feature types.

Being residual, redeposited pieces, the former group of finds has little to no research potential, and as almost all finds from the two possible occupation layers are simple reduction waste, the second group also has little research potential. The finds from layer (306), as well as those from layer (767), includes one blade and two microblades, dating these sub-assemblages to the pre-Bronze Age period.

Dating

A number of elements are important to the dating of the lithic assemblage, 1) raw material preferences; 2) typology; and 3) technology. Due to the residual nature of most of the assemblage, radiocarbon-dates and association with pottery styles are less relevant.

Raw materials

Three raw materials are important to the dating of the collection: materials of the chalcedony family, black exotic flint and Arran pitchstone. As shown in other reports on assemblages from

107

this area (Coles 1971; Nicol and Ballin 2019), in the Tay estuary materials of the chalcedony family (chalcedony proper, carnelian, jasper and agate) tend to dominate Mesolithic assemblages whereas late Upper Palaeolithic, Neolithic and Bronze Age ones tend to be dominated by flint.

During the middle and late Neolithic periods large amounts of mottled-grey and black flint with excellent flaking properties were imported from the greater Yorkshire area (Ballin 2011; 2025; forthcoming a), the former tending to date to the middle Neolithic and the latter to the late Neolithic period. Truncated blade CAT 55 may represent late Neolithic importation. And three pieces of Arran pitchstone (CAT 26, 66 and 139) are more likely to represent early Neolithic exchange than an influx of material from any earlier or later periods (Ballin 2015; 2017; Ballin et al. 2018).

Typology (Figure 56)

The collection includes a number of more or less diagnostic tool types - edge-blunted microlith CAT 34, kite-shaped point CAT 152, combined scraper/scale-flaked knife CAT 22 and three fire-flints (CAT 1-3). Microliths are generally datable to the Mesolithic period, and microblade-based pieces like CAT 55 tend to date to the late Mesolithic (Ballin 2021). Leaf-shaped arrowheads are generally of early Neolithic date, with kite-shaped variants being datable to the later part of this period (Green 1980, 85; Ballin forthcoming b). The combined scraper/knife is dated by its invasive retouch to the Neolithic-early Bronze Age period (Clark 1936). And fire-flints tend to be post-medieval, representing fire-making by the application of a steel strike-a-light (Ballin 2005).

Technology

There are few diagnostic technological elements, the most notable one being a relatively large number of microblades. Microblade production characterises the late Mesolithic period (Ballin 2021), whereas broadblades may be datable to a number of pre-Bronze Age periods. The association of the site's microblades with the late Mesolithic is supported by the presence microblade-based microlith CAT 34. Invasive retouch is a form of tool modification used during the Neolithic-early Bronze Age period (Clark 1936).

Radiocarbon-dates

A large number of samples were taken, but no radiocarbon-dates were associated with contexts 306 and 767, the only contexts from which undisturbed lithic assemblages were recovered. However, these two possible late Mesolithic occupation layers may or may not be datable by UBA-54830, which indicates a visit to the site during the late Mesolithic (5987 – 5803 cal BC). UBA-54851 suggests a visit to the site during the early Mesolithic period (9129 – 8655 cal BC), which is interesting as no Scottish sites or finds have been radiocarbon-dated. Unfortunately, the assemblage includes no diagnostic early Mesolithic pieces.

Conclusion

Following the above characterisation of the lithic finds, it must be concluded that the assemblage has low to no research potential. Most of the objects represent residuality and redeposition in connection with the Iron Age construction work at the site (particularly the digging of the many trenches), and only the finds from the two possible occupation layers (306 and 767) may be roughly *in situ*. However, practically all the finds from these two contexts are plain waste (chips and flakes) with little information value. The lithic assemblage tells us little more than that the site was visited during the late Mesolithic (the microlith), the early Neolithic (the kite-shaped point), the late Neolithic (the truncated blade of black flint) and the post-medieval period (the fire-flints).

Note

In addition to the prehistoric artefacts dealt with above, a broken arrowhead was retrieved from the fill of a pit (995/996) within the central area of the fort. There is no doubt that the raw material is obsidian (NOT Arran pitchstone), and the piece must have been buried and refound deliberately during the excavation, probably as a joke. The piece is a side-notch or dovetail arrowhead, a type commonly found in the United States. The proximal base has been rounded by retouch, and the arrowhead has full retouch of both lateral sides. The piece broke in the notch. Pieces like this are made by flintknappers at many American archaeological sites and monuments and then sold to visitors/tourists.

Stone Artefacts

By Beverley Ballin Smith

Introduction

The excavations of the hillfort at Broxy Kennels on the Cross Tay Link Road route produced a small assemblage of eleven worked stones from the ditch fills, colluvium deposits and the occasional pit. Most of the tools identified are probably prehistoric although there are one or two which suggest activities of later periods.

The stones were brushed or washed before examination. Where possible they have been examined to identify their lithology, weighed, measured, photographed and examined in detail for tooling or wear marks. The assemblage was analysed according CIfA's *Standards and Guidance for the collection, documentation, conservation and research of archaeological materials* (2014, revised 2020).

The raw material origins

The geology of the area surrounding the hillfort is primarily bedrock of Devonian sandstone, with superficial glaciofluvial deposits of gravels and sand with lenses of clay and slit. To the immediate south of the site are raised marine beach deposits of similar composition. The course of the River Tay with its alluvium banks lies a few hundred metres to the east (BGS 2024).

The worked stone comprises utilised cobbles of various sizes along with two slate pieces. The cobbles include mica schist and schist, quartz, quartzite and sandstone. It is likely that the sandstone is a locally derived river-bed cobble, but the other stones were probably brought down by the River Tay from the central highland region of Scotland as water worn/glacial pieces. There was little stone noted in the exposed sands and gravels into which the hillfort had been dug and it is reasonable to assume that the river was the nearest source of these raw materials.

Two materials have been quarried, the slates and the fragment of Cumbrian tuff. The provenance of the slates, one a schist and the other

unidentified, is not presently known although there are slate quarries to the north at Dunkeld (pers. comm. Dr Joan Walsh), which are located immediately north of the Highland Boundary Fault. It is likely these quarries supplied the local area with roofing slates. A fragment of Cumbrian tuff was derived from quarries established in the Neolithic on the Great Langdale in the Lake District, North of England.

Results of the analysis (For further details and images Appendix 5)

Axehead fragment

SF 184 is a fragment of a polished Neolithic axehead of Cumbrian tuff. It was found in the fill (666) of a pit (665) at the base of the southern slope of the hillfort, along with other unworked stone, burnt bone and carbonised organic material.

The fragment is part of petrology Group VI, identifying it as derived from the Great Langdale axe factory (McK Clough 1988, Table 3). Although broken across its shaft close to what would have been its cutting edge, analysis has shown that it is a complex piece. The rounded cutting edge was facetted on one surface where a large and two small flaking scars were not removed during polishing. It also appeared to have discrete lateral facets running up the piece from the cutting edge (Figure 57). After breakage the fragment has been used in several ways. A flake was struck off it from the longest surviving side, thinning the piece at its broken edge. A thin 5.1 – 6.8 mm wide facet has been ground down beneath the cutting edge, and which has also been polished through use. Both edges of the facet, including the remodelled cutting edge are abraded, have been darkened through the piece being used as a polisher. Parts of the upper polished surface of the piece are also darker in colour, perhaps from being held in the hand or fingers.

Polished edged implements are not unknown as several were found at Overhowden and Airhouse (Ballin 2011, 27-29) and are discussed further in Ballin (2021, 67-68) where examples have been found in the Mesolithic and more importantly for SF 184, in the later Neolithic.

Figure 57: Cutting edge of polished stone axe SF 184.

Cobble tools

Two cobble tools are grinders. SF 4, from colluvium in the north of the excavated area, is a rounded and well-used quartz piece that fits well in the hand. It has facetted areas of wear around its circumference on the sides that have been worn through the action of grinding.

SF 88 a grinder/hammerstone of quartzite, found in the upper fill of Ditch 1N, with one end facetted from grinding. The other end is slightly damaged and indented where it has been used as a hammer. There is surface damage to one side, possibly through natural erosion.

Two further cobbles are probably anvils. SF 72 is of mica schist and was located in the earliest fill of the recut of Ditch 1N. It is a flattened cobble with a ground hollow in one surface that measures 43 by 43 mm and is approximately 10 mm deep. The hollow has been formed by a rotary action but it is not smooth due to the laminated properties of the stone. There is also some modern damage on the stone's surfaces.

The other cobble, SF 87, from the upper fill of Ditch 1N is a denser stone of quartzite with much mica. The cobble is small with an area of dark polish on one side and a shallow, irregular concavity on one face caused by pecking or hammering where it has been used as an anvil.

Whetstones/polishers

Three of these stones are cobbles and one is a bar-shaped stone. SF 92 is a bar of schist with areas of smooth dark polish on one surface and one side where it has possibly been used as a whetstone. It was found in the recut of Ditch 1S.

SF 152A and SF 152B are both quartzite cobbles from the recut of Ditch 2S. The former is a split cobble with some surviving surfaces. An area of dark polish is visible on one surface and on one rounded edge indicating it was used as a whetstone or polisher. SF 152B is a heavily burnt cobble, with one surviving and preserved surface. The slight concavity of the surface suggests its use was as a polisher.

The remaining stone in this category is Sample 948 a small cobble of sandstone from the fill (666) of pit (665) at the base of the south slope of the hillfort. Most of its surfaces have been naturally sand blasted, but the smallest face is smooth and possibly worn to a slight hollow. It is an uncertain polisher. It was also found together with SF 184, the fragment of a polished stone axehead.

Roofing slate fragments

Two unstratified roofing slate fragments were found on the excavation. SF 41 is possibly schist but SF 42 is a fine grained grey slate, both could be local slates but it is not confirmed. The perforation through the former is oval in shape and measures c. 5 by 5 mm and in SF 42 it is elongated measuring 7.5 by 6 mm. Both holes were cut by the thin pick end of a slaters hammer. It is suspected that these slates were from abandoned or demolished recent farm buildings in the area of the hillfort.

Possible quern SF 205 was not located.

Discussion

The small number of artefacts found associated with the hillfort is not unexpected. Structural remains within the hillfort are not numerous; stone suitable for tool use is rarely found in the deep subsoil; and stone tools associated with the middle Iron Age/Roman Iron Age in Lowland

Scotland tend to low in numbers because of the widespread use of iron. Other factors affect the numbers of stone artefacts. It would have been easy to dispose of an unwanted tool by throwing it off the hillfort to land somewhere downslope in colluvium, such as grinder SF 004. The sand and gravel composition of the subsoil has had a sand-blasting effect on some stones, such as SF 088, where surface marks of use could be naturally removed by soil movement and therefore some tools could have been lost from the record.

Some of the worked stones that have survived are earlier than the activities that took place on top of the hillfort. For example, the reused fragment of polished Neolithic stone axe came from near the base at the southern slope, and Sample 948 and uncertain polisher was also found in the vicinity.

Three whetstones/polishers were found in the recuts of Ditch 1S and Ditch 2S, suggesting they were tools used while activities took place on the top of the hillfort but after the remodelling of the ditches. Two anvils and a grinder/hammerstone were found in the fills of Ditch 1N and the two roof slate fragments were unstratified. SF 72, one of the anvils is radiocarbon dated from its inclusion in a deposit to 750 – 410 cal BC (UBA 54880). None of the other stone artefacts are dated.

A larger number of stone tools were found at Eildon Hill in the Southern Uplands, mostly pounders/grinders, whetstones, hammerstones, anvils, a quern and quern rubbers, mainly from the house platforms but dated to the late Bronze Age to the early Iron Age with later activities taking place in the middle or Roman Iron Age (Dalland, 57-60 and Clarke Appendix 1 in Owen 1992). Other hillforts, such as the Brown and White Caterthuns in Angus (Dunwell and Strachan 2007, 58, 86) also indicated a paucity of stone tools: two hammerstones and a possible rubbing stone from the former and five possible rubbing stones and a pounder/grinder from the latter. The Brown Caterthun was occupied in the late Bronze Age through to as late as the middle Iron Age (ibid, 68-71). The White Caterthun did not produce any dating evidence.

The Prehistoric Pottery

By Beverley Ballin Smith

Introduction

The pottery collection from Broxy Kennels fort is an assemblage of contrasts. The most interesting part of it is related to the Bronze Age remains at the base of the southern slopes of the Iron Age hillfort, where early Bronze Age Beaker pottery dominates. Pottery related to the use of the fort on top of the hill has been severely affected by burning and the information retrieved from it is sparse.

Methodologies

The assemblage is a collection of prehistoric pottery. The majority of the pottery was retrieved by hand during the excavation of the fort, with additional smaller fragments found during the processing of soil samples. All the sherds were brushed before analysis and were examined using a x6 hand lens. Their attributes and statistics were compiled in an archivable table devised using Microsoft Excel. The assemblage was analysed according to the revised guidelines for the study of prehistoric pottery of the Prehistoric Ceramics Research Group (2010) and its *Standard for Pottery Studies in Archaeology* (2016), as well as the CIfA's *Standards and Guidance for the collection, documentation, conservation and research of archaeological materials* (2014, revised 2020).

Analysis and description of the pieces (see also Appendix 6)

The assemblage comprises a total of 475 sherds, of which 24 are rims, seven are base or base edge sherds and 387 are body sherds. Fragments less than 10 by 10 mm are not included in these numbers. The total weight of the assemblage is 2794 g.

The majority of sherds on the south side of the fort were recovered from pits, colluvium and a possible occupation surface. The remainder of the pottery was found in the ditch fills forming the fort defences with two fragments only from the souterrain.

The manufacture of prehistoric pottery most often reflects the local geology (bedrock and superficial deposits), but in this case the River Tay lying to the east of the fort may have been the most obvious resource providing clay from its banks, with the river bed providing sand, gravel and other stones. Without rock outcrops in the vicinity of the fort, and with only the rare boulder or cobble found in the subsoil, the majority of stone used as mineral temper would have come from cobbles found in the river-bed. Quartz sand, broken-quartz rock and an unidentified dark mineral, possibly dolerite, formed the main inclusions in the pottery, along with vegetable temper of dried grasses or cereal straw.

The early Bronze Age pottery from the site was well-made, with mineral temper being hard to identify in the fine pots produced. The wall thicknesses of these vessels averaged between 6 mm and 7 mm in width, but a later Bronze Age funerary vessel had a wall thickness of over 16 mm. However, by the Iron Age, fine stones added to the clay for pottery manufacture were replaced on this site by much larger and heavier ones, suggesting variations in the available resources and changes in manufacturing techniques. During this later period the wall thickness of sherds of one vessel are recorded in excess of 20 mm. The composition of the clay/mineral size and organic temper largely depended on the type of pot required, the function to which it was put, and the skill of the potter.

Post depositional changes

At the base of the southern slope of the fort, the Bronze Age pottery that was buried in pits remained in good condition, with its decoration often found to be crisp and fresh-looking and surface finishing surviving well. Where pottery sherds had moved from their original place of deposition, such as in colluvium, they and their decoration were worn and abraded. Fragments often suffered from breakages, but this may also have been due to excavation or recovery techniques in the difficult geological background of the fort.

The pottery fragments found in the fort ditch fills contrasted greatly with those from the Bronze Age on the south side. Most of the sherds were highly fragmented, heavily abraded (rolled), and burnt. They were probably discarded into the open ditches but the pre-deposition firing/ burning had caused distortion and spalling of the pieces. The filling-in of the ditches and their recutting caused further abrasion and loss of characteristics of the sherds found there.

Earliest pottery

One sherd is tentatively identified as possibly being Neolithic in date derived from colluvium on the south side of the hill, in soil that had most likely tricked down from its top. Vessel 11 (Figure 58), is a heavily abraded fragment of a rounded and everted rim. The top of the rim is either unevenly moulded or simply abraded, with a short concave neck formed when the rim coil was added to the vessel body. Finger moulding marks are visible on its internal surface, along with quartz sand, quartz rock and the impressions of vegetable temper. The external surface has largely been removed through weathering. The shape of the piece suggests it is a late vessel from the early Neolithic.

Bronze Age pottery

The Beakers

Fragments of eight Beakers were found together in pit (348) at the base of the south slope of the fort, with other fragments coming from the occupation layer (767). The Beakers were well-made with, fine to medium-sized mineral temper that had been added to the clay. In most cases only the rare piece of quartz or quartz sand was identified, but all sherds had organic temper. The generally sparse inclusions in the clay enabled the potter(s) to make very fine vessels. Vessel 5 for example, had a wall thickness of only c.4.5 mm. The vessels were also well-finished, and also internally, which is unusual. Vessels were not simply smoothed, as six of them were polished by burnishing.

The *rims* of Vessels 4 and V8 (Figure 58) are flattened or gently rounded on the top and are also everted slightly from the neck of the vessel, producing vessel shapes that were slightly S-shaped. The rims of both these vessels suggest a rim diameter of c. 180 mm. Only c. 4% of the rim of Vessel 4 survived, while c. 20.5% of that of Vessel 8 is present.

Vessel 7 is a fragment of a similar shaped rim to those of Vessels 4 and 8 but its fabric is much heavier, producing a sherd with a thickness of 10.5 mm. Just below the rim is a well-formed cordon - a characteristic of some Beaker vessels (Figure 58). The rim top is fragmentary and it was not possible to measure its diameter. The sherd is plain, but the cordon carries a negative impression from a probable cereal grain.

Two individual *base* and *base edge* sherds were found with the rims and body sherds. Both are flat-bottomed with rounded base edges. Vessel 12 from colluvium deposits had a basal diameter of 70 mm and only 7.5% of it was present, but it had two parallel, horizontal lines of impressed cord above the base edge. This and Vessel 1 body sherds are the only examples to be decorated with twisted cord from this site. Vessel 3 is only a small fragment of a base-edge sherd, without further diagnostic features.

Vessel 2 is interesting as it has three small non-joining base/base-edge sherds found together with three conjoined body sherds that are likely to be part of the same pot as a decorated body sherd, which conjoins with two other plain sherds (Figure 58).

Decoration is note on the majority of Beaker sherds from the site. It includes impressed twisted cord already noted on Vessel 1, while Vessels 2, 5 and 6 are comb impressed, Vessel 4 has stab decoration and Vessel 8 has fingernail pinch marks.

The belly of Vessel 2 has a very clear design made with a comb-like implement with four to six teeth, each approximately 2 mm wide and with a very slight gap between them (Figure 58). The decoration consists of a single example of a bordered but plain lozenge that would have formed a row around the pot, with infilled

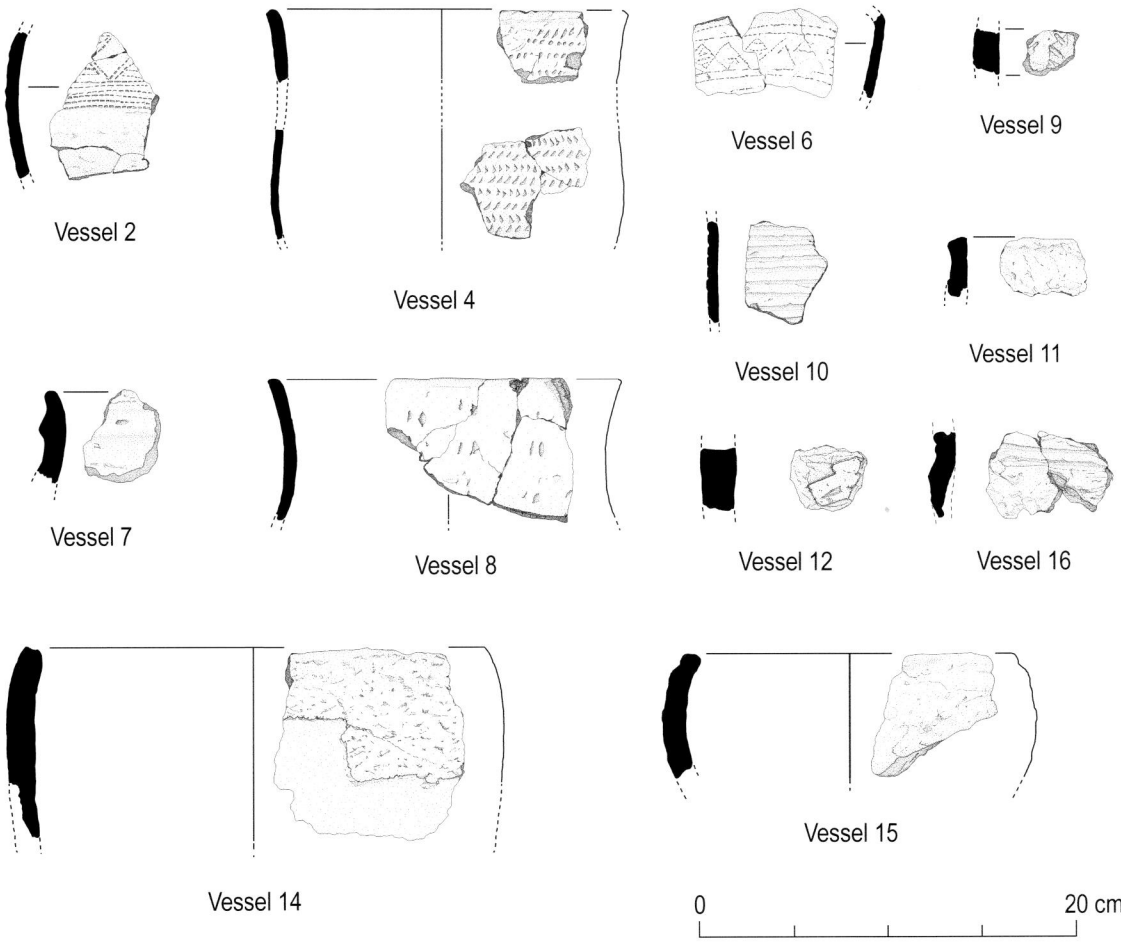

Vessel 2

Vessel 4

Vessel 6

Vessel 9

Vessel 10

Vessel 11

Vessel 7

Vessel 8

Vessel 12

Vessel 16

Vessel 14

Vessel 15

0   20 cm

Figure 58: Earliest vessel V11, Beaker pottery V2, V4, V6, V7, V8, V10, later Bronze Age vessels V14, V14, Iron Age vessels, V 15 and V16.

triangles between. Only the lower border to this decoration is present and it is of formed of six fairly equally spaced horizontal comb impressed lines, and below them is a large blank field probably to the base of the vessel.

A similar design decorates heavily abraded Vessel 6. A band of alternating plain and filled lozenges within a blank field but bordered top and bottom with two horizontal lines has been created by a toothed implement (Figure 58). This pot comprises two conjoined sherds that are probably the lower part of a small vessel with a distinct carination that suggests a more distinctive S-shaped form with a more acute angle between its belly and its base.

Vessel 4 appears to have an all-over decoration of stabbed motifs, most likely created using a small bone, possibly a bird bone (Figure 58). The decoration begins just below the rim and continues in fairly evenly spaced horizontal rows down the vessel. The angle of each row of motifs alternates from right to left.

The motif that decorates the surviving rim and body sherds of Vessel 8 was formed by pinching the clay with the nails of the thumb and first finger (Figure 58). The gap between each motif is fairly widely spaced at approximately 20-30 mm. The motif created both vertical and horizontal rows, with some evidence that it could also be offset.

Vessel 10 is a problematical body sherd. It was found in the colluvium deposits on the south side of the hill but its fine composition and polished finish, but not its decoration, is similar to that of Beaker Vessel 2 both internally and externally. It is an almost straight piece, minus any other diagnostic features (Figure 58). It has 7-9 horizontal incised lines, up to 2 mm in width, which cover the piece, they are not entirely regularly spaced but they form a corrugated design scratched into the surface. However, detailed examination of the sherd indicates that its horizontal lines are incised quite roughly and shallowly through its surface to largely remove a previous design of either horizontal impressed cord, or most likely, impressed comb tooth marks. Comparison with late Neolithic Grooved Ware sherds from Seggie Farm, Guardbridge (Ballin Smith 2025), indicates that the incised line

decoration on Vessel 10 has been made when the surface of the vessel was dry, but before firing. The lines are not cleanly incised, and traces of the previous decoration can be seen. This piece clearly indicates a late decoration change of a Beaker vessel.

Other Bronze Age Vessels

Two single sherds from two different vessels (Vessels 9 and 13) were found together with the majority of Beakers in pit (348). In contrast to the Beaker sherds these are thick-walled pieces, measuring from c. 13 mm to 18 mm in sherd width. They have medium to coarse quartz rock, possibly other minerals as well as organic temper present in the clay mix. Vessel 13 retains a well- finished exterior surface, which is highly smooth and may have been burnished. It also has carbonised food deposits internally. The Vessel 9 sherd is smaller and also more abraded. However, both are decorated.

Vessel 13 has the remains of two 3 mm broad but parallel stab marks, but the side of one of them has been lost. Vessel 9 seems to have had an open V-shaped design with the remains of three parallel oblique incisions c. 2 mm wide surviving on one side of the sherd and only one on the other (Figure 58). The decoration, combined with the fact that these were substantially built vessels, may indicate they are the only remains of two Food Vessels on the site.

A third, large and heavy sherd, Vessel 14 (Figure 58) comprises four sherds from the south slope of the hill. The largest has a flat, slightly inverted rim and is coarsely gritted with unidentified mineral temper. Its surface is also abraded and any finishing of the vessel has been lost. Its rim suggested a large vessel c. 340 mm in diameter and was probably a later Bronze Age funerary urn, known as flat-rimmed ware.

Iron Age pottery

Although there are a large number of small, highly burnt and distorted fragments and sherds from the ditches in the northern side of the fort, mainly Ditch 1, only three vessels have been identified, Vessel 15, a rim sherd is from the fill (580) of the terminus of Ditch 3N, and Vessel 16 was located in the fills (045 upper and 071 lower) of the same ditch. This ditch is later than ditches 2 and 4 and is intimately associated with the construction of the souterrain in ditch 2N and any structure contemporary with it. Two radiocarbon dates: 750 – 410 cal BC (UBA-54835) and 538 – 395 cal BC (UBA- 54832) dated the fills (045 and 071) of Ditch 3N and indicate that the disposal of the pottery took place during the early Iron Age. Vessel 17 was found in the fills of Ditch 2S on the southern slope of the hill.

Vessel 15 is a rounded and inturned rim with finger runnel formed below it to create a short neck to a heavy and thickly made bulbous body (Figure 58). The rim diameter was c. 170 mm, and 8% of it is present. In contrast to the earlier pottery described above, the mineral temper of quartz and possibly dolerite is much coarser but organic temper was still added to the clay. The marks produced in moulding the vessel are noticeable and have not been removed in the finishing process. The large fragments of mineral temper protrude through the surface of the sherd, and cracks have formed around them. This vessel is likely to have been a cooking pot or storage vessel.

A total of nine sherds form Vessel 16 and all share the same characteristics. The pottery is badly damaged and distorted because of being subject to high temperature burning and also abrasion in its burial contexts. In addition, it was not well-made as several sherds have parted at coil joins. As with Vessel 15 the composition of the clay body included coarse to very coarse temper with quartz and possibly dolerite grit present, often showing through the vessel's surfaces. It would also have been thick-walled vessel, with walls measuring up to 15.5 mm in width. Each sherd of this vessel has one or two deep incised horizontal lines positioned below the rim (Figure 58), but these are not decoration. They have been created through use, such as tying a cord around the vessel in order to hang it up, or to tie an organic cover on it. The incised lines area the products of considerable wear and use of the pot. The finishing of the exterior of the vessel has not survived, but carbonised food residues are present on the interior surfaces of some sherds, suggesting it too was a storage vessel or cooking pot.

Vessel 17 includes two large sherds of up to 16.5 mm in wall thickness. One of them includes a distorted flattened rim with extremely large stone temper measuring in excess of 20 by 20 mm. The vessel shape cannot be determined because of the high degree of burning and spalling. The large pieces of temper, the presence of finger moulding marks and food deposits suggests this was a cooking pot.

Comparison with other sites

Despite the generally poor condition of most of the sherds, others have survived well enough to provide useful information about the activities at the base of the hill and on its summit. The earliest is a single rim sherd from an early Neolithic vessel. Its occurrence is not unusual as the prominent hill top would have been used by people passing through or camping in the area at that time.

The Bronze Age

The story of the pottery becomes more interesting with the occurrence of eight early Bronze Age Beaker sherds in one pit, and the remains of two others in the near vicinity. The best preserved of these vessels show little use and their burial together in a pit at the base of the hill suggests a specific occasion, perhaps a celebration. It is not accidental that these vessel fragments are buried together and suggests a deliberate act. As these sherds were reasonably well-preserved, it indicates that they were not subject to much disturbance, and therefore the question remains as to whether the vessels were purposely broken up with only certain parts of them buried together as a commemorative act or an act of remembrance. Certainly, rims and decorative sherds were preferred, and the individual Beakers might represent individual or community identities. The inclusion with the Beakers of two fragments of possible early Bronze Age Food Vessels normally associated with burial customs, gives further weight to a social gathering related to an important event such as a burial or cremation. Sheridan (2004, 261) indicates that the use of Food Vessels overlapped in currency with Beakers during this early period of the Bronze Age.

The grouping of a collection of sherds in a pit is not unheard of. Recently, a group of three pits at Northbar, Erskine near the River Clyde was found during excavation to contain between them the remains of 14 Beakers and a piece of worked flint, with the majority of the vessels found in the largest pit (Ballin Smith forthcoming a). The radiocarbon date associated with the pit produced a date range of very end of the late Neolithic and into the first half of the Chalcolithic 2462 – 2208 cal BC (UBA-49250), suggesting these are early Beakers. It is likely that the Broxy Beakers are later. Four Beakers were also identified by Sheridan (2008) from a pit at Eweford West, on the A1, and suggested that the remains were not associated with funerary rites but perhaps feasting or other ritual activity as the pit was close to a cairn and cereal grains were present.

In Portree in 2006-07 (Johnson 2013, 35-36, illus 28) two pits with Beaker pottery were excavated, with one containing 39 different Beaker vessels together with lithic artefacts and a single grain of bread wheat, Triticum aestivum. Further investigation into the activities at this site in connection with the Beaker pottery did not take place.

The remains of a urn Vessel 14 indicates that Bronze Age activities, including a possible burial, continued at the site during this period but further evidence of them there, such as settlement is sparse to non-existent.

The Iron Age

The pottery from this period is mainly confined to the fort ditch fills, but its condition indicates that there was a large fire (or fires) in the vicinity, possibly in the northern part of the site, where the majority of it was found. The fills of the souterrain produced only two fragmentary and undiagnostic body sherds. This is not unusual, as finds are generally sparse in these structures. The souterrain at Carlunge 1 in Angus, excavated in the middle of the twentieth century, produced some sherds of locally produced courseware with an inturned rim, large grits and pronounced vegetable temper, and referred to as common southern Scottish early Iron Age pottery (Stevenson, in Wainwright 1963, 147-8). Finds from the souterrain at Ardestie, Angus amounted to 12 sherds of coarseware but included a large vessel with an everted rim and bulbous profile to a narrow base (ibid, 131).

The pottery from the ditches indicates that at the time of it being discarded, they were open or partly open, and that the defensive system was in operation. The location of the discarded pottery close to the souterrain suggests the vessels were probably associated with a wooden structure beside it or overlying it. Only three vessels were identified and only one has been radiocarbon dated to the early Iron Age, but the high numbers of small fragments of pottery suggest they were part of one or more clearance operations and the most convenient place to dump the material was a ditch or ditches.

Clay and Fired Clay

By Beverley Ballin Smith

Introduction

Burnt pebbles of daub and cobble-sized pieces of loosely bonded clay, stones and organic material, referred to as mixed clay were both found at the Broxy Kennels hillfort. Both materials suggest there episodes of burning associated with wooden structures there. The mixed clay cobbles were retrieved by hand mostly from contexts associated with the ditches forming the fort. The majority of the daub pebbles were found during the processing of soil samples from across the project area. All were weighed and examined with a X6 hand lens and most were photographed.

As its name suggests daub or fired clay is the burnt remains of clay used for construction, mixed with organic material such as animal dung and straw, and occasionally with small stones. It is generally a relatively soft material when found in archaeological contexts compared to fired pottery, and it is only hardened by exposure to fire. Unfired clay is light in weight and generally does not survive burial conditions, taphonomic processes or the post-excavation processing of samples particularly well. However, the presence of fragments of burnt clay is important for site interpretation, as it can support or enhance the understanding of abandoned or demolished structures.

The use of clay in construction

Pieces of fired clay found on excavations are largely raw clay, dug from deposits in the subsoil, or a stream side, to which an organic binder, usually straw or dung material was added to make the clay more pliable. It sometimes has the addition of gravel or the occasional small stone as a strengthener, and is generally referred to as 'daub'.

Daub was used as a constructional material together with withies (willow/hazel/alder wands) for hurdle-type wooden constructions, where its main function was as an infilling and insulating material. This combination of wooden withies and clay is traditionally known as wattle work or 'stake and rice' in Scotland (Walker and McGregor

1996, 38). If protected from the weather it was both a windproof and somewhat impermeable barrier. In the archaeological record this relatively soft clay substance was used as a building material for light weight, non-load bearing structures such as the walls of prehistoric timber buildings and for smaller structures such as ovens, hearths and furnaces. It has a long history of use, not just in Britain but also worldwide, and the different base materials and additives produced different variants such as *adobe, cob* and *daub* (Graham 2004, 27).

The natural generally yellowish-brown colour of the subsoil clay in Scotland reflects that of the underlying bedrock, but when daub made from it is burnt it changes to grey/buff to orange/red hues. On archaeological sites this would normally occur through the burning down of a house or structure, or through the prolonged heat of a furnace or hearth. In Scotland much of the fired clay material is lost from the archaeological record due to taphonomic processes (mainly water and root penetration, and mechanical abrasion), especially if it was not hardened sufficiently through burning. Fired clay pieces normally survive as irregular, abraded and soft clay lumps. Table 39 indicates the number of pieces of daub and mixed clay from the site and the weight from the different contexts in which this material was found.

Results of the analysis

The total weight of fired clay and mixed clay pieces is c. 3635.8 g and individual pieces range in size from a few millimetres in diameter up to 100 by 80 by 40 mm. Natural clay, or clay that appears unaltered (SF 118 and SF 223) apart from being burnt, appears in the samples, and in addition there are two categories: daub and a heavier mixed clay.

Daub from this site is characterised as small, heavily abraded, rounded or irregularly rounded pebbles of soft burnt clay. Most have small vesicles where fine organic material added to the clay has burnt away, and rare grass marks can be occasionally be seen on some surfaces. The occurrence of small fragments of mineral within the clay is rare apart from Sample 130, which included a single small stone. Noticeably absent are curved depressions in the clay from it being pressed against roundwood withies in a construction. In total there are 66 small (40 by 40 mm or less in size) pebbles of daub that together weigh 101.6 g, and the individual average weight is 1.5 g. Sample 971 from (712) stakehole part of fill of fire-pit (694) below Ditch 4S in the south-west corner of the excavated area was dated to the early to middle Iron Age by charcoal producing a date of 514 – 385 cal BC (UBA- 54842).

Mixed clay has been separated from the samples as its consistency is quite different from daub. It is an unusual find in that larger cobble-sized clay pieces with small stones and seemingly larger fragments of charcoal and organic material are bonded together loosely. Some of the largest pieces of this material indicate evidence of being partly burnt. The inclusion of stone has made this

material heavier at a combined weight of 3461.1 g, and with estimated average weights of c. 90 g.

Some of the pieces from SF 81 (Figure 59) have rounded edges, and although this could be a product of natural abrasion, one or more surfaces of these pieces are flat to flattish. SF 77 (Figure 60) is notable, as it too has one relatively flat surface. The thickness and size of the fragments of this material suggests it could have been used, for example to make a level floor surface within a wooden building. It is not well compacted and is not sufficiently burnt to indicate it was used for a formal hearth. The flat surfaces and rounded edges may indicate its use on the floor in certain parts of a building, but its lack of compaction indicates it was not well-used.

SF Nr	Sample	Context	Total Nr pieces	Total Weight g	Identification
	3	(016) fill of (006) Ditch 1N	1 S	0.4	Daub
116		(257) fill of posthole (274) by Slot G in Ditch 1S	1 S	4.6	Daub
	299	(196) sand in base of (005) Ditch 1S	4 S	1.6	Daub
76		(075) top fill of Ditch 2N	3 small	8.5	Daub
77		(076) top fill of pit (083) in terminal of Ditch 2N	2 large, 5 medium 11 S	1547	Mixed clay
78		(076) top fill of pit 083) in terminal of Ditch 2N	3 L, 2 M	921	Mixed clay
81		(084) fill of pit (083) in terminal of Ditch 2N	1 L, 1 M, S	363	Mixed clay
81		(078) fill of (008) Ditch 2N	1 S	4.4	Daub
90		(150) near base of fill of (008) Ditch 2N	1 S	10.1	Mixed clay
	130	(150) fill of (008) Ditch 2N	10 S	16.5	Daub
	898	(580) fill of (010) fill of Ditch 3N	7 S	3.9	Daub
79		(1075) curvilinear S-shaped alignment of postholes on top of hillfort	1 L, 3 M, 8 S	620	Mixed clay
188		(003) hill wash overlying subsoil on south slope of hillfort	3 S	1.8	Natural clay
189		(667) under hill wash (305) on south slope of hillfort	8 S	3.5	Daub
	3	(304) part of palisade ditch (294) at base of south slope of hillfort	8 S	42	Mostly daub
	971	(712) stakehole part of fill of fire-pit (694) below Ditch 4S in SW corner	23 S	16.2	Daub
223		u/s	1 L	71.3	Natural clay
		Totals	108	3635.8	

Table 39: List of daub and clay materials from the project area organise by context location.
S = small M= Medium L= Large

Discussion

Fired clay or daub pieces are not datable in themselves but the radiocarbon dates suggest periods of occupation from the Mesolithic to the late Iron Age (see Table 1). These pieces are generally very small and their distribution includes ditch fills (Ditch 1N and S, Ditch 2N and Ditch 3N) post- and stake- holes and the 'palisade' at the south-western foot of the hillfort as well as from colluvium. This suggests the material was quite wide-spread and indicates its use in a building or buildings across the top of the hillfort. The dispersal of this material to the north and south and its location in the open ditches especially, suggests the clearance of structures within the hillfort. It is important evidence that indicates or reinforces the presence of wooden structures within the area of the hill top bounded by the ditch systems.

The distribution of the mixed clay material is also interesting in that Ditch 2N and especially its terminal received much of this material which was encountered at its base and at the top of its infilling deposits. Stratigraphically this is important, as it implies that it was present in the ditch before the insertion of the souterrain and the construction of any accompanying roundhouse. Its association with also the curvilinear structures (1075) on top of the hillfort may reinforce the idea that it may have been used as a flooring material.

Taphonomic conditions and weathering of soils on the top and sides of the hillfort may have been severe and the survival of fired clays is extraordinary. On sites with gentler contours such as at Ayr Academy, for example (Ballin Smith 2019), fragments of daub from the early Bronze Age survived well but it was not present from the later Bronze Age and Iron Age structures at Braehead, Glasgow (Ellis 2007) on the floodplain of the River Clyde. It must be stressed that both natural weathering and subsequent uses of the site have had a significant bearing on the survival of this material.

Figure 59: SF 81 Mixed clay with rounded edges

Figure 60: SF 77 mixed clay with flat surface

119

Metalwork

By Gemma Cruickshanks and Leanne Demay

XRF result abbreviations: Cu (copper), Sn (tin), Pb (Lead), Zn (zinc).

The Brooch SF 184 *(Figure 61)*

This brooch has proved challenging to parallel and an exact age remains elusive, particularly given its unstratified context. While quatrefoil brooches are found in the medieval period (e.g. Egan and Pritchard 2002, 257, fig 165: 1342) they tend to be entirely quatrefoil, unlike this example which has an annular outer circumference. The pins on medieval brooches tend to be wound around the frame and extend across the front of the brooch, whereas SF 184 has a more modern style of hinged pin attached to the back. Using enamelling as decoration in this way is also not a feature of medieval brooches. A post-medieval or later date therefore seems most likely, though no closely comparable examples have been found to confirm this.

Dating aside, the brooch is fairly small and finely made, suggesting it was a decorative rather than functional piece; it would have been a struggle to fasten it through a particularly heavy fabric and could not have supported much weight. The back of the frame shows signs of attachments at 90° to the current pin, suggesting that there may have been an earlier pin which was replaced, implying it was a valued piece of jewellery. The replacement pin is missing, which may have led to its accidental loss on this site.

Description: Annular copper alloy brooch with circular outer and quatrefoil central void. The frame is adorned with glass or enamel insets: four lentoid blue glass insets are placed perpendicular to the frame at the four widest points, each bordered by semi-circular yellow/brown insets, with four white/brown insets at each of the narrowest parts of the frame. The glass or enamel is fairly degraded and may not show the original colour. The back has a bent loop attached to one side and the base of a hinged pin at the other, the pin is missing. The remains of attachments at 90° to this suggest the last pin was a replacement. XRF: Cu with low Pb, Sn and Zn. Diameter 23 mm, Thickness 2 mm, Weight 9 g. Unstratified.

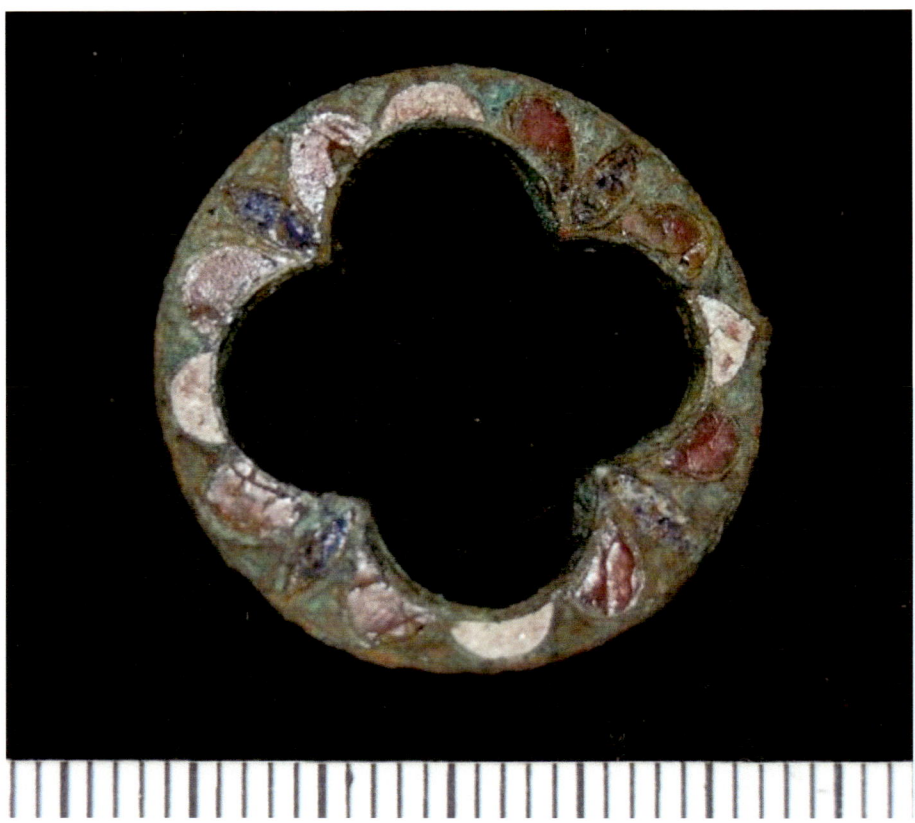

Figure 61: The Brooch SF 184

The Pommel SF 027 (Figure 62)

A perforated hollow copper alloy sphere (SF 027) was probably a pommel from the end of a dagger or sword handle, the former more likely given its size. Pommels secured a dagger's handle to the tang but were also often highly decorative. Examples of this form are known from the medieval period (e.g. Ward Perkins 1940, 30) though it is likely such simple forms continued to be made and used into the post-medieval period.

Description: the pommel is a hollow copper alloy sphere with an uneven circular perforation at one end and opposing square perforation at the other. Patches of lead are visible inside, probably from soldering to the handle. XRF: Cu and Zn with low Pb and Sn. Diameter 20 mm, Height 15 mm, round perforation Diameter 7 mm, square perforation Width 8 mm, weight 11.3 g. Unstratified.

Figure 62: Medieval pommel SF 027

Other Metalwork

All finds were found during the metal-detecting survey and were therefore unstratified in topsoil.

SF 014 Discoidal lead button-weight with pair of cylindrical perforations (Diameter 2 mm) set within a central circular recess (Diameter 7 mm). Other side is plain, edge flat. Very similar to SF 083. Eighteenth to early twentieth century AD. These weights were sewn into dress or cloak hems (or curtains) to help keep them down in wind. Diameter 23 mm, Thickness 3 mm, Weight 15.2 g.

SF 019 XRF analysis revealed the presence of zinc within the alloy, indicating a Roman or later date. The object is too fragmentary to determine its original form but its porous structure may suggest it was unfinished or miscast. It is a fragment of cast copper alloy, flat on one side, and porous on the other, with all edges broken. May be an unfinished or miscast fragment. XRF: Cu with low Pb and Zn. 25 by 18 by 8 mm. Weight 7.2 g.

SF 083 Discoidal lead button weight with pair of cylindrical perforations (Diameter 2 mm) set within a central circular recess (Diameter 8 mm). Other side is plain, edge rounded. Same as SF 014. Diameter 22 mm, Thickness 3.5 mm, Weigh 13.8 g.

SF 123 Part of a fragmentary composite object, surviving only where curved bands of leather were attached either side of a thicker piece of leather using small copper alloy rivets. A mass of iron corrosion at one end indicates an iron element too. Its original function remains unclear. Length 68 mm, Width 8 mm, Thickness 8 mm.

SF 139 Discoidal copper alloy button with four perforations arranged in a square, set into a central dome, dished on other side. Slight raised rim around the outer edge. Eighteenth-nineteenth century AD. Diameter 16 mm, Thickness 1 mm, Weight 1.3 g.

SF 182 Flat, ovoid lead sack seal with Dutch crest (shield, crown and lion) on one side, surrounded by a ring of raised dots, and 'R&A 327' on the other side. Nineteenth century AD. Measures 20 by 16 by 4 mm, Weight 9 g.

SF 183 Flat, ovoid lead sack seal with Dutch crest (shield, crown and lion) on one side, surrounded by a ring of raised dots, and 'R&A ?4?' on the other side. 19th century AD. Measures 20 by 16 by 4 mm, Weight 8.4g.

SF 185 Discoidal copper alloy button with four perforations arranged in a square, set into a central dome, dished on other side. Eighteenth-nineteenth century AD. Diameter 17 mm, Thickness 1 mm, Weight 1.5 g.

SF 186 Copper alloy watch winder with shield-shaped plate displaying very worn writing ('WATCH MAKERS AND JEWELLER' on one side, unclear on the other side, but presumably a company name). Iron rod protruding from the lower edge. Watch winders with advertisements on them are likely to be late eighteenth/nineteenth century in date. Length 29 mm, Width 12 mm, Thickness 2 mm, Weight 2.5 g.

SF 187 Hollow domed uniform button with shield motif. Loop on back is now detached. Nineteenth-twentieth century AD. Diameter 24 mm, Thickness 8 mm, Weight 4.8 g.

SF 215 The end of a tin-lead alloy bar with triangular section and fairly flat end, the other end is broken or cut. Shape suggests it was part of a bar ingot and the alloy composition suggests it may have been used as solder. XRF: Sn, Pb with low Cu and Zn. Length 32 mm, Width 22 mm, Thickness 11 mm, Weight 35.3 g.

SF 366 Small domed lead fragment, slightly flattened on top. Probably broken from a lead weight or shot. Age unknown. XRF: Pb with low Sn and Cu. Diameter 17 mm, Height 7 mm, Weight 11.8 g.

Vitrified Material

By Gemma Cruickshanks (National Museums Scotland)

Summary

A small assemblage of 1.6 kg vitrified material was retrieved during excavations at Broxy Kennels (summarised in Table 40). Vitrified material can be produced during a range of high temperature processes, from specialist crafts to domestic hearth activity. This material is dominated by ironworking debris, mainly iron smelting (producing metal from ore) along with a smaller quantity of undiagnostic material. The material was recovered from fills of Ditches 1, 2 and 3; none was *in situ* and no ironworking features were identified. Ironworking evidence is scarce on Iron Age sites in Perthshire, particularly in the early Iron Age making this a significant find.

The Assemblage

The material was visually examined and classified using common terminology (e.g. Crew and Rehren 2002; Lucas and Paynter 2010; McDonnell and Milns 2015) based upon characteristics such as, colour, size, morphology and density. The assemblage is summarised below and a full catalogue is in the archive.

Bog Iron Ore

A single small fragment of bog iron ore (SF 208) with typical granular and slightly porous texture was an unstratified find on the east slope. Bog iron ore forms from accumulating iron minerals in areas of slow-moving water such as bogs or loch margins and was the ore of choice in Scotland from the early Iron Age into the medieval period (Cruickshanks 2017). While the presence of one small fragment does not necessarily indicate

Material	Feature				Total (g)
	Ditch 1 (C.107, C.108, C.188, C.193)	Ditch 2 (C.402, C.403)	Ditch 3 (C.897)	Topsoil/ unstratified	
Bog iron ore				6.6	6.6
Smelting slag		691.2	264.2	459.1	1414.5
Undiagnostic iron slag	96.6				96.6
Tuyère	83.3				83.3
Vitrified ceramic	56.9				56.9
Coke				3.1	3.1
Total (g)	236.8	691.2	264.2	468.8	1661

Table 40: Summary of vitrified material assemblage.

it was collected for use, the presence of other ironworking evidence on the site adds weight to this being related to that activity.

Iron Smelting Slag

Nine amorphous fragments (SF 144, SF 153, SF 255 and SF 415) of fairly dense, fractured iron slag with frequent charcoal impressions and voids are characteristic of iron smelting slag. Such slag is the waste product of extracting metallic iron from ore in a smelting furnace. The smelting fragments were retrieved from fills in Ditch 2N (context 402 and 403), Ditch 3S (context 897) and topsoil on the north side of the fort.

Undiagnostic Iron Slag

Five small fragments of iron slag (SF 85) from a fill (context 107) of Ditch 1N were too small to determine which part of the ironworking process they originated.

Tuyère and Vitrified Ceramic

A range of small fragments of vitrified ceramic (SF 86, SF 103 and SF 109) were recovered, all from fills of Ditch 1N (contexts 108, 188 and 193). The fragments typically comprise orange fine clay with one face blackened and porous from exposure to intense heat. One of the fragments within SF 086 shows the edge of a possible perforation, suggesting it was part of a ceramic tuyère. Tuyères were generally disc or tubes of clay or sometimes stone, which protected the bellows nozzle from the heat of a metalworking hearth or furnace. Another of the fragments in SF 086 shows two layers of vitrification, indicating the tuyère or hearth lining had been patched up and used again.

Coke

A small fragment of black, porous coke was an unstratified find on the north slope of the hill. Coke forms during burning of fuel, often coal, during a range of processes.

Discussion

This small assemblage indicates that iron smelting, probably using bog iron ore, took place nearby. The pieces were distributed across the site; no concentrations were noted which may have hinted at the location of a furnace. That the fragments were dispersed throughout a number of fills and locations suggests that either smelting was a regular activity over a long period, or there was a great deal of redeposition here which scattered a discrete dump over time. It is difficult to interpret the scale of ironworking activity with only a few scattered fragments, but the piece of relined vitrified ceramic (SF 086) suggests at least some repeated activity.

None of the contexts which produced vitrified material were directly dated, but radiocarbon dates from a range of other contexts throughout Ditches 1, 2 and 3 returned mainly early Iron Age dates. However, there are scattered middle Iron Age and later dates around the site and it is possible some of the upper ditch fills include later material. Early Iron Age iron smelting is rare in Scotland and without directly dates from the contexts which produced slag, such an identification remains tentative.

Recent excavations on other hillforts in Perthshire have produced parallels, though they remain scarce. Glasgow University undertook small-scale excavation on ten hillforts as part of their SERF Project, but only one, Dunknock, produced ironworking debris (Cruickshanks and Hunter 2019). Interestingly, the Dunknock ironworking debris was also from a ditch fill with early Iron Age dates (Tessa Poller pers. comm.). A small quantity of redeposited blacksmithing debris was retrieved from Moredun fort but none from nearby Moncreiffe fort (McLaren 2023, 136). Securely-dated Iron Age ironworking evidence is relatively scarce across other site types in Perthshire too, with the notable exception of a recently discovered furnace associated with a middle Iron Age roundhouse at Logierait terraces (Ellis, Cruickshanks and Hall et al. 2021). The limited evidence therefore suggests access to ironworking was restricted in this region, implying Broxy Kennels held some degree of influence and status in order to host this specialist craft. This small assemblage is therefore a significant addition to our understanding of the organisation of ironworking in Iron Age Perthshire.

PART 4: Discussion

By Kenneth Green with a contribution by Beverley Ballin Smith

Environmental and archaeological evidence earlier than the fort

By Beverley Ballin Smith

The geographical setting of both Broxy Kennels and Scone situated close to the River Tay and its confluence with the River Almond was important to prehistoric people. It allowed them movement through the landscape but also provided safe places to visit and eventual settle. River networks were vital means of communication by facilitating navigation through a forested landscape as often noted in the recovery of Mesolithic camp site remains such as along the River Dee in Aberdeenshire (Murray and Murray 2021), also Ferniegair, Hamilton, in South Lanarkshire (Atkinson 2023). Rivers and streams exposed raw materials for tool and pottery-making, they were also a source of food, and made woodland resources more easily available for shelter, tool making, and the hunting of larger mammals. Two radiocarbon dates from the tenth and sixth millennia BC (c. 9100 to c.5800 BC) from willow charcoal together with the evidence from the survival of worked flint (microblades, see *The Lithic Assemblages,* above) from this period, indicate Mesolithic peoples' use of this landscape.

The next recorded human use of the area was during the early Neolithic, during the fourth millennium (from c. 3900 to 3650 BC). The hill at Broxy Kennels with its commanding view across the River Tay and its flood plain to the east must have been an attractive place for a temporary encampment. An area at the base of the hill along its southern slope and towards the east was the site of a small number of pits and a large accumulation of hearth waste that included burnt bone and the carbonised remains of hazel wood. The contents of two linear pits to the south-west and two smaller ones indicated they were the remains of fire-pits of early Neolithic date. However, additional evidence of larger pits and postholes on the drier edges of the fertile flood plain around Scone suggested semi-permanent dwellings or encampments, sometime during the Neolithic or the Bronze Age.

The material cultural evidence of the Neolithic came in various forms of lithic (flint, chalcedony, quartz and pitchstone - the latter from the Isle of Arran) found both at Scone, where there may have been a deliberate deposition disturbed by the later burnt mound, and also at Broxy Kennels. The most prominent artefact came in the shape of a fragment of a polished axehead in tuff, from the Langdale Axe factory in the Lake District. It was found in a pit, in an area demonstrated to have been inhabited during the Bronze Age, at the base of the southern slope of the Broxy Kennels Hill. The axehead clearly came from Cumbria. The early Neolithic pitchstone, and black flint used for a late Neolithic knife, together with the Cumbrian tuff demonstrate the long-distance communication and exchange networks in operation between communities throughout the Neolithic.

Evidence of the local environment during this period is extremely slim, but the analysis of soil samples from the Scone investigations indicated that alder and willow trees were present and also birch. These species tolerate damp/wet conditions and suggest that birch, especially, was a coloniser on damper ground. In addition, there were traces of oak, hazel and also hazel nutshells. Hazel likes light and grows along woodland margins, perhaps indicating that at elevations above the floodplain, oak woodland was present.

The presence of people at the very end of the Neolithic and into the early Bronze Age from c. 2460 to at least 2290 BC is established by a single radiocarbon date and the location of a large pit (738), surrounded by numerous stakeholes. It was considered that the stakeholes represented the presence of a single structure, but further examination indicates that they may have been the remains of windbreaks, or lightweight tents. The large pit was used over a long period, with at least six firings, and produced evidence of hazel, alder, oak, willow and cherry-type wood, with barley grain and hazel nut shells. The wood in the surrounding stake-holes was generally of, alder, oak, some hazel and also willow, but in pit (665), which produced the tuff axehead, there was also evidence of the use of elm wood.

To the immediate east and south of the large pit were two irregular pits, interpreted as tree boles, the southern one appeared to be associated with grain storage or processing, due to the large amount of barley found there. It was also considered that the grain may have been stored in a container made of hazel wands because of the dominance of hazel charcoal in the pit. A significant amount of barley had also been processed and used as packing around the stake in the stake or posthole (717) located between the two tree boles. This evidence also indicates that somewhere in the vicinity of the hill, there was a field or more planted with barley that had been harvested along with the gathering of hazel nuts during the late summer and early autumn.

A pit and an occupation deposit approximately 10 m to the north-east of the large pit and stakeholes produced similar evidence of the range of tree species used as firewood, and also of barley. Most of the Bronze Age pottery came from the pit (348) and consisted of sherds from eight Beaker vessels, a possible food vessel and a funerary urn, all from the early Bronze Age (see *Prehistoric Pottery*, above). The collection of Beaker vessels suggest a gathering of people, perhaps in celebration of a good harvest, or marking the passing of a deceased person or their burial. Whatever the event, they left behind important evidence of their visit.

Scone 2 produced evidence of a burnt mound which is likely to be later Bronze Age in date, than the artefacts discussed above. It is, however, one more indicator, of a long period of human presence near the River Tay, even though there does not appear to have been any permanent settlement in the areas investigated until the Iron Age. The evidence for early prehistoric activity in and around Broxy Kennels fort mirrors that from other forts in Perthshire such as Moncreiffe and Castle Law at Abernethy (Strachan et al. 2023, 49 and 233).

The establishment of the fort

By Kenneth Green

The fort on the hill at Broxy Kennels came into existence sometime between 575 – 465 cal BC during the early Iron Age. Changes took place in the organisation of society across Britain and Europe due to the growth in population, the gathering of wealth through the ownership of cattle, land and prestige goods. These changes became expressed physically in the construction of fortified structures to protect land, wealth and communities. Prominent landscape formations such as hill tops and promontories across Scotland were selected for the building of forts using earth, wood and/or stone for ramparts, accompanied by encircling ditches (Figure 63).

In the Perthshire area, a network of smaller forts controlled river crossings or routeways through a landscape in which larger forts were situated. Broxy Kennels fort was one of these – its presence validated the land ownership and prestige of its inhabitants (Armit and McKenzie 2013, 496).

The fort was a prominent feature in the landscape situated relatively close to the lowest crossing of the River Tay at the location of the present-day city of Perth. A number of other Iron Age forts and hillforts existed on both sides of the River Tay suggesting small communities were established across the region that formed part of a larger network of defended settlements in the area (Figure 64). Strachan (et al. 2023, 240-1) discusses the possibility of relationships between forts in the area of the lower River Tay such as the Roundel and Dow Hill which were built on low terrain and of a similar size to each other, and located at roughly the same distances from Moredun on either side of the hill, allowing them to control the landscape surrounding the larger hillfort and the lower reaches of the river, assuming these settlements were all contemporary with Moredun. The fort at Broxy

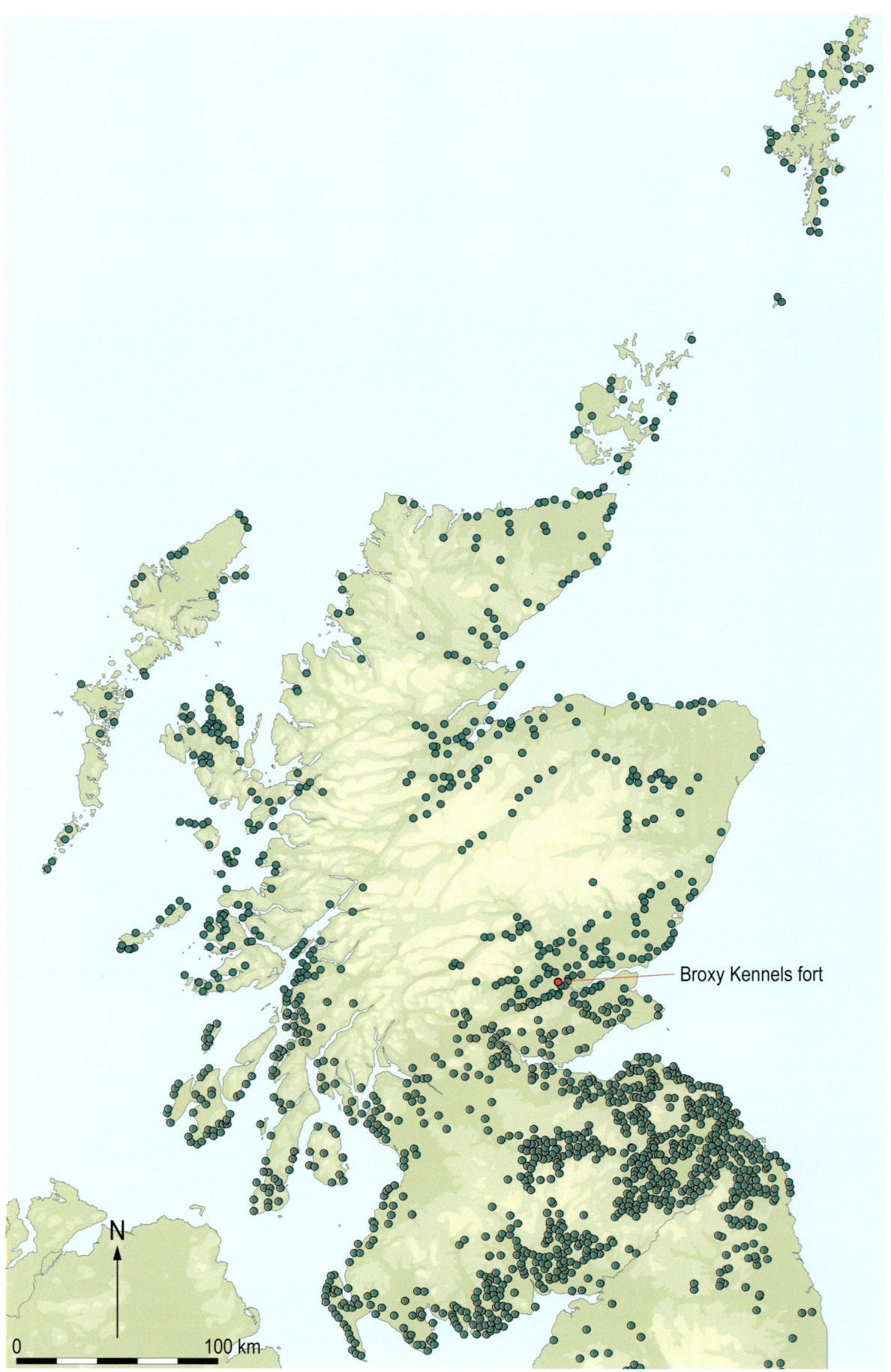

Figure 63: Map of forts across Scotland and Northern England © GUARD Archaeology Ltd.

Broxy Kennels fort

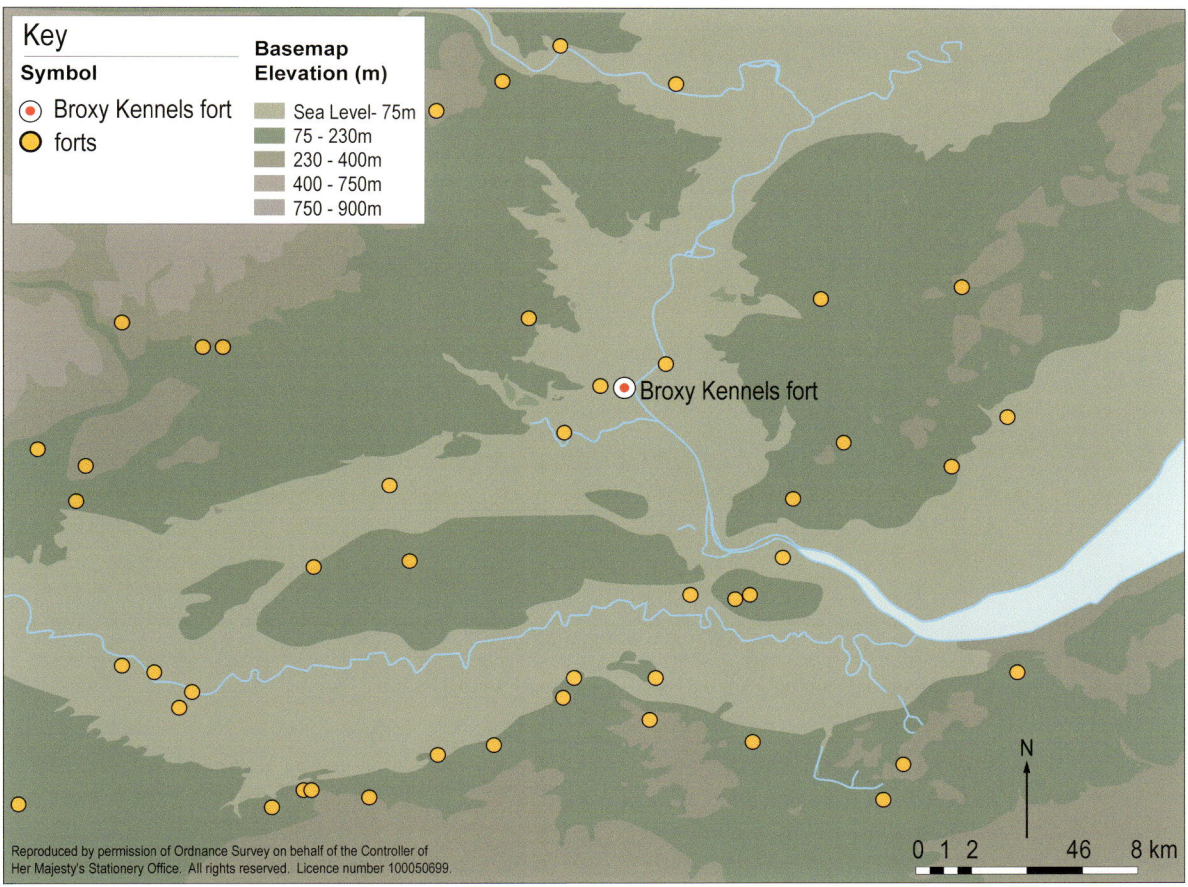

Figure 64: Map of forts in the vicinity of Broxy Kennels © GUARD Archaeology Ltd & Perth & Kinross Heritage Trust.

Kennels seems not to be paired with another fort but it is possible that it was visible from forts situated further inland such as Moneydie and Kinvaid along the Schochie Burn valley to the north-west, Rosemount across the River Tay to the north-east and possibly Pitcairngreen to the south-west on the side of the River Almond valley (see Lock and Ralston 2017), depending on whether they were near contemporary structures. However, none of these forts have been archaeologically investigated or dated.

Other contemporary forts such as the Castle Law forts in Abernethy and Forgandenny, Knock Farril, Strathpeffer, and Finavon in Angus were designed with outer ramparts to make the forts more visible in the landscape. Multi-vallation of these sites, similar to that at Broxy Kennels may have been an indicator of social status of the communities inhabiting these enclosed settlements, as monumental constructions as well as for defence (Banks 2000, 276; Harding 2017, 121).

The construction of the fort - ditches

Broxy Kennels fort was principally a multivallate fort which was constructed sometime in the sixth to fifth centuries BC and continued in use until at least around the early fourth century BC in its first phase of inhabitation. It had four large ditches, three of which appear to have enclosed the entirety of the small hill, although they may not necessarily have been constructed in one event (Figure 65).

Ditches 1 and 2, the innermost, surrounded the hill entirely, broken only by an entrance on the fort's north-east side. Ditch 3 was dug only around the fort's entrance area and was a later phase of activity when part of Ditch 2 was backfilled and the entrance to the hillfort was modified. Ditch 4, the outermost ditch, again surrounded the entire fort while respecting Ditch 3 on the north side, which suggests Ditch 4 was either contemporary with or later than Ditch 3.

127

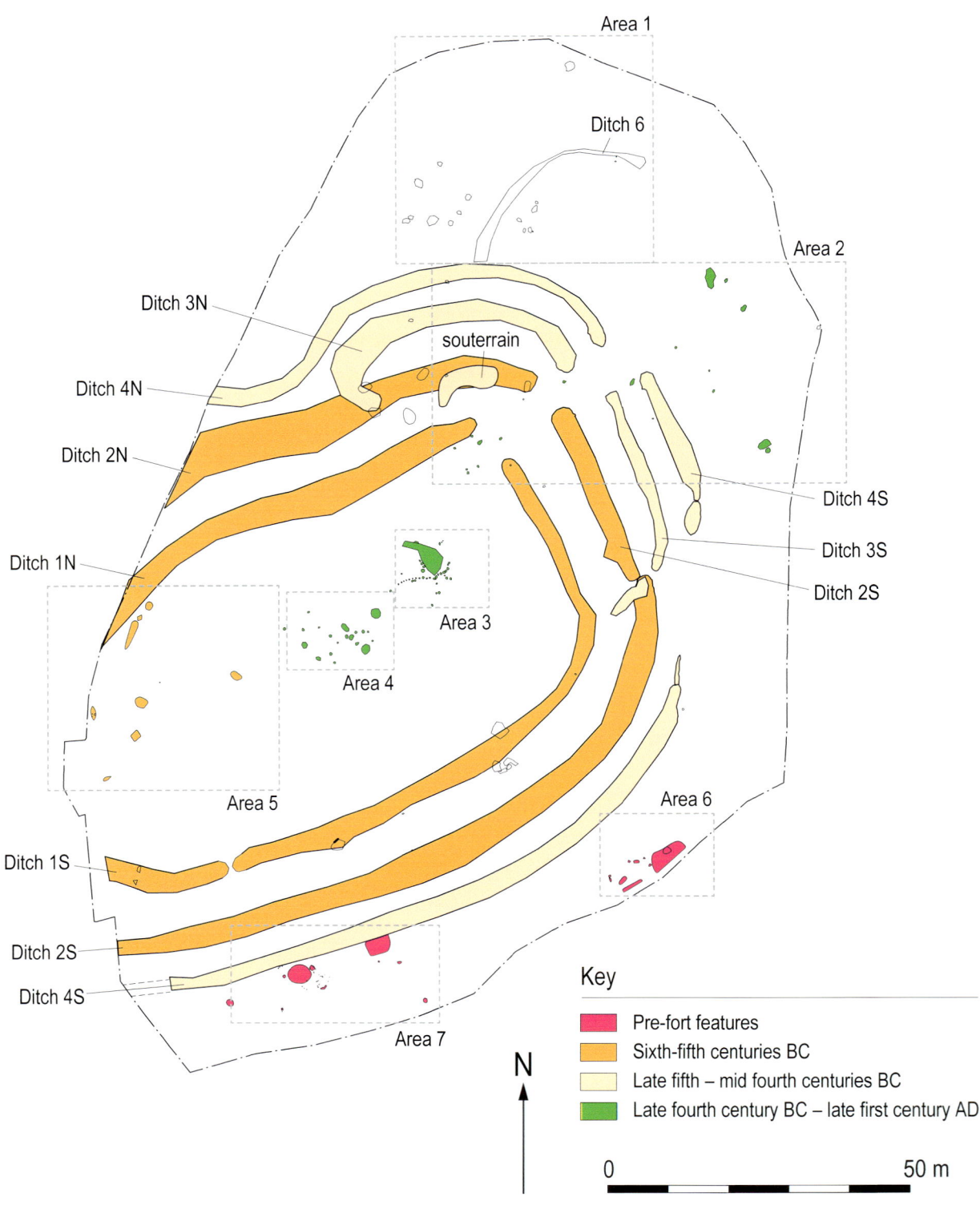

Area 1

Ditch 6

Area 2

Ditch 3N

souterrain

Ditch 4N

Ditch 2N

Ditch 4S

Ditch 1N

Ditch 3S

Ditch 2S

Area 3

Area 4

Area 5

Area 6

Ditch 1S

Ditch 2S

Ditch 4S

Area 7

N

Key

- Pre-fort features
- Sixth-fifth centuries BC
- Late fifth – mid fourth centuries BC
- Late fourth century BC – late first century AD

0   50 m

Figure 65: Phase plan of the development of Broxy Kennels fort © GUARD Archaeology Ltd.

At some point probably during the fifth century BC, Ditch 2 was backfilled or partially backfilled by its north terminus. Into this backfill a souterrain was later constructed, which may be contemporary with the digging of Ditches 3 and 4. The souterrain was excavated into material which provided radiocarbon dates of 755 cal BC – 416 cal BC (UBA-54873), 751 cal BC – 410 cal BC (UBA-54870) and 408 cal BC – 235 cal BC (UBA-54868) while material found around the paved floor of the souterrain and above it was radiocarbon dated to 540 cal BC – 391 cal BC (UBA-54872) and 513 cal BC – 383 cal BC (UBA-54881) suggesting the souterrain was constructed around the late fifth-early fourth century BC near the end of this first fort. This first phase of the hillfort spanned about 70 to 200 years and which included the construction of the souterrain (see *Radiocarbon Dating and Chronological Modelling*).

A subsequent phase of inhabitation of the fort began sometime around the fourth-third centuries BC and ended around the late first century AD albeit with heavy caveats given the less precise ranges for the start and end dates (see *Radiocarbon Dating and Chronological Modelling)*. This second phase of the settlement spanned about 90 – 305 years and may have been essentially an unenclosed hilltop settlement surrounded by the decaying ramparts and filled in ditches of the previous phase, comparative to the post-hillfort settlements at Broxmouth in East Lothian (Armit and McKenzie 2013, 93). Like Broxmouth, it was only during this latter phase that much in the way of activity was apparent across the hilltop summit. The pits and postholes within the four areas of the interior suggested occupation, but there was little evidence of what it was and there was no pattern to the features. Area 2 consisted of a number of pits and postholes around the entrance to the fort, two of which returned radiocarbon dates of 175 cal BC – 2 cal BC (UBA-54877) and 41 cal BC – cal AD 116 (UBA-54846) and may be contemporary with the backfilling of the souterrain in Ditch 2. Area 3 consisted of two curvilinear alignments of postholes which may have formed parts of structures dated to sometime between the fourth and first centuries BC (349 cal BC – 88 cal BC, UBA-54852 and 342 cal BC – 52 cal BC, UBA-54855). Area 4 consisted of a number of

seemingly random pits: one was radiocarbon dated to near the end of this second phase of the Iron Age fort (116 cal BC – cal AD 7; UBA-54860) while a second pit was dated to the early medieval period (cal AD 574 - cal AD 648, UBA-54856). The group of assorted pits within Area 5 of the fort was returned dates from the earlier Iron Age phase of inhabitation of the fort, 540 cal BC – 399 cal BC (UBA-54878) and 733 cal BC – 401 cal BC (UBA-54879).

Outside the fort entrance, Area 1 to the north consisted of a small curvilinear Ditch 6, possibly a late addition, and a cluster of pits, one of which returned an early Mesolithic radiocarbon date of 9129 cal BC – 8709 cal BC (UBA-54851) presumably from residual material.

The ditches surrounding multivallate Iron Age forts are often found to be further strengthened by the construction of ramparts around their inside edges but these did not survive at Broxy Kennels, although they are assumed to have existed. Excavations at the nearby fort at Moncreiffe Hill identified at least four ramparts around the hillfort constructed from a combination of stone blocks, rubble and soil (Strachan et al. 2023, 27-33). Prior to its excavation, the Broxy Kennels hill had been under arable crops and use for pasture for many years, most likely centuries if not millennia, resulting in any ramparts that may have survived being eroded into the ditches and completely ploughed away. Analysis of the ditch sediments (see *Micromorphology*) suggests that the material filling them is the same material that was excavated from them, suggesting the ditches were naturally or deliberately backfilled with the earthen ramparts and material from the interior area of the fort, including also material that had an earlier origin (see *Radiocarbon Dating and Chronological Modelling)*.

The stratigraphy recorded through the ditches at Broxy Kennels fort suggests that all four were recut at least once, although the number and location of the recuts varied across each ditch. The stratigraphic evidence taken with that of pollen (see *Archaeobotany*) and micromorphology does not seem to suggest the ditches were recut seasonally, but ditch maintenance was probably necessary on a regular basis. Due to the fact the ditches were dug into soft sandy silts forming the hill, the exposure of ditch sides probably quickly led to their erosion with subsequent deposition into the base of the ditch. A process of natural infilling was set in motion as soon as the ditches were dug, exacerbated by the presence of ramparts composed of the same loose material. Ditches were modified however, such as the northern terminus of Ditch 2 which was backfilled prior to the construction of the souterrain. The northern arm of Ditch 3 was also constructed around the same time and also cut Ditch 2, but it is unclear if this occurred before or after the construction of the souterrain. The southern terminus of Ditch 3 was also modified. It was recut and a new terminus was constructed slightly to the south-east of the original; the reason for this may have been related to the entrance way into the fort.

The entrance through the ditches

Pope et al. (2020) suggest that in the fourth century BC, some hillforts may have had several entrances for both humans and animals and thereby creating a focal point in the landscape for communities to gather together. This, however, was not the case at Broxy Kennels, which only had one entrance throughout the lifetime of the fort. This entranceway may have acted like a funnel channelling people and their livestock directly into the centre of the fort. The alignment of the entrance with the contours of the hill and an easy access to the River Tay reinforces Pope's (*ibid*) idea that the proximity of the entrance (gates) to water may emphasise the importance of cattle to Iron Age societies. With the fort situated within a rich agricultural landscape and with its proximity to the river, it implies it acted as a focal point for the local agricultural community (Figure 66).

There was little archaeological evidence, however, for any gates securing the entranceway such as those described as part of the process of bi- or multivallation at other forts. Some gates were significant constructions, such as those at Eddisbury which had a 0.55 m diameter tree trunk forming one of the gate posts. At Broxy Kennels random small pits and postholes were identified around the ditch termini, and especially around Ditch 1 at the top of the incline to the fort interior, and a few externally in front of the entrance. There was no substantial feature to suggest that the ditches had gates except for a possible further ditch from Ditch 3S to almost Ditch 4S. It was not mirrored on the north side of the entrance and therefore any relevance for the presence of gates is speculative.

Structures within the fort

Small concentrations of features were identified within the interior of the fort, which were divided into three main parts: Areas 3, 4 and 5. In Area 3, nearest the entrance were two possible structures of curved alignments of pits and postholes. These structures were considered to be the remains of roundhouses, although both lacked occupation deposits, ring-ditches or any of the other usual features associated with Iron Age roundhouses no doubt due to plough truncation. There was also a distinct lack of material culture from the postholes making their function difficult to characterise. It is possible that the two possible structures identified may represent fence line divisions or some other kind of small enclosures rather than more domestic roundhouses.

Radiocarbon dates taken from several of the pits, postholes and deposits within these three areas within the fort interior suggest that activity there occurred generally in the second to late first centuries BC during the second phase of the fort. Some of the features towards the west side of the fort in Area 5 may belong to the earlier phase, while other features returned radiocarbon dates of around the turn of the first millennia and into the early medieval periods. This suggests that the effect of plough truncation masks a long period of use and reuse of the top of the hill and the fort interior, from possibly as early as the late Bronze Age, predating the construction of the ditches, punctuated throughout the Iron Age, to after the fort was abandoned. The reuse of the hill top, erosion of deposits and the truncation of features by subsequent activities, including ploughing, have left extremely sparse evidence of what exactly the fort interior was used for.

Figure 66: Broxy Kennel Fort during sixth-fifth centuries BC. Artist's reconstruction.

The souterrain

The radiocarbon dates for the souterrain are slightly later than most of those from the ditch fills, tending more towards the end of the first phase of the fort, during the late fifth-early fourth century BC, suggesting that the souterrain was an after-thought to the layout of the ditches. The *Radiocarbon Dating and Chronological Modelling* suggests the overall timespan for this first phase of the fort was a minimum of 70 years to a maximum of 200 years, and that included the construction of the souterrain.

It would seem plausible that the fort was modified when the souterrain was constructed, with Ditch 2 being either partially or wholly backfilled when the souterrain was built. The positioning of Ditches 3 and 4 respected the location of the souterrain and it is possible that they were dug

to modify the fort during the souterrain phase, while Ditch 1 and maybe the termini of Ditch 2 were backfilled. Questions remain as to whether the original function of the fort changed with the construction of the souterrain and why it was considered a necessity at this specific location within the fort (Figure 67). A similar comparison is evident at Castlelaw in Midlothian where a souterrain was inserted into the backfilled middle ditch of a hillfort, albeit much later, in the late second century AD (Childe 1933, 386).

The souterrain was dug into material that backfilled Ditch 2, that was of early Iron Age to early-middle Iron Age in date. The tight radiocarbon dating suggests that the northern terminus of Ditch 2 was backfilled sometime between the late sixth and middle fifth centuries BC, with the souterrain being constructed and in use between the early fifth and middle fourth

Figure 67: Broxy Kennel Fort during late fifth to middle fourth centuries BC. Artist's reconstruction.

centuries BC. There was very little material culture recovered from the souterrain, none of which was diagnostic enough to suggest dates of use for the structure.

Geochemical analysis (see *Multi-element Analysis*) was carried out across the primary floor deposits of the souterrain. The results, however, were inconclusive, suggesting that human activity had taken place within the structure, but heavy leaching of the soils meant that particular activities, their nature and intensities could not be identified. Further analysis of the deposits (see *Micromorphology*) within the souterrain suggested that it was filled in with amalgamated soils over a long period of time, not as one single event. The souterrain did not appear to have ever been reused and once abandoned it slowly filled in naturally with soils from the surrounding ground surface.

Analysis of the basal deposits of the souterrain (see *Archaeobotany*) contained willow and oak charcoal possibly suggesting that the walls or roof of the souterrain was covered with wattle panels with oak supports. There was a scatter of hearth waste and occasional barley and indeterminate cereal grains, but not enough to suggest processing or storage of grain inside it. But if it was not used for storage of grain harvests, the question remains as to what it was used for.

The abandonment of the souterrain appears to have occurred at the end of the first phase of the fort as no material culture was recovered from it that dated to the subsequent phase of the settlement. Some souterrains such as the one at Newmill, Perthshire (Watkins and Barclay 1981) may have been deliberately abandoned much later in time than that at Broxy Kennels. A radiocarbon date from within the Newmill souterrain interior seemed to date its destruction to the second or third centuries AD.

Features contemporary with the souterrain

Ditch 4, the outermost ditch generally returned dates of the late sixth to mid-fourth centuries BC, which was slightly earlier than the sampled floor deposits from the souterrain. They may suggest that the souterrain, Ditch 3 and Ditch 4 were contemporary but the ditches may have started to silt up earlier than the abandonment of the souterrain.

A pit and a posthole in Area 5 to the western end of the fort's interior both appear to be contemporary with the deposits filling Ditch 2 into which the souterrain was inserted. In Area 7 just outside the fort to the south was an isolated fire-pit (694) whose use was contemporary with that of the floor deposits in the souterrain and alder wood was used as its fuel.

Material culture of the fort

As with most Iron Age settlements in Perthshire contemporary material cultural remains are not prolific and are mixed with earlier evidence. The lithic assemblage from Broxy Kennels represents a scatter of artefacts from across several earlier periods which found their way into the fort as residual objects. Three fire-flints also demonstrate probable post-medieval period activity on the site.

The small assemblage of coarse stone tools, using local stone: two grinders, a hammerstone, two anvils along with a possible third anvil, a whetstone and at least two polishers, were largely found in the ditch fills and in colluvium deposits indicating that they could be early, contemporary with or later than the fort. The assemblage was small and typical of lowland Iron Age sites where iron implements were gradually replacing those in stone. The artefacts from Broxy Kennels seem to be typical of stone tool assemblages found in similar settlements across Perthshire. In the lower River Tay forts small assemblages of mostly hand tools, using mostly local stone was the norm (Strachan et al. 2023). Moredun Fort, however, had a larger and more diverse assemblage than other hillforts (*ibid.*).

A small assemblage of Iron Age pottery was found at Broxy Kennels, most of which was recovered from the fills in the four ditch termini, particularly the northern terminus of Ditch 1. Three possible cooking pots were identified (see *Prehistoric Pottery*) and may represent general refuse or an intentional clearing event within the fort. The pottery assemblage appears to be fairly typical for contemporary sites in Perthshire. Sites such as Moncrieffe Fort, Moredun Fort, Castle Law, Kay Craig and Rossie Law have all yielded similar small assemblages of pottery. These pots were often large, wide-mouthed bucket or barrel shaped vessels with slightly inturned rims. Excavations at Broxmouth (Cool 1982, 247-249) identified two main types of pottery from the Iron Age (early thick-walled vessels and later thinner walled ones) which all the Perthshire assemblages generally conform to. The small assemblages recovered from these Iron Age sites may suggest that other, organic materials such as wood were being used in place of pottery (MacSween in Ellis 2007).

A small assemblage of metal objects was recovered from the topsoil during the metal detecting survey of Broxy Kennels hillfort prior to the topsoil strip. These included a brooch (SF 184), a pommel (SF 027) probably from a dagger or sword and a bronze object (SF 019). Analysis revealed zinc in the alloy of the unidentified bronze object (SF 019), suggesting that it was no earlier than Roman period and probably much later (see *Metalwork*). From the design of the copper alloy pommel (SF 027) it was likely soldered to a knife handle from as early as the medieval period to as late as the post-medieval period. The brooch (SF 184) was post-medieval or later in style (Hattatt 1989, 233, Fig 112). These three unstratified objects were all lost at a time long after the fort had been abandoned.

However, a small dispersed assemblage of bog iron ore, iron slag and a piece of vitrified clay, which may represent part of a tuyere - a protective part for bellows used in smelting – may derive from the Iron Age occupation of the site (see *Vitrified Material*). The analysis indicates that there were two layers of vitrification on the tuyere, suggesting it had been used at least twice. This assemblage was found distributed across the site, suggesting smelting activities were carried out over a long period of time, although it is possible that one discreet dump of material had been disturbed and spread around. Within other Iron Age settlements in Scotland, similar wide scatters of iron smelting debris found spatially and stratigraphically across sites have often originated from one specific smelting hearth (McLaren 2023, 143-144). The presence of smelting slag is extremely uncommon amongst Iron Age forts in Scotland and tends to be evident only in fairly complex Iron Age settlements such as Broxmouth hillfort in East Lothian or specialised craftworking centres such as Culduthel in the Highlands (McDonnell 2013; Dungworth and McLaren 2021). The evidence suggests iron smelting took place within the fort as a contemporary activity, and although the amount of material is small this may be an indication of the Broxy's inhabitants' role within the local social network and economy of Iron Age Perthshire.

Environmental evidence from the fort

Macro-botanical and pollen evidence survived in the sampled deposits from the fort (see *Archaeobotany*). The ditches were the most informative features of the fort, usually containing domestic hearth waste materials. Ditch 1S had hazel and cherry charcoal along with large amounts of willow, hazel roundwood and oak suggesting possible wattle structures, also found in the ditch recuts. In its Slot F particularly, close to the location of several fire-pits and possible kiln bases, there were large quantities of oak charcoal suggesting industrial processes took place nearby. The presence of alder charcoal in Slot H may have indicated a structural origin. Further evidence of hazel charcoal in sufficient quantities indicated a wattle hurdle or fence from both Ditch 4S and Ditch 1N. Ditch 2N had a quantity of carbonised heather, broom or gorse which may indicate nearby vegetation or the gathering of those species for other uses, such as bedding, fodder or fuel. A rare fragment of elm came from Ditch 3N along with further burnt wattle panels including a large amount of willow roundwood, and also alder charcoal, perhaps used as furnace fuel. Evidence of mixed charcoal in the lower deposits of the souterrain suggests the possibility that there may have been a wooden structure over the top of it that subsequently burnt down.

Samples from the features in and around the fort also contained scattered hearth waste with traces of possible oak posts from two postholes in Area 2. Some cereal grain was recovered from both Structures 1A and 1B, while other features contained midden waste. The central area in the fort, Area 4, material was identified possibly indicating the presence of a burnt structure.

The Broxy Kennels archaeobotany assemblage appears to be typical for prehistoric settlement in the region. For example, excavations at Moredun Fort (Robertson in Strachan 2023, 179) revealed a monumental roundhouse where there was evidence of a catastrophic fire, and cereals had become accidentally scattered across its contexts. There was also some evidence of food waste, while sedge and weed seeds may have suggested thatched buildings. Oak and alder was selected for construction with large structural elements made from the former (*ibid*, 182). The presence of alder, hazel and willow and cherry, like at Broxy Kennels suggests wattle screens were employed in the construction of Moredun. In addition, there was evidence of heather used for its building's roofs. Together these indicate that native plant species were widespread and obtainable locally to the forts. The diversity of species around Moredun indicates that the landscape comprised pockets of woodland as well as open moorland.

Further afield at Braehead in Glasgow (Ellis 2007), barley and some less common wheat grains were recovered from the excavated Iron Age roundhouses together with a small amount of chaff possibly used as kindling, while peat and wood were used as fuel.

The Broxy Kennels environmental remains demonstrate changes to the landscape from the early Bronze Age into the early Iron Age, with the development of fields for cereal cultivation, the use of woodland species, many taken from wet or damp areas near the river, others from surviving woodland in the vicinity of the fort. The use of hazel roundwood for wattle panels could indicate coppicing and woodland management in areas local to the fort, while heather species denote there were also areas of more open moorland or uncultivated land,

Inferring occupation in the interior of the fort is difficult as most of the evidence from the ditch deposits contained scattered hearth material and domestic midden waste. However, the occurrence of hazel roundwood in Ditch 1 may indicated wattle panels could have been use in or on the ramparts, or as structural items to buildings in the fort interior. Large quantities of oak charcoal in Ditch 1S could suggest possible industrial processes occurring in that area, and the presence of a large amount of alder charcoal in Ditch 3N also suggests structural or industrial processes in this area, possibly related to the souterrain.

Only a small assemblage of mammal bone was recovered from the deposits excavated at Broxy Kennels (see *Animal Bone*). Many of the samples could not be identified due to their fragmentation and poor preservation. However, evidence suggests sheep or goats, pigs and cattle were kept during the Iron Age with little evidence of wild species. Similar assemblages to this were recovered from hillforts at Castle Law, Abernethy, and Moredun Fort on Moncreiffe Hill (Strachan et al. 2023), suggesting a common local pattern of reliance on animal husbandry as part of the local agricultural economy of Iron Age forts in the Perthshire area.

Understanding the fort and souterrain

The archaeological evidence at Broxy Kennels suggests the fort had an initial defensive function with at least two ditches (Figure 66). The sporadic and thin evidence of postholes in its interior support the presence of structures, possibly roundhouses using wattle panelling. It is also likely that wattle panels were used in connection with the ditches and their ramparts. Much of the archaeobotanical remains are typical of hearth and midden waste suggesting people were living and working in and around the hillfort, which implies it also had a domestic function. Changes to the fort took place with the filling in of the terminus of Ditch 2N, while Ditches 3 and 4 were created along with the souterrain, and presumably its associated settlement. Although these modifications were carried out over the lifetime of the fort, they do not seem to have changed the function of it significantly. The presence of structures and the later construction of the souterrain suggest that the fort was occupied on a permanently basis.

The digging of the ditches created the fort. Ditches 1 and 2 were the original defences, and were recut at least once during the fort's occupation. Later, Ditch 2 was partially backfilled and the souterrain constructed into it. Ditch 3 was added to encompass the new structure as part of the same event while Ditch 4 was excavated to encompass the entire hill (Figure 67). This chronology is complicated by that part of Ditch 4S that returned some of the earliest radiocarbon dates from the fort, 1047 cal BC – 901 cal BC (UBA-54859) and 3653 cal BC – 3522 cal BC (UBA-54861), from late Bronze Age and early Neolithic. One possible explanation for this is that the interior of the fort was refurbished and relevelled with residual deposits from much earlier phases of occupation of the site dumped into the ditch. The recutting of the ditches was important for them to function, but natural silting and the dumping of large amounts of waste, including structural material and pottery, necessitated further cleaning, clearing, redigging and finally closure or abandonment of the site.

The function of the souterrain remains elusive. The archaeobotanical results indicated the possibility of wattle panelling with oak supports lining or dividing its internal space, along with a general deposition of hearth waste. Cereal grains were present, some of barley but mostly indeterminate grain, but not enough to suggest the processing or storage of grain took place in the structure. Geochemical analysis for specific activities could not be conclusively demonstrated, and the soil micromorphology indicated it was left open for a long period of time and gradually filled in. Its roofing is a problem, but oak timber with wattle panelling may have been used to cover the structure. There was no surviving evidence of a roundhouse being built over the top of the souterrain.

There are approximately 200 Iron Age souterrains known to exist in Scotland (Hunter and Carruthers 2012; Figure 68) along with early medieval souterrains in Ireland and similar Iron Age structures in Cornwall, to which the Broxy Kennels souterrain can be compared (Table 41). The nearby Loak Farm souterrain, north of Luncarty, possibly had a corbelled roof, as it was a smaller structure than that at Broxy Kennels. However, it contained stone tools, pottery and iron slag, iron objects and paving slabs but produced little evidence for a surface structure

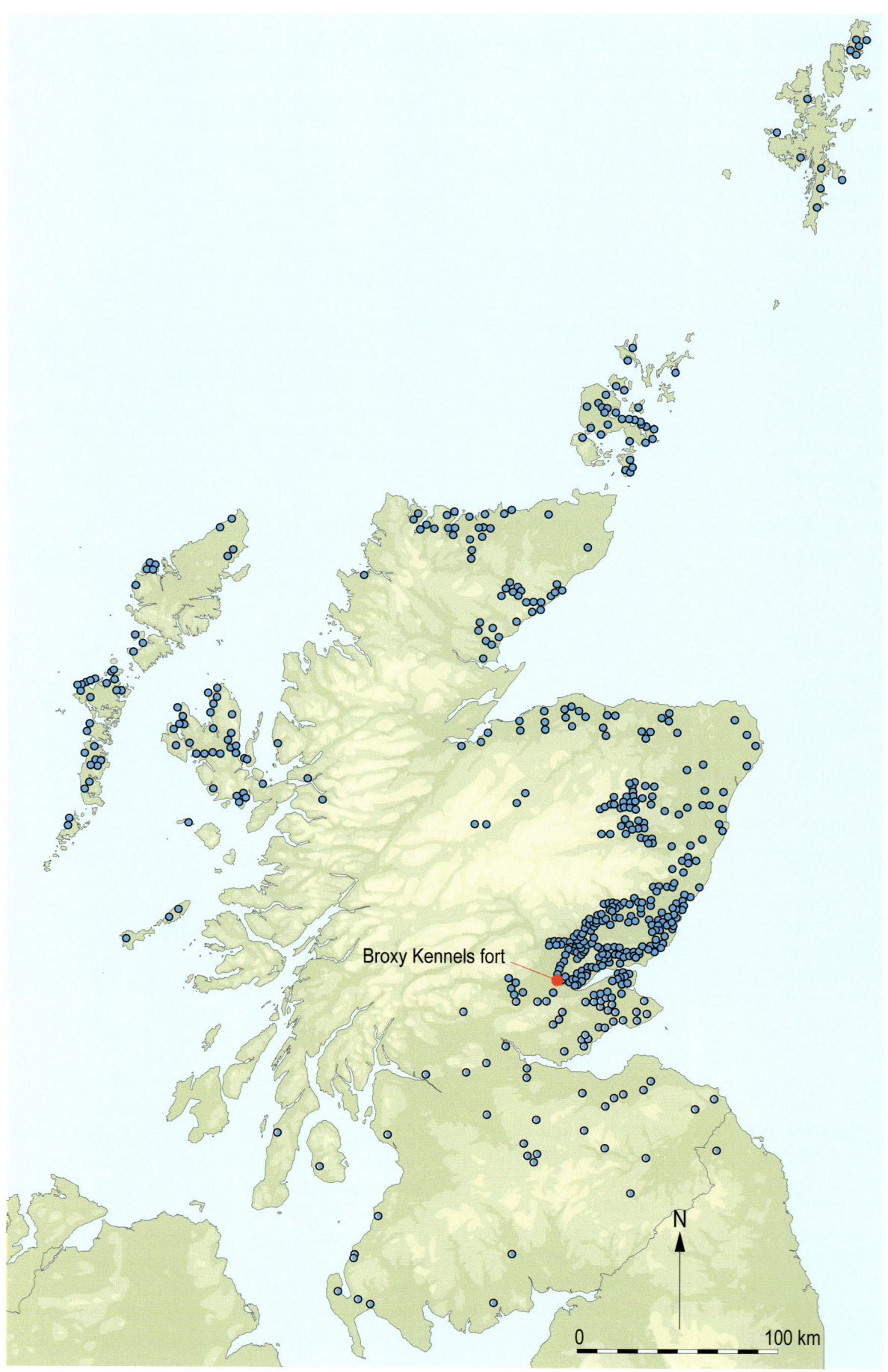

Figure 68: Map of souterrains across Scotland and Northern England © GUARD Archaeology Ltd.

(Demay 2021). The Newmill souterrain near Bankfoot, Perthshire did not appear to have any floor deposits, but charcoal was recovered from it. The structure appeared to have been deliberately abandoned and filled in at one event and there was no evidence of its roof (Watkins and Barclay 1981). Observations by Wainwright (1963) based on excavations at Ardestie and Carlungie, both north of Dundee, suggest that souterrains may have sometimes been dismantled deliberately rather than left to ruin as both of these examples had been partially demolished and filled in, although the settlements surrounding them had continued to be occupied (Armit 1999).

Another, but much longer souterrain with two chambers was excavated at Pitcur, Forfarshire. It had three entrances and some of the stones used in the structure had cup marks. Samian pottery and a Roman coin were recovered during its excavation along with 'many other finds' now all lost (MacRitchie 1900).

The Shanzie souterrain, Alyth, Perthshire was first used c. 200 BC and had a primary fill which contained many Iron Age finds including metalworking debris along with Romano-French Samian pottery, hulled barley and some oats. When it was abandoned at the end of the first century AD it lay open and was filled in naturally, with its roof stones collapsed into its chamber. The abandonment and infilling was dated by a Roman stone (Coleman and Hunter 2002).

Further afield, in Cornwall, the Boden Vean Fogue (Gossip 2003) measured 9.8 m in length and was likely to have been originally longer and may have joined another earth-cut passage. It had been roofed with slabs and was backfilled in a single event. This structure contained a basal deposit over the natural stone floor. The word fogue is derived from the Cornish word for cave and there are 11 such structures known in Cornwall but it is likely that there were more. They also date to the Iron Age, drawing comparisons with souterrains.

The paucity of material culture and the amount of environmental remains recovered from Broxy Kennels fort is typical of other Perthshire forts especially when compared to the majority of sites investigated by Strachan et al. (2023) and the hillforts excavated by the Glasgow University SERF project (Poller et al. 2007).

Souterrain	Length (m)	Width (m)	Height (m)
Broxy Kennels	9.66 m	4 m	1.08 to 1.17 m
Loak Farm (Demay 2022)	10 m	1.7 to 2.5 m	1.6 m
Newmill (Watkins and Barclay 1981)	20.75 m	1.8 to 4 m	2 m
Pitcur (MacRitchie 1900)	58 m	1.5-2m	?
	18 m	3m	?
Shanzie (Coleman and Hunter 2002)	25 m	2 m	1.6 m
Boden Vean Fogue (Gossip 2003)	9.8 m	1.2-1.9 m	1.5 m

Table 41: Measurements of souterrains.

The spatial distribution of artefacts and environmental remains aids our recognition of activities in parts of the Broxy Kennels fort to a limited extent. The finds and samples dumped or accumulated in Ditch 1N (Slot trenches A and B) - sherds of pottery, flint, stone tools, animal bone, slag, vitrified clay and charcoal might suggest the remains of a nearby structure or structures within the interior space, but there was no physical evidence to corroborate this. However, they suggest both domestic and industrial processes took place fairly near to the fort entrance.

Several pits identified as possible fire-pits or kilns were located close to the outer edge of Ditch 1S (Slot F) and contained large quantities of oak charcoal suggesting an industrial process had taken place in that location (see *Archaeobotany*). There were insufficient material cultural remains from this area to suggest what the industrial processes might have been. Ditch 2N (Slot D) contained an abundance of heather, broom and gorse charcoal which could suggest the presence of bread ovens within the fort, or alternatively this material could have been used for animal bedding or fodder. Associated with this material were medieval or later finds, suggesting much later activities in this area.

The pollen analysis (see *Archaeobotany*) from Ditch 1N gives more detail concerning the changes to the local environment over the course of the lifespan of the Broxy Kennels fort. After Ditch 1N was recut, cereal pollen increased indicating higher levels of farming in the immediate landscape. An increase in herbaceous pollen also suggests that domestic animals may have been allowed to graze on, or close to, the fort at around the same time. Also recorded was a slight increase in cereal pollen after the ditch was recut suggesting an increase in the rate or amount of arable farming. Tree and shrub pollen suggest woodland had been depleted over time and it was not present close to the fort when the ditch was dug, but in order to gather hazel wood (from the numerous charcoal fragments) the inhabitants of the fort would have had to travel further afield. Altogether this evidence suggests that, over the course of the use of Broxy Kennels fort, there was an intensification of both arable and pastoral farming around the site with a reduction in tree cover.

Although Broxy Kennels appears to have been abandoned before the end of the first century AD, the remains of the settlement may still have been visible to Roman soldiers who arrived in this area about the same time to establish their fort at Bertha c. end of the 1st to the 3rd century AD The Roman Gask Project 2005) to the immediate south of Broxy Kennels.

Evidence for Roman interest or influence at Broxy Kennels fort is non-existent. The souterrain at Broxy Kennels did not contain any Roman material unlike other souterrains such as Pitcur, Shanzie and Loak Farm discussed above, which suggests that there was contact between people living at or near these sites. This did not happen at Broxy Kennels presumably because it had been abandoned by this time.

Broxy Kennels was abandoned, probably for a number of reasons. Evidence for burnt wattle in some of its ditches suggests that the fort may have been cleared out at some point. Given the lack of later Iron Age dates from the ditches, the ramparts may have long since eroded away and filled in the ditches by the time the subsequent Iron Age settlement was abandoned. However, other mundane reasons could include the demise or the dispersal of the community that lived in the vicinity of the fort where resources were easier to obtain. That the arrival of the Romans caused its abandonment is a remote possibility, because the archaeological evidence points to Broxy Kennels having been abandoned prior to the establishment of Bertha Roman fort.

It is quite possible the people from the fort moved not far away from it as still may have 'belonged' to them. The flood plain of the River Tay was not necessarily a good choice for a new settlement as it may have had heavy soils and was liable to flood. The obvious movement was probably inland, where a new farming settlement could be established. Redgorton, some 800 m north-west from the hillfort, is perhaps an example of such a farm whose origins could stretch back into the Iron Age.

The local, regional and national context of the fort

Perth and Kinross region is known to have a large number of hillforts which are comparable to Broxy Kennels fort, some of them being multivallate. The *Atlas of Hillforts* (Lock and Ralston 2017) describes Broxy Kennels as a contour fort with a single enclosure. This is the same for most of the forts in Perthshire, although Ben Effray is categorised as a promontory fort and Moredun Top is described as a contour fort with multiple enclosures (Figure 69). None of these other hillforts, however, have a souterrain like that at Broxy Kennels, the closest example being the hillfort at Castlelaw in the Pentland hills south of Edinburgh (Childe 1933).

The radiocarbon dates returned from Broxy Kennels placed the fort broadly in the early Iron Age but comparison should be made with other similar forts to put it into a chronological sequence. The nearby fort of Moncreiffe appears to begin around 595 to 405 cal BC and ends 400 to 135 cal BC (Strachan et al. 2023, 39) similar to the span at Broxy Kennels. The roundhouse at Moredun Top was the earliest structure there dating to 325 to 240 BC, and activity ended c. 325 to 15 BC. Castle Law at Abernethy returned only one suitable sample that was dated to the middle Bronze Age but it may have been a reused or portable object that was brought into the site. Bone recovered during Victorian excavations at Castle Law was dated to the early Iron Age.

The SERF project run by the University of Glasgow investigated a number of hillforts in Perthshire, some of which have published radiocarbon dates (Poller et al. 2007 and Lock and Ralston 2017).

These include Dun Knock which was dated to between 800 and 400 cal BC; Rossie Law which returned dates of between 1200 to 800 cal BC, 800 to 400 cal BC and 400 cal BC to 50 cal AD; Kay Craig which dated to between 800 to 400 cal BC; Castle Craig which returned later dates of between 50 and 400 cal AD and post 800 AD; and Ben Effray which was dated to between 800 and 400 cal BC. This evidence places most of the hillforts in Perthshire broadly into the pre-Roman Iron Age suggesting many were roughly contemporary with the occupation of Broxy Kennels at some time or another.

Some forts such as Rossie Law and Castle Craig have later dates ranging from the late Iron Age into the medieval period. The Brown Caterthun in Angus was dated to the early to middle Iron Age and emphasises what appears to have been a period of intense fort-building across Scotland (Dunwell and Strachan 2007). A few others such as Guardbridge (Kilpatrick et al. 2005) seem to have their origins in the early Iron Age, while others continued either sporadically or continuously throughout the Iron Age and into the early medieval period (Toolis 2021, 265; Muir and Toolis 2024, 125-130).

While Broxy Kennels appears to conform to the general chronology of hillforts, having been constructed in the early Iron Age, other forms of monumental building took place in Scotland. At Moredun (Strachan et al. 2023) for example, a monumental roundhouse may predate the construction of the fort's ditches. Brochs such as Leckie (MacKie 2016); Fairy Knowe (Main et al. 1999) and Castle Craig (James 2012) are likely to be later in date than the hillforts (Figure 69). Macinnes (1984) suggests that most of the dating evidence from these structures comes from Roman material such as Samian ware, glass and metalwork dating to the first and second centuries AD, rather than the structures themselves. The changes made to the Broxy Kennels fort such as recutting of ditches and the excavation of new ditches and the souterrain may reflect widespread societal changes in the middle to late Iron Age.

In terms of restricted attributes at Broxy Kennels, there was evidence of iron working in the form of some slag and a fragment of a tuyere that came from a deposit in the recutting of Ditch 1. Most of the slag and vitrified material at Broxy Kennels came from secure contexts, from fills above recuts suggesting that this was an activity which came late to the fort. Metalworking was not part of the initial activities that took place at the fort and may relate to the modification of ditches and the construction of the souterrain.

Although rare, evidence for metalworking has been found at other hillfort sites in Perthshire. The three forts discussed by Strachan et al. (2023) produced small amounts of metal working and vitrified material. A small amount of vitrified clay was recovered from Moncreiffe and small amounts of ferrous metalworking waste indicative of blacksmithing was found at Moredun Top, although no *in situ* smithing evidence was located. Part of a crucible which may have been for copper working along with some vitrified material was recorded Castle Law.

Although the original function of the Broxy Kennels souterrain cannot be explicitly determined, its presence on the site suggests a level of social significance for its inhabitants. There is a wide variation in form and size of souterrains across Scotland such as Gress Lodge in Lewis (MacRitchie 1916) and Pitcur in Angus (MacRitchie 1900) making attempts to determine their function difficult. They would, however, have been required a large amount of intensive labour to dig, quarry and transport the stone required for their building, possibly requiring skills and expertise brought in from outside the immediate community (Armit 1999, 582).

Souterrains were often found in farming settlements throughout the Scottish Lowlands with a large concentration in Perthshire, Angus, Fife and Aberdeenshire. Some have speculated that this may have distinguished their builders culturally, ethnically or politically from their surrounding neighbours (Armit 1999, 583) but the distribution of souterrains across Scotland (Figure 68) demonstrates that Iron Age societies across Scotland were open to the building and occupation of souterrains but that Iron Age societies further south were not (Toolis 2021, 267). The souterrain at Broxy Kennels does not, however, add any further insight into why this enigmatic structure was built where it was and why.

Inter-regional settlements around Perthshire include the number of forts already discussed above such as those excavated by Strachan et al. (2023) and the SERF project, along with the oblong enclosure at Finavon and Forgandenny (Harding 2017, 85) and forts such as the Caterthuns in Angus. The Brown Caterthun is thought to have been a communal meeting place for the inhabitants of the surrounding landscape (Dunwell and Strachan 2017, 72-74). A number of homesteads and settlements have been identified and discussed by Harding (2017, 95) across central and eastern Scotland (Figure 69) including both palisaded homesteads such as that at Bannockburn (Rideout 1997), and Douglasmuir in Angus which dates to around middle of the first millennium BC, similar to Broxy Kennels (Kendrick 1995).

Immediately north of Broxy Kennels was another souterrain at Newmill near Bankfoot suggesting a like-minded community in that area. Upland stone-built settlements (Harding 2017, 102) such as Dalruzion are thought to span the middle to late Iron Age, suggesting a continuity of structures that were fairly uninterrupted by the Romans. Around Loch Tay were a number of crannogs (Atkinson 2016, 34-35), which would have exploited nearby agricultural land and natural resources. These buildings on water continued to be built throughout the Iron Age and the medieval period. The Croftvellich building, near to Ben Lawers, was occupied by Iron Age people, and Tombreck was occupied during later Iron Age. The latter was a homestead made up of a series of roundhouses dating to 400 to 200 BC (Atkinson 2016, 59). Taylor (1990) looked at the

Figure 69: Map of sites mentioned in the discussion.

Litigan homestead, dating to around 840 to 1020 AD, which began as a monumental roundhouse with a continuation of homesteads lasting into the early medieval period.

The large body of research into settlements in the Iron Age in Scotland suggests that, although hillforts such as Broxy Kennels were common, various other forms of settlement occurred around Perthshire and beyond. Despite the name, hillforts may not always have been purely defensive. Collis (1981) argues that they were built for prestige, with impressive facades but with minimal defences to the rear. This suggests that hillforts and other forms of monumental structure were built to impress visitors and give an impression of wealth and grandeur. Strachan et al. (2023, 251) adds that although construction of forts may have required some guidance from external experts, constructing and maintaining the forts required a large local workforce. These structures may have, much like the Brown Caterthun, acted as a focus for gatherings of the community, bringing people together to fulfil social and communal obligations (Ralston 1996, 145; Sharples 1991, 263). It is likely that the workforce required to build a hillfort was much larger than the community that lived permanently there, though reciprocal obligations may have motivated this rather than simply coercion.

In its wider context the occupation of Broxy Kennels was similar in its structure, dates and material cultural assemblage to that of other contemporary sites such as Moncreiffe, Moredun and Abernethy (Strachan et al. (2023). However, Hamilton and Manley (2001) suggested that as the early Iron Age progressed into the latter half of the first Millennium BC, around the floruit of Broxy Kennels and its contemporaries, there was

a re-working of social politics in society. There is little evidence for centralised production, exotic goods or trade networks associated with these hillforts, suggesting that the sites were 'monumentalised' and played a role in bringing together dispersed communities around a central topographical place. As time went on hillforts were being constructed in similar locations and in similar forms but by less homogenous, more dispersed communities who needed a central location to focus on.

Around the beginning of the first millennium AD there appeared to be a general move away from many former enclosed settlements such as Broxy Kennels. However not all enclosed settlements disappeared, with extremely large hilltop settlements such as Traprain Law in East Lothian and Tap O'Noth in Aberdeenshire (Figure 69) re-emerging at the same time until the very early medieval period, when small but complex hierarchically organised fortified settlements began to reappear in the settlement record. Though some early medieval enclosed settlements such as Rhynie in Aberdeenshire were entirely new constructions, several other early medieval forts such as Dunadd in Argyll and Edinburgh Castle Rock may have been largely continuously occupied from the Iron Age, while others such as Trusty's Hill in Galloway and Tinnis in the Scottish Borders were re-occupied after a period of abandonment (Noble et al. 2019; Lane and Campbell 2000; Driscoll and Yeoman 1997; Toolis and Bowles 2017; Muir and Toolis 2024).

Where prominent early medieval households may have reused the locations of past forts, this did not occur at Broxy Kennels, as the hillfort became part of the agricultural landscape and its monumentality was ploughed into the ground.

Bibliography

Adderley, W P, Wilson, C A, Simpson, I A and Davidson, D A 2010 Anthropogenic Features, 569-588, *in* Stoops, G Marcelino, V and Mees, F (eds.) *Interpretation of Micromorphological Features of Soils and Regoliths*. Amsterdam: Elsevier.

Ahmed, A A, Leinweber, P and Kuhn, O 2023 Advances in understanding the phosphate binding to soil constituents, *Science of The Total Environment* 887, 163692.

AMS Ltd 2021 Cross Tay Link Road: A Written Scheme of Archaeological Investigation Pre-construction Version P05. Unpublished document.

Armit, I 1999 The abandonment of souterrains: evolution, catastrophe or dislocation? *Proceedings of the Society of Antiquaries of Scotland* 129, 577-596.

Armit, I and McKenzie, J 2013 *An Inherited Place: Broxmouth Hillfort and the South-East Scottish Iron Age*. Edinburgh: Society of Antiquaries of Scotland.

Arroyo-Kalin, M 2014 Anthropogenic sediments and soils: Geoarchaeology, 279-284, *in*, Smith, C (ed.) *Encyclopaedia of Global Archaeology*.: New York, Springer.

Ashman, M and Puri, G 2013 *Essential soil science: a clear and concise introduction to soil science.* Oxford: Blackwell Publishing.

Ashmore, P J 1999 Radiocarbon dating: avoiding errors by avoiding mixed samples, *Antiquity* 73, 124-130.

Atkinson, J A 2016 Ben Lawers, an archaeological landscape in time: results from the Ben Lawers Historic Landscape Project, 1996-2005. *Scottish Archaeological Internet Reports* 62. Available from: https://journals.socantscot.org/index.php/sair/issue/view/91

Bailie, W and Ramsay, S 2022 Cross Tay Link Road, Perth Project-Wide Sampling Strategy. Unpublished document, GUARD Archaeology Ltd.

Ballin, T B 2005 Lithic artefacts and pottery from Townparks, Antrim Town, *Ulster Archaeological Journal* 64, 12-25.

Ballin, T B 2008 Quartz Technology in Scottish Prehistory. *Scottish Archaeological Internet Reports* 26. Available from: http://www.sair.org.uk/sair26.

Ballin, T B 2009 Archaeological Pitchstone in Northern Britain. Characterization and interpretation of an important prehistoric source. British Archaeological Reports British Series 476. Oxford: Archaeopress.

Ballin, T B 2011 *Overhowden and Airhouse, Scottish Borders: characterization and interpretation of two spectacular lithic assemblages from sites near the Overhowden henge*. Oxford: BAR: British Series 539.

Ballin, T B 2015 Arran pitchstone (Scottish volcanic glass): New dating evidence, *Journal of Lithic Studies* 2 (1), 5-16. Available from: http://journals.ed.ac.uk/lithicstudies/article/view/1166

Ballin, T B 2017 Pitchstone from radiocarbon-dated pits – an update, *PAST* 87, 14-15.

Ballin, T B 2018 The procurement of Rhum bloodstone and the Rhum bloodstone exchange network – a prehistoric social territory in the Scottish Inner Hebrides? *Archäologische Informationen* 41 (Early View). Available from: http://vg01.met.vgwort.de/na/37e29030e27c4afd9c263be32e3ee102?l=https://journals.ub.uni-heidelberg.de/index.php/arch-inf/article/download/56945/48309

Ballin, T B 2021 *Classification of Lithic Artefacts from the British Late Glacial and Holocene Periods*. Oxford: Archaeopress Publishing Ltd.

Ballin, T B 2025 The lithic assemblage, *in* Kilpatrick, M et al. *Guardbridge, Fife: A multi-period settlement with a multi-vallate fort*, Archaeology Reports Online 61. Available from: https://www.archaeologyreportsonline.com/PDF/ARO61_Guardbridge.pdf

Ballin, T B forthcoming a: The lithic assemblage, *in* Rees, A Guardbridge, Fife.

Ballin, T B forthcoming b: The lithic assemblage, *in* Sheridan, A *The chambered tomb at Strath Glebe, Isle of Skye*.

Ballin, T B and Faithfull, J 2009 Gazetteer of Arran Pitchstone Sources. Presentation of exposed pitchstone dykes and sills across the Isle of Arran, and discussion of the possible archaeological relevance of these outcrops. *Scottish Archaeological Internet Reports* 38. Available from: http://www.sair.org.uk/sair38

Ballin, T B, Ellis, C and Bailie, W 2018 Arran pitchstone – different forms of exchange at different times? *CIfA Scottish Group Newsletter*, Spring 2018.

Ballin Smith, B 2019 Fired Clay in Arabaolaza, I Beside the River Ayr in prehistoric times: excavations at Ayr Academy, *Archaeology Reports Online* 33. Available from: https://www.archaeologyreportsonline.com/reports/2019/ARO33.html

Ballin Smith, B 2025 The prehistoric pottery, *in* Kilpatrick, M et al. *Guardbridge, Fife: A multi-period settlement with a multi-vallate fort*.

Ballin Smith forthcoming b: The prehistoric pottery, *in* Atkinson, J-J and McNicol, D *Bronze Age ritual monuments and domestic occupation at Northbar, Erskine*.

Banks, I 2000 Excavation of an Iron Age and Romano-British enclosure at Woodend Farm, Johnstonebridge, Annandale, 1994 and 1997, *Proceedings of the Society of Antiquaries of Scotland* 130, 223-81.

Barnetson, L 1986 Animal bone from Clatchard Craig, 178, *in* Close-Brooks, J Excavations at Clatchard Craig, Fife, *Proceedings Society Antiquaries Scotland* 116, fiche 1:B1–C14.

BGS = British Geological Survey 2024 *Geology of Britain Online Viewer*. Available from: https://www.bgs.ac.uk

Bronk Ramsey, C 1995 Radiocarbon calibration and analysis of stratigraphy: the OxCal program, *Radiocarbon* 37, 425-430.

Bronk Ramsey, C 1998 Probability and dating, *Radiocarbon* 40, 461-474.

Bronk Ramsey, C 2001 Development of the radiocarbon calibration program, *Radiocarbon* 43, 355-363.

Bronk Ramsey, C 2009 Bayesian analysis of radiocarbon dates, *Radiocarbon* 51, 337-360.

Brophy K and Noble G 2012 Within and beyond pits: deposition in lowland Neolithic Scotland, 63-76, *in* Anderson-Whymark H and Thomas J (eds.) *Regional Perspectives on Neolithic Pit Deposition*: Beyond the Mundane. Oxford: Oxbow Books.

Brown, A G, Davis, S R, Hatton, J, O'Brien, C, Reilly, F, Taylor, K, Emer Dennehy, K, O'Donnell, L, Bermingham, N, Mighall, T, Timpany, S, Tetlow, E, Wheeler, J and Wynne, S 2016 The Environmental Context and Function of Burnt-Mounds: New Study of Irish Fulachtaí Fiadh, *Proceedings of the Prehistoric Society* 82, 259-290.

Buck, C E, Cavanagh, W G and Litton, C D 1996 *Bayesian approach to interpreting archaeological data*. Chichester: John Wiley and Sons, Ltd.

Bullock, P, Federoff, N, Jongerius, A, Stoops, G, Turina, T and Babel, U 1985 *Handbook for Soil Thin Section Description*. Albrighton: Waine Research.

Burton, E 2018 Appendix F: Geophysical Survey Report of Cross Tay Link Road, *in* Shaw, C Report 4855: Cross Tay Link Road Archaeological Watching Brief and Geophysical Survey. Unpublished Archaeology Data Structure Report, GUARD Archaeology Ltd.

Cappers, R T J, Bekker, R M and Jans, J E A 2006 *Digital Seed Atlas of the Netherlands*, Groningen Archaeological Studies 4. Eelde, The Netherlands: Barkhuis Publishing.

Chartered Institute for Archaeologists (CIfA) 2014 (revised 2020) *Standard and guidance for the collection, documentation, conservation and research of archaeological materials*. Reading: CIfA. Available from: http://www.archaeologists.net/sites/default/files/CIfASandGFinds_1.pdf

Childe, V G 1933 Excavations at Castlelaw Fort, Midlothian, *Proceedings of the Society of Antiquaries of Scotland* 67, 362-88.

Christison, D and Anderson, J 1899 On the recently excavated fort on Castle Law, Abernethy, Perthshire, with notes on finds, *Proceedings of the Society of Antiquaries of Scotland* 33 (1898-9), 13-33.

Clark, J G D 1936 Report on a Late Bronze Age Site in Mildenhall Fen, West Suffolk, *The Antiquaries Journal* 14, 29-50.

Coleman, R and Hunter, F 2002 The excavation of a souterrain at Shanzie Farm, Alyth, Perthshire, *Tayside and Fife Archaeological Journal* 8, 77-101.

Coles, J M. 1971 The Early Settlement of Scotland: Excavations at Morton, Fife, *Proceedings of the Prehistoric Society* 37, 284-366.

Collis, J A 1981 Theoretical Study of Hillforts, 66-67, *in* Guilbert, G. (ed.) *Hillfort Studies Essays for AHA Hogg*. Leicester: Leicester University Press.

Crew, P and Rehren, T 2002 High temperature workshop residues from Tara: iron, bronze and glass, 83-102, *in* Roche, H (ed.) *Excavations at Ráith na Ríg, Tara, Co Meath, 1997*. Dublin: Royal Irish Academy, Discovery Programme Reports 6.

Cruickshanks, G 2017 Iron in Iron Age Scotland: a long term case study of production and use, c.800BC to AD 800. Unpublished PhD thesis, University of Edinburgh.

Cruickshanks, G and Hunter F 2019 Metalworking Debris and Other Vitrified Materials from Dunknock, Perth and Kinross.

Unpublished Specialist Report, National Museums Scotland.

Davidson, D, Wilson C, Meharg A A, Deacon C and Edwards K J 2007 The legacy of past manuring practices on soil contamination in remote rural areas, *Environment International* 33 (1), 78-83.

Demay, L 2021 Land at Loak Farm, Bankfoot, Perth and Kinross Strip, map and record: phase 2b. Unpublished Data Structure Report, AOC Archaeology Group.

Driscoll, S T and Yeoman, P 1997 *Excavations within Edinburgh Castle in 1988–91*. Edinburgh: Society of Antiquaries of Scotland.

Dungworth, D and McLaren, D 2021 Metal, 142-167, *in* Hatherley, C and Murray, R *Culduthel: An Iron Age Craftworking Centre in North-East Scotland*. Edinburgh: Society of Antiquaries of Scotland.

Dunwell, A J and Strachan, R 2007 *Excavations at Brown Caterthun and White Caterthun Hillforts, Angus, 1995-1997*. Perth: Tayside and Fife Archaeological Committee Monograph 5.

Egan, G and Pritchard, F 2002 *Dress Accessories 1150-1450: medieval finds from excavations in London*. London: Museum of London.

Ellis, C 2007 Total excavation of a later prehistoric enclosure at Braehead, Glasgow, *Proceedings of the Society of Antiquaries of Scotland* 137, 179-264.

Ellis, C, Cruickshanks, G, Hall, D, Bjarke Ballin, T, Ramsay, S and Anderson, S 2021 The Logierait terraces, a place of significance, *Tayside and Fife Archaeological Journal* 22, 8-22.

Gale, R and Cutler, D 2000 *Plants in Archaeology*. Otley: Westbury Publishing.

Gossip, J 2009 The evaluation of a multi-period prehistoric site and fogou at Boden Vean, St Anthonyin-Meneage, Cornwall, 2003, *Cornish Archaeology* 52, 1-98.

Graham, T 2004 Wattle and Daub: Craft, Conservation and Wiltshire Case Study. Unpublished MSc dissertation, University of Bath.

Green, H S 1980 *The Flint Arrowheads of the British Isles. A detailed study of material from England and Wales with comparanda from Scotland and Ireland.* BAR British Series 75 (i). Oxford: British Archaeological Reports.

Halliday, S 2019 How many hillforts are there in Scotland? Revisited, 37-52, *in* Romankiewicz, T, Fernández-Götz, M, Lock, G and Büchsenschütz, O (eds.) *Enclosing Space, Opening New Ground: Iron Age Studies from Scotland to Mainland Europe.* Oxford: Oxbow Books.

Hamilton, S and Manley, J 2001 Hillforts, monumentality and place: a chronological and topographic review of first millennium BC hillforts of south-east England, *European Journal of Archaeology* 4 (1), 7-42.

Hamilton, W D and Kenney, J 2015) Multiple Bayesian modelling approaches to a suite of radiocarbon dates from ovens excavated at Ysgol yr Hendre, Caernarfon, North Wales, *Quaternary Geochronolog* 25, 72-82.

Hamilton, W D, and Haselgrove, C 2019 Exploring settlement dynamics through radiocarbon dating, 111-120, *in* Romankiewicz, T, Fernández-Götz, M. Lock, G. and Büchsenschütz O. (eds.) *Enclosing Space, Opening New Ground: Iron Age Studies from Scotland to Mainland Europe.* Oxford: Oxbow.

Harding, D W 2017 *The Iron Age in Northern Britain: Britons and Romans, Natives and Settlers.* Abingdon: Routledge.

Hattatt, R 1989 *Ancient Brooches and Other Artefacts.* Oxford: Oxbow Books.

HES = Historic Environment Scotland 2016 *Scotland's Archaeology Strategy.* Edinburgh: Historic Environment Scotland.

Hunter, F and Carruthers M 2012 *Iron Age.* Scottish Archaeological Research Framework: Society of Antiquaries of Scotland. Available from: https://tinyurl.com/vpla6yx

James, H 2012 Castle Craig 2012, Unpublished SERF Data Structure Report, University of Glasgow.

Johnson, M 2013 Prehistoric pottery, 35-40, *in* Suddaby, I Excavation of post-built roundhouses and a circular ditched enclosure at Kiltaraglen, Portree, Isle of Skye 2006-07, *Scottish Archaeological Internet Report* 54. Available from: https://journals.socantscot.org/index.php/sair/issue/view/84

Kendrick, J 1995 Excavation of a Neolithic enclosure and an Iron Age settlement at Douglasmuir, Angus, *Proceedings of the Society of Antiquaries of Scotland* 125.

Kilpatrick, M, Barbour, J, Muir, T and Hunter, C 2025 *Guardbridge, Fife: A multi-period settlement with a multi-vallate fort*, Archaeology Reports Online 61. Available from: https://www.archaeologyreportsonline.com/reports/2025/ARO61.html

Kühn, P, Aguilar, J, Miedema, R, and Bronnikova, M 2018 Textural pedofeatures and related horizons, 377-423, *in* Stoops, G Marcelino, V and Mees, F (eds.) *Interpretation of Micromorphological Features of Soils and Regoliths.* Amsterdam: Elsevier.

Laing, D 1976 *The soils around Perth, Arbroath and Dundee.* The Soil Survey of Scotland. Dundee: Macaulay Land Use Research Institute.

Lane, A and Campbell, E 2000 *Dunadd: An Early Dalriadic Capital.* Oxford: Oxbow Books.

Lang, C 2014 The hidden archive of historical human inhumations locked within burial soils. Unpublished Ph.D Thesis, University of York.

Lindbo, D L, Stolts, M H and Vepraskas, M L 2010 Redoximorphic Features, 129-185, *in* Stoops, G Marcelino, V and Mees, F (eds.) *Interpretation of Micromorphological Features of Soils and Regoliths.* Amsterdam: Elsevier.

Lock, G and Ralston I 2017 *Atlas of Hillforts of Britain and Ireland.* Available from: https://hillforts.arch.ox.ac.uk

Lucas, V A and Paynter, S 2010 *Whitby Cliff, Whitby, North Yorkshire – an assessment of metalworking debris from the Whitby Cliff Excavations.* English Heritage Research Department Report Series, 31.

MacKie, E W 2016 *Brochs and the Empire: The impact of Rome on Iron Age Scotland as seen in the Leckie broch excavations*. Oxford: Archaeopress Publishing Ltd.

MacInnes, L 1984 Brochs and the Roman occupation of lowland Scotland, *Proceedings of the Society of Antiquaries of Scotland* 114, 235-49.

Macphail, R I and Goldberg, P 2010 Archaeological material, 589-622, *in* Stoops, G Marcelino, V and Mees, F (eds.) *Interpretation of Micromorphological Features of Soils and Regoliths*. Amsterdam: Elsevier.

MacRitchie, D 1900 Description of an Earth-House at Pitcur, Forfarshire, *Proceedings of the Society of Antiquaries of Scotland* 34, 202-214.

Main, L, Barber, J, Boyd, W E, Caldwell, D, Clarke, A, Collins, G and Young, A 1999 Excavation of a timber round-house and broch at the Fairy Knowe, Buchlyvie, Stirlingshire, 1975-8, *Proceedings of the Society of Antiquaries of Scotland* 128, 293-417.

McDonnell, G 2013 Metallurgical and vitrified material, 393-402, *in* Armit, I and McKenzie, J *An Inherited Place: Broxmouth Hillfort and the south-east Scottish Iron Age*. Edinburgh: Society of Antiquaries of Scotland.

McDonnell, J G and Milns, J 2015 Ferrous and non-ferrous metalworking, 392-428, *in* Dockrill, S, Bond, J, Turner, V, Brown, L, Bashford, D, Cussans, J and Nicholson, R *Excavations at Old Scatness, Shetland Volume 2: The Broch and Iron Age Village*. Lerwick: Shetland Heritage.

McK Clough, T H 1988 Introduction, 1-11, *in* Clough, T H McK and Cummins, W *A Stone Axe Studies Vol 2: The petrology of prehistoric stone implements from the British Isles.* CBA Research Report 67. Dorset: CBA.

McLaren, D 2023 The metal-working waste and associated vitrified materials, 136-45, in Strachan, D, Cook, M and McLaren, D *Three Forts on the Tay: Excavations at Moncrieffe, Moredun and Abernethy, Perth and Kinross 2014-17*. Oxford: Archaeopress Publishing Ltd.

Moore, P D, Webb, J A and Collinson, M E 1991 *Pollen Analysis*. 2nd edition. Oxford: Blackwell Scientific Publications.

Muir, T and Toolis R 2024 Tinnis Fort, 125-137, *in* Toolis, R, Gilmore, A, Muir, T, Muser, L and Woodward, A Unearthing Ancient Tweeddale: Tinnis Castle, Thirlestane Barrows and Merlin's Grave, *Archaeology Reports Online* 56. Available from:https://www.archaeologyreportsonline.com/reports/2024/ARO56.html

Murray, H K and Murray, J C 2021 Nether Park Quarry, Aberdeenshire: a small Mesolithic and Neolithic site on the banks of the River Dee, *Archaeology Reports Online* 43. Available from: https://www.archaeologyreportsonline.com/reports/2021/ARO43.html

Nicol, S and Ballin, T B 2019 Freeland Farm, Perth and Kinross – a mainly Late Mesolithic carnelian assemblage from the Lower Strathearn, *Archaeology Reports Online* 36. Available from: https://www.archaeologyreportsonline.com/reports/2019/ARO36.html

Noble, G, Gondek, M, Campbell, E, Evans, N Hamilton, D and Taylor, S 2019 Rhynie: a powerful place of Pictland, 58–80, *in* Noble, G and Evans, N (eds.) *The King in the North: The Pictish Realms of Fortriu and Ce*. Edinburgh: Birlinn.

Oades, J M 1984 Soil organic matter and structural stability: mechanisms and the implications for management, *Plant and Soil* 76, 319-337.

Oonk, S, Slomp, C P, Huisman, D J and Vriend, S P 2009 Effects of site lithology on geochemical signatures of human occupation in archaeological house plans in the Netherlands, *Journal of Archaeological Science* 36(6), 1215-1228.

Owen, O 1992 Eildon Hill North, 21-71, *in* Rideout, J S, Owen, O A and Halpin, E *Hillforts of Southern Scotland*. Edinburgh: AOC Scotland Ltd/Historic Scotland.

Paterson. E 2011 *Geochemical atlas of Scottish topsoils*. Aberdeen: Macaulay Land Use Research Institute.

Pettitt, R and Hession, J 2019 Perth Transport Futures Project: Phase 2 – Cross Tay Link Road, Perth, Perthshire Archaeological Evaluation. Unpublished Data Structure Report CTLR19. Rubicon Heritage Services Ltd.

Pickering M D, Ghislandi S, Usai M R, Wilson C, Connelly P, Brothwell D R and Keeley B J 2018 Signatures of degraded body tissues and environmental conditions in grave soils from a Roman and an Anglo-Scandinavian age burial from Hungate, York, *Journal of Archaeological Science* 99, 87-98.

Pierce, C, Adams, K R and Stewart, J D 1998 Determining the fuel constituents of ancient hearth ash via ICP-AES analysis, *Journal of Archaeological Science* 25(6), 493-503.

Poller, T, Goldberg, M and Driscoll, S. 2007 The Strathearn Environs and Royal Forteviot Project (SERF) - Jackschairs Hillfort, Perth and Kinross (Forgandenny parish), excavation, 155-156, *Discovery and Excavation in Scotland* 8.

Pope, R, Mason, R, Hamilton, D, Rule, E, and Swogger, J 2020 Hillfort gate-mechanisms: a contextual, architectural reassessment of Eddisbury, Hembury, and Cadbury hillforts, *Archaeological Journal* 177 (2), 339-407.

Prehistoric Ceramics Research Group 2010 *The Study of Prehistoric Pottery. General Policies and Guidelines for Analysis and Publication*, PCRG Occasional Papers 1 and 2 (3rd edition). Salisbury: Wessex Archaeology.

Ralston, I 2015 The hillforts and enclosed settlements of Scotland: an overview, 201-10, *in* Hunter, F and Ralston, I (eds.) *Scotland in Later Prehistoric Europe*. Edinburgh: Society of Antiquaries of Scotland.

Reimer, P J, Austin, W E N, Bard, E, Bayliss, A, Blackwell, P G, Ramsey, C B, Butzin, M, Cheng, H, Edwards, R L, Friedrich, M, Grootes, P M, Guilderson, T P, Hajdas, I, Heaton, T J, Hogg, A G, Hughen, K A, Kromer, B, Manning, S W, Muscheler, R, Palmer, J G, Pearson, C, Plicht, J v d, Reimer, R W, Richards, D A, Scott, E M, Southon, J R, Turney, C S M, Wacker, L, Adolphi, F, Büntgen, U, Capano, M, Fahrni, S M, Fogtmann-Schulz, A, Friedrich, R, Köhler, P, Kudsk, S, Miyake, F, Olsen, J, Reinig, F,

Sakamoto, M, Sookdeo, A, Talamo, S 2020 The IntCal20 Northern Hemisphere Radiocarbon Age Calibration Curve (0–55 cal k BP), *Radiocarbon* 62, 725-757.

Rideout, J S 1997 Excavation of a promontory fort and a palisaded homestead at Lower Greenyards, Bannockburn, Stirling, 1982-5, *Proceedings of the Society of Antiquaries of Scotland* 126, 199-269.

Robertson, J 2023 Animal bone analysis, *in* Strachan, D, Cook, M and McLaren, D *Three Forts on the Tay: Excavations at Moncrieffe, Moredun and Abernethy, Perth and Kinross 2014–17*. Oxford: Archaeopress Publishing Ltd.

The Roman Gask Project 2005. Available from: https://www.theromangaskproject.org/the-roman-gask-project-1997/

Salisbury, R B 2020 Advances in archaeological soil chemistry in central Europe, *Inderdisciplinaria Archaeologica: Natural Sciences in Archaeology* 11(2), 199-211.

Savory, G 2019 Excavation of a double-ditched enclosure at Winchburgh, *Scottish Archaeological Internet Reports* 82. Available from: http://journals.socantscot.org/index.php/sair/article/view/10133.

Schweingruber, F H 1990 *Anatomy of European Woods*. Berne and Stuttgart: Haupt.

Sharples, N 1991 *Maiden Castle: Excavations and field survey 1985-6*. Archaeological Report, vol. 19. London: English Heritage.

Sheridan, A 2004 Scottish Food Vessel Chronology, 243-269, *in* Gibson, A and Sheridan A (eds.) *From Sickles to Circles: Britain and Ireland at the time of Stonehenge*. Stroud: Tempus Publishing Ltd.

Sheridan, J A 2008 Battle axeheads; the types and uses of cinerary urns; Early Neolithic Carinated Bowl pottery, *in* Lelong, O and MacGregor *The Lands of Ancient Lothian: Interpreting the Archaeology of the A1*, 108, 110, 213; see also archive reports on pottery from several sites. Edinburgh: Society of Antiquaries of Scotland.

Soil Survey of Scotland = Scotland's soils 2024. Available from: https://soils.environment.gov.scot/maps/soil-maps/national-soil-map-of-scotland/

Stafford, J 2024 Archaeology tours return to Arthur's Stone for a final year of excavations. *The University of Manchester, University Alumni Magazine 2024*.

Stoops, G 2003 *Guidelines for Analysis and Description of Soil Regolith Thin Sections*. Soil Science Society of America, Inc. USA.

Stace, C 1997 *New Flora of the British Isles.* (2nd edition). Cambridge: Cambridge University Press.

Steier, P and, Rom, W 2000 The use of Bayesian statistics for ^{14}C dates of chronologically ordered samples: a critical analysis, *Radiocarbon* 42, 183-198.

Strachan, D 2020 *Hillforts of the Tay.* Perth: Perth and Kinross Heritage Trust.

Strachan, D, Cook, M and McLaren, D 2023 *Three Forts on the Tay: Excavations at Moncrieffe, Moredun and Abertnethy, Perth and Kinross, 2014-17*. Oxford: Archaeopress Publishing Ltd.

Stuiver, M and Polach, H A 1977 Reporting of ^{14}C data, *Radiocarbon* 19, 355-363.

Taylor D B 1990 Circular homesteads in North West Perthshire, *Abertay Historical Society* 29.

The Roman Gask Project 2005 Available from: https://www.theromangaskproject.org/the-roman-gask-project-1997/

Toolis, R 2015 Iron Age settlement patterns in Galloway, *Transactions of the Dumfriesshire and Galloway Natural History and Antiquarian Society* 89, 17-34.

Toolis, R 2021 Shifting perspectives on 1st-millennia Scotland, *Proceedings of the Society of Antiquaries of Scotland* 150, 247-278.

Toolis, R 2022 Project 5764: Broxy Kennels Fort Archaeological Research Framework (Appendix J). Unpublished report. GUARD Archaeology Ltd.

Toolis, R and Bowles, C 2017 *The Lost Dark Age Kingdom of Rheged: The Discovery of a Royal Stronghold at Trusty's Hill, Galloway*. Oxford: Oxbow Books.

Wainwright, F T 1963 *The souterrains of Southern Pictland.* London: Routledge Kegan Paul.

Walker, B and McGregor C 1996 *Earth Structures and Construction in Scotland.* Edinburgh: Historic Scotland.

Ward, G K and Wilson, S R 1978 Procedures for comparing and combining radiocarbon age determinations: a critique, *Archaeometry* 20, 19-32.

Ward Perkins, J B 1940 *The London Museum Medieval Catalogue*. London: HMSO.

Watkins, T and Barclay, G 1981 Excavation of a settlement and souterrain at Newmill, near Bankfoot, Perthshire, *Proceedings of Society of Antiquaries of Scotland* 110, 165-208.

Wilson, C, Davidson, D and Cresser, M S 2007 Evaluating the use of multi-element soil analysis in archaeology: a study of a post-medieval croft (Olligarth) in Shetland, *Atti della Societa Toscana di Scienze Naturali* - Memorie serie A, 112, 69-79.

Wilson, C, Davidson, D and Cresser M S 2008 Multi-element soil analysis: an assessment of its potential as an aid to archaeological interpretation, *Journal of Archaeological Science* 35 (2), 412-424.

Appendices

Appendix 1: Tables 2-28 botanical results
Table 2

				D1S-A						
Area										
Context	012	014	020	033	035	049	051	053	068	
Sample	2	4	18	19	35	24	31	30	42	
Description	Upper fill of ditch (005) slot A	Fill of small pit (013)	Intermediate fill of (065) - recut ditch 1 (005)	Lower fill of ditch 1 (005)	1st fill of recut (030) in ditch 1 (005)	Fill of posthole (048)	Fill of fire pit (050)	Fill of posthole (052)	Fill of slot A ditch 1	
Volume of charcoal >4mm	2ml	1ml	<1ml	-	5ml	1ml	15ml	2ml	20ml	
% charcoal >4m identified	1	100%	100%	-	100%	100%	100%	100%	100%	
Charcoal										
Alnus cf glutinosa — alder	-	-	1 (0.03g)	-	7 (0.41g)	-	-	-	29 (1.33g)	
Betula spp — birch	1 (0.02g)	-	-	-	-	1 (0.04g)	21 (1.48g)	4 (0.17g)	2 (0.06g)	
Corylus cf avellana — hazel	2 (0.07g)	1 (0.02g)	-	-	3 (0.21g)	-	24 (1.19g)	3 (0.02g)	33 (1.65g)	
Cytisus / Ulex — broom / gorse	-	1 (0.01g)	-	-	-	-	-	-	-	
Prunoideae — cherry type	-	-	-	-	-	-	-	-	1 (0.05g)	
Quercus spp — oak	2 (0.02g)	-	1 (0.02g)	-	1 (0.01g)	-	1 (0.08g)	1 (0.02g)	11 (0.51g)	
Salix spp — willow	-	-	-	-	1 (0.04g)	-	9 (0.52g)	-	6 (0.34g)	
Indet charcoal — indet charcoal	-	-	-	-	-	1 (0.02g)	-	-	-	
Indet cinder — indet cinder	-	-	-	-	-	12 (0.21g)	-	-	-	
Cereals (carbonised)										
Avena spp — oat	-	-	-	-	-	-	7	-	-	
Hordeum vulgare sl — barley	-	-	-	-	-	-	15	-	-	
cf Hordeum vulgare sl — cf barley	-	-	-	-	-	-	76	-	-	
Indet cereal — indet cereal	1	-	-	-	-	1	575	-	-	
Seeds etc (carbonised)										
Bromus spp — brome grass	-	-	-	-	-	-	1	-	-	
Chenopodium album — fathen	-	-	-	-	-	-	132	-	-	
Corylus avellana nutshell frags — hazel nutshell	-	-	6 (0.04g)	-	-	-	-	-	-	
Fallopia convolvulus — black bindweed	-	-	-	-	-	-	1	-	-	
Lamiaceae — dead nettle family	-	-	-	-	-	-	1	-	-	
Persicaria maculosa — redshank	-	-	-	-	-	-	204	-	-	

Table 2 continued

Area		D1S-B					D1S-C			
Context		138	139	141	142	524	205	206	208	209
Sample		103	104	105	107	867	367	368	370	371
Description		Fill of ditch recut (140) slot B	Fill of ditch recut (140) slot B	Basal fill of ditch recut (140) slot B	Fill of ditch 1 (005) slot B	Fill of posthole (523)	Fill of (005) slot C	Fill of (005) slot C	Fill of (005) slot C	Fill of (005) slot C
Volume of charcoal >4 mm		80ml	1ml	2ml	-	<1ml	5ml	4ml	<1ml	1ml
% charcoal >4m identified		50%	100%	100%	-	100%	100%	100%	100%	100%
Charcoal										
Alnus cf glutinosa	alder	-	-	-	-	-	-	-	-	-
Betula spp	birch	-	-	-	-	-	-	-	-	-
Corylus cf avellana	hazel	9 (1.63g)	6 (0.20g)	2 (0.15g)	-	1 (0.02g)	10 (0.31g)	2 (0.12g)	-	4 (0.14g)
Cytisus / Ulex	broom / gorse	-	-	-	-	-	-	-	-	-
Prunoideae	cherry type	-	-	1 (0.06g)	-	-	-	-	-	-
Quercus spp	oak	1 (0.11g)	-	-	-	-	5 (0.12g)	6 (0.23g)	-	2 (0.06g)
Salix spp	willow	28 (7.91g)	-	-	-	1 (0.01g)	5 (0.16g)	2 (0.12g)	1 (0.05g)	-
Indet charcoal	indet charcoal	-	-	-	-	-	-	-	-	-
Indet cinder	indet cinder	-	-	-	-	-	-	-	-	-
Cereals (carbonised)										
Avena spp	oat	-	-	-	-	-	-	-	-	-
Hordeum vulgare sl	barley	-	-	-	-	-	-	-	-	-
cf Hordeum vulgare sl	cf barley	-	-	-	-	3	-	-	-	-
Indet cereal	indet cereal	-	-	-	-	-	-	-	-	-
Seeds etc (carbonised)										
Bromus spp	brome grass	-	-	-	-	-	-	-	-	-
Chenopodium album	fathen	-	-	-	-	-	-	-	-	-
Corylus avellana nutshell frags	hazel nutshell	-	-	-	-	1 (<0.01g)	5 (0.02g)	1 (0.01g)	-	-
Fallopia convolvulus	black bindweed	-	-	-	-	-	-	-	-	-
Lamiaceae	dead nettle family	-	-	-	-	-	-	-	-	-
Persicaria maculosa	redshank	-	-	-	-	-	-	-	-	-

Table 3

Area	D1S-F							D1S-E					D1S-D		
Context	321	196	191	190	189	189	188	174	175	171	168	183	163	161	160
Sample	812	299	297	296	SF106	295	294	201	200	217	163	287	286	284	283
Description	Fill of fire-pit (317)	Fill of ditch (005)	Fill of cut ditch (192)	Fill of cut ditch (192)	Fill of cut ditch (192)	Fill of cut ditch (192)	Fill of cut ditch (192)	Fill of (173)	Fill of (173)	Fill of ditch 1 (005)	Fill of (167)	Fill of channel base of slot D ditch 1 (005)	Fill of slot D ditch 1 basal (005)	Fill of slot D ditch 1 (005)	Fill of slot D ditch 1 uppermost (005)
Volume of charcoal >4 mm	400ml	<1ml	2ml	20ml	100ml	30ml	5ml	6ml	10ml	<1ml	5ml	2ml	4ml	10ml	8ml
% charcoal >4m identified	25%	100%	100%	100%	100%	100%	100%	100%	100%	100%	100%	100%	100%	100%	100%
Charcoal															
Alnus cf glutinosa (alder)	-	-	-	4 (0.17g)	-	5 (0.10g)	-	2 (0.05g)	17 (0.63g)	-	1 (0.11g)	-	-	9 (0.19g)	8 (0.18g)
Betula spp (birch)	-	-	-	6 (0.26g)	-	2 (0.07g)	1 (0.01g)	-	-	-	-	-	-	-	8 (0.19g)
Corylus cf avellana (hazel)	-	-	-	17 (0.63g)	5 (2.01g) rw	29 (1.19g)	10 (0.29g)	3 (0.12g)	23 (1.00g)	-	6 (0.18g)	5 (0.12g)	6 (0.18g)	10 (0.41g)	10 (0.27g)
Ericales (heather type)	-	-	-	-	-	-	1 (0.03g)	-	-	-	-	-	-	-	-
Prunoideae (cherry type)	-	-	-	2 (0.09g)	-	4 (0.42g)	-	6 (0.33g)	-	-	-	-	-	-	1 (0.03g)
Quercus spp (oak)	373 (20.55g)	2 (0.04g)	9 (0.21g)	3 (0.16g)	48 (25.22g)	9 (0.35g)	3 (0.07g)	-	2 (0.06g)	6 (0.03g)	1 (0.08g)	4 (0.09g)	12 (0.43g)	7 (0.33g)	3 (0.07g)
Salix spp (willow)	-	-	1 (0.13g)	29 (0.36g)	-	46 (2.42g)	10 (0.27g)	11 (0.26g)	5 (0.12g)	1 (0.02g)	7 (0.39g)	4 (0.17g)	2 (0.10g)	15 (0.43g)	6 (0.16g)
Ulmus spp (elm)	-	-	-	-	-	-	-	-	1 (0.19g)	-	-	-	-	-	-
Indet charcoal (indet charcoal)	-	-	-	-	-	-	-	-	-	-	-	-	-	-	1 (0.05g)
Seeds etc (carbonised)															
Corylus avellana nutshell frags (hazel nutshell)	24 (0.20g)	-	1 (0.03g)	1 (<0.01g)	-	-	2 (0.01g)	-	3 (0.02g)	1 (0.01g)	-	6 (0.02g)	-	-	2 (0.04g)

Table 4

Area	D1S-G				D1S-H							D1S-I			D1S-J
Context	197	199	265	267	213	214	215	221	227	257	259	243	248	291	286
Sample	326	325	823	824	314	315	316	321	313	526	525	518	486	536	535
Description	Basal fill slot G (005)	2nd fill slot G (005)	Fill of (457) posthole	fill of (457) posthole	Bottom fill of cut (005)	Bottom fill of cut (005)	Fill of recut (216)	Fill of recut (216)	Bottom fill of recut (216)	Fill of recut (256)	Lower fill of recut (258)	Bottom fill of (232) 005 l	Middle fill of 005 l	Band of clay within recut (279) slot l	Upper fill of (275) in slot J of inner ditch
Volume of charcoal >4 mm	50ml	15ml	<1ml	1ml	30ml	1ml	15ml	15ml	80ml	12ml	50ml	10ml	12ml	4ml	25ml
% charcoal >4m identified	50%	100%	100%	100%	100%	100%	100%	100%	50%	100%	100%	100%	100%	100%	100%
Charcoal															
Alnus cf glutinosa — alder	-	13 (0.21g)	-	-	23 (2.93g)	-	3 (0.16g)	11 (0.28g)	4 (0.32g)	12 (0.41g)	61 (8.36g)	1 (0.06g)	2 (0.10g)	1 (0.07g)	11 (0.85g)
Betula spp — birch	19 (0.69g)	5 (0.18g)	-	-	-	-	-	1 (0.10g)	-	2 (0.05g)	-	5 (0.28g)	3 (0.15g)	1 (0.01g)	4 (0.18g)
Corylus cf avellana — hazel	62 (2.55g)	27 (1.09g)	-	2 (0.03g)	18 (1.10g)	1 (0.02g)	12 (0.47g)	23 (1.65g)	46 (4.75g)	18 (0.76g)	13 (0.76g)	20 (0.57g)	18 (0.68g)	6 (0.17g)	43 (2.06g)
Ericales — heather type	-	-	2 (0.06g)	-	-	-	-	-	-	-	-	-	-	-	-
Prunoideae — cherry type	-	1 (0.05g)	-	1 (0.04g)	-	1 (0.03g)	3 (0.17g)	-	1 (0.02g)	-	-	-	-	-	6 (0.31g)
Quercus spp — oak	-	1 (0.02g)	-	1 (0.01g)	-	3 (0.05g)	13 (1.01g)	10 (0.31g)	1 (0.21g)	-	-	1 (0.06g)	1 (0.01g)	1 (0.02g)	2 (0.04g)
Salix spp — willow	9 (0.37g)	3 (0.08g)	-	1 (0.03g)	10 (0.39g)	4 (0.09g)	17 (0.99g)	6 (0.53g)	10 (0.75g)	7 (0.27g)	-	9 (0.31g)	6 (0.26g)	2 (0.29g)	12 (0.50g)
Seeds etc (carbonised)															
Corylus avellana nutshell frags — hazel nutshell	1 (0.02g)	1 (<0.01g)	-	-	1 (0.02g)	-	-	-	-	-	-	-	2 (0.01g)	-	-

Table 5

	D2S-A				D2S-D	D2S-E			D2S-E/M		D2S-F		
Area													
Context	018	037	038	041	358	326	327	370	748	751	318	365	366
Sample	5	28	29	27	774	727	728	762	1003	1000	739	760	761
Description	Fill of ditch 2 (007) slot (25A)	Lower main fill of ditch 2 (007) slot A	Lowest fill of ditch 2 (007) slot A	Charcoal rich fill of ditch 2 (007) slot A	Fill of ditch 2 cut 007 slot D	Fill of (007) slot E	Fill of (007) slot E	Fill of (007) ditch slot E	Fill of (007) Slot M	Fill of (007) Slot M	Mid fill of Ditch 2S Slot F	2nd fill of Ditch 2S Slot F	Basal fill of Ditch 2S Slot F
Volume of charcoal >4 mm	<1ml	10ml	<1ml	80ml	4ml	1ml	4ml	15ml	5ml	<1ml	10ml	<ml	1ml
% charcoal >4m identified	100%	100%	100%	100%	100%	100%	100%	100%	100%	100%	100%	100%	100%
Charcoal													
Alnus cf glutinosa — alder	-	5 (0.39g)	-	51 (2.40g)	3 (0.06g)	-	7 (0.41g)	5 (0.23g)	2 (1.15g)	1 (0.01g)	26 (1.19g)	-	-
Betula spp — birch	-	3 (0.16g)	-	2 (0.08g)	-	3 (0.09g)	-	17 (0.88g)	-	-	1 (0.02g)	-	-
Corylus cf avellana — hazel	-	5 (0.16g)	-	18 (0.69g)	5 (0.23g)	1 (0.03g)	2 (0.05g)	19 (0.79g)	-	-	5 (0.16g)	-	-
Maloideae — rowan type	-	-	-	1 (0.04g)	-	-	-	-	-	-	-	-	-
Prunoideae — cherry type	-	3 (0.64g)	-	15 (0.72g)	-	-	-	4 (0.14g)	-	-	-	-	-
Quercus spp — oak	1 (<0.01g)	6 (0.21g)	2 (0.01g)	6 (0.24g)	4 (0.14g)	-	1 (0.04g)	4 (0.12g)	-	-	2 (0.03g)	1 (0.01g)	-
Salix spp — willow	-	8 (0.21g)	-	27 (1.90g)	-	-	2 (0.09g)	4 (0.16g)	-	-	5 (0.10g)	1 (0.01g)	-
Indet charcoal — indet charcoal	-	-	-	-	-	-	-	-	-	-	-	-	4 (0.16g)
Seeds etc (carbonised)													
Corylus avellana nutshell frags — hazel nutshell	-	9 (0.14g)	-	-	-	-	-	-	-	-	-	-	-

153

Table 6

	D2S-G			D2S-H	D2S-I			D2S-J				D2S-L	
Area													
Context	341	343	352	332	402	403	405	430	431	434	477	396	420
Sample	744	746	750	759	785	786	788	804	805	808	839	781	799
Description	Fill of ditch (007) slot G	Fill of ditch (007) slot G	Bottom fill of ditch (007) slot G	Basal fill of (007) slot H	Ditch (007) slot I	Ditch (007) slot I	Basal fill of (007) slot I	fill of (007) slot J	fill of (007) slot J	fill of (007) slot J	Fill of (007) Slot J	Fill of (007) slot L poss PH remnant	Fill of (007) slot C
Volume of charcoal >4 mm	<1ml	2ml	1ml	10ml	7ml	2ml	1ml	100ml	10ml	4ml	1ml	<1ml	2ml
% charcoal >4m identified	100%	100%	100%	100%	100%	100%	100%	50%	100%	100%	100%	100%	100%
Charcoal													
Alnus cf glutinosa — alder	1 (0.02g)	-	-	4 (0.35g)	5 (0.11g)	3 (0.12g)	-	22 (8.62g)	32 (1.03g)	11 (0.37g)	-	1 (0.02g)	9 (0.25g)
Betula spp — birch	-	-	-	3 (0.11g)	-	-	-	-	-	-	-	-	-
Corylus cf avellana — hazel	-	5 (0.07g)	-	15 (1.08g)	13 (0.72g)	-	3 (0.21g)	3 (0.20g)	-	-	3 (0.03g)	-	5 (0.07g)
Prunoideae — cherry type	-	-	-	-	6 (0.26g)	-	-	-	2 (0.07g)	1 (0.03g)	-	-	-
Quercus spp — oak	-	-	1 (0.09g)	4 (0.10g)	2 (0.07g)	-	1 (0.04g)	1 (0.09g)	2 (0.04g)	-	2 (0.03g)	-	-
Salix spp — willow	-	2 (0.02g)	-	3 (0.45g)	1 (0.04g)	-	-	1 (0.14g)	-	-	-	-	1 (0.02g)
Cereals (carbonised)													
Hordeum vulgare sl — barley	-	1	-	-	-	-	-	-	-	-	1	-	-
Seeds etc (carbonised)													
Bromus spp — brome grass	-	-	-	-	-	-	-	3	-	-	-	-	-
Carex spp — sedge	-	-	-	-	-	-	-	4	-	-	-	-	-
Corylus avellana nutshell frags — hazel nutshell	-	-	-	-	1 (0.01g)	-	-	-	-	1 (0.03g)	-	-	-
Danthonia decumbens — heath grass	-	-	-	-	-	-	-	3	-	-	-	-	-
Poaceae — grass	-	-	-	-	-	-	-	1	-	-	-	-	-

Table 7

Area						D3S-A					D3S-B	Linear 311	
Context	045	071	096	097	166	179	181	856	862	340	313	314
Sample	63	41	64	65	162	246	248	1091	1095	743	732	733
Description	Top fill of (009) ditch	3rd fill of (046)	3rd fill (009) ditch	4th fill of (009) ditch	Bottom fill of (164)	Top fill of (009) terminus	Bottom fill of (009) terminus	Fill of ditch (048) Slot C Lower	Fill of ditch (009) - lowest	Fill of (046) slot B	Fill of possible linear (311)	Fill of possible linear (311)
Volume of charcoal >4 mm	3ml	2ml	2ml	<1ml	30ml	10ml	1ml	5ml	-	2ml	4ml	6ml
% charcoal >4m identified	100%	100%	100%	100%	100%	100%	100%	100%	-	100%	100%	100%
Charcoal												
Alnus cf glutinosa alder	6 (0.17g)	-	-	1 (0.01g)	30 (1.00g)	-	-	-	-	-	-	-
Betula spp birch	-	1 (0.02g)	-	-	-	2 (0.16g)	-	2 (0.10g)	-	-	3 (0.10g)	2 (0.07g)
Corylus cf avellana hazel	4 (0.13g)	4 (0.14g)	2 (0.06g)	-	70 (4.15g)	23 (0.94g)	-	6 (0.31g)	-	3 (0.11g)	2 (0.03g)	19 (0.24g)
Prunoideae cherry type	1 (0.03g)	1 (0.05g)	-	-	2 (0.17g)	1 (0.06g)	-	-	-	1 (0.05g)	-	-
Quercus spp oak	1 (0.03g)	-	1 (0.01g)	-	6 (0.39g)	-	3 (0.02g)	4 (0.36g)	-	1 (0.02g)	2 (0.05g)	2 (0.11g)
Salix spp willow	4 (0.07g)	1 (0.11g)	1 (0.05g)	-	8 (0.38g)	1 (0.13g)	1 (0.02g)	2 (0.06g)	-	2 (0.04g)	5 (0.35g)	3 (0.25g)
Seeds etc (carbonised)												
Corylus avellana nutshell frags hazel nutshell	-	-	-	-	-	1 (0.01g)	-	5 (0.05g)	-	2 (0.02g)	-	2 (0.01g)

Table 8

		D4S-A					D4S-B		D4S-C		
Area											
Context		080	081	082	1055	306	889	893	469	479	536
Sample		57	58	66	1224	614	1121	1125	836	849	891
Description		Fill of ditch (047) slot A	Fill of ditch (077) slot A	Fill of ditch (047)	Fill of pit (1054)	Fill of (299) slot B	Fill of (912)	Fill of (912)	Fill of post hole (468) in (047) slot F	Fill of Ditch (047) Slot F	Fill of (535)
Volume of charcoal >4 mm		15ml	50ml	20ml	-	25ml	1ml	<1ml	<1ml	2ml	-
% charcoal >4m identified		100%	50%	100%	-	100%	100%	100%	100%	100%	-
Charcoal											
Alnus cf glutinosa	alder	9 (1.43g)	16 (0.73g)	33 (1.21g)	-	16 (0.56g)	1 (0.05g)	-	-	-	-
Betula spp	birch	1 (0.02g)	-	6 (0.22g)	-	-	1 (0.01g)	-	-	-	-
Corylus cf avellana	hazel	6 (0.27g)	27 (1.75g)	34 (1.43g)	-	33 (2.40g)	1 (0.01g)	2 (0.02g)	-	4 (0.16g)	-
Maloideae	rowan type	-	-	1 (0.30g)	-	-	-	-	-	-	-
Prunoideae	cherry type	1 (0.03g)	2 (0.10g)	-	-	-	1 (0.03g)	-	-	-	-
Quercus spp	oak	2 (0.07g)	6 (0.26g)	6 (0.23g)	-	1 (0.05g)	1 (0.02g)	-	1 (0.02g)	1 (0.02g)	-
Salix spp	willow	12 (0.85g)	25 (0.88g)	11 (0.45g)	-	30 (2.13g)	-	-	-	-	-
Cereals (carbonised)											
Hordeum vulgare sl	barley	-	-	-	-	13	-	-	-	-	-
Indet cereal	indet cereal	-	-	-	-	10	-	-	-	-	-
Seeds etc (carbonised)											
Corylus avellana nutshell frags	hazel nutshell	2 (0.01g)	1 (<0.01g)	-	-	7 (0.02g)	2 (<0.01g)	-	-	-	-

156

Table 9

	D4S-D	D4S-E			D4S-F	D4S-G		D4S-H	D4S-I	
Context	495	637	638	640	644	655	688	653	691	746
Sample	862	922	923	925	947	927	951	931	957	984
Description	Fill of (047)	Fill of (476)	Fill of (476)	Basal fill of (476)	Fill of ditch (476)	Fill of (476)	Fill of (476) Basal layer	Fill of (476)	Fill of (476)	Burnt deposit within fill (691)
Volume of charcoal >4mm	-	1ml	<1ml	-	4ml	20ml	2ml	<1ml	2ml	4ml
% charcoal >4mm identified	-	100%	100%	-	100%	100%	100%	100%	100%	100%
Charcoal										
Alnus cf glutinosa — alder	-	-	-	-	-	-	-	1 (0.06g)	4 (0.18g)	-
Betula spp — birch	-	-	-	-	-	1 (0.11g)	-	-	-	-
Corylus cf avellana — hazel	-	-	-	-	-	3 (0.12g)	-	-	-	18 (0.57g)
Prunoideae — cherry type	-	-	-	-	-	52 (1.95g)	-	-	2 (0.05g)	-
Quercus spp — oak	-	1 (0.01g)	-	-	6 (0.12g)	-	12 (0.18g)	-	2 (0.10g)	-
Cereals (carbonised)										
Hordeum vulgare sl — barley	-	-	-	-	1	-	-	-	-	-
Seeds etc (carbonised)										
Corylus avellana nutshell frags — hazel nutshell	-	-	-	-	-	2 (<0.01g)	-	-	-	-

Table 10

Area	D1N-A					D1N-B						
Context	016	017	055	056	064	103	105	107	109	110	112	598
Sample	3	10	23, 44	45	85, SF114, SF117, SF167	101	112	111	113	88, SF175, SF225	89, SF169	913
Description	Fill of ditch terminus (006)	Top fill of ditch (006)	Fill of ditch terminus (006) slot A	Fill of ditch terminus (006) slot A (basal layer)	Fill of ditch 1 (006) slot B	Fill of ditch (006) slot B	Fill of ditch 1 (005) slot B	Fill of ditch 1 (005) slot B	Fill of ditch 1 (005) slot B	Fill of ditch 1 (006) slot B	Fill of ditch 1 (006) slot B	Fill of (006) Slot B
Volume of charcoal >4 mm	3ml	1ml	12ml	4ml	1625ml rw	80ml	300ml	120ml	-	40ml	150ml	3ml
% charcoal >4m identified	100%	100%	100%	100%	c.90%	50%	20%	50%	-	100%	100%	100%
Charcoal												
Alnus cf glutinosa	3 (0.06g)	1 (0.10g)	6 (0.15g)	8 (0.45g)	3 (9.01g)	-	41 (5.13g)	-	-	-	-	-
Betula spp	-	-	10 (0.56g)	-	-	1 (0.08g)	-	-	-	-	-	-
Corylus cf avellana	4 (0.11g)	-	10 (0.38g)	1 (0.04g)	242 (144.49g)	36 (2.69g)	10 (1.27g)	51 (11.85g)	-	-	7 (16.39g)	6 (0.31g)
Prunoideae	2 (0.04g)	-	-	-	1 (0.12g)	-	3 (0.27g)	-	-	-	1 (1.12g)	-
Quercus spp	13 (0.31g)	-	26 (1.05g)	2 (0.10g)	28 (15.44g)	3 (0.22g)	-	11 (0.87g)	-	4 (4.28g)	6 (0.17g)	2 (0.27g)
Salix spp	-	-	7 (0.26g)	-	141 (181.36g)	43 (4.47g)	31 (4.00g)	10 (0.88g)	-	12 (4.84g)	8 (14.45g)	4 (0.09g)
Cereals (carbonised)												
Indet cereal	1	-	-	-	-	-	-	-	-	-	-	-
Seeds etc (carbonised)												
Corylus avellana nutshell frags	-	-	-	-	2 (0.01g)	-	-	-	-	1 (0.01g)	3 (0.02g)	-

Table 11

	Area	D1N-C				D1N-D				D1N-E			D1N-F			
	Context	115	184	185	186	100	125	126	228	133	134	135	121	123	128	129
	Sample	84	341	340	339	69	80	81	332	96	97	98	73	75	90	91
	Description	Base fill of ditch 1 (006) slot C	Basal fill (210)	Fill (006) C	Fill (006) C	Fill below (088) in slot D (006)	Fill of (006) slot D below (124) and above (125)	Fill of (006) slot D below (124) and above (125)	Bottom fill of ditch (006) slot D	Fill of ditch (006) slot E	Fill of ditch (006) slot E	Fill of ditch (006) slot E	Fill of ditch (006) slot F	Fill of ditch (006) slot F	Fill of ditch (006) slot F	Fill of ditch (006) slot F
Volume of charcoal >4 mm		15ml	25ml	15ml	20ml	10ml	15ml	7ml	8ml	-	1ml	1ml	200ml	6ml	1ml	<1ml
% charcoal >4m identified		100%	100%	100%	100%	100%	100%	100%	100%	-	100%	100%	25%	100%	100%	100%
Charcoal																
Alnus cf glutinosa	alder	35 (1.46g)	25 (1.05g)	9 (0.39g)	8 (0.21g)	7 (0.32g)	18 (0.74g)	7 (0.24g)	-	-	1 (0.03g)	2 (0.06g)	-	-	-	1 0.01g
Betula spp	birch	1 (0.02g)	11 (0.37g)	3 (0.10g)	5 (0.53g)	3 (0.32g)	14 (0.74g)	5 (0.15g)	-	-	-	-	-	1 (0.05g)	-	-
Corylus cf avellana	hazel	9 (0.34g)	28 (1.32g)	22 (1.63g)	24 (0.71g)	15 (0.60g)	17 (0.59g)	9 (0.27g)	16 (0.79g)	-	-	1 (0.03g)	9 (0.36g)	1 (0.04g)	-	-
Prunoideae	cherry type	-	-	2 (0.07g)	3 (0.24g)	2 (0.15g)	2 (0.10g)	-	-	-	-	-	15 (0.58g)	-	-	-
Quercus spp	oak	2 (0.11g)	2 (0.11g)	-	1 (0.06g)	9 (0.48g)	2 (0.08g)	-	3 (0.10g)	-	2 (0.07g)	2 (0.02g)	28 (1.49g)	3 (0.24g)	3 (0.10g)	1 (0.01g)
Salix spp	willow	6 (0.42g)	24 (1.24g)	14 (0.81g)	22 (0.98g)	8 (0.25g)	5 (0.20g)	5 (0.50g)	-	-	3 (0.05g)	-	118 (3.99g)	9 (0.17g)	1 (0.02g)	-
Cereals (carbonised)																
Hordeum vulgare sl	barley	-	-	-	-	-	-	-	1	-	-	-	-	-	-	-
Indet cereal	indet cereal	-	-	-	-	1	-	-	-	-	-	-	-	-	2	-
Seeds etc (carbonised)																
Corylus avellana nutshell frags	hazel nutshell	1 (0.02g)	-	-	-	-	-	-	-	4 (0.02g)	-	2 (<0.01g)	-	-	-	-

Table 12

Area		D2N-A													D2N-E	
Context	076	077	079	084	090	117	136	145	146	150	152	153	154	155	807
Sample	52	53	54	61	56	71	121	125	126	130	120	123	132	124	1051
Description	Fill of pit (083)	Fill of pit (083)	Basal fill recut (089) ditch 2N	Fill of ditch (008)	Fill of post hole pit (089)	Fill of cut posthole (116)	Fill of (008) ditch fill	Fill of (008) ditch fill	Fill of (008) ditch fill	Fill of (008) ditch fill	Fill of (008) ditch fill	Fill of (008) ditch fill	Fill of (008) ditch fill	Fill of (008) ditch fill	Fill of ditch 2 (008) Slot E Base
Volume of charcoal >4 mm	2ml	5ml	5ml	1ml	7ml	<1ml	1ml	4ml	1ml	20ml	<1ml	4ml	3ml	<1ml	<1ml
% charcoal >4m identified	100%	100%	100%	100%	100%	100%	100%	100%	100%	100%	100%	100%	100%	100%	100%
Charcoal															
Alnus cf glutinosa (alder)	4 (0.09g)	16 (0.43g)	5 (0.19g)	-	3 (0.16g)	-	-	-	-	17 (0.50g)	-	-	-	-	-
Betula spp (birch)	1 (0.02g)	-	2 (0.04g)	-	3 (0.14g)	-	1 (0.02g)	-	-	-	-	-	-	-	-
Corylus cf avellana (hazel)	5 (0.11g)	7 (0.23g)	7 (0.26g)	8 (0.33g)	9 (0.55g)	-	2 (0.07g)	7 (0.50g)	2 (0.04g)	19 (0.89g)	1 (0.01g)	6 (0.59g)	2 (0.11g)	-	-
Prunoideae (cherry type)	-	1 (0.07g)	-	1 (0.08g)	3 (0.08g)	3 (0.12g)	-	-	-	16 (0.73g)	-	-	1 (0.03g)	-	-
Quercus spp (oak)	2 (0.07g)	-	5 (0.16g)	-	-	1 (0.03g)	1 (<0.01g)	-	-	1 (0.10g)	-	2 (0.06g)	-	1 (0.03g)	1 (0.04g)
Salix spp (willow)	1 (0.10g)	5 (0.33g)	3 (0.09g)	-	3 (0.15g)	-	-	-	-	18 (1.26g)	-	-	7 (0.12g)	-	-
Ulmus spp (elm)	-	-	-	-	-	-	-	-	-	-	-	-	-	-	-
Seeds etc (carbonised)															
Corylus avellana nutshell frags (hazel nutshell)	-	2 (0.04g)													

Table 13

	D2N/3N-B						D2N-C					D2N-D					
Area / Context	580	569	791	795	797	898	528	529	532	533	611	574	576	577	578	579	800
Sample	898	911	1033	1037	1039	1154	870	871	874	875	1030	1046	905	1047	1048	906	1049
Description	Basal fill of Ditch 3N Slot B	Fill of pit (593)	Fill of (008) Slot B	Void	Fill of (010) Slot B	Fill of pit (900) Slot B	Hillwash layer fill of (008) C	Uppermost fill of (008) C	Basal fill of Ditch 2N Slot C	Basal fill of Ditch 2N Slot C	Fill of (008) Slot C	Fill of ditch (008) Slot D	Fill of ditch (008) Slot D	Fill of ditch (008) Slot D	Fill of ditch (008) Slot D	Fill of ditch (008) Slot D	Fill of ditch (008) Slot D
Volume of charcoal >4 mm	120ml	2ml	2ml	10ml	1ml	1ml	1ml	1ml	1ml	1ml	-	-	15ml	<1ml	<1ml	<1ml	<1ml
% charcoal >4m identified	25%	100%	100%	100%	100%	100%	100%	100%	100%	100%	-	-	100%	100%	100%	100%	100%
Charcoal																	
Alnus cf *glutinosa* — alder	34 (2.41g)	-	-	11 (0.34g)	1 (0.03g)	1 (0.03g)	-	-	-	2 (0.11g)	-	-	-	-	1 (0.02g)	-	-
Betula spp — birch	11 (0.59g)	-	-	1 (0.02g)	-	-	-	-	-	-	-	-	-	1 (0.02g)	-	1 (0.01g)	-
Corylus cf *avellana* — hazel	32 (2.41g)	1 (0.02g)	-	-	-	-	1 (0.02g)	2 (0.06g)	1 (0.03g)	1 (0.02g)	-	-	-	-	-	-	-
Cytisus / *Ulex* — broom / gorse	-	-	-	-	-	-	-	-	-	-	-	-	9 (0.85g)	-	-	-	-
Ericales — heather type	-	-	-	-	-	-	-	-	-	-	-	-	154 (2.63g)	-	-	-	-
Prunoideae — cherry type	6 (0.42g)	1 (0.04g)	1 (0.03g)	7 (0.32g)	1 (0.04g)	-	-	-	-	-	-	-	-	-	-	-	-
Quercus spp — oak	-	6 (0.14g)	-	3 (0.09g)	1 (0.04g)	-	5 (0.09g)	-	-	-	-	-	-	-	-	-	-
Salix spp — willow	6 (0.41g)	-	2 (0.05g)	6 (0.58g)	-	1 (0.03g)	-	-	1 (0.03g)	-	-	-	-	-	1 (0.05g)	1 (0.01g)	1 (0.09g)
Ulmus spp — elm	-	-	-	-	-	-	-	-	-	-	-	-	-	-	-	-	-
Indet charcoal	-	-	-	-	-	-	-	3 (0.07g)	-	-	-	-	-	-	-	-	-
Cereals (carbonised)																	
Hordeum vulgare sl — barley	-	-	-	-	-	-	-	1	-	-	-	-	-	-	-	1	-
Indet cereal	-	-	-	-	-	-	-	1	-	-	-	-	-	-	-	-	-
Seeds etc (carbonised)																	
Corylus avellana nutshell frags — hazel nutshell	-	-	1 (<0.01g)	1 (<0.01g)	-	-	-	-	-	-	-	-	-	-	-	-	-

Table 14

	D3N-A					D3N-C					D3N-D		D3N-E
Context	019	029	029	032	087	620	623	624	631	632	798	863	857
Sample	6	13	SF67	17	50	1015	1019	1018	1013	1012	1040	1096	1155
Description	Fill of ditch 3 cut (010)	Basal fill in recut ditch 3 north, 010 slot A	Basal fill in recut ditch 3 north, 010 slot A	Fill of ditch 3 cut (010) A	Fill of cut (085)	Basal fill of Ditch (010)	Fill of Ditch Recut (622)	Fill of Ditch Recut (622)	Basal fill of Ditch recut (630)	Fill of Ditch Recut (630)	Fill of (010) Slot D	Fill of ankle breaker (010) Slot D	Basal fill of (010) Slot E
Volume of charcoal >4 mm	1ml	<1ml	150ml	5ml	10ml	-	-	-	2ml	<1ml	200ml	-	<1ml
% charcoal >4m identified	100%	100%	100%	100%	100%	-	-	-	100%	100%	100%	-	100%
Charcoal													
Alnus cf glutinosa alder	4 (0.09g)	4 (0.07g)	-	7 (0.23g)	6 (0.27g)	-	-	-	5 (0.15g)	1 (0.02g)	63 (19.23g)	-	-
Betula spp birch	-	-	-	-	-	-	-	-	1 (0.03g)	-	-	-	-
Corylus cf avellana hazel	2 (0.05g)	-	1 (0.15g)	5 (0.28g)	6 (0.16g)	-	-	-	-	-	4 (0.53g)	-	1 (0.01g)
Prunoideae cherry type	-	-	-	-	3 (0.18g)	-	-	-	-	-	5 (0.48g)	-	-
Quercus spp oak	2 (0.04g)	-	107 (25.25g)	4 (0.12g)	5 (0.23g)	-	-	-	1 (0.05g)	-	-	-	-
Salix spp willow	-	-	28 (8.98g)	-	5 (0.41g)	-	-	-	1 (0.06g)	-	-	-	1 (0.01g)
Ulmus spp elm	-	-	-	-	2 (0.12g)	-	-	-	-	-	-	-	-
Seeds etc (carbonised)													
Corylus avellana nutshell frags hazel nutshell	-	-	-	-	-	1 (0.02g)	-	-	-	-	1 (<0.01g)	-	-

Table 15

Table 15

	D4N-A				D4N-B			D4N-C			D4N-D			D4N-E			
Context	025	026	059	062	454	455	456	462	464	466	804	805	809	825	869	982	990
Sample	15	16	36	39	818	819	820	834	831	833	1044	1045	1054	1068	1103	1187	1192
Description	Fill of ditch (021)	Fill of ditch (021)	Fill of recut (058)	4th fill of (021)	Fill of ditch (021)	Fill of ditch (021)	Fill of ditch (021)	Fill of ditch (021)	Fill of ditch (021)	Fill of ditch (021)	Fill of ditch (021)	Fill of ditch (021)	Fill of ditch (021)	Lower fill of (021)	Lower fill of (021)	Fill of pit (981)	Fill of pit (981)
Volume of charcoal >4 mm	10ml	2ml	15ml	-	-	<1ml	-	160ml	<1ml	<1ml	1ml	-	-	1ml	<1ml	100ml	1ml
% charcoal >4m identified	100%	100%	100%	-	-	100%	-	25%	100%	100%	100%	-	-	100%	100%	50%	100%
Charcoal																	
Alnus cf glutinosa — alder	25 (1.03g)	4 (0.19g)	25 (0.65g)	-	-	1 (0.02g)	-	20 (1.43g)	-	-	-	-	-	3 (0.06g)	-	31 (3.22g)	-
Betula spp — birch	-	-	4 (0.08g)	-	-	-	-	1 (0.09g)	-	-	-	-	-	-	-	-	-
Corylus cf avellana — hazel	5 (0.25g)	-	23 (0.72g)	-	-	-	-	45 (1.94g)	-	-	1 (0.01g)	-	-	3 (0.07g)	-	17 (1.04g)	-
Cytisus / Ulex — broom / gorse	-	-	-	-	-	-	-	21 (1.16g)	-	-	-	-	-	-	-	4 (0.19g)	-
Prunoideae — cherry type	2 (0.22g)	-	1 (0.05g)	-	-	-	-	-	-	-	-	-	-	-	-	1 (0.08g)	-
Quercus spp — oak	5 (0.14g)	1 (0.03g)	-	-	-	-	-	24 (1.38g)	1 (0.02g)	-	-	-	-	3 (0.10g)	1 (0.02g)	37 (3.56g)	2 (0.04g)
Salix spp — willow	3 (0.10g)	1 (0.03g)	5 (0.11g)	-	-	-	-	15 (0.60g)	-	-	1 (0.02g)	-	-	-	-	-	-
Indet charcoal — indet charcoal	-	-	-	-	-	-	-	-	-	2 (0.09g)	-	-	-	-	-	-	1 (0.03g)

Table 16

Area			785	786	787	911	915	927	928	929
		Context				Ditch 6				
		Sample	1027	1020	1021	1136	1139	1151	1152	1153
		Description	4th fill of (779) Slot C	1st fill of terminus Slot A	2nd fill of terminus Slot A	Fill of ditch (779) Slot D	Lower fill of ditch (779) Slot E	Top fill of ditch (799) Slot F	Basal fill of ditch (779) Slot F	Mid clay fill of ditch (779) Slot F
Volume of charcoal >4 mm			1ml	30ml	1ml		1ml	5ml	1ml	1ml
% charcoal >4m identified			100%	100%	100%		100%	100%	100%	100%
Charcoal										
Alnus cf glutinosa	alder		-	27 (0.98g)	1 (0.02g)	-	-	4 (0.31g)	-	-
Betula spp	birch		-	3 (0.17g)	1 (0.05g)	-	-	1 (0.02g)	-	-
Corylus cf avellana	hazel		-	30 (1.39g)	2 (0.02g)	-	3 (0.15g)	5 (0.17g)	5 (0.09g)	1 (0.02g)
Quercus spp	oak		3 (0.03g)	2 (0.04g)	1 (0.02g)	-	-	2 (0.03g)	-	-
Salix spp	willow		-	25 (0.93g)	1 (0.01g)	-	-	2 (0.02g)	1 (0.01g)	1 (0.04g)
Seeds etc (carbonised)										
Corylus avellana nutshell frags	hazel nutshell		-	9 (0.03g)	-	-	-	-	-	1 (0.03g)

Table 17

		Souterrain													
Area	Sample	027	042	069	073	074	095	144	156	157	182	235	315	316	353
	Context	47, SF66, SF105, SF242, SF244	33, SF69, SF241	93	49	48	724, SF248	512, SF247	165, 168, 389	172, 204, 218, 220, 723	271	449	685	725	751
	Description	fill of cut (044) souterrain (043)	Fill of souterrain cut (044)	Fill of (044) slot B	Fill of cut (044) souterrain slot A	Fill of cut (044) souterrain slot A	Bulk sample fill of (043) basal	Fill of (043)	Grid G4 fill of (043)	Grid G6 fill of (043)	Grid A2 fill of (043)	Grid V2 fill of (043)	Grid X3.2 fill of (043)	Bulk sample fill of (043) basal	Top fill of charcoal lined poss fence line
Volume of charcoal >4 mm		c.60ml	1030ml	15ml	60ml	40ml	40ml	35ml	20ml	20ml	5ml	15ml	<1ml	15ml	10ml
% charcoal >4m identified		100%	30%	100%	50%	100%	100%	100%	100%	100%	100%	100%	100%	100%	100%
Charcoal															
Alnus cf glutinosa (alder)		24 (1.38g)	-	13 (0.39g)	3 (0.14g)	1 (0.10g)	24 (3.31g)	18 (2.86g)	5 (0.77g)	-	1 (0.10g)	-	-	4 (0.16g)	-
Betula spp (birch)		5 (0.64g)	-	6 (0.15g)	1 (0.02g)	-	3 (0.10g)	10 (1.78g)	5 (0.21g)	4 (0.13g)	-	1 (0.35g)	-	5 (0.19g)	-
Corylus cf avellana (hazel)		27 (2.92g)	13 (093g)	28 (1.47g)	2 (0.04g)	27 (2.59g)	41 (2.46g)	167 (1.14g)	31 (1.05g)	46 (1.85g)	7 (0.34g)	5 (0.11g)	-	15 (0.39g)	17 (0.51g)
Ericales (heather type)		-	-	-	-	-	-	-	-	-	-	67 (2.51g)	-	-	-
Maloideae (rowan type)		-	-	-	-	-	1 (0.24g)	-	-	-	-	-	-	-	-
Prunoideae (cherry type)		4 (0.31g)	-	1 (0.46g)	1 (0.05g)	-	3 (0.33g)	-	1 (0.23g)	1 (0.03g)	4 (0.17g)	2 (0.12g)	-	5 (0.20g)	-
Quercus spp (oak)		27 (6.36g)	187 (23.06g)	2 (0.03g)	112 (5.54g)	18 (0.14g)	2 (0.10g)	4 (0.62g)	5 (0.15g)	4 (0.19g)	3 (0.10g)	-	1 (<0.01g)	4 (0.15g)	-
Salix spp (willow)		21 (1.56g)	123 (27.37g)	7 (0.26g)	7 (1.62g)	33 (2.34g)	5 (0.310g)	3 (0.31g)	10 (0.61g)	7 (0.39g)	2 (0.05g)	-	-	14 (0.80g)	13 (1.26g)
Cereals (carbonised)															
Hordeum vulgare sl (barley)		-	-	2	-	-	-	-	-	-	-	-	-	-	-
Indet cereal (indet cereal)		-	-	2	-	-	-	-	-	-	-	-	1	4	-
Seeds etc (carbonised)															
Corylus avellana nutshell frags (hazel nutshell)		1 (<0.01g)	4 (0.02g)	-	-	-	-	-	-	-	-	-	-	-	-

Table 17 continued

Area			Souterrain													
Context			827	841	844	865	866	867	870	882	883	884	885	886	992	1069
Sample			1066	1069	1074	1098	1099	1102	1104	1114	1115	1116	1117	1118	1191	1230
Description			Soil behind Souterrain wall North	Fill behind wall of Souterrain	Lower fill of Souterrain cut (044) - North wall	Second fill of Souterrain south wall	3rd fill of Souterrain south wall	Deposit between Souterrain floor stones within Slot	Deposit beneath Souterrain floor stones within slot	Top fill of Souterrain Slot - Partially ditch (008) fill	2nd fill of Souterrain Slot - Partially ditch (008) fill	3rd fill of Souterrain Slot - Partially ditch (008) fill	4th fill of Souterrain Slot - Partially ditch (008) fill	5th fill of Souterrain Slot - Partially ditch (008) fill	Fill of pit (991)	Basal fill of ditch 2 (008) in souterrain
Volume of charcoal >4 mm			35ml	2ml	2ml	1ml	<1ml	1ml	4ml	10ml	1ml	2ml	10ml	2ml	2ml	Souterrain
% charcoal >4m identified			100%	100%	100%	100%	100%	100%	100%	100%	100%	100%	100%	100%	100%	100%
Charcoal																
Alnus cf glutinosa (alder)			64 (2.58g)	2 (0.03g)	5 (0.14g)	3 (0.06g)	1 (0.02g)	-	7 (0.24g)	18 (0.64g)	1 (0.02g)	-	12 (0.51g)	-	-	-
Betula spp (birch)			3 (0.16g)	1 (0.04g)	-	-	-	1 (0.01g)	2 (0.04g)	-	-	-	-	-	4 (0.08g)	-
Corylus cf avellana (hazel)			14 (0.62g)	6 (0.17g)	2 (0.03g)	1 (0.01g)	-	-	3 (0.06g)	7 (0.20g)	-	3 (0.11g)	12 (0.30g)	1 (0.03g)	2 (0.08g)	-
Prunoideae (cherry type)			2 (0.11g)	-	-	-	-	1 (0.05g)	1 (0.03g)	2 (0.14g)	-	-	1 (0.02g)	1 (0.02g)	-	-
Quercus spp (oak)			4 (0.11g)	-	-	-	-	-	3 (0.08g)	1 (0.03g)	-	-	-	3 (0.06g)	1 (0.03g)	1 (0.04g)
Salix spp (willow)			6 (0.19g)	1 (0.01g)	1 (0.06g)	-	-	-	-	2 (0.20g)	-	5 (0.22g)	9 (0.53g)	-	-	-
Seeds etc (carbonised)																
Corylus avellana nutshell frags (hazel nutshell)			2 (0.01g)	-	-	-	-	-	-	4 (0.01g)	-	-	-	-	-	-

Table 18

	Area							Area 1						
Context	407	438	442	444	774	776	778	983	1004	1006	1007	1010	1014
Sample	796	813	814	845	996	997	1005	1185	1201	1202	1203	1204	1208
Description	Fill of pit (406)	Fill of pit (437)	Fill of pit (441)	Fill of (443)	Fill of pit (772) Area 1, nr Ditch 6	Fill of pit (775)	Fill of pit (777)	Fill of (984)	Pit (1003) Area 1	Pit (1005) Area 1	Pit (1008) Area 1	Pit (1009) Area 1	Fill of pit (1015)
Volume of charcoal >4 mm	3ml	10ml	-	-	-	1ml	1ml	-	-	-	2ml	-	-
% charcoal >4m identified	100%	100%	-	-	-	100%	100%	-	-	-	100%	-	-
Charcoal													
Betula spp (birch)	-	4 (0.18g)	-	-	-	-	-	-	-	-	2 (0.21g)	-	-
Corylus cf avellana (hazel)	2 (0.04g)	-	-	-	-	-	-	-	-	-	-	-	-
Quercus spp (oak)	7 (0.26g)	5 (0.36g)	-	-	-	5 (0.05g)	1 (0.06g)	-	-	-	2 (0.11g)	-	-
Salix spp (willow)	2 (0.07g)	26 (0.80g)	-	-	-	-	-	-	-	-	-	-	-
Cereals (carbonised)													
Hordeum vulgare sl (barley)	-	-	-	-	-	-	-	-	-	-	1	-	-
Seeds etc (carbonised)													
Corylus avellana nutshell frags (hazel nutshell)	-	-	-	-	1 (<0.01g)	-	-	-	-	-	-	-	-

Table 19

Area	159	231	234	252	347	386	392	394	397	424	472	483	493	1053	1071
Context	159	231	234	252	347	386	392	394	397	424	472	483	493	1053	1071
Sample	336	375	399	426	747	772	779	780	782	801	838	844	848	1223	1231
Description	Fill of posthole158)	Fill of possible posthole (230)	Fill of posthole (233)	Fill of pit (251)	Fill of pit (346) posthole	Fill of posthole (385)	Lower fill of pit (390)	Fill of pit (393)	Fill of pit (395)	Fill of oval feature (423)	Lower fill of pit (476)	Fill of pit (482)	Fill of pit (492)	Fill of pit (1052)	Basal fill of posthole (1070)
Volume of charcoal >4 mm	1ml	1ml	1ml	100ml	2ml	5ml	-	7ml	-	10ml	<1ml	<1ml	<1ml	2ml	<1ml
% charcoal >4m identified	100%	100%	100%	50%	100%	100%	-	100%	-	100%	100%	100%	100%	100%	100%
Charcoal															
Alnus cf glutinosa (alder)	1 (0.04g)									22 (1.35g)					
Corylus cf avellana (hazel)	3 (0.04g)	4 (0.06g)	2 (0.08g)			10 (0.29g)				13 (0.62g)			1 (0.05g)	4 (0.12g)	1 (0.04g)
Ericales (heather type)			2 (0.10g)		3 (0.08g)										
Prunoideae (cherry type)		1 (0.01g)				1 (0.02g)				2 (0.07g)					
Quercus spp (oak)		1 (0.01g)		207 (8.81g)	2 (0.04g)	3 (0.05g)		45 (1.67g)						6 (0.18g)	
Salix spp (willow)		1 (0.04g)			2 (0.06g)					8 (0.26g)					
Indet charcoal												1 (0.02g)			
Cereals (carbonised)															
Indet cereal															4
Seeds etc (carbonised)															
Corylus avellana nutshell frags (hazel nutshell)				4 (0.06g)							1 (0.02g)	1 (<0.01g)		6 (0.02g)	

Table 20

		345	350	351	414	458	460	497	499	517	520	522	525	527	538
Area									**Area 3**							
Context		345	748	749	789	821	822	1101	1100	863	865	866	868	869	878
Sample		769	748	749	789	821	822	1101	1100	863	865	866	868	869	878
Description		Fill of (345)	Fill of posthole (346)	Fill of pit (349) lower	Fill of posthole (413)	Fill of posthole (457)	Fill of posthole (457)	Fill of pit (496)	Fill of pit (498)	Fill of posthole (516)	Fill of posthole (519)	Fill of posthole (521)	Lower fill of posthole (521)	Fill of posthole (526)	Fill of posthole (537)
Volume of charcoal >4 mm		15ml	4ml	1000ml	2ml	1ml	3ml	2ml	1ml	8ml	10ml	4ml	1ml	5ml	-
% charcoal >4m identified		100%	100%	20%	100%	100%	100%	100%	100%	100%	100%	100%	100%	100%	-
Charcoal															
Alnus cf glutinosa	alder	1 (0.02g)	-	-	-	-	-	-	-	-	16 (0.48g)	-	-	-	-
Betula spp	birch	11 (0.37g)	2 (0.05g)	-	1 (0.08g)	-	-	-	-	1 (0.05g)	17 (0.57g)	1 (0.04g)	-	4 (0.08g)	-
Corylus cf avellana	hazel	19 (0.59g)	13 (0.41g)	-	1 (0.01g)	1 (0.04g)	-	4 (0.10g)	1 (0.01g)	12 (0.62g)	12 (0.48g)	2 (0.07g)	-	2 (0.03g)	-
Ericales	heather type	-	-	-	-	-	-	-	-	-	-	-	1 (0.02g)	-	-
Prunoideae	cherry type	2 (0.10g)	-	-	-	-	1 (0.08g)	-	-	-	-	-	-	-	-
Quercus spp	oak	6 (0.25g)	2 (0.05g)	c. 800 (41.12g)	4 (0.21g)	1 (0.02g)	3 (0.14g)	5 (0.12g)	1 (0.01g)	-	1 (0.03g)	1 (0.02g)	-	2 (0.05g)	-
Salix spp	willow	16 (0.72g)	4 (0.09g)	-	2 (0.03g)	-	6 (0.14g)	-	-	16 (0.65g)	6 (0.16g)	7 (0.62g)	1 (0.15g)	1 (0.49g)	-
Cereals (carbonised)															
Avena spp	oat	1	-	-	-	-	-	-	-	-	-	-	-	-	-
Hordeum vulgare sl	barley	1	-	-	-	-	-	-	-	-	-	-	-	-	-
Indet cereal	indet cereal	2	-	-	-	-	-	-	-	-	-	-	-	-	-
Seeds etc (carbonised)															
Corylus avellana nutshell frags	hazel nutshell	3 (0.02g)	-	-	-	-	-	-	-	-	-	-	-	-	-

Table 20 continued

Area		540	541	544	549	551	553	555	557	560	562	564	571	589	592
							Area 3 (cont)								
Context		540	541	544	549	551	553	555	557	560	562	564	571	589	592
Sample		879	880	882	883	884	885	886	887	889	890	892	896	903	907
Description		Fill of posthole (539)	Fill of posthole (542)	Fill of posthole (543)	Fill of posthole (548)	Fill of posthole (548)	Fill of posthole (552)	Fill of posthole (554)	Fill of posthole (556)	Backfill in posthole (558)	Fill of posthole (561)	Fill of posthole (563)	Fill of stakehole (570)	Fill of posthole (588)	Fill of shallow pit (591)
Volume of charcoal >4 mm		<1ml	1ml	2ml	20ml	1ml	1ml	-	4ml	-	2ml	1ml	-	1ml	5ml
% charcoal >4m identified		100%	100%	100%	100%	100%	100%	-	100%	-	100%	100%	-	100%	100%
Charcoal															
Betula spp	birch	-	-	-	4 (0.65g)	1 (0.02g)	4 (0.11g)	-	-	-	1 (0.01g)	1 (0.05g)	-	1 (0.02g)	-
Corylus cf avellana	hazel	1 (0.02g)	4 (0.06g)	4 (0.09g)	19 (0.95g)	-	-	-	1 (0.02g)	-	1 (0.06g)	-	-	1 (0.02g)	1 (0.37g)
Quercus spp	oak	3 (0.04g)	1 (0.02g)	6 (0.12g)	3 (0.10g)	-	2 (0.10g)	-	16 (0.46g)	-	-	-	-	-	-
Salix spp	willow	-	3 (0.04g)	1 (0.08g)	35 (1.19g)	5 (0.14g)	-	-	6 (0.22g)	-	3 (0.07g)	-	-	-	-
Cereals (carbonised)															
Avena spp	oat	-	-	-	9	-	1	-	2	-	-	-	-	-	-
Hordeum vulgare sl	barley	-	1	-	10	-	1	-	3	-	-	-	-	-	-
cf Hordeum vulgare sl	cf barley	-	-	-	5	-	-	-	2	-	-	-	-	-	-
cf Triticum spp	cf wheat	-	-	-	14	-	-	-	1	-	-	-	-	-	-
Indet cereal	indet cereal	-	-	-	-	2	-	-	4	-	-	-	-	-	-
Seeds etc (carbonised)															
Corylus avellana nutshell frags	hazel nutshell	-	-	-	-	-	2 (<0.01g)	-	-	-	-	-	-	-	-

Table 20 continued

		608	934	935	937	942	944	949	965	966	976	978	980	994
Area							Area 3 (cont)							
	Context	928	1160	1161	1162	1163	1164	1166	1174	1175a	1183	1184	1194	1193
	Sample	Fill of poss. posthole (607)	Fill of post-pipe in posthole (933)	Fill of posthole (933)	Fill of posthole (936)	Fill of posthole (941)	Fill of posthole (943)	Lower fill of posthole (947)	Fill of poss. post-pipe in posthole (936)	Fill of poss. post-pipe in posthole (936)	Fill of posthole (975)	Fill of posthole (977)	Fill of posthole (979)	Fill of posthole (993)
	Description													
Volume of charcoal >4 mm		1ml	-	1ml	<1ml	<1ml	<1ml	-	-	-	-	1ml	2ml	<1ml
% charcoal >4m identified		100%	-	100%	100%	100%	100%	-	-	-	-	100%	100%	100%
Charcoal														
Alnus cf glutinosa	alder	-	-	-	-	2 (0.04g)	-	-	-	-	-	-	-	1 (0.03g)
Betula spp	birch	1 (0.04g)	-	-	-	-	-	-	-	-	-	6 (0.23g)	-	-
Corylus cf avellana	hazel	1 (0.02g)	-	-	-	-	-	-	-	-	-	-	-	-
Ericales	heather type	-	-	2 (0.03g)	2 (0.03g)	-	-	-	-	-	-	-	5 (0.09g)	-
Quercus spp	oak	1 (0.02g)	-	-	-	-	-	-	-	-	-	2 (0.06g)	-	-
Salix spp	willow	-	-	-	-	-	1 (0.01g)	-	-	-	-	1 (0.01g)	-	-
Cereals (carbonised)														
Avena spp	oat	-	-	-	-	-	-	-	-	-	-	1	-	-
Hordeum vulgare sl	barley	-	-	-	-	-	-	-	-	-	-	-	1	1

Table 21

Area 4

Context	1002	946	940	974	972	968	670	658	616	614	606	600	595	587	585	583	573
Sample	1205	1171	1170	1200	1182	1176	937	932	919	918	917	914	908	902	901	900	897
Description	Fill of pit (1001)	Fill of poss. Posthole (945)	Fill of posthole (938)	Fill of posthole (973)	Fill of poss. posthole (971)	Fill of pit (967)	Deposit nr centre of fort	Fill of pit (657)	Fill of pit (615)	Fill of pit (613)	Fill of posthole (605)	Fill of posthole (599)	Fill of posthole (594)	Fill of posthole (586)	Fill of posthole (584)	Lower fill of pit (581)	Fill of posthole (572)
Volume of charcoal >4 mm	5ml	3ml	<1ml	7ml	3ml	6ml	1000ml	3ml	15ml	<1ml	2ml	5ml	4ml	2ml	4ml	5ml	3ml
% charcoal >4m identified	100%	100%	100%	100%	100%	100%	10%	100%	100%	100%	100%	100%	100%	100%	100%	100%	100%
Charcoal																	
Alnus cf glutinosa (alder)	-	-	-	16 (0.51g)	-	1 (0.06g)	19 (2.08g)	1 (0.17g)	-	1 (0.02g)	-	-	-	6 (0.20g)	2 (0.09g)	-	2 (0.03g)
Betula spp (birch)	-	1 (0.03g)	-	1 (0.07g)	8 (0.25g)	2 (0.08g)	-	-	6 (0.64g)	-	-	1 (0.01g)	2 (0.09g)	-	2 (0.06g)	6 (0.15g)	9 (0.37g)
Corylus cf avellana (hazel)	7 (0.45g)	4 (0.17g)	-	3 (0.12g)	7 (0.28g)	4 (0.17g)	5 (0.26g)	2 (0.06g)	17 (1.47g)	-	1 (0.52g)	-	13 (0.35g)	-	9 (0.22g)	10 (0.31g)	-
Prunoideae (cherry type)	-	-	-	-	-	-	-	-	1 (0.03g)	-	-	-	-	-	-	-	-
Quercus spp (oak)	1 (0.04g)	4 (0.05g)	1 (0.02g)	1 (0.01g)	1 (0.02g)	-	176 (12.78g)	3 (0.12g)	6 (0.29g)	-	1 (0.02g)	2 (0.05g)	1 (0.03g)	1 (0.01g)	-	2 (0.08g)	-
Salix spp (willow)	-	3 (0.04g)	-	1 (0.02g)	-	7 (0.50g)	61 (3.74g)	1 (0.03g)	5 (0.49g)	-	-	8 (0.37g)	1 (0.06g)	2 (0.09g)	4 (0.31g)	1 (0.03g)	2 (0.06g)
Cereals (carbonised)																	
Hordeum vulgare sl (barley)		-	-	-	-	-	-	-	-	-	-	2	-	-	-	-	-
cf Hordeum vulgare sl (cf barley)	-	-	-	-	-	-	-	-	-	-	-	3	-	-	-	-	-
Indet cereal (indet cereal)	-	-	-	-	-	-	-	-	-	-	-	-	-	1	-	-	-
Seeds etc (carbonised)																	
Corylus avellana nutshell frags (hazel nutshell)	68 (0.72g)	7 (0.02g)	-	2 (<0.01g)	-	-	-	-	7 (0.07g)	-	1 (0.03g)	-	1 (<0.01g)	1 (<0.01g)	1 (<0.01g)	6 (0.08g)	-

172

Table 22

		895	896	960	1012	1013	1040	1046	1047	1049	1051	1057
Area							Area 5					
Context		895	896	960	1012	1013	1040	1046	1047	1049	1051	1057
Sample		1126	1127	1173	1206	1207	1222	1225b	1226	1227	1228	1225a
Description		Top fill of linear terminus (894)	Clay fill of linear terminus (894)	Main fill of pit (958)	Fill of pit (1011)	Fill of pit (1011)	Fill of posthole (1039)	Fill of linear (1045)	Fill of pit (1063)	Fill of posthole (1048)	Fill of posthole (1050)	Fill of pit (1022)
Volume of charcoal >4 mm		150ml	70ml	10ml	1ml	-	<1ml	30ml	2ml	1ml	3ml	<1ml
% charcoal >4m identified		50%	50%	100%	100%	-	100%	100%	100%	100%	100%	100%
Charcoal												
Alnus cf glutinosa	alder	-	-	-	-	-	1 (0.02g)	19 (0.69g)	-	-	6 (0.13g)	1 (0.06g)
Betula spp	birch	-	-	3 (0.30g)	-	-	-	-	-	-	1 (0.03g)	-
Corylus cf avellana	hazel	61 rw (2.35g)	36 (1.92g)	8 (0.38g)	-	-	-	85 (3.90g)	6 (018g)	1 (0.05g)	3 (0.06g)	-
Cytisus / Ulex	broom / gorse	-	-	-	-	-	-	1 (0.04g)	-	-	-	-
Quercus spp	oak	2 rw (11.36g)	2 (0.30g)	7 (0.65g)	-	-	-	6 (0.23g)	-	-	-	-
Salix spp	willow	17 rw (0.73g)	17 (5.66g)	3 (0.14g)	-	-	-	8 (0.29g)	-	4 (0.13g)	2 (0.12g)	-
Indet cinder	indet cinder	-	-	-	4 (0.30g)	-	-	-	-	-	-	-
Wood		-	-	-	-	100ml	-	-	-	-	-	-
Coniferales	conifer	-	-	-	-	>30 (23.09g)	-	-	-	-	-	-
Cereals (carbonised)												
Hordeum vulgare sl	barley	-	2	-	-	-	-	-	-	-	-	-
Seeds etc (carbonised)												
Corylus avellana nutshell frags	hazel nutshell	5 (0.02g)	-	-	-	-	-	-	-	-	-	-

Table 23

Area				Area 6										
Context	481	505	507	508	831	838	839	843	951	953	956	962	964
Sample	842	850	851	852	1071	1072	1073	1070	1168	1167	1158	1177	1175b
Description	Fill of small pit (480)	Fill of pit (504)	Upper fill of pit (506)	Lower fill of pit (506)	Fill of pit (830)	Fill of pit (830)	Burnt deposit (839)	Fill of pit (842)	Fill of possible feature (950)	Fill of posthole (952)	Fill of pit (955)	Fill of pit (961)	Fill of pit (963)
Volume of charcoal >4 mm	60ml	<1ml	1ml	2ml	6ml	8ml	90ml	5ml	-	-	2ml	-	2ml
% charcoal >4m identified	100%	100%	100%	100%	100%	100%	50%	100%	-	-	100%	-	100%
Charcoal													
Alnus cf glutinosa — alder	-	-	1 (0.02g)	-	15 (0.31g)	3 (0.09g)	-	-	-	-	-	-	-
Corylus cf avellana — hazel	5 (0.30g)	1 (0.03g)	1 (0.03g)	-	14 (0.27g)	18 (0.85g)	29 (1.17g)	21 (0.78g)	-	-	10 (0.23g)	-	6 (0.19g)
Quercus spp — oak	71 (5.48g)	-	-	9 (0.20g)	1 (0.02g)	5 (0.22g)	229 (8.95g)	-	-	-	4 (0.13g)	-	2 (0.05g)
Salix spp — willow	2 (0.22g)	-	-	1 (0.04g)	6 (0.25g)	12 (0.25g)	3 (0.16g)	-	-	-	2 (0.11g)	-	1 (0.05g)
Seeds etc (carbonised)													
Corylus avellana nutshell frags — hazel nutshell	-	-	-	1 (<0.01g)	1 (0.01g)	2 (0.05g)	3 (0.02g)	3 (0.08g)	-	-	-	-	-

Table 24

	Area	Area 7 - Features associated with deposit (767)								
	Context	348	348	348	348	721	675	767	767	767
	Sample	949	949	SF197B	949	976	940	992	993	SF220
	Description	Fill of cist - spit 1	Fill of cist - spit 2	Fill of cist - spit 2	Fill of cist - spit 3	Fill of cist - spit 4	Deposit in (667)	Fill of (767)	Fill of (767)	Fill of (767)
Volume of charcoal >4 mm		4ml	5ml	2ml	10ml	2ml	60ml	20ml	30ml	6ml
% charcoal >4m identified		100%	100%	100%	100%	100%	50%	100%	100%	100%
Charcoal										
Alnus cf glutinosa	alder	-	-	-	7 (0.39g)	-	84 (4.72g)	-	24 (1.28g)	-
Betula spp	birch	-	-	-	-	-	-	-	2 (0.07g)	-
Corylus cf avellana	hazel	10 (0.63g)	13 (0.71g)	-	15 (0.69g)	1 (0.02g)	-	34 (1.84g)	38 (3.09g)	7 (1.02g)
Quercus spp	oak	3 (0.04g)	9 (0.28g)	6 (0.20g)	9 (0.43g)	2 (0.05g)	-	44 (1.89g)	30 (1.76g)	-
Salix spp	willow	-	1 (0.02g)	-	1 (0.04g)	-	-	5 (0.29g)	-	-
Cereals (carbonised)										
Hordeum vulgare sl	barley	-	-	-	-	-	-	-	2	-

Table 25

Area 7 - Bronze Age structure

	693	697	707	733	662	680	682	684	687	690	709	711	714	716	718	720	723
Sample	953	959	958	973	934	942	943	944	950	952	960	961	962	963	966	964	965
Description	Fill of stakehole (692)	Fill of stakehole (696) (9)	Fill of stakehole (706) (10)	Fill of stakehole (732)	Fill of (661)	Fill of stakehole (679)	Fill of stakehole (681)	Fill of stakehole (683)	Fill of ditch (476) Slot C	Fill of stakehole (689)	Fill of stakehole (708)	Fill of stakehole (710)	Fill of stakehole (713)	Fill of stakehole (715)	Fill of stakehole (717)	Fill of stakehole (719) (16)	Fill of stakehole (722)
Volume of charcoal >4 mm	-	-	<1ml	<1ml	100ml	-	-	-	1ml	<1ml	1ml	<1ml	-	<1ml	5ml	-	<1ml
% charcoal >4m identified	-	-	100%	100%	50%	-	-	-	100%	100%	100%	100%	-	100%	100%	-	100%
Charcoal																	
Alnus cf glutinosa — alder	-	-	-	1 (0.03g)	-	-	-	-	-	-	-			-	-	-	2 (0.05g)
Corylus cf avellana — hazel	-	-	-	-	119 (7.25g)	-	-	-	-	1 (0.01g)	1 (0.01g)	-	-	-	21 (0.67g)	-	-
Quercus spp — oak	-	-	-	-	3 (0.16g)	-	-	-	5 (0.07g)	-	1 (0.07g)	3 (0.04g)	-	1 (0.01g)	-	-	-
Salix spp — willow	-	-	1 (0.01g)	-	-	-	-	-	-	-	-	-	-	-	-	-	-
Cereals (carbonised)																	
Hordeum vulgare sl — barley	-	-	-	-	410	-	-	-	-	1	-	-	-	1	61	-	-
cf Hordeum vulgare sl — cf barley	-	-	-	-	115	-	-	-	-	-	-	-	-	-	54	-	-
Indet cereal — indet cereal	-	-	-	-	175	1	2	-	-	2	4	-	3	3	115	-	-
Seeds etc (carbonised)																	
Corylus avellana nutshell frags — hazel nutshell	-	-	-	-	-	-	-	-	1 (<0.01g)	-	-	-	-	-	-	-	-

Table 26

Area	Area 7 - southern stakes			Area 7 - stakeholes around tree bowl (663)					Area 7 - Bronze Age pit						
Context	727	735	737	672	674	731	725	739	741	742	743	744	745	755	729
Sample	968	974	975	938	939	972	967	978	979	980	981	982	983	986	969
Description	Fill of Stakehole (726)	Fill of (734)	Fill of (736)	Fill of stakehole (671)	Fill of stakehole (673)	Fill of stakehole (730)	Fill of stakehole (724) (18)	Fill of (738)	Fill of (738)	Fill of (738)	Fill of (738)	Fill of (738)	Fill of (738)	Fire affected deposit (755)	Fill of stakehole (728)
Volume of charcoal >4 mm	-	-	<1ml	-	-	<1ml	2ml	10ml	30ml	10ml	6ml	<1ml	8ml	2ml	-
% charcoal >4m identified	-	-	100%	-	-	100%	100%	100%	100%	100%	100%	100%	100%	100%	-
Charcoal															
Alnus cf glutinosa — alder	-	-	1 (0.01g)	-	-	-	1 (0.11g)	-	28 (0.97g)	-	9 (0.33g)	-	13 (0.51g)	-	-
Corylus cf avellana — hazel	-	-	-	-	-	-	1 (0.01g)	25 (1.05g)	47 (3.10g)	14 (0.56g)	7 (0.32g)	1 (0.01g)	3 (0.80g)	5 (0.07g)	-
Prunoideae — cherry type	-	-	-	-	-	-	-	-	-	-	2 (0.06g)	-	-	-	-
Quercus spp — oak	-	-	-	-	-	2 (<0.01g)	-	4 (0.16g)	2 (0.13g)	7 (0.22g)	6 (0.10g)	-	8 (0.26g)	-	-
Salix spp — willow	-	-	-	-	-	-	-	4 (0.11g)	6 (0.26g)	15 (1.40g)	-	1 (<0.01g)	1 (0.04g)	1 (0.02g)	-
Cereals (carbonised)															
Hordeum vulgare sl — barley	-	-	-	1	-	-	-	17	-	-	-	-	-	-	-
cf Hordeum vulgare sl — cf barley	-	-	-	-	-	-	2	26	-	-	-	-	-	-	-
Indet cereal — indet cereal	-	-	-	-	1	3	-	35	-	-	-	-	-	1	-
Seeds etc (carbonised)															
Corylus avellana nutshell frags — hazel nutshell	-	-	-	-	-	-	-	-	11 (0.31g)	2 (0.05g)	17 (0.13g)	-	1 (<0.01g)	2 (0.01g)	-

Table 27

Area		660	666	669	677	695	712	740	757	759	763
Context		660	666	669	677	695	712	740	757	759	763
Sample		933	948	936	941	970	971	977	988	989	990
Description		Fill of stakehole (659)	Fill of pit (665)	Fill of (668) stakehole	Fill of posthole (676)	Upper fill of fire-pit (694)	Lower fill of fire-pit (694)	Outer fill of (694) fire-pit	Fill of (756)	Fill of (758)	Fill of (767)
Volume of charcoal >4 mm		15ml	15ml	4ml	2ml	60ml	2000ml	2ml	60ml	25ml	1ml
% charcoal >4m identified		100%	100%	100%	100%	50%	5%	100%	50%	100%	100%
Charcoal											
Alnus cf glutinosa	alder	30 (1.35g)	11 (0.39g)	-	-	89 (5.05g)	103 (16.81g)	2 (0.06g)	-	-	-
Corylus cf avellana	hazel	4 (0.13g)	29 (1.93g)	14 (0.24g)	1 (0.04g)	-	9 (0.72g)	-	2 (0.09g)	2 (0.05g)	-
Quercus spp	oak	-	3 (0.11g)	-	1 (0.09g)	-	-	-	157 (6.84g)	73 (1.91g)	3 (0.05g)
Salix spp	willow	-	3 (0.42g)	4 (0.35g)	-	-	-	-	-	-	-
Ulmus spp	elm	-	1 (0.03g)	-	-	-	-	-	-	-	-
Seeds etc (carbonised)											
Corylus avellana nutshell frags	hazel nutshell	1 (<0.01g)	-	-	-	-	-	-	-	2 (<0.01g)	-

Area 7 - other pits and postholes

Table 28

	Area	Palisade		Scone 1	Scone 2		
	Context	295	304	084	044	053	061
	Sample	543	3	28	20	6	12
	Description	Fill of (294) slot F	Fill of (294) slot G	Fill of pit (083)	Fill of burnt mound	Fill of pit (052)	Fill of possible posthole (058)
Volume of charcoal >4 mm		-	200ml	4ml	25ml	4ml	6ml
% charcoal >4m identified		-	25%	100%	100%	100%	100%
Charcoal							
Alnus cf glutinosa	alder	-	63 (10.12g)	-	41 (1.67g)	3 (0.09g)	-
Betula spp	birch	-	-	-	39 (2.00g)	-	-
Corylus cf avellana	hazel	-	18 (2.12g)	-	8 (0.32g)	2 (0.04g)	7 (0.42g)
Quercus spp	oak	-	3 (0.23g)	-	10 (0.98g)	9 (0.21g)	13 (0.69g)
Salix spp	willow	-	-	20 (0.60g)	4 (0.18g)	-	1 (0.02g)
Seeds etc (carbonised)							
Corylus avellana nutshell frags	hazel nutshell	-	-	-	-	-	3 (0.01g)

Appendix 2: Tables 29 and 30 botanical results

Species	Overall Depth / Context	1cm	6cm	11cm	15cm	20cm	25cm	29cm	34cm	39cm	43cm	48cm	53cm	57cm	62cm	67cm
Sample			108		187				107			112			110	
	Context	290	290	290	290	290	290	291	291	291	292	292	292	292	292	292
Trees & Tall Shrubs																
Alnus	alder	33	51	7	7	44	5	9	14	33	6	11	-	25	8	8
Betula	birch	-	-	-	-	-	-	-	-	-	-	-	-	1	1	-
Coryloid	hazel type	54	67	26	7	72	30	33	60	88	10	33	6	186	66	72
Fraxinus	ash	-	-	-	-	-	-	-	-	-	-	1	-	-	-	-
Quercus	oak	1	-	-	-	-	-	1	-	-	1	-	-	6	2	1
Salix	willow	-	-	-	-	-	-	-	2	2	-	-	-	3	2	2
Heaths																
Calluna	heather	29	41	14	8	142	79	36	19	87	3	11	18	9	103	47
Herbs																
Poaceae	grass	127	92	14	12	60	20	32	53	120	330	105	14	107	20	36
Poaceae (>37 um)	cereal	2	1	-	-	1	-	-	-	-	10	-	1	1	-	-
Cyperaceae	sedge	5	3	-	-	3	1	4	4	10	5	2	1	17	6	6
Anthemis type	chamomile type	-	2	1	-	3	1	1	-	-	2	2	-	1	1	-
Apiaceae	carrot family	-	-	-	-	-	-	-	-	-	-	1	-	1	-	-
Artemisia	mugwort	1	-	-	-	-	-	1	-	-	-	-	-	-	-	-
Aster type	daisy type	-	-	-	-	-	3	-	-	1	4	1	-	-	-	-
Caryophyllaceae	pink family	26	11	5	1	13	9	24	4	5	20	67	11	26	16	41
Cirsium	thistle	-	-	-	-	1	-	-	-	-	-	-	-	-	-	-
Lactuceae	dandelion type	3	7	-	-	2	1	-	1	2	7	9	-	12	1	1
Lamium type	deadnettle type	-	-	-	-	-	1	2	-	-	-	-	-	3	-	-
Persicaria maculosa	redshank	2	1	1	-	2	-	-	-	-	-	2	-	-	-	-
Plantago lanceolata	ribwort plantain	16	21	3	-	9	4	48	7	10	11	20	3	3	2	4
Plantago major/media	greater/hoary plantain	6	13	-	-	6	1	77	3	12	10	5	1	8	2	4
Potentilla type	cinquefoil type	1	-	-	-	-	-	-	-	1	-	-	-	-	-	-
Ranunculus acris group	meadow buttercup group	37	25	8	2	10	12	51	9	18	13	22	2	34	6	8
Rumex acetosa type	common sorrel type	-	-	1	-	-	-	1	4	1	1	-	1	6	3	1
Sinapis type	mustard type	8	5	2	-	-	-	8	4	1	-	7	3	18	1	4
Stellaria holostea	greater stitchwort	-	3	2	-	2	1	6	-	2	2	2	-	2	3	2
Succisa pratensis	devil's-bit scabious	150	171	483	464	188	402	167	318	118	87	205	459	32	274	420
Trifolium type	clover type	-	-	-	-	-	1	1	-	-	-	-	-	-	-	-
Veronica type	speedwell	-	-	1	-	-	-	2	-	1	-	1	-	1	-	1
Total Land Pollen (TLP)		*501*	*514*	*567*	*501*	*558*	*571*	*503*	*502*	*512*	*522*	*507*	*519*	*501*	*517*	*658*
Aquatic types																
Menyanthes	bogbean	-	-	-	-	-	-	-	-	-	-	-	-	-	-	-
Myriophyllum vertilatum	whorled water milfoil	-	1	-	-	-	-	-	1	-	-	-	-	1	-	1
Total Land Pollen + Aqu		*501*	*515*	*567*	*501*	*558*	*571*	*503*	*503*	*512*	*522*	*507*	*519*	*502*	*517*	*659*
Pteridophytes																
Filicales	ferns	45	44	1	4	17	10	38	77	89	14	29	22	70	33	43
Lycopodium	clubmoss	1	1	-	-	1	2	-	-	1	-	-	-	1	-	-
Polypodium	polypody fern	97	73	77	78	69	124	63	444	89	23	55	258	604	103	388
Pteridium	bracken	-	-	-	-	-	-	1	-	-	1	-	-	-	1	2
Sphagnum	bogmoss	1	1	1	-	2	-	2	4	6	1	3	8	7	6	6
Total Land Pollen + Pter		*645*	*633*	*646*	*583*	*647*	*707*	*605*	*1027*	*697*	*560*	*594*	*807*	*1184*	*660*	*1097*

Table 30

Species	Overall Depth	1cm	6cm	11cm	15cm	20cm	25cm	29cm	34cm	39cm	43cm	48cm	53cm	57cm	62cm	67cm
	Context	108			187				107				112		110	
	Sample	290	290	290	290	290	290	291	291	291	292	292	292	292	292	292
Trees & Tall Shrubs																
Alnus	alder	6.6	9.9	1.2	1.4	7.9	•	1.8	2.8	6.4	1.1	2.2	-	5.0	1.5	1.2
Betula	birch	-	•	-	-	-	-	-	-	-	-	-	-	•	•	•
Coryloid	hazel type	10.8	13.0	4.6	1.4	12.9	5.3	6.6	12.0	17.2	1.9	6.5	1.2	37.1	12.8	10.9
Fraxinus	ash	-	-	-	-	-	-	-	-	-	-	•	-	•	•	-
Quercus	oak	•	-	-	-	-	-	•	-	•	•	-	-	1.2	•	•
Salix	willow	-	-	-	-	-	-	•	•	•	-	-	-	-	•	•
Total Trees & Shrubs (% TLP)		*17.6*	*22.9*	*5.8*	*2.8*	*20.8*	*6.2*	*8.6*	*15.2*	*24.0*	*3.2*	*8.9*	*1.2*	*44.1*	*15.3*	*12.6*
Heaths																
Calluna	heather	5.8	8.0	2.5	1.6	25.4	13.8	7.2	3.8	17.0	•	2.2	3.5	1.8	19.9	7.1
Total Heaths (% TLP)		*5.8*	*8.0*	*2.5*	*1.6*	*25.4*	*13.8*	*7.2*	*3.8*	*17.0*	*0.6*	*2.2*	*3.5*	*1.8*	*19.9*	*7.1*
Herbs																
Poaceae	grass	25.3	17.9	2.5	2.4	10.8	3.5	6.4	10.6	23.4	63.2	20.7	2.7	21.4	3.9	5.5
Poaceae (>37 um)	cereal	•	•	-	-	•	-	-	-	-	1.9	•	-	•	•	-
Cyperaceae	sedge	-	•	•	-	•	•	-	•	2.0	•	•	•	3.4	1.2	•
Anthemis type	chamomile type	-	•	•	-	•	•	•	-	-	•	•	•	•	-	-
Apiaceae	carrot family	-	-	-	-	-	-	•	-	-	-	•	-	•	-	-
Artemisia	mugwort	•	-	-	-	-	-	-	-	-	-	-	-	-	-	-
Aster type	daisy type	-	-	-	-	-	-	-	•	•	-	-	-	-	-	-
Caryophyllaceae	pink family	5.2	2.1	-	-	2.3	1.6	4.8	-	•	3.8	13.2	2.1	5.2	3.1	6.2
Cirsium	thistle	-	-	•	•	-	-	-	-	-	-	-	-	-	-	-
Lactuceae	dandelion type	-	1.4	-	-	-	-	-	-	-	1.3	1.8	-	2.4	-	-
Lamium type	deadnettle type	-	-	•	-	-	•	•	•	•	-	•	•	•	•	•
Persicaria maculosa	redshank	•	•	•	-	•	•	•	•	-	-	•	•	-	-	-
Plantago lanceolata	ribwort plantain	3.2	4.1	•	-	1.6	•	9.5	1.4	2.0	2.1	3.9	•	1.6	-	•
Plantago major/media	greater/hoary plantain	1.2	2.5	-	-	1.1	-	15.3	-	2.3	1.9	•	-	-	-	-
Potentilla type	cinquefoil type	•	-	-	-	-	•	-	-	-	-	-	-	-	-	-
Ranunculus acris group	meadow buttercup group	7.4	4.9	1.4	•	1.8	2.1	10.1	1.8	3.5	2.5	4.3	•	6.8	1.2	1.2
Rumex acetosa type	common sorrel type	-	-	•	-	-	-	1.6	•	•	•	1.4	-	1.2	•	•
Sinapis type	mustard type	1.6	•	•	-	-	-	1.2	•	-	-	-	-	-	-	-
Stellaria holostea	greater stitchwort	-	-	-	-	-	-	-	•	-	-	1.4	-	3.6	•	•
Succisa pratensis	devil's-bit scabious	29.9	33.3	85.2	92.6	33.7	70.4	33.2	63.3	23.0	16.7	40.4	88.4	6.4	53.0	63.8
Trifolium type	clover type	-	•	-	-	-	-	-	-	-	-	-	-	-	-	•
Veronica type	speedwell	-	-	-	-	-	-	•	-	-	-	-	-	-	-	-
Total Herbs (% TLP)		*49.9*	*50.4*	*89.2*	*93.2*	*42.3*	*76.4*	*76.9*	*69.7*	*33.6*	*30.1*	*67.9*	*92.5*	*29.1*	*59.8*	*73.1*
Aquatic types																
Menyanthes	bogbean	-	-	-	-	-	-	-	-	-	-	-	-	-	-	-
Myriophyllum verticillatum	whorled water milfoil	-	•	-	-	-	-	-	•	-	-	-	-	•	-	•
Total Aquatics (% TLP + Aq)		*0.0*	*0.2*	*0.0*	*0.0*	*0.0*	*0.0*	*0.0*	*0.2*	*0.0*	*0.0*	*0.0*	*0.0*	*0.2*	*0.0*	*0.2*
Pteridophytes																
Filicales	ferns	7.0	7.0	•	•	2.6	1.4	6.3	7.5	12.8	2.5	4.9	2.7	5.9	5.0	3.9
Lycopodium	clubmoss	•	•	-	-	•	•	-	-	•	-	-	-	•	-	-
Polypodium	polypody fern	15.0	11.5	11.9	13.4	10.7	17.5	10.4	43.2	12.8	4.1	9.3	32.0	51.1	15.6	35.4
Pteridium	bracken	-	-	-	-	-	-	-	-	-	-	-	-	-	•	-
Sphagnum	bogmoss	-	-	-	-	-	-	•	-	-	-	-	-	-	•	•
Total Pter (% TLP + Pter)		*22.3*	*18.8*	*12.2*	*14.1*	*13.8*	*19.2*	*16.7*	*51.1*	*26.5*	*6.8*	*14.6*	*35.7*	*57.7*	*21.7*	*40.0*

Appendix 3: Average Element Concentrations (%) of Broxy Kennels samples

Sample	Ba	Zr	Sr	Rb	Zn	Fe	Mn	Cr	V	Ti	Ca	K	Al	P	Si	S	Mg
control 358	0.043	0.019	0.013	0.006	0.014	4.531	0.133	0.015	0.013	0.551	0.65	2.13	10.269	0.107	35.86	0.022	1.016
control 359	0.041	0.014	0.012	0.004	0.007	2.742	0.044	0.009	0.008	0.359	0.364	1.463	8.025	0.102	41.131	0.011	0.519
control 360	0.033	0.032	0.012	0.004	0.007	4.024	0.087	0.013	0.007	0.603	0.747	1.261	7.138	0.211	33.107	0.058	1.11
control 361	0.028	0.028	0.014	0.005	0.007	3.27	0.065	0.013	0.01	0.562	0.462	1.588	9.308	0.143	34.738	0.048	1.107
control 362	0.042	0.03	0.012	0.004	0.013	4.074	0.111	0.013	0.009	0.664	0.607	1.537	8.881	0.136	36.103	0.023	1.026
control 363	0.053	0.049	0.015	0.007	0.01	3.674	0.041	0.011	0.013	0.66	0.705	1.989	9.371	0.16	31.301	0.034	0.4
control 364	0.044	0.018	0.013	0.005	0.006	4.296	0.134	0.013	0.01	0.485	0.587	1.891	9.597	0.113	32.846	0.028	1.458
control 365	0.043	0.03	0.013	0.005	0.007	4.519	0.14	0.011	0.011	0.643	0.684	1.442	8.372	0.12	35.591	0.018	0.985
grid A3	0.04	0.027	0.014	0.006	0.014	3.224	0.087	0.013	0.011	0.619	0.585	1.874	11.241	0.269	42.014	0.022	1.096
grid B3	0.041	0.029	0.013	0.005	0.009	3.091	0.087	0.008	0.008	0.583	0.487	1.478	8.188	0.198	33.982	0.013	0.785
grid C3	0.048	0.027	0.014	0.006	0.009	3.326	0.094	0.01	0.012	0.72	0.665	1.85	10.802	0.258	40.403	0.024	1.064
grid D3	0.044	0.029	0.013	0.005	0.005	2.922	0.086	0.008	0.01	0.619	0.615	1.774	10.775	0.221	42.223	0.021	1.542
grid E3	0.035	0.027	0.014	0.005	0.011	3.092	0.101	0.012	0.007	0.693	0.653	1.811	10.533	0.248	40.526	0.019	0.864
grid F3	0.044	0.033	0.014	0.005	0.01	2.957	0.107	0.01	0.011	0.6	0.61	1.72	9.704	0.253	39.519	0.017	0.91
grid G3	0.034	0.028	0.013	0.006	0.008	3.038	0.093	0.011	0.012	0.704	0.615	1.868	11.439	0.304	41.676	0.024	1.416
grid H3	0.05	0.026	0.014	0.006	0.016	3.271	0.116	0.013	0.009	0.65	0.587	1.858	11.006	0.287	40.573	0.024	0.654
grid I3	0.042	0.028	0.014	0.006	0.008	3.239	0.12	0.012	0.011	0.654	0.74	1.801	10.542	0.229	39.341	0.027	0.981
grid J3	0.046	0.026	0.013	0.006	0.012	3.32	0.088	0.013	0.01	0.621	0.621	1.807	10.241	0.224	38.443	0.021	1.395
grid K3	0.041	0.028	0.013	0.006	0.006	2.947	0.085	0.009	0.01	0.592	0.583	1.48	8.605	0.193	35.348	0.02	1.158
grid L3	0.042	0.029	0.013	0.005	0.008	3.223	0.099	0.011	0.015	0.739	0.605	1.663	10.199	0.239	39.451	0.023	1.303
grid M3	0.033	0.037	0.013	0.005	0.007	3.101	0.087	0.009	0.006	0.709	0.678	1.73	10.588	0.239	41.898	0.023	0.885
grid N3	0.041	0.032	0.014	0.006	0.011	3.268	0.115	0.016	0.012	0.704	0.617	1.883	11.234	0.261	40.284	0.029	0.774
grid O3	0.034	0.031	0.014	0.006	0.009	3.134	0.081	0.012	0.012	0.668	0.556	1.737	10.214	0.241	39.795	0.035	1.228
grid P3	0.04	0.03	0.013	0.005	0.008	3.129	0.073	0.01	0.01	0.677	0.587	1.696	9.874	0.221	40.322	0.027	0.88
grid Q3	0.049	0.028	0.013	0.005	0.012	3.196	0.059	0.013	0.012	0.711	0.684	1.796	11.204	0.219	41.685	0.025	1.265
grid R3	0.04	0.029	0.013	0.005	0.008	2.909	0.067	0.012	0.011	0.667	0.662	1.651	10.781	0.228	42.153	0.025	1.06

grid																
grid S3	0.029	0.031	0.013	0.005	0.009	3.116	0.055	0.01	0.005	0.604	0.551	1.503	8.64	0.208	36.401	0.024	0.4
grid T1	0.037	0.026	0.013	0.005	0.008	3.332	0.145	0.011	0.01	0.68	0.628	1.823	10.848	0.243	40.561	0.029	1.136
grid U1	0.05	0.032	0.013	0.006	0.013	3.262	0.081	0.014	0.009	0.771	0.595	1.845	11.108	0.299	40.666	0.036	1.191
grid V3	0.043	0.033	0.014	0.005	0.008	3.223	0.071	0.012	0.013	0.722	0.683	1.842	11.925	0.246	42.391	0.028	1.102
grid W3	0.039	0.025	0.013	0.006	0.019	3.274	0.058	0.014	0.009	0.713	0.613	1.795	10.677	0.238	38.938	0.031	1.059
grid X3	0.039	0.027	0.014	0.005	0.011	3.06	0.05	0.012	0.009	0.667	0.638	1.71	10.557	0.239	40.218	0.03	1.006
grid Y3	0.037	0.032	0.013	0.005	0.007	2.894	0.046	0.011	0.009	0.707	0.607	1.833	11.189	0.238	41.099	0.029	0.4
grid Z3	0.042	0.029	0.013	0.005	0.007	3.126	0.046	0.013	0.013	0.675	0.622	1.869	10.777	0.251	40.533	0.034	1.475
grid AA3	0.04	0.03	0.014	0.006	0.014	3.167	0.044	0.014	0.009	0.717	0.549	1.856	10.736	0.24	39.448	0.027	0.699
grid BB3	0.028	0.03	0.013	0.005	0.008	2.932	0.033	0.012	0.008	0.652	0.584	1.622	9.322	0.194	39.656	0.028	0.924
grid CC3	0.042	0.027	0.013	0.005	0.01	3.221	0.082	0.012	0.008	0.63	0.529	1.723	9.901	0.233	38.597	0.027	0.911
grid DD3	0.034	0.031	0.013	0.005	0.007	3.073	0.07	0.011	0.008	0.665	0.597	1.691	9.615	0.246	39.296	0.034	1.043
grid EE3	0.048	0.03	0.013	0.005	0.009	3.137	0.059	0.011	0.011	0.574	0.511	1.636	9.652	0.219	38.218	0.023	0.862
grid FF3	0.043	0.029	0.014	0.005	0.008	3.221	0.198	0.011	0.009	0.695	0.545	1.786	11.184	0.244	40.136	0.044	1.146
grid GG3	0.03	0.027	0.014	0.005	0.014	3.207	0.073	0.014	0.006	0.653	0.588	1.847	11.042	0.218	40.963	0.036	0.652
grid K1.2	0.039	0.029	0.014	0.006	0.008	3.146	0.089	0.011	0.011	0.731	0.631	1.767	10.656	0.251	40.659	0.026	0.784
grid K2.2	0.045	0.031	0.014	0.006	0.009	3.167	0.099	0.011	0.011	0.691	0.614	1.734	10.253	0.207	41.356	0.021	1.022
grid K3.2	0.036	0.025	0.013	0.006	0.011	3.296	0.098	0.013	0.011	0.683	0.592	1.857	11.4	0.239	41.996	0.026	1.257
grid K4.2	0.041	0.03	0.013	0.005	0.009	3.111	0.093	0.01	0.007	0.639	0.575	1.614	9.312	0.203	37.661	0.021	1.083
grid K5.2	0.043	0.026	0.013	0.006	0.012	3.122	0.05	0.013	0.011	0.725	0.604	1.874	11.351	0.261	42.163	0.025	0.894
grid K6.2	0.04	0.03	0.013	0.005	0.008	3.076	0.074	0.011	0.012	0.747	0.593	1.73	10.304	0.251	40.37	0.025	1.109
grid K2	0.039	0.032	0.014	0.005	0.009	3.098	0.085	0.014	0.009	0.698	0.622	1.756	10.885	0.226	40.721	0.026	1.144
grid K4	0.035	0.034	0.015	0.005	0.013	3.105	0.075	0.013	0.008	0.66	0.618	1.796	11.334	0.233	41.357	0.028	1.273
grid K5	0.045	0.033	0.014	0.005	0.013	3.006	0.102	0.011	0.009	0.644	0.562	1.734	10.131	0.208	40.399	0.036	0.559

Appendix 4: Catalogue of Animal Bone fragments by context, small find no (SF) or bulk sample no (BS)

Job no	SF	BS	Context	Wt of sample (g)	Area	Species	Bone/element	Part	number of fr.	Burnt/unburnt	Comments	General	Abrasion	Density	Friability	Condition total
5764	002		u/s	2.8	S slope	IM		fragment	10	calcined			2	2	2	8
5764	002		u/s		S slope	cf cattle	metapodial	distal	1	calcined	small fragment		2	3	2	8
5764	004		u/s	2.2	S slope	rabbit	R innominate	R half pelvis	1	unburnt			3	3	3	12
5764	179		u/s	40.9		IM		fragment	60	calcined	small stones fused c		1	1	2	6
5764	180		069	2.1	souterrain fill	IM		fragment	30	calcined			2	2	2	8
5764	180		069		souterrain fill	?SU	LBSF	diaphysis	1	calcined	unfused		2	2	2	8
5764	263		069	0.4	souterrain fill	IM		fragment	1	calcined	medium mammal		2	2	2	8
5764	084		100	0.3	D1N-D	IM		fragment	2	calcined			2	2	2	8
5764	1031 (sic)		110		D1N-B	IM		fragment	40	calcined	small stones fused c		1	1	1	6
5764	083		113	1.5	D1N-C	IM		fragment	13	calcined			2	2	2	8
5764	093		115	1.3	D1N-C	IM		fragment	35	calcined			2	2	2	8
5764	110		124		D1N-D	cattle	mandible	oral	1	unburnt	2 conjoining fragme		2	2	2	8
5764	110		124		D1N-D	cattle	mandible	oral	1	unburnt	2 conjoining fragme		2	2	2	8
5764	110		124		D1N-D	cattle	mandible	fragment	20	unburnt			2	2	2	8
5764	111		156		souterrain dep	IM		fragment	8	calcined			2	2	2	8
5764	101		188	8.8	D1S-F	IM		fragment	3	calcined			2	2	2	8
5764	101		188		D1S-F	LU	scapula	blade	1	burnt	2 conjoining fragme		2	2	2	9
5764	107		189	0.4	D1S-F	IM		fragment	3	calcined			3	3	2	9
5764	115		189	1.9	D1S-F	IM	LBSF	fragment	1	calcined			2	3	2	10
5764	100		193	1.4	D1S-F	IM		fragment	3	calcined			2	2	2	8
5764	102		196	6.4	D1S-F	IM		fragment	8	calcined			2	2	2	8
5764	118		295	1.2	S palisade	IM		fragment	1	calcined			2	2	2	8
5764	139		326	1.7	D2S-E/M	IM		fragment	12	calcined			2	2	2	8
5764	138		328	0.5	D2S-E/M	IM		fragment	4	calcined			2	2	2	8
5764	141		353	2.2	souterrain fill	IM	LBSF	fragment	3	calcined			2	2	2	8
5764	142		363	1.5	D2N-E	IM		?rib	1	calcined			2	2	2	8
5764	142		363		D2N-E	IM		fragment	1	calcined			2	2	2	8
5764	165		569	0.2	D2N/D3N-B	IM		fragment	7	calcined			1	1	1	5
5764	173		580	1.4	D2N/D3N-B	IM		fragment	1	calcined			2	2	2	8
5764	237		761	0.4	D2-E pit	IM		fragment	2	calcined	?fire pit		2	2	2	8
5764	112		890	2.1	D4S-B	IM	LBSF	fragment	1	calcined			3	2	2	9
5764	253		902		N slope	horse	tooth	up M/PM	1	unburnt	in wear		3	3	3	11
5764	253		902		N slope	horse	L scapula	blade	1	unburnt	in 2 conjoining fragn		3	2	2	9
5764	253		902		N slope	horse	R scapula	blade	1	unburnt	in 3 conjoining fragn		3	2	2	9
5764	253		902		N slope	horse	vertebra	thoracic	4	unburnt	some arthritic extra		3	2	2	9
5764	253		902		N slope	cf horse	vertebra	centrum	1				3	2	2	9
5764	253		902		N slope	cf horse	rib	articulation	2				3	2	2	9
5764		035	035		D1S-A	LU cf cattle	tooth	enamel	1	?burnt	fragments		1	2	1	5
5764	112		105	31.1	D1N-B	cf cattle	phalanx 3	articulation	1	calcined	posterior fragment		2	2	2	8
5764		1100	499	0.1	pit 498, N slope pig	cf cattle	tooth	enamel	1	?burnt	small cusp fragment		1	2	2	6
5764		1171	946	0.7	Area 4, PH fill	sheep/goat	metapodial	distal	1	calcined	small fragment		2	2	2	8
5764		1187	982		D4N-E	ungulate	tooth	enamel	100	burnt	tiny fragments		2	2	1	6
									391							

Abbreviations

IM	indeterminate mammal
LU	large ungulate
SU	small ungulate
L	left
R	right
LBSF	long bone shaft fragment

Appendix 5: Stone Artefacts Catalogue

Stone SF	Area	Context	Geological type	No. of Pieces	Weight (g)	Brief description	Length (mm)	Width (mm)	Thick-ness (mm)	Contextual location
004		044	Quartz	1	608	Cobble, fits well in the hand, with facetted areas ground through use on the sides. **Grinder**	78.5	71.3	54	Colluvium to the N
041	North Area	u/s	Slate	1	176	Part of a **roofing slate**, perforated. Fine-grained grey slate	113.5	60.8	13.8	u/s

| 042 | u/s | u/s | Slate | 1 | 584 | Part of a **roofing slate**, perforated. Fine-grained grey slate | 192 | 186 | 8.2 | u/s |
| 072 | - | North Slope | Mica schist | 1 | 456 | Flattened cobble with pecked and ground hollow in one surface. Some modern damage. **Anvil** | 107 | 93.5 | 29.2 | Earliest fill of recut of Ditch 1 N |

087	-	North Slope	101	Quartzite?	1	313	Small cobble with area of dark polish on one side and a rough shallow concavity on one face where the stone has been used as an **anvil**.	93.3	68	32.8	Upper fill of Ditch 1 N
088	-	North Slope	101	Quartzite?	1	252	Small cobble with one facetted end from grinding. The other end is indented when used as a hammer. Surface damage to one side, possibly through natural erosion. **Grinder hammerstone**.	75.8	62.8	41.3	Upper fill of Ditch 1 N
092	-	South Slope	160	Schist	1	272	Bar of schist with dark polish on one surface and one side. Used as a **whetstone/polisher**.	137	39.6	24.7	Recut in Ditch 1 S

| 184 | - | South Slope | 666 | Cumbrian tuff | 1 | 53.7 | Cutting edge fragment of a highly **polished stone axe.** Has a ground facetted edge to the cutting edge | 64 | 39.5 | 15.4 | Fill of pit South Slope |

| 152A | - | South Slope | 401 | Quartzite | 1 | 384 | Split cobble with surviving surfaces. Polish visible on one surface and rounded edge. Possible **whetstone/polisher** | 95.3 | 64.3 | 49.3 | Recut in Ditch 2 S |
| 152B | | South Slope | 401 | Quartzite | 1 | 357 | Heavily burnt cobble, with one surviving preserved surface that suggests its use was as a **polisher**. Slight concavity at this point. | 70.6 | 62.4 | 59.9 | Recut in Ditch 2 S |

| 948 | - | Area 7 | 666 | Sandstone | 1 | 206.6 | Small cobble, most of the surface is sand blasted, but the smallest face is smooth and possibly worn to a slight hollow. **Uncertain polisher.** | 57.4 | 53.1 | 49.7 | Fill of pit South Slope |

Appendix 6: Prehistoric Pottery Catalogue

Context and location	Vessel description	Image
Vessel Nr. 1 Context 348 pit and 767 occupation layer South slope	SF 135/221 SF135 EBA Beaker fine sherd decorated with 5 fine incised lines, most likely cord. Has a little quartz and quartz sand temper. Has a smooth exterior but has been burnt. SF 221 with two lines of similar decoration, possibly part of the same vessel. Total two sherds Wt. 4.5 g, wall thickness 7.7mm	
Vessel Nr. 2 Context 348 pit and 767 occupation layer, South slope	SF 190/198/219A BA Beaker with clearly defined toothed design. All fragments join forming part of the belly of the vessel. The decoration comprises a square plain lozenge, bordered by two rows of comb impressed lines, with triangles to either side, with infilled horizontal lines. Below this are six fairly equally spaced horizontal comb impressed lines, and below that a blank field to the base (?). Comb with 2 mm wide teeth, with slight gap between them. SF 190, 3 body sherds join - from just above the base. Has a rounded base edge to the flat, slightly burnt base. SF 219A 3 comb impressed sherds and a curved piece from a rim or base edge. Total, 12 sherds. Wt. 65g. wall thickness 7.3 mm, base 10 mm.	
Vessel Nr. 3 Context 348 pit, South slope	SF 192 EBA Beaker base sherd possibly with evidence of the base edge. Wt. 5.8 g, wall thickness 7.2 mm	Not illustrated
Vessel Nr. 4 Context 348 pit, South slope	SF 191/196/199 SF 199 rim with stab decoration of EBA Beaker, likely to be part of the same vessel as SF 196 but much abraded. The rim is rounded and very slightly everted. Four lines of horizontal stab decoration are present. Non-joining with the other sherds. SF 196 3 conjoined body sherds with fine stab decoration presented in 8 horizontal rows of alternate facing stabs. Possibly made by a fine bone or twig. The motif is 3-4 mm in length and c. 1 mm wide. Total 6 sherds. Wt. 41.4 g, wall thickness 6 mm, rim 7 mm. Rim diameter c. 180 mm, c. 7.5 % present	

Vessel Nr. 5	SF 196A/202

SF 202 EBA Beaker sherds but worn comb decoration. Three small sherds join, possibly from the belly of the vessel. Blank fields of 6-8.5 mm in width are present on four sherds. Three sherds join. Well-made and well-finished fine pottery as SF 196A.

Context 348 pit, South slope

SF 196A fine sherd with 5 fine -toothed impressed horizontal lines. Deeply impressed but at an irregular intervals. Part of the neck to a carination. Some suggestion of breakage along coil joins. Total of 6 sherds.
Wt. 12.5 g, wall thickness 4.2 mm to 4.5 mm.

Vessel Nr. 6

Context 348 pit, South slope

SF 197
EBA small Beaker - two large sherds joining with decoration, but very abraded. Possible neck to a vessel? Decorated with fine toothed impressions. Two horizontal lines, quite wide spaced border a field c. 20 mm wide with infilled lozenges with plain triangles to either side. Minimum diameter c. 100 mm.
Total of 4 sherds.
Wt. 6.2 g, wall thickness 6.2 mm.

Vessel Nr. 7

Context 348 pit, South slope

SF 200
Fragment of a sherd, possibly an EBA Beaker? with a rounded and everted rim, and a rounded cordon formed by pinching just below it, but on quite a thick sherd for an EBA Beaker. Cordon c. 10 mm wide.
Wt. 22.2 g, wall thickness 10.5 mm.

Vessel Nr. 8

Context 348 pit, South slope

SF 137/194/195
SF 137 Plain rim sherd of an EBA Beaker. Flat topped slightly everted rim. Possibly burnt.
SF 194 Plain, flat-topped slightly everted rim with neck in two pieces. Has two pinch marks, comprising two impressions, in a vertical line, 15 mm apart, and a third offset to the side, between them.
SF 194 conjoins with SF 195
Plain, flat-topped, slightly everted rim and neck conjoin. Broken at a coil join, has two pinch marks, comprising two impressions, in a vertical line, 15 mm apart. Total of 5 sherds.
Wt. 82.7 g, wall thickness 7.5- 8 mm.
Rim c. 180 mm in diameter, 20.5% present.

Vessel Nr. 9

Context 348 pit,
South slope

SF 193
Thick piece not a Beaker sherd (may have
some uncertain decoration comprising three
oblique broad stab marks.
Wt. 8.8,g wall thickness 13.4 mm.

Vessel Nr. 10

Context 170 = 305
colluvium

SF 091
EBA Beaker possibly the neck of a vessel.
Seems to have been decorated initially with a
toothed implement but it was changed to a
straight horizontal incised line, which has
eradicated most of the tooth impressions. A
total of 7-9 horizontal lines survive but the
gaps between them vary from 3 to 5 mm. The
incised lines are 1.5-2 mm wide. The
decoration forms a corrugated design.
Wt. 17.9 g, wall thickness 6.9 mm.

Vessel Nr. 11

Context 170 = 305
colluvium

SF 001
Rounded and everted rim possibly EN?.
Exterior surface heavily abraded and burnt.
Uncertain date.
Wt. 17.6 g, wall thickness 11 mm.
Rim diameter not measured.

Vessel Nr. 12

Context 739 upper
fill pit 738, South
slope

SF 213
EBA Beaker base, flat with rounded base edge.
Burnt. Two horizontal lines of impressed cord
are noted above the base edge, but badly
abraded. Total of two sherds.
Wt. 14.6 g, base thickness 11.7 mm. Base
diameter c. 70 mm, 7.5% present.

Vessel Nr. 13

Context 348 pit,
South slope

SF 201
Heavy sherd, close to base of vessel, With two
marks that may be oblique stab marks.
Wt. 21.9 g, wall thickness 18 mm.

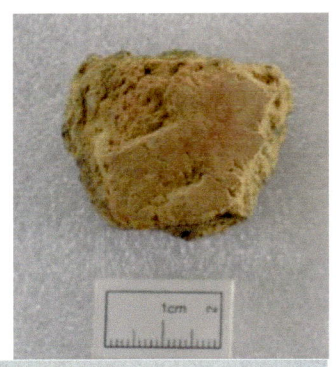

Vessel Nr. 14

Context 310 (void)
South slope

SF 131
Large sherd with flat, slightly inverted rim
from a BA urn. Separate rim sherd and 2 body
sherds. With grits showing through the
exterior surface. Some loss of surface.
Total of 4 sherds.
Wt. 270.5 g, wall thickness 16.2 mm.
Diameter c. 340 mm, c. 7.5% present.

Vessel Nr. 15

Context 580 fill of
Ditch 3 terminus

SF 172
Rounded inturned rim, with finger runnel to
form a short neck and bulbous body. Temper
shows through the pot surface. IA?
Wt. 54.8 g, wall thickness 13 mm.
Rim diameter c. 170 mm, c. 8% present.

Vessel Nr. 16

Context 45 top fill
and 71 lower fill of
Ditch 3

SF 059/063/074
SF 059 three sherds, two conjoin with up to
two incised lines - from wear. They are not
decorated. Damaged at coil join. Probably
burnt, and not well made. Large grits show
through one surface.
SF 063 same vessel as SF 74. Two very
abraded sherds with one deep incised mark
through the use of an organic material.
Possibly burnt.
SF 074 thick sherds with 2 deep horizontal
incised lines, made through use of organic
material/twine. Sherds are burnt. Largest
sherd is broken at coil join. Total of 9 sherds.
Wt 85.8 g, wall thickness 12.5-15.5 mm.

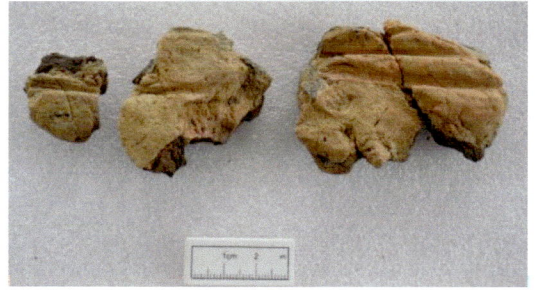

Vessel Nr. 17

Context 343 upper
fill Ditch 2

SF 140
Distorted flattened rim with v large stone
temper in excess of 20 by 20 mm. Burnt with
spalling. Badly made cooking pot. IA?
Total 10 sherds.
Wt. 142.8 g, wall thickness 16.5 mm. Rim
diameter not measured.

Index